Build

your own

Computer

Book Owner:

All reasonable precautions have been taken in the preparation of this book. However, information is provided on an 'as is' basis and is without guarantee. The author/publisher does not accept liability for any loss or damage allegedly caused by following any instructions or advice contained in this book. Nor does the author accept responsibility for mentioned websites, other than his own, or guarantee that they remain active or appropriate. Readers are advised to confirm technical and pricing details of components for themselves. The prices mentioned for components and software are indicative of retail prices in American dollars at the time of writing. Prices and availability of components and software vary over time and among different regions of the world.

Brands and products mentioned in this book that are known to be trademarked are listed in a following table of trademarks. The author would welcome information about any overlooked trademark holders or any revised pricing and availability information for mention in future editions. Fractal Design supplied a Fractal Design R6 case, Sea Sonic provided a Prime Titanium 600 W fanless modular PSU, Noctua provided an NH-U12S SE-AM4 U-Type tower cooler, and Thor Technologies provided a SmartProtect surge protector for evaluation in the system featured in this book.

Wherever possible, Lightening Source-printed copies of this book are printed on paper that has received Chain-of-Custody certification from the Forest Stewardship Council®, the Sustainable Forestry Initiative®, and the Program for the Endorsement of Forestry Certification.

First edition 2015. Second, 2016, edition incorporated corrections; updates (such as instructions for using Windows 10); additional material (such as instructions about system benchmarking) and details of components released since the first edition. Third, 2017 edition, included an introduction to case modeling; additional overclocking information, and responses to readers' suggestions. Fourth, extensively revised and updated 2019 edition, includes instructions for building an AMD Ryzen 2000 series-based system; additional information about selecting RAM modules; more detailed information about thermal compounds and surge protectors, as well as typographical corrections. Constructive criticisms about the book are welcomed at the book's website: www.Pittman-Progressive-Publishing.com.

Main typeface: Cambria, Roman font, 11.5; secondary typeface: Calibri, Roman font, 10.
Fourth edition ISBN: 978-0-9942213-6-0.
1. Microprocessors — Design and Construction — Amateurs' manuals.
2. Microprocessors — Maintenance and Repair — Amateurs' manuals.
Publisher: Pittman Progressive Publishing

List of Trademarks

Trademark Holder	Trademarks
Abelssoft (Ascora GmbH & Co. KG)	HackCheck, EasyBackup, Ashampoo Registry Cleaner, Office 2018; WashAndGo utility
Adesso Inc.	iMouse Ergonomic Mouse
Adobe Systems Software Ireland Ltd.	Adobe Premiere Pro CC, Photoshop CS4; Adobe PageMaker 7.0
Advanced Micro Devices Inc.	CrossFireX, Radeon GPUs, R9 290X GPU; Radeon R9 295X2, AM A10-7800 FM+ CPU, Gemini GPU, Radeon Pro SSG, Ryzen, Threadripper; Wraith Prism RGB cooler, FreeSync 2; Eyefinity; Radeon Vega GPU
AgentGOD (publisher)	IntelBurnTest
Agylstor Inc.	Agylstor M.4 NVMe SSD
Alex Ciobanu	PROJECT ISOLATION computer model
AnandTech	SYSMark
Apple Computer Inc.	Macintosh, macOS, High Sierra OS, FireWire (IEEE 1394); iMac
AQVOX AUDIO DEVICES	AQVOX USB Low-Noise Isolated Power Supply; USB Low-Noise 5 V Isolated Linear Power Supply
Araca Noae LLC	ArcaOS 5.0
ASRock Inc.	X99 WS-E/10G motherboard, X470 Master SLI/ac ATX Form-factor Motherboard; GeForce GTX 1080 Ti GPU
ASUSTeK Computer Inc. (ASUS); Republic of Gamers brand (ROG)	NCL-DS1R1 socket 604 SCSI motherboard, X99-E-10G WS motherboard, STRIX GTX 1080 O8G Gamming GPU, ROG MAXIMUS VIII Formula ATX motherboard, ROG Strix GPU, EK-FC1070 GTX Ti waterblock, XONAR DGX 5.1, mini-ITX X370 motherboard, Z97-A motherboard, Zenith Extreme Motherboard; 2.5-inch FX external hard drive
Atheros & Zebralet	TWO-FACE computer model
ATTO Technology	Dual-channel X4 PCIe to Ultra 320 SCSI controller card
Audacity	Audacity 2.3 audio software
Audio-Technica Corporation	PBHS1 headset
Autodesk Inc.	AutoCAD 2017
Avast Software s.r.o.	Avast Free Antivirus
AVEXIR Technologies Corp.	Raiden RAM modules
Back To The Beach Software, LLC	Web Studio 5.0
Bandisoft	Bandicam 3.2.4
Beepa Pty. Ltd.	Fraps 3.5.99
BenQ Corporation	GW2760S monitor; 32-inch 4K Thunderbolt 3 Monitor
Bethesda Softworks LLC	The Elder Scrolls V: Skyrim
Binary Fortress Software	DisplayFusion
BIOSMAN	POST card
Bitdefender	Antivirus Free Edition
BitFenix Co. Ltd.	Alchemy LED Strips
Blue Microphones	Blue Yeti microphone; Blue Compass microphone arm
Blu-ray Disc Association	Blu-ray; Ultra HD Blu-ray
Buffalo Americas Inc.	Buffalo MediaStation 6X BDXL Blu-ray writer
Business Applications Performance Corporation (BAPCo)	SYSMark standardized benchmarks
Cambridge Quantum Computing Ltd.	t|ket> quantum OS
Canonical Ltd.	supporters of Ubuntu
CaseLabs	MAGNUM SMA8 case

Chord Electronics Ltd.	Qutest DAC
Cobblestone Software Inc.	PaperDisk
Cool Force	Nanoxia power cables
Cooler Master Corp.	SI3 twin 120-mm fan pack
Corel Corporation	VideoStudio Pro X6
Corsair	AX1500i Digital ATX PSU, Vengeance LPX DDR 4, SF600 600 W SFF PSU, AX1600i 1600W ATX TITANIUM Modular PSU, II RGB RAM Cooler; Hydro H75 liquid cooler, Obsidian 1000D Super-Tower case, Dominator Airflow Platinum RAM cooler; Modular Gold-rated SF 600 W PSU
Creative Technology Ltd.	Sound Blaster Z, Sound Blaster ZxR soundcard; Sound BlasterX AE-5 Soundcard
Dany Technologies	Dany T.View TV tuner
DarkSide	High Density Cable Sleeving - Commando UV; Dimmable Rigid LED Strip – UV
Datamancer LLC	Aviator keyboard
DCS Reviews, LLC	FPS Review
Deepcool Industries Co. Ltd.	Castle 240/280 RGB AIO Cooler
Dell Inc.	U3014 IPS monitor, PowerEdge 342-2082 600 GB SAS HD, UltraSharp 4K UP3216Q 31.5" monitor; UP3218K 8K monitor
Denso Wave Inc.	QR code
Dolby Laboratories Inc.	audio encoding/compression technologies
D-Wave Systems Inc.	D-Wave 2000Q System quantum computer
Encyclopædia Britannica Inc.	Encyclopædia Britannica Online
F&M Technology	Inateck Withdrawable HDD Enclosure
FiiO Electronics Technology Co. Ltd.	FiiO K1 USB DAC/headphone amplifier
FileMaker Inc.	Aaker Pro 12 Advanced
Fractal Design	Design Core 3000 USB 3.0 case, Design R6 case; Mini C tower
Frank Delattre (author)	CPU-Z
Free Software Foundation	GNU (GNU Not UNIX)
FreeBSD Foundation	FreeBSD
Futuremark c/o UL	GALAXY Overclocking Contest
G.SKILL International Enterprise Co. Ltd.	TridentZ RGB Series 128 GB DDR 4 3600 SDRAM, DDR 4 Ripjaws modules; Turbulence Cooler
GELID Solutions	Slim Hero CPU cooler
George Woltman	Prime95
GIGA-BYTE Technology Co., Ltd.	GA-6PXSVT 10-Gigabyte Ethernet motherboard, Ultra Durable 4 Classic motherboards, GA-X99P-SLI motherboard, GA-Z170X-Designare motherboard, Aorus GTX 1080 graphics card; X299 UD4 LGA 2066 ATX motherboard
Golden Emperor International Ltd.	GeIL RAM
Google	Gmail, Google Docs, Android OS; Google G Suite
Guru3D.com	various benchmarks
Harman International Industries, Inc.	JBL Pulse Bluetooth speakers
Hasso-Plattner-Institute	Identity Leak Checker
Henkel AG & Co.	Loctite 222
Hitachi Ltd.	Ultrastar He10 hard drive; HGST Ultrastar He10 10 TB 7,200 rpm 256MB Cache 3.5-inch Hard Drive
HP Development Company, L.P.	ioDrive2 3 TB Internal Solid-State Drive, All-in-One 22-c0025xt desktop computer; 805358-256 2,400 MHz ECC Quad Rank DDR

HTC Corporation	HTC Vive VR tracking headset
HWBOT (Frederik Colardyn, Founder)	HWBOT overclocking website
IBM	OS2/Warp operating system; WAV (with Microsoft)
IDrive Inc.	IDrive Cloud backup service
In Win Development	Infinity HALO case
Infraware, Inc.	Polaris Office
Innovative Concepts and Design LLC (Gemini)	SC-1 external sound card
Institute of Electrical and Electronics Engineers	Gigabit Ethernet standard
Intel Corporation	Core i7 CPU, X540T1 Ethernet Network Adapter, Core i5-4770, ATX, Compute Stick2.0, Thunderbolt, Extensible Firmware Interface (EFI), Skylake motherboard chipset, Skylake CPU, Xeon Pltnm 8176 Processor, Xeon Phi 7290 72-core Coprocessor, 3D XPoint Optane memory, Compute Stick CS325, Core i5 CPU, MINX OS, Haswell-E CPU, Skylake-X CPU, 3D XPoint (with Micron Technology), 4004 CPU, Atom Processor C3758, Knights Landing (Xeon Phi) co-processor, Next Unit of Computing (NUC) computer format, Core i9-9980XE CPU; Haydes Canyon NUC
iXsystems Inc.	TrueOS
JBL	Pulse 3 Speaker
Jim Hall	FreeDOS operating system
Kingston Technology Corporation	HyperX dual-channel DDR 3 RAM, DataTraveler Ultimate GT flash drive; HyperX Pulsefire Surge RGB mouse
KitGuru Tech	component evaluation and buying advice service
Koninklijke Philips N.V (Phillips)	Amibglow monitor
Kordz Pty. Ltd.	PRO Series DisplayPort 1.4 cable
Lamptron	FC6 5.25-inch Fan Controller Faceplate, FC 10 5.25-inch Fan Controller; FC5 6 Channel LED Fan Controller V3
lewing@isc.tamu.edu	Tux (Linux mascot)
LG Electronics Inc.	Ultra HD Blu-ray Player
Lifi Labs, Inc.	Z LED light strap
Linus Torvalds	Linux
LSI Corporation	MegaRAID 9361-8i SAS RAID controller
Mad Catz Interactive Inc.	RAT ProX gaming mouse
Mayhems Solutions Ltd.	Pastel Coolant; Chameleon coolant
Memory Cube Consortium	hybrid v-DRAM
Microsoft	Sculpt keyboard, Windows OS, DirectX API, Internet Explorer, WPS Office Free, LIQUi|> quantum computer simulator, Actual Multiple Monitors 8.13, Windows Defender antivirus; Waveform Audio File Format (WAV) (with IBM)
Micro-Star Int'l. Co. Ltd. (MSI)	MSI Afterburner; GTX 960 GPU
Millenniata Inc.	M-DISC
Mobi Systems Inc.	OfficeSuite V 4.6
modDIY	modSticker
Molex Connector Company	Molex power supply cables
Moving Picture Experts Group (developers)	MP3
Mozilla Foundation	Firefox Quantum web browser
MYOB Technology Pty. Ltd.	AccountEdge Pro

NCH Software	WavePad Sound Editor v 5.55
Nero Ltd.	Nero
Nimbus Data	3D NAND 100 TB ExaDrive DC100 SSD
Ningbo Qidian Mechanical & Electrical Equipment Co. Ltd.	QDIY transparent case
Noctua	NH-U12S SE-AM4 U-Type tower cooler, Noctua NF-S12 B cooler, NF-S12 B Redux 120 mm fan; Chromax NA-SAVP1 anti-vibration pads
NovaTech Network	NovaBench 3.0.4
Nuance Communications Inc.	Dragon Dictate
Nvidia Corporation	SLI API, Quadro GV100, Scalable-Link Interfacing (SLI), G-SYNC, GT 1030 GPU; GeForce 256 GPU
NZXT Corp.	Kraken G10 bracket, NZXT Sentry Fan Controller; E Series semi-digital ATX PSU
Oculus VR, LLC	Oculus Rift VR headset; Oculus Quest VR headset
OCZ Storage Solutions	RevoDrive 350 PCIe SSD; OCZ RevoDrive 350 960 GB PCIe SSD
Oleh Yuschuck	PaperBack
Open Source	Open365 (beta version)
Open Source (supported by Xiph.Org Foundation)	Free Lossless Audio Codec (FLAC)
Oracle Corporation	Oracle Solaris OS; UNIX OS; Virtual Box
Overclock.net community Freezer' Burn	Freezer' Burn overclocking competition
PassMark Software	MemTest 86 V8.0, PassMark PerformanceTest v 8.0; BurnInTest 8.1
Pazera Free Audio Extractor	Jacek Pazera
PC Building Simulator	PC Building Simulator
Peripheral Component Interconnect Special Interest Group (PCI-SIG)	Peripheral Component Interconnect (PCI); PCIe
Phanteks	ENTHOO ELITE Super Tower Computer Case
Pioneer Electronics Australia Pty. Ltd.	Pioneer 16X Bluray Burner DVD/CD; Ultra HD Blu-ray Player
Piriform Ltd.	CCleaner; Speccy
Python Software Foundation	Python 3.7
Qualcomm Technologies Inc.	Snapdragon CPU
Quantum Corporation	DAT 72 CD72SH-SSTU SATA 40 GB, TD3100-801 Travan 40 GB tape; Quantum TC-L52AN-EY-C LTO-5 1.5 TB SAS tape drive
Razer Inc.	Blackwidow Chroma mechanical keyboard, Naga Hex MOBA/Action-RPG Gaming Mouse-Red, Firefly Micro Textured Surface Hard Gaming Mouse Mat, Nommo Chroma speakers; Core X external graphics enclosure
Realtek Semiconductor Corporation	ALC892 audio chip
Red Hat Inc.	Red Hat Enterprise Linux
RME	AIO HDSPe AIO -PCIe digital audio card sound
ROG	Maximus VIII Formula motherboard
Rosewill Inc.	Rosewill Blackbone case
S.PiC	VEGA computer model
Samsung Electronics Co. Ltd.	850 Evo solid-state drive XP941 M.2 SSDs, 1 Tb T1 portable SSD, PM1633a SSD, 8 TB NVMe NGSFF SSD, 500 GB USB 3.0 T1 SSD; 512 GB 970 M.2 PRO PCIe NVMe SSD
SanDisk Corporation	64 GB Ultra CZ800 USB 3.1 flash drive

Sea Sonic Electronics Co. Ltd.	Prime Titanium 660 W fanless PSU, E Series semi-digital ATX PSU, SSP-300SUB 300W 1U Flex ATX PSU; SSP-300SUG ATX PSU
Seagate Technology PLC	HDD ST3,000DM001 3 TB 64MB Cache SATA 6.0Gb/s, 3.5-inch Internal Hard Drive Bare Drive, IronWolf 12 TB spinning hard drive; 2 TB Backup+ Ultra Slim Portable spinning hard drive
Sega	Total War: Rome II
Serenity Systems International	eComStation 2.1 operating system
Serif (Europe) Ltd.	Page Plus; Ability Office V6
SGI (trademark managed by Gold Standard Group)	OpenGL 6
Shure Incorporated	X2U XLR-to-USB Signal Adapter
Silicon Graphics	OpenGL API
Silicon Power	Silicon Power DDR 4 RAM
SilverStone Technology C. L.	Silent Foam
SiS LLC	Sandra Lite v 30.16
SK Hynix Inc.	DDR 4 2,400 MHz ECC RAM, https://www.amazon.com/Hynix-PC4-19200-2400MHZ-
Skype	Skype VoIP telephony service
SODIAL	SODIAL Diagnostic Card Tester
SONY	MPF 920 internal floppy disk drive; Sony C800GPAC Studio Condenser Microphone
Sun Microsystems (Oracle)	VirtualBox
Tandberg Data	QuikStor RDX SATA 5.25 Inch Internal Docking Station, QuikStor 1 TBA removable cartridge; Data LTO-6 HH Internal 2.5 TB Ultrium SAS tape drive
The Apache Software Foundation	Apache OpenOffice 4.4
The Document Foundation	LibreOffice 6.04
The GIMP Team	GIMP 2.9.4
The Open Group	UNIX trademark
The Serial ATA International Organization	SATA connection standard, mini-SATA; eSATA
Thermaltake Technology Co. Ltd.	C-Pro tube compression fittings, Extreme 3.0 Plus card reader, Toughpower DPS G RGB 1250 W Titanium PSU; Floe Riing RGB 360 CPU Liquid Cooler
Thor Technologies Pty. Ltd.	SmartProtect surge protector
TL Sourcing Ltd.	CableMod ModMesh C-Series AXi; HXi & RM Cable Kit
Ubuntu Foundation	Ubuntu
UHD Alliance	HDR10 (high dynamic range) standard; 4K Ultra HD Premium
UNIGINE Corp.	Heaven Bench Mark 4.0
Valve Corporation	Steam digital distribution platform
Velcro Industries B.V.	Velcro
Video Electronics Standards Association (VESA) (developers)	DisplayPort
VideoLAN non-profit organization	VLC media player
Western Digital Technologies Inc. (HGST Inc.)	Ultrastar He10 hard drive, Ultrastar He8 8 TB helium spinning hard drive; My Passport Wireless 250 GB External SSD
win.rar GmbH, publisher of RARLAB products	WinRAR
Yuri Bubly (@1usmus)	developer of the DRAM Calculator for Ryzen
Zemana Ltd.	ANTILogger

Zotac (Nvidia Corporation)	GeForce GTX 1080 Ti AMP Extreme GPU

Charles Babbage (1791-1871)
British mathematician; inventor of the first mechanical computer. Given the honorary title:
'The Father of Computing'.

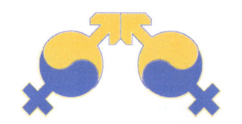

© <u>**Pittman Progressive Publishing**</u>

Contents

Professional Review

List of Tables

List of Figures

I once had a life. But now that I have a computer and an Internet connection, my mantra is, 'I am logged in, therefore I am.'

1. Introduction

This book provides a practical guide to building a modern personal desktop computer (PC) hardware system. It is intended for people with limited knowledge of computers. Therefore, technical concepts are carefully explained. Indeed, some complex concepts, such as calculating component bandwidths, are presented multiple times in various contexts. A glindex of Information Technology (IT) terms is also provided.

Bill Sydnes, Lead Engineer at IBM in 1982, originally defined a PC as 'a computer built from third-party hardware and software'. That definition was later popularly re-defined to refer to 'a stand-alone, non-Apple desktop computer used by one person at a time'. Nowadays, some people also consider portable computing devices such as laptops to be personal computers. Nevertheless, in this book, the term 'personal computer' refers to a non-Apple desktop computer that an ordinary person can build from third-party components for their personal or professional use.

The instructions provided in this book primarily relate to PCs that run on Windows, UNIX, or Linux-based operating systems (OSs). These instructions cover every step of PC-building — from selecting components to system testing and troubleshooting. The instructions are supported with numerous photos. The book is not about building Hackintosh computer systems. A Hackintosh is a non-Apple PC running a Mac operating system. Hackintoshes are problematic to build, unreliable, and not supported by Apple.

Computer technology advances so quickly that by the time you research and build a PC, some of its components will be superseded. The strategy advocated in this book is to use currently available components that meet your technical needs; are within your budget and provide enough flexibility to meet your perceived future needs. Prices of hardware and software also change quickly. Mentioned prices are in American dollars unless otherwise indicated.

You might recognize the cartoon character, Ding Duck, from *The Swamp* cartoons. In this book, we see two sides of Ding's personality. One side offers friendly advice; the other side gives stern warnings about common mistakes. To remind you that computer building should be satisfying, not stressful, Ding sometimes cracks jokes. In fact, his second joke is below.

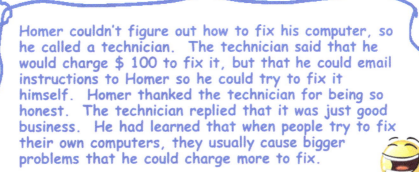

Ding's friendly side.

Ding's annoyed side.

Homer couldn't figure out how to fix his computer, so he called a technician. The technician said that he would charge $ 100 to fix it, but that he could email instructions to Homer so he could try to fix it himself. Homer thanked the technician for being so honest. The technician replied that it was just good business. He had learned that when people try to fix their own computers, they usually cause bigger problems that he could charge more to fix.

There is some confusion in the IT industry about units of measurement. This confusion mainly results from the use of two systems called the 'metric system' (i.e., 'decimal system') and the 'binary system'. The official name of the metric system, the *Système International*, is abbreviated as 'SI'. The metric system uses units that are multiples of 1,000, which are powers of 10. For instance, 1,000 equals 10^3, which is 10 X 10 X 10 in the metric system. So, 1 kilobyte in the metric system is 1,000 bytes. The binary system uses units that are multiples of 1,024, which are powers of two. For instance, 2^{10}, which is 2 X 2 X 2 X 2 X 2 X 2 X 2 X 2 X 2 X 2, equals 1,024. So, 1 kilobyte equals 1,024 bytes in the binary system. The IT industry originally used the binary system because, until recently all computers could only use two binary digits, which could only have values of '0' or '1'.

The IT industry historically used the same unit names, such as 'kilobyte', 'megabyte' and 'gigabyte', and their respective abbreviations, 'KB', 'MB', and 'GB', to refer to corresponding units in both systems. For instance, '1 kilobyte' was used to refer to both '1,024 binary system bytes' and '1,000 metric system bytes'.

People working in the IT industry usually know which system units are intended. Nevertheless, there are some situations where confusions can occur. For instance, many computer hardware manufacturers use metric units to refer to flash memory capacities but use binary units to refer to main and cache memory capacities. Also, some operating systems and software programs use binary units when referring to main memory, secondary memory, and file sizes but use metric units when referring to transmission and processor speeds. Moreover, different operating systems use different units. Windows reports file sizes and storage device capacities using binary units, and the Linux kernel also uses binary prefixes when booting up. However, Ubuntu has used decimal units since its 10.10 release — as has the Mac OS since version 10.6.

The International Electrotechnical Commission (IEC) and some other standards organizations decided to eliminate the confusion between the metric and binary systems in 1998. To do that, they adopted International Standard IEC 60027-2. It contained a list of new binary prefixes that only refer to powers of 1,024. The third edition of Standard IEC 60027-2, published in 2005, extended that list up to 'yobi' to match the corresponding metric prefix units.

The new prefixes of the binary system units start with the first two letters of the names of the corresponding SI unit prefixes. However, the next two letters are 'bi' (for 'binary'). For example, 'ki' + 'bi' = 'kibi'. So, in the binary system, 'kibibyte' means 'kilo binary byte to the power of 1', or '1,024'. Similarly, 'mebibyte' means 'kilo binary byte to the power of 2', which is $(2^{10})^2$, or 1,048,576 bytes.

The first syllables of the names of the binary units should be pronounced the same way as the first syllables of the names of the corresponding SI prefixes. The second syllables should be pronounced 'bee.'

Most authorities, such as the US National Institute of Standards and Technology, prescribe that unit names in both systems are treated as common nouns and are not capitalized. Also, most authorities say that periods should not be used with abbreviations of unit names in either system. The division slash '/' meaning 'per' may be used once in both metric and binary units.

From 1998, traditional unit prefixes were only supposed to be used to refer to decimal-system units. For example, 'kilobyte' was only supposed to denote '1,000 bytes' and 'megabyte' was only supposed to denote '1,000,000 bytes'. The International Bureau of Weights and Measures, which maintains the SI system of units, now prohibits the use of the traditional prefixes to denote binary values. The values and names of the units in the two systems are shown in Table 1.1.

Table 1.1: Binary and Decimal IT Measuring Systems

Binary and Metric Units									
Binary Units									
Names	byte	kibibyte	mebibyte	gibibyte	tebibyte	pebibyte	exbibyte	zebibyte	yobibyte
Short Forms	B	KB[1]	MB	GB[2]	TB	PB	EB	ZB	YB
Binary Powers	-	$1{,}024^1$	$1{,}024^2$	$1{,}024^3$	$1{,}024^4$	$1{,}024^5$	$1{,}024^6$	$1{,}024^7$	$1{,}024^8$
Powers of 10	-	$(2^{10})^1$	$(2^{10})^2$	$(2^{10})^3$	$(2^{10})^4$	$(2^{10})^5$	$(2^{10})^6$	$(2^{10})^7$	$(2^{10})^8$
Bytes	1	1,024	1,048,576	1,073,741,824	1,099,511,627,776	1,125,899,906,842,624	1,152,921,504,606,846,976	1,180,591,620,717,411,303,424	1,208,925,819,614,629,174,706,176
Metric Units									
Names	byte	kilobyte	megabyte	gigabyte	terabyte	petabyte	exabyte	zettabyte	yottabyte
Short Forms	B	KiB[1]	MiB	Gib[2]	TiB	PiB	EiB	ZiB	YiB
Powers of 10		10^3	10^6	10^9	10^{12}	10^{15}	10^{18}	10^{21}	10^{24}
Powers of 1,000	-	$1{,}000^1$	$1{,}000^2$	$1{,}000^3$	$1{,}000^4$	$1{,}000^5$	$1{,}000^6$	$1{,}000^7$	$1{,}000^8$
Bytes	1	1,000	1,000,000	1,000,000,000	1,000,000,000,000	1,000,000,000,000,000	1,000,000,000,000,000,000	1,000,000,000,000,000,000,000	1,000,000,000,000,000,000,000,000

Notes: 1. 'Kilobyte' is sometimes unofficially abbreviated as 'kB', 'Kbyte', and 'K'. However, in the SI, the capital 'K' by itself is reserved to represent the Kelvin unit of temperature. So, in the metric system, only the lower-case 'k' should be used to informally represent 'kilobyte'. 2. 'GIG' is sometimes used informally to mean 'giga'.

The metric system (i.e., the SI) is the most commonly used system, and therefore, it is used wherever possible in this book. However, many products and concepts that were traditionally measured with binary system units are still described with traditional binary system unit names. Moreover, there has been little industry acceptance of the new SI binary unit names. Therefore, in accordance with current popular usage, traditional binary unit names are still also used in this book. If popular usage changes to exclusively favor the usage of the new SI binary unit names, they will be exclusively adopted in future editions of this book. Table 1.2 lists the units of measurement that are used in this book.

Table 1.2: Information Technology Units of Measure

Units	Short Forms	Meanings
alternating current	ac	often abbreviated as AC, A/C, ACT, A.C. or A-C but 'ac' non-capitalized is recommended by the Institute of Electrical and Electronics Engineers (IEEE)
bit	b	a binary digit which represents either a single On or Off signal
bit rate	b/s	speed with which bits of data are transmitted over a channel
Byte	B	a group of 8 bits
candelas per meter squared	(cd/m^2)	historically, the light emitted by a common 'standard' candle — although the modern SI definition is much more technical[1]
decibel	dB (or DB)	measure of amplitude (i.e., loudness) of an audio signal
floating-point operations per second	FLOP	the speed at which a computer can make calculations using approximate numbers with a limited number of significant digits
gigabit	Gb (or Gbit)	1,000,000,000 bits
gigabit Ethernet[2]	GbE (or GigE)	1,000,000,000 bits per second
gigapixels	GP	1,000,000,000 pixels
gigatexel	GT	1,000,000,000 filtered textured pixels
hertz	Hz	1 Hz = 1 operational cycle per second
in/out operations per second	IOPS	the number of reads and writes a device can manage in one second
joule	J	amount of work needed to produce one watt of power for one second (symbol is capitalized [J] but the word is not capitalized)
kilobit	kb	1,000 bits
kilohertz	kHz	1,000 Hz
megabit	Mb	1,000,000 bits
megahertz	MHz	1,000,000 cycles per second
megapixels	MP	1,000,000 pixels
millisecond	ms	1/1,000 of a second
nanosecond	ns	1/1,000,000,000 of a second
petaFLOP	–	1,000,000,000,000,000 floating-point operations per second
revolutions per minute	rpm	number of rotations of 360 degrees per minute
total harmonic distortion + noise	THD+N	the total energy in the sound output by a device, excluding the input energy that is often expressed as a ratio of the distortion plus noise divided by the pressure of the total signal, which is expressed as a percentage
volt	V	electromotive force between two points on a wire carrying a current of one ampere when the power moved between the points is one watt
watt	W	electrical current flow of one ampere with the force of one volt
Watts per meter-Kelvin	W/mK	1 W/mK is the passage of 1 W per second through a contact surface of 1 m^2 between contacting materials that differ in temperature by 1-degree Kelvin (K)[3]

Notes: 1. Luminescence is also measured by the non-SI-unit, 'nit'. One nit equals one candela per square meter. 2. Ethernet is a set of networking technologies used to transmit Ethernet frames over a network. '10 GbE' means 'at a rate of 10 gigabits (i.e., 10 billion bits) per second' in accordance with the IEEE 802.3ae-2002 standard. 'IEEE' stands for the 'Institute of Electrical and Electronics Engineers'. One of its services is developing global industry standards. 3. 1° Kelvin is the same as 1°C, but the Kelvin scale starts at absolute zero, and its freezing temperature of water is 273.15 degrees K.

The conventions for separating groups of digits in numbers have varied in different countries. Traditionally, writers in English-speaking countries used commas as the delimiters between groups of three digits. However, some writers who used that comma-standard, used commas in four-digit numbers such as '2,020', while others did not. Writers in many non-English-speaking European countries used periods for the same purpose. To try to standardize the matter, the International Organization for Standardization recently published the SI/ISO 31-0 standard that prescribed the use of spaces between groups of three digits. For example, that standard would require the use of '20 020' instead of '20,020' or '20.200'. Since 2003, the use of spaces as digit-separators has also been endorsed by the International Bureau of Weights and Measures.

Nevertheless, in this book, the traditional English standard of separating every third digit with commas is used in numbers with more than three digits. That is because commas provide clearer, more positive visual signals than blank spaces. Those clearer signals make it easier to accurately and confidently write and read numbers.

'Bit' is not defined in the SI. However, the International Electrotechnical Commission specifies that 'bit' should be represented by a lower-case letter 'b'. The Metric Interchange Format stipulates that the upper-case letter 'B' should be reserved to represent 'byte'. Historically, 'byte' had no standard meaning either. Its size related to whatever size units were used by various hardware drivers. However, international standard IEC 80000-13 has now standardized it to mean '8 bits'. The " symbol represents 'inch'. One inch equals about 2.54 cm.

Some confusion also exists about the various terms used to refer to the parts of connections between IT components. Part of the reason is that some of these terms have meanings that overlap somewhat. Table 1.3 provides clarifications of the meanings of these terms.

Table 1.3: IT Connection Terms

Terms	Meanings
connector	A connector is a part of a cable, wire, port, expansion card, or slot that can make a data or power connection with another piece of hardware. For example, the connector on the end of a USB cable allows it to be connected to a USB port, which is also a connector.
female	A female connector has a hole or holes able to accept a male connector.
header	A header is a group of connector pins. Connectors with female pinholes can be connected to headers. Headers are often used to allow electrical connections to be made to motherboards.
jack	A jack is a circular female port that allows a compatible circular plug to be plugged into it. Jacks are most often used to connect cables carrying audio signals. There are three standard sizes of jacks: 2.5 mm (3/32") 3.5 mm (1/8") and 6.3 mm (1/4").
male	A male connector has a protruding plug or pins able to plug into a female connector.
pin	A pin is a small wire male connector that can be plugged into a female pinhole connector to enable the transmission of an electrical current.
plug	A plug is a male end part of a cable that inserts into a socket or port. For example, the plug on the end of the power supply unit cord can be inserted into a mains power source socket.[1]
port	A port is a female docking point used to connect an external device to a motherboard. For example, the PS/2 ports on the backs of many older motherboards allow keyboards and mice with PS/2 plugs to be connected to them. PS/2 has been a legacy architecture since 2001. More recent motherboards are likely to have USB ports instead. Expansion cards also have ports to enable them to connect to external devices such as speakers.

Table 1.3 continued on next page

slot	A slot is a connector on a motherboard formed from a row of pinholes that allows an expansion card or random access memory (RAM) module to be attached to it. The term is sometimes incorrectly used interchangeably with 'socket'. This may be because some early types of central processor units (CPUs) could be attached to motherboards by slots.
socket	A socket is a type of connector on a motherboard that allows mechanical and electrical connections to be made with a CPU. The term 'socket' also refers to a mains electrical power point outlet that accepts a power plug.[1]

Note: 1. Americans often refer to 'mains power' as 'wall power' or 'grid power'.

Recently there has been much discussion in the IT media about the future of modular desktop computers. Some commentators argue that modular desktop PCs will soon be superseded by mobile devices with central processing units (CPUs) soldered onto motherboards — just as audio processor units often are already. Indeed, all-in-one computers that even include monitors are already available. For example, an HP All-in-One 22-c0025xt model with a 21.5" screen, an Intel Core i3 CPU, a 1 TB spinning hard drive, 8 GB of DDR 4 memory, two internal speakers, and an Intel 630 UHD graphics card costs only $ 560. It requires a third-party external 90 W power supply unit, however. The HP All-in-One computer is shown in Figure 1.1. An even more extreme all-in-one concept is Intel's Compute Stick CS325. It is barely the size of a large USB flash (i.e., thumb) drive, yet it contains a basic computer with an HDMI (High-Definition Multimedia Interface) monitor cable plug. It costs about $ 400. An example is also shown in Figure 1.1.

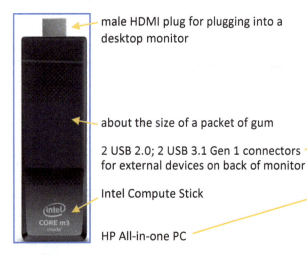

male HDMI plug for plugging into a desktop monitor

about the size of a packet of gum

2 USB 2.0; 2 USB 3.1 Gen 1 connectors for external devices on back of monitor

Intel Compute Stick

HP All-in-one PC

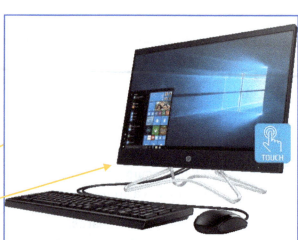

Figure 1.1: Non-modular Computers

Although such factory-built all-in-one computers are economical and offer some advantages, they do not provide the power, features, flexibility, repairability, and expandability of modular desktop PCs. Even ordinary factory-built computers are invariably compromised. In other words, they have performance bottlenecks. For instance, the bottleneck might be a weak integrated graphics processor unit, a motherboard with insufficient expansion slots, or a case that doesn't provide enough front USB 3.0 or USB 3.1 ports. By designing our systems, we can avoid such bottlenecks.

Do-it-yourself (DIY)-built PCs can also be less expensive than factory-built ones. This is partially because we can reuse components such as cases, fans, LED lights, and secondary storage devices. It is also because we can avoid paying for unwanted bundled software, such as operating systems (OSs) and applications, that usually come with factory-built computers.

For instance, UNIX and Linux users usually must buy Windows or Mac OSs when they buy factory-built computers — even though they might not want either of those OSs. Similarly, we can avoid paying for hardware components that we do not want. Instead, we can shop for the best-priced components that we do want.

Moreover, we can save more money because we don't have to pay for someone to build and test our computers. Nor do we have to pay premiums merely to have commercial brand names on our modular computers. We can save yet more money by repairing our self-built computers rather than always taking them to service technicians.

Personally-built modular systems can also last longer than off-the-shelf systems because we can select better quality components than might be installed in factory-built systems. Moreover, components can be upgraded or replaced when necessary.

Building a PC is an excellent practical way to learn about information technology. This experience may even help some people start careers in the IT industry. The experience can be shared by socializing in local computer clubs, as shown in Figure 1.2. Online PC-building forums offer other social computer-building opportunities. Some examples of online computer-building forums are:www.forums.custompcreview.com, www.reddit.com/r/buildapc, and www.forums.mysuperpc.com.

Figure 1.2: Social Aspect of DIY Computer-building

The famous Canadian philosopher of communication theory, Marshall McLuhan, predicted some time ago that, 'The age of automation is going to be the age of "Do it yourself".' We should take advantage of the DIY-opportunity still available to us during this automation age. As long as we do so, third-party manufacturers will continue to develop new components. Two notable recent examples were provided by AMD and Intel. AMD recently released its revolutionary Ryzen CPUs, which are featured in this book. Intel recently announced that they are developing their first graphic card for release in 2020 (which might be featured in a future edition of this book). Another encouraging fact is that more than fifty-five new motherboards were launched at Computex in 2019. If such third-party computer components were discontinued, we would lose the chance to build computers tailored to our individual needs. Computex is the main international ICT (Information and Communication Technology) trade exhibition, which is held in Taipei, Taiwan.

When DIY personal computer components first became available in the mid-1970s. They usually came bundled in kits. The amount of primary memory (i.e., RAM) typically provided in those first-generation kits was 65 kb. The 'kb' abbreviation refers to 'kilobits' — not 'kilobytes'! Do-it-yourself builders needed considerable electronic skills to build those weak computers.

Sometimes, DIY-builders even had to solder memory chips and circuit boards onto motherboards. Solder is a metal with a low melting temperature, such as lead or tin, used for joining two pieces of other metals that have higher melting temperatures.

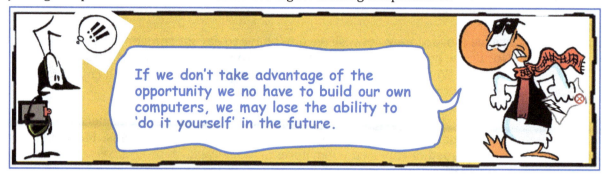

> If we don't take advantage of the opportunity we no have to build our own computers, we may lose the ability to 'do it yourself' in the future.

That might be why some people still think that building computers is difficult. However, these days, personal computers are built from standardized components that are assembled with standardized, mainly toolless, connections. That makes building a PC almost foolproof. There are, nevertheless, two possible disadvantages to building personal computers.

1. Although DIY-builders might save money, those savings come at a cost. That cost is time. It takes most people many hours to plan and build their first computers. So, people with little free time might have no option but to accept factory-built PCs.

2. Factory-built PCs carry manufacturer warranties on their entire systems, whereas there is no single place to take self-built computers for warranty support. However, that usually isn't a disadvantage because brand-name boxed hardware components have their own warranties. Indeed, those individual warranties are often better than the warranties that come with factory-built computers. Moreover, DIY-builders are often able to take advantage of extended warranty options for boxed components. The components within factory-built retail computers are usually only covered by the warranties provided for the entire computers.

Table 1.4 provides a checklist that you can use to assess whether building a computer is a good idea for yourself. This checklist will encourage you to consider the matter objectively. You should score at least 6 to have enough motivation to satisfactorily build your own computer.

Table 1.4: Reasons for Building your own Computer

Reasons	Very Important	Somewhat Important	Not Important
build a PC to meet your needs	2	1	0
enrich your knowledge of Information Technology (IT)	2	1	0
lead to an IT business or career	2	1	0
save money on the cost of computer	2	1	0
repair and upgrade your computer in the future	2	1	0
gain confidence from completing a technical project	2	1	0
ensure that your PC has high-quality components	2	1	0
enjoy social contact with other computer-builders	2	1	0
enjoy creative design or fabrication[1]	2	1	0
Column Total Points			
Grand Total of all Columns			

Note: 1. For builders who enjoy case-designing or modeling. The 'modelling' spelling is used in most countries, aside from the United States, where 'modeling' is preferred.

2. Planning the Build

Planning and building your first PC can be daunting, expensive, and even dangerous if you are unprepared. However, building your own custom PC will be easy, economical, and safe if you prepare yourself.

The first thing to consider is what you want to use your computer for. A computer has only one function: running software. Therefore, the question you need to answer is, 'What are the main software programs I want to run?' For instance, ask yourself: 'Do I mainly intend to use an Internet browser and an email client application for emails? Do I want to use a sophisticated desktop publishing program or just an ordinary word processor? Do I want to use video-editing software? Do I want to play sophisticated video games? Do I want to create high-quality podcasts? Do I want to use virtual reality (VR) programs?' You need to know the answers to such questions to select the right software. Only then can you sensibly select the correct hardware to run that software.

Your first software decision is to decide which operating system (OS) you want to use. A computer OS is, after all, software. An OS controls all a computer's operations, including its memory and installed software and hardware.

Some novice computer-builders think that there are only two OSs, Microsoft's Windows for personal computers and Apple's macOS for Apple computers. (Apple used to spell the name of its operating system 'Mac OS' but since 2016 has spelled it as 'macOS'.) However, there are hundreds of other OSs that you could use instead of Windows. One example is FreeDOS. It is a free DOS-compatible operating system that can run legacy DOS software. FreeDOS is an improved version of the old MS-DOS and PC-DOS command-line operating systems. 'DOS' stands for 'Disk Operating System'. DOS was the only type of OS before graphical user interface (GUI) OSs such as oNLine System, Star, Apple Lisa, Apple Macintosh, and Windows were developed. Another example is eComStation 2.1. It is an updated version of OS/2 Warp, which IBM stopped selling in 2006. Since 2015 it has been developed and marketed as ArcaOS by Arca Noae. The personal edition costs $ 129. The basic version of Microsoft Windows at the time this book was written was Windows 10 Home Edition. It cost $ 119.99 from the online Windows shop. Microsoft is also working on a lite version of Windows, which probably will be branded 'Lite'.

Most non-Windows PC OSs are based on Linux. Linux was developed in 1991 by Finnish student Linus Torvalds. Linus designed Linux as a clone of another OS, UNIX. A clone is a program that operates like another program but does not necessarily have a similar user interface. So, although Linux works like UNIX, it does not necessarily look like UNIX. Nowadays, there is not just one Linux OS. Rather, there are many versions called 'distributions'.

Nevertheless, all Linux OS distributions share two essential components. They all have the Linux kernel, which is still maintained by Torvalds. They all also have a set of tools that provide users with a method of interacting with the Linux kernel. This set of tools is called GNU and is sponsored by the Free Software Foundation. 'GNU' is a recursive acronym meaning 'GNUs' Not UNIX!' That means that, although GNU is designed like UNIX, it does not contain UNIX code. Somewhat confusingly, there is also a Linux distribution called GNU. Because all the Linux distributions need both the Linux kernel and the GNU tools, many people refer to them as 'GNU/Linux' OSs. Although that name is more complex that 'Linux', it is not a complex as Linux's original name, which was 'Yggdrasil Linux/GNU/X'! Linux distributions offer three significant advantages over Windows. 1) They are more reliable. 2) They are not as vulnerable to security issues such as viruses. 3) They are open-source software, and their source code is freely available for anyone to use.

'Source code' refers to the essential parts of a computer program that are written in a high-level language which can be read and modified by programmers. For example, Google programmers developed the Android operating system that is used on mobile devices from Linux's source code. Android is not normally used as an OS on desktop PCs because it has some limitations. For instance, it:

- can only open one screen application at a time,
- can only open one window on a screen at a time,
- only provides basic support for mice, and
- does not support right-clicking.

Nevertheless, if you are interested in the challenge of using Android as the OS on your PC, you could follow the instructions provided in an article by Juderson published on TechNorm's website entitled, *How to Install and Run Android OS on Your PC the Easy Way*.

The three advantages of Linux mentioned previously are the reasons that many large enterprises use Linux distributions. For example, Red Hat Enterprise developed the Linux Red Hat distribution for the commercial server market. A server is a powerful computer and software system that provides data and/or services to other computers.

The disadvantage of most Linux distributions is that they are complicated to install and use. For that reason, they are mostly used by 'power users' with advanced computing skills. Only a few Linux distributions are relatively easy to install and use. The most popular user-friendly distribution is Ubuntu. It is reasonably easy for beginners to install and use and has a modern graphical user interface. What is more, it is free. At the time that the fourth edition of this book was written, the latest version of Ubuntu was 18.04. That is a long-term support release. That means that it will be supported for at least five years by Canonical Ltd. Canonical is the private company which maintains Ubuntu. Even though Ubuntu is fairly easy to use, some users still find it to be too complex. Fortunately, even simpler free alternatives are available. One user-friendly distribution is named 'elementary OS'; another is 'Manjaro'.

In 2010 Microsoft CEO Steve Ballmer declared that 'Linux is a cancer'. Yet, as the fourth edition of this book was being produced, Microsoft released its own Linux distribution, called Azure Sphere OS. Microsoft is now promoting it as a more secure OS for Internet-connected devices than Windows. Microsoft has also partnered with Canonical to develop a Windows Subsystem for Linux (WSL) to enable Ubuntu to be installed directly inside Windows. WSL allows users to run Ubuntu within Windows without setting up a virtual machine. Microsoft provides instructions for installing the WSL at https://docs.microsoft.com/en-us/windows/wsl/install-win10.

The original version of UNIX was developed AT&T's Bell Laboratories in the early-1970s. It is a highly portable OS that can be used on all types of computers — including mainframes. 'Mainframe' is a loosely defined term referring to an expensive, high-performance computer used for large-scale computing tasks that require greater reliability and power than ordinary desktop computers can provide. The UNIX trademark is now controlled by The Open Group. The Open Group is an industry consortium that was established in 1996 to develop open technology standards and certifications. UNIX is often written as 'Unix' or 'UNIX', but the open group specifies 'UNIX'.

As most Mac computer users know, macOS is based on UNIX and Apple released the latest version of macOS, 10.13.4 High Sierra, as a free upgrade in 2018. As mentioned in the introduction, it is possible to use the macOS on non-Mac PCs because, these days, Apple uses Intel CPUs in its computers. However, it is a breach of Apple's end-user license agreement to use a Mac OS on a non-Apple computer. Moreover, installing a Mac OS on a PC with Windows OS already installed is usually a complex procedure that involves running a virtual computer.

You can, however, simplify the process of running some operating systems alongside Windows by using the VirtualBox utility. For instance, you might want to try a UNIX OS or a Linux distribution without worrying about your installed Windows OS and files being affected. Sun Microsystem's free VirtualBox is offered by Oracle at www.virtualbox.org/wiki/Downloads. To use it, you will need to insert a CD/DVD disc with a Windows 10 ISO into the PC's optical drive. Appendix 7 provides instructions for creating a Windows 10 ISO on a USB device, which could be adapted. Then,

1. Select the correct package for your system's host operating system and then download VirtualBox 6.0.10, as shown in Figure 2.1.

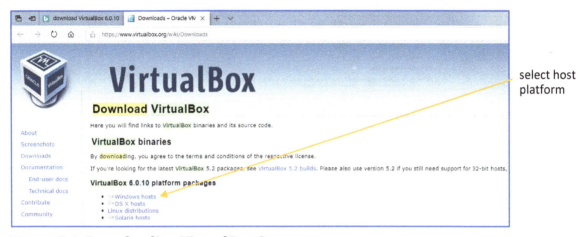

Figure 2.1: Downloading VirtualBox Screen

2. Save and then run the downloaded VirtualBox file.

3. On the pop-up Oracle VM VirtualBox Manager box, click the Next button and then follow the Oracle VM wizard's installation instructions. Click the Finish button when the installation is complete.

4. On the next Oracle pop-up box, click 'Machine' from the main menu, as shown in Figure 2.2—step 1 and then click 'New…' from the pop-up menu.

5. Then select the OS Type and enter a name for the OS you want to try, as shown in Figure 2.2—step 2. Also, select the OS version, in this case, 'Oracle Solaris 11 (64-bit)', as shown in Figure 2.2—step 3. Then, click the 'Next' button, as shown in Figure 2.2—step 4.

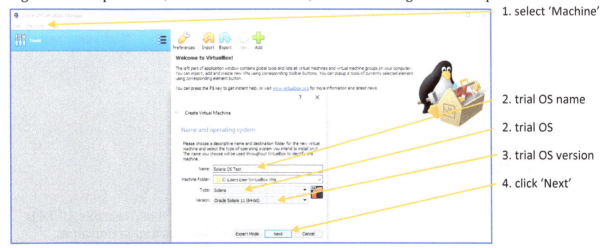

Figure 2.2: Selecting Trial OS in VirtualBox

6. On the pop-up Memory size screen, click 'Next' to accept the memory size of 1,536 MB.

7. On the next pop-up Hard Disk screen, click the Create button to a create a Virtual hard disk of 16.00 GB. Then, click the Next button on the next Hard disk file type pop-up screen to accept the default VDI file type.

8. On the next pop-up Storage on physical hard disk screen, click the Next button to accept a dynamically allocated file size.

9. On the next pop-up File location and size screen, click the Create button to accept the file name, and size, as shown in Figure 2.3.

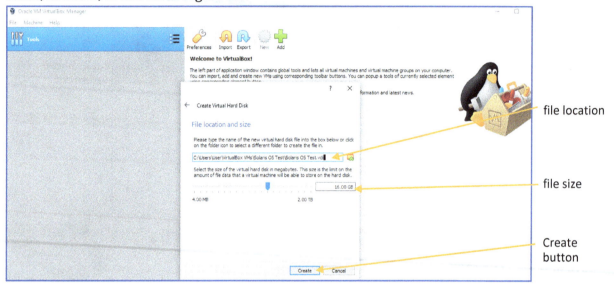

Figure 2.3: Selecting VirtualBox File Location and Size

10. On the next pop-up Oracle VM VirtualBox Manager screen, click the green Start arrow, as shown in Figure 2.4.

Figure 2.4: Selecting Oracle VirtualBox

Like Linux, UNIX is more stable than Windows and has better built-in security features. Moreover, it supports greater processing potential than Windows. For those reasons, UNIX is normally used on powerful vital scientific and commercial workstations and mainframes.

Nowadays, there are five main versions of UNIX. Many DIY computer-builders aren't aware that three of these versions can be used for free on their ordinary personal computers just as well as they can be used on the biggest mainframe computers in the world. These versions even have user-friendly graphical user interfaces similar to Microsoft Window's GUI.

One of those versions is Solaris (previously named Sun Solaris). It is owned by Oracle. Oracle allows anyone to download and use the latest version of Solaris, 11.4, for free. However, their license conditions only permit Solaris to be used as a 'development platform' — not for 'commercial or production' purposes.

Another free UNIX OS is FreeBSD. It is available without the restriction imposed by Oracle. FreeBSD has been developed by a large worldwide community of users for more than thirty-five years. The FreeBSD version being prepared for release while the fourth edition of this book was being written was 12.0. There is also another free OS based on FreeBSD called TrueOS. TrueOS offers some additional features, such as support for the latest Intel graphic chipsets, and disk encryption. Its current version is 18.06.

Comparing the hundreds of OSs would be extremely time-consuming. Fortunately therefore, many of them are assessed and compared by G2 Crowd, an American business solutions review service. An example of a matrix from their website is shown in Figure 2.5. According to that matrix, the high-performance OSs that best combine 'user satisfaction' and 'market presence' in the small business and home sector might be Ubuntu or CentOS.

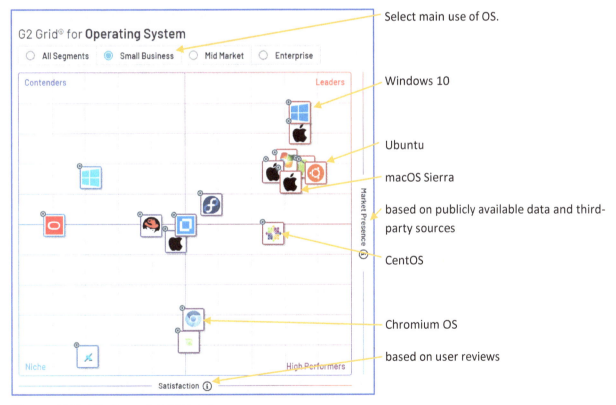

Figure 2.5: G2 Crowd OS Matrix

The logos of some popular contemporary PC operating systems are shown in Figure 2.6.

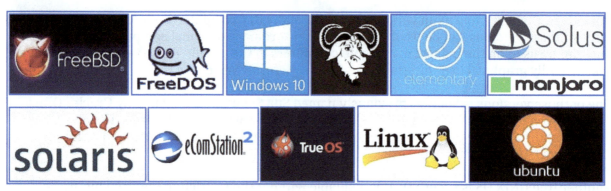

Figure 2.6: PC Operating System Logos

Although many operating systems have been mentioned in this section, I have not yet mentioned what is probably the most common PC OS in the world. Most ordinary DIY computer-builders are not even aware of this OS. But, given the huge number of Intel CPUs installed in computers, the most common PC OS is probably MINIX. MINIX is a UNIX-like OS that has been embedded within Intel chipsets for the last decade or so. Since 2008, these chipsets have contained tiny microprocessors called the Intel Management Engine (Intel ME).

These engines are actually entire computer control systems. They have their own tiny CPU cores, ROMs and RAMs. Intel ME runs on secret code written by Intel, which, in turn, apparently runs the MINIX operating system independently of system main operating systems. MINIX controls systems' memories, motherboard bus drivers, file systems, and other critical system operations.

Recently the global IT security firm, Positive Technologies, reported that this system presented serious vulnerabilities. For example, they discovered that MINIX controls web servers and allows unauthorized people to remotely connect to computers — and even to access the computer's CPUs! What is more, it allowed that access even when system firewalls are turned on — and even when systems are not running!

In November 2017, Intel acknowledged MINIX's security risks. Intel has since provided a detection tool that can show if a microprocessor's management engines are vulnerable. Users can download the INTEL-SA-00086 Detection Tool for Windows or the SA00086_Linux.tar.gz tool for Linux.

AMD's Ryzen CPUs are not entirely free from similar issues. Since 2013 AMD CPUs have incorporated a somewhat similar AMD Secure Technology. However, as near as I can figure out, the potential vulnerabilities discovered with that technology do not allow unauthorized remote access. Moreover, AMD has prepared a firmware security update that is automatically installed whenever Ryzen-system UEFI-BIOS updates are downloaded. That is one reason I chose a Ryzen CPU for the project described in this book.

Since 2008, most PCs have been capable of operating in either 32-bit or 64-bit modes. So, whatever OS you choose, you need to decide whether you want a 32-bit or a 64-bit version. 'Thirty-two-bit' and '64-bit' refer to the sizes of the data paths used by central processor units. Sixty-four-bit data path systems handle blocks of memory that are twice the size of 32-bit systems. That means that they can make full use of the capabilities of modern 64-bit CPUs and work faster with applications, such as games and video encoders, that must quickly process large batches of data.

What is more, 64-bit OSs can access more than 4 gigabytes (GB) of memory, whereas 32-bit OSs can only support up to 4 GB of memory. In the future, nearly all applications will be 64-bit applications. An application is a program that allows a user to complete a task. For all these reasons, your best choice is likely to be a 64-bit OS.

The amounts of memory that can be used by OSs include all the types of memory within their systems — not just their random access memories. For instance, if a graphics processor unit used 1 GB of video RAM, a 32-bit OS could then only access 3 more GB of RAM — regardless of how much more RAM was installed. Other factors, aside from the OS, such as motherboard buses and chipsets, also limit the amount of RAM that can be effectively used by systems. Table 2.1 lists the amounts of RAM supported by some contemporary OSs.

Table 2.1: RAM Supported by OSs

Operating Systems	RAM Supported (GB)
Windows 98	1
Windows XP	4
Windows 8 64-bit Home Basic	128
Windows 10 32-bit	4
Windows 10 Home 64-bit	128
Windows 10 Pro 64-bit	512
Ubuntu 18.04 32-bit	64[1]
Ubuntu 18.04 64-bit	16,777,216,000 (or 16,777,216 TB)[2]
UNIX (Solaris 11.4)	100,000 (or 100+ TB)[3]

Notes: 1. Canonical recently stopped providing the 32-bit version of Ubuntu Server. 2. 'TB' means 'terabyte'. One TB = 1,000 GB. In practice, the amount of RAM is limited by hardware restrictions to 256 TB. 3. The computer that Oracle sells running the Solaris OS which can support the most RAM is the SPARC M6-32. It can support up to 32 TB of RAM.

The latest version of Ubuntu is only available in a 64-bit version. Microsoft has been foreshadowing the possibility that it would likewise provide only a 64-bit version of Windows since before Windows 7 was released. However, Windows 10, which was released in mid-2015, was still available in 32 and 64-bit versions. That decision was probably influenced by the chipsets that were provided on motherboards at the time.

If you do select a 64-bit operating system, the hardware and the software applications you install will need to support 64-bit architecture. 'Architecture' refers to the overall structure of a hardware device or software program. If you install a 64-bit version of Windows 8.1 or 10, you will not be able to run old legacy 16-bit architecture programs. Even many 32-bit software applications will not run properly on 64-bit OSs — although some 32-bit applications will run on 64-bit systems. Also, some older device drivers do not support 64-bit architecture. A device driver is a program that allows an OS to control a device.

You can check how compatible many hardware drivers and software applications are with the latest Windows OSs at the Windows compatibility center at www.microsoft.com/en-us/windows/compatibility/CompatCenter/. You can also check if a Windows 10 system is running in 32 or 64-bit mode by entering 'system' in the Windows' Cortana Type here to search dialog box. Then, in the menu box that appears, select 'About your PC' as shown in Figure 2.7. An example of the type of report you will receive is also shown in Figure 2.7.

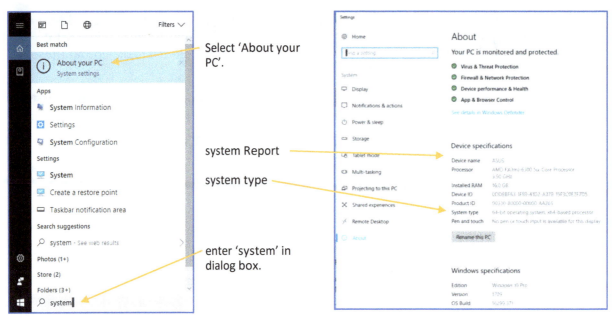

Figure 2.7: Windows 10 System Search and Report

It would be possible to develop a 128-bit operating system. However, then 128-bit CPUs, motherboards, device drivers and software programs would have to be developed to work with the 128-bit OS. But we have not yet made full use of the potential of 64-bit systems. It therefore seems unlikely that IT companies would spend the large amounts necessary to develop 128-bit operating systems in the near future. It seems more likely that they might develop an entirely new type of OS.

In fact, Cambridge Quantum Computing has recently developed a new type of OS named 't|ket>'. It can operate traditional supercomputers as well as new quantum computers. A few years ago, in 2015, a Cambridge Quantum Computing Limited representative announced that t|ket> was an integral part of quantum computing that would soon 'have profound and far-reaching effects on a vast number of aspects of our daily lives'.

Besides an OS, you will likely want to install a suite of office applications that includes a word processor. The standard Microsoft suite at the time the fourth edition of this book was written was Office 365 Home. It includes Word, Excel, PowerPoint, OneNote, Outlook, Publisher, and Access, as well as touchscreen support. OneNote is a sort of digital notebook that allows documents to be shared among users on a network such as the Internet. Microsoft charges Office 365 Home customers a subscription fee of $ 69.99 every year. Over five years, the cost amounts to $ 349.95!

Many other more economical office suites are also available. For example, Serif's Ability Office V6 provides a Word-like word processor, a spreadsheet, and a presentation-creator for a one-off cost of $ 39.99. Ashampoo also offer their Office 2018 suite, which includes a Microsoft-compatible word processor, a spreadsheet, and a presentation program for about $ 20. An even less-expensive office suite is provided for free by Google. The Google Docs suite includes a word processor and a spreadsheet as part of the Google Drive service. The Google Docs suite also allows users to collaboratively edit documents online in real-time similar to the way they could using OneNote. Google also offers its Google G Suite of programs with extra features for $ 60 per year.

The price of most Linux-based office suites is $ 0. Most Linux distributions come with integrated suites of office applications. For example, Ubuntu comes with the free LibreOffice 6.04 office suite, as well as the recently released Firefox Quantum web browser.

LibreOffice is probably the most popular Linux-based office suite. Two other popular free office suites are Apache OpenOffice 4.4 and Mobi Systems basic OfficeSuite V 4.6. Microsoft also offers a free suite called WPS Office Free. It is a basic lightweight version of MS Office that displays ads. A free Microsoft Office look-alike office suite called Smart Office has even been developed to run on Android. Polaris Office is a free cross-platform Windows/macOS suite that also displays ads. A computing platform is the environment, including the hardware and software — typically including the operating system — that runs a software program or hosts a service.

Table 2.2 provides an example checklist to stimulate your thinking about the OS and applications that you want to install. A blank checklist is provided for your use in Appendix 1.

Table 2.2: Software Selection Stimulation List

Task	Software Possibilities	Main Use	Some Use	Poss-ible Use
OS	Ubuntu 18.04 or Windows 10	✓		
desktop publishing	PagePlus X9		✓	
Internet browsing	Google Chrome 2018	✓		
email client service[1]	Gmail 2018	✓		
office suite	Apache OpenOffice 4.4	✓		
voice dictation/writing	Dragon Dictate 14		✓	
audio editing	WavePad v 8.4		✓	
game-playing /VR[2]	The Elder Scrolls V: Skyrim	✓		
photo editing/storage	GIMP 2.9.8		✓	
programming	Python 3.7[3]			✓
online study/research	Encyclopædia Britannica for Win10		✓	
VoIP[4] calls	Skype		✓	
web page design	Web Studio		✓	
computer-aided design (CAD)	AutoCAD 2017			✓
accounting	AccountEdge Pro			✓
video editing	VideoStudio Pro 2018			✓
other_____				
other_____				

Notes: 1. An email client service is a computer application that enables users to send and receive emails. 2. 'VR' stands for 'virtual reality'. VR is the computer-generated simulation of three-dimensional environments that people can interact with using special electronic equipment. 3. Version 3.7 was a beta version when the fourth edition of this book was being prepared. 4. Voice over Internet Protocol (VoIP) allows telephone calls to be transmitted over the Internet.

The next planning step is to research the hardware system requirements of the applications that you intend to install. You might need that information later on when selecting some of your system's components. An example list provided in Table 2.3. The term 'secondary storage' used in this table refers to non-volatile mass storage devices such as spinning hard drives, tape drives, solid-state drives (SSDs) and optical drives. At this stage, you do not need to fully understand all the other technical terms mentioned in Table 2.3. A blank Software System Requirements form is provided in Appendix 2 for your use.

Table 2.3: Example Software System Requirements

Software	CPU	RAM	Secondary Storage	Audio/Visual
Dragon Professional 14	2.2 GHz dual-core with 2 MB L2 cache	4 GB	3.2 GB	16-bit recording audio
Microsoft 64-bit Windows 10	1+ GHz 64-bit	2 GB	20 GB	DirectX 9 +; monitor at least 800 X 600-pixel resolution[1]
Adobe PageMaker 7.0.2	—[2]	512 MB	100 MB	1,024 X 600 or higher monitor resolution
Microsoft 365 Business 64-bit	64-bit with SSE2	2 GB	3.0 GB	DirectX 10 or higher graphics card and a 1,024 X 576 or higher resolution monitor
Adobe Premier Pro CC (video-editing)	64-bit Intel Core2 Duo or AMD Phenom II	8 GB	multiple 10+ GB RAID 0[3] fast spinning hard drives or SSDs	1,280 X 800, 16-bit color or above monitor and Adobe-certified graphic card[4]; 1 GB+ VRAM[4]
The Elder Scrolls V: Skyrim (game)	quad-core Intel or AMD	4 GB	6 GB	DirectX compatible audio on Nvidia GeForce GTX 260 or higher; ATI Radeon 4890 or higher; graphic card with 1 GB VRAM
AutoCAD 2017 64-bit	Athlon with SSE2 technology or Pentium 4 with EM64T support and SSE2 technology	4+ GB	6 GB	Direct 3-D-capable workstation-class graphics card with Pixel Shader 3.0 or greater, and a 1,280 X 1,024 True color video display adapter with 128+ MB VRAM
Encyclopædia Britannica	—	—	4 GB	—
Web Studio 5.0.23 (web page design)	Pentium 4 CPU or AMD equivalent	1 GB	200 MB	CD/DVD optical drive
Python 3.7[5]	—	—	—	—
Audacity 2.2.2 music editor	—	—	—	—
FileMaker Pro 16 (database manager)	1+ GHz	2 GB	—	1,024 X 768+ graphic card and monitor, and an optical drive

Notes: 1. A pixel is a single dot on a screen. 2. '—' indicates that no specification is provided. 3. RAID (Redundant Array of Independent Disks) 0 is a system that automatically copies files to a group of disk drives. 4. 'VRAM' means 'video RAM'. 5. Python is a free programming language.

We can make three significant observations from Table 2.3.

1. Some applications require at least 8 GB of random access memory (RAM).

2. Collectively, the applications require about 62 GB of secondary storage space.

3. Some applications have highly specified audio/visual support requirements.

If you don't have the time or inclination to research the hardware requirements of the programs you intend to install, you should at least consider the general types of tasks you intend to undertake. Every system will be somewhat different. Nevertheless, Table 2.4 provides some general suggestions about the hardware requirements for typical types of systems.

Table 2.4: Basic Minimum Hardware Requirement Suggestions

System	CPU	RAM	Secondary Storage	Audio/ Visual	Case & Power Supply
basic word-processing and game playing	dual-core[1] to support multitasking [2]	4 GB	DVD/CD burner, and a 100+ GB SATA hard drive	onboard video and sound	inexpensive mid-tower ATX case, and a 300+ watt power supply
serious game playing	3+ GHz AMD or Intel quad-core	16+ GB	fast 500+ GB SATA or SCSI hard drive and an Ultra HD Blu-ray	2 X 1+ GB linked high specification ATI or Nvidia graphic cards	mid-tower ATX case, and 600+ watt power supply
video-editing	quad-core for multi-threaded codecs[3]	8+ GB	two fast 1 TB+ hard drives with RAID	fast graphics card with 1+ GB VRAM	mid-tower ATX case, and 500+ watt power supply
server[4]	AMD Athlon or Pentium 4 or better	8+ GB	at least two 2 TB RAID hard drives	Gigabit Ethernet port	full-ATX tower, and 500+ watt power supply
virtual reality	AMD FX 8350 or better, or Intel i5-4590 or better	16+ GB	fast 1 TB+ hard drive	Oculus Rift[5] or HTC Vive VR tracking headset; graphic card that can render 180 f/s, OS with Direct X 12; HDMI 1.4 video	mid-tower ATX case, and 600+ watt power supply, and at least two USB 3.0 ports and one USB 3.1 port

Notes: 1. 'Dual-core' means that a single physical central microprocessor contains two virtual CPUs. 2. Multitasking is carrying out two or more different operations or running two or more programs at the same time. 3. A codec is a combined hardware and software system used to convert analog signals into digital signals and back again. 4. A server is a computer and software system that provides data and/or services to other computers. For example, a network server is used as a central database shared by users across a network. 5. Oculus Rift is a virtual reality headset developed by Oculus VR. It will require USB 3.0 ports to enable Oculus Touch in the future. In 2019, Oculus VR released their Oculus Quest VR headset with its own Snapdragon processor and 64 GB of memory for $ 400. It was probably the best value-for-money VR headset at that time.

Some of the requirements listed in Table 2.4 are recommendations — not minimum requirements. This table, once again, shows that some applications require at least 8 GB of RAM and that some have highly specified graphic support requirements.

Once you have identified the main hardware specifications necessary to support your intended software, you may begin thinking intelligently about what components and peripheral devices you'll need. Later on, you'll see how the final selection of some of these components and devices will become more complex because of the ways that they interrelate.

For example, if you intend to connect some external devices, such as camcorders or musical instruments, to your PC, you will need to ensure that your motherboard or expansion card has the correct ports to connect them. For another example, if you want to use dual, high-resolution monitors, you might need to install a highly specified graphic card with dual high-bandwidth High-Definition Multimedia Interface (HDMI) cable connectors. An example is the ASUS ROC GeForce GTX 1080 Ti graphic card, which costs about $ 1,300.

Table 2.5 provides an example typical list of essential components and peripheral devices to jog your thinking. A copy of this table, without the checkmarks, is provided in Appendix 3 for your use.

Table 2.5: System Components and Essential Peripheral Devices

Peripherals and Options	Essential	Desirable	Possible
case	✓		
central microprocessor (CPU)	✓		
keyboard (wired or wireless)	✓		
monitor	✓		
primary memory (RAM)	✓		
motherboard	✓		
mouse (wired or wireless)	✓		
optical drive (CD/DVD, BD, or Ultra HD Blu-ray)[1]	✓		
power supply unit (PSU)	✓		
surge protector (i.e., power board)		✓	
floppy disk drive			✓
solid-state hard dive		✓	
audio card (if not integrated on the motherboard)			✓
external speakers			✓
spinning hard drive[2]	✓		
graphic card (if not integrated on the motherboard)			✓
Ethernet NIC[3] (if not integrated into the motherboard)		✓	
modem			✓
tape drive			✓
other_____			
other_____			
other_____			
other_____			

Note: 1. 'BD' means 'Blu-ray device' and 'Ultra HD Blu-ray' means 'Ultra-high-definition Blu-ray'. 2. Essential if no SSD is installed. 3. Ethernet is a system of protocols for connecting computer systems into networks that avoid simultaneous transmissions by systems. 'NIC' stands for 'network interface card'.

People who don't make project budgets are likely to impulsively buy expensive components.

When you have worked out the list of hardware components you want to include in your system, you will be able to start thinking about an approximate budget for your project. Of course, you cannot know exactly how much the components and software will cost until you select them.

Nevertheless, preparing an initial overall budget at this early stage of planning will help you refine your selection of components later-on. If you don't bother to make an initial budget for your project, it will be harder for you to control your spending.

You have some flexibility in budgeting for a PC that you build yourself. That is partially because you can upgrade components and devices in the future. For instance, you might not be able to afford as much RAM as you would like when you build your computer; however, you could easily add more in the future.

You could use Table 2.6 to help you estimate the cost of your system. At one extreme, it shows the least amount you might spend to build a basic system. At the other extreme, it shows the amount you might spend on a highly specified system. Those extreme suggestions are merely rough estimates to start you thinking about your project budget. Write down the amounts that you expect to spend for your system in the 'Likely Amount' column. This exercise will help you start forming a realistic project budget.

The prices listed in Table 2.6 are in American dollars. At the time the fourth edition of this book was written, $ 1 US was approximately equal to £ 0.67, ¥ 5.6 CH, ₹ 65.7, $ 1.13 CAN, $ 1.16 AUS, € 0.76, R 0.000012, or 0.64 Ⓑ.

Table 2.6: Computer System Budget

Hardware and Software	Least Amount	Likely Amount	Maximum Amount
Software			
operating system	$ 0 for Ubuntu 18.04		$ 199.99 for Windows 10 Pro
office applications	$ 0 for LibreOffice or Apache		$ 349.99 for MS Office 365 Personal for five years
other applications	$ 150		$ 2,500
Subtotal	**$ 150**		**$ 3,049.98**
Hardware			
essential computer hardware	$ 550		$ 1,500
desirable non-essential hardware	—		$ 500
Subtotal	**$ 550**		**$ 2,000**
Misc.	—		$ 500
Grand Total	**$ 700**		**$ 5,549.98**

Reviewing Table 2.6 should help you appreciate the following three points.

1. There is a great range of possible system costs.

2. The total cost of your system's software might be more than the cost of all of its hardware.

3. Highly specified hardware systems running sophisticated software programs are extremely expensive.

To reinforce point 3, consider Table 2.7. It shows the prices of some highly specified hardware components available when the fourth edition of this book was written. You can see from this table how impulse buying, without the discipline of following a budget, could be extremely costly. Moreover, bear in mind that the total cost in Table 2.7 does not include the costs of any software programs.

You can see that the cost implications of selecting components are huge. Indeed, you can see that some expensive individual components cost more than an entire basic system. You can also see that the total hardware cost shown in Table 2.7 is about seventy-four times greater than the minimum system hardware and software costs estimated in Table 2.6!

Table 2.7: Prices of Highly specified Components and Peripherals

Components	$ US	£	¥ (CH)
HP ioDrive 3 TB Internal Solid-State Drive	17,500	12,930	111,219
Xeon Pltnm 8176 CPU	9,250	6,830	58,780
Nvidia Quadro GV100	8,999	6,648	57,192
Intel's Xeon Phi 7290 72-core Coprocessor with 36 MB of cache	6,294	4,650	40,000
Cyberton CLX Triple-Liquid-cooled Z270 4.7 GHz ASUS motherboard	2,490	1,839	15,820
G.SKILL TridentZ RGB Series 128 GB DDR 4 3,600 RAM[1]	2,250	1,662	14,300
Dell UltraSharp 4K[2] UP3216Q 31.5" LCD monitor	1,100	812	6,990
Phanteks ENTHOO ELITE Super Tower case	890	657	5,655
OCZ RevoDrive 350 960 GB PCIe[3] SSD	790	583	5,020
Datamancer Aviator keyboard	725	535	4,607
CORSAIR AX1600i 1600W ATX TITANIUM modular power supply unit	500	369	3,177
HGST Ultrastar He10 10 TB 7,200 rpm 256MB Cache 3.5-inch hard drive	430	317	2,732
Thermaltake Floe Riing RGB[4] 360 CPU liquid cooler	280	206	1,779
Pioneer 16X Blu-ray Burner DVD CD optical drive	250	184	1,588
Creative's Sound Blaster ZxR soundcard	234	172	1,487
Mad Catz Interactive Inc's RAT ProX gaming mouse	220	162	1,398
Total	52,202	38,556	331,744

Notes: 1. This amount of RAM would require a motherboard with 8 RAM slots. Such motherboards are now available. Indeed, a few motherboards with 16 RAM slots are even available. However, motherboards with more than 4 RAM slots are likely to be large EATX or SSI EEB form-factor motherboards. A form-factor is the architectural standards of a component. 2. A '4K resolution' refers to approximately 4,000 horizontal pixels (actually 3,840 pixels on consumer 4K devices). 3. 'PCIe' stands for 'PCI Express'. 4. 'RGB' is a color model based on red, green, and blue lights. DIY computer-builders use 'RGB' to refer to 'RGB Light Emitting Diode (LED) lighting' in particular.

The values of currencies fluctuate; the prices of components usually fall over time, and different suppliers in different countries sometimes offer different prices. The only way to find out the actual prices of components is to inquire with suppliers at the time and location you want to buy them.

A useful strategy for sensibly controlling your project's expenditure is to allow a percentage of the total system cost for each component. Suggested expenditures for components, expressed as percentages of total system costs, in a typical balanced system, are provided in Table 2.8. The percentages shown in Table 2.8 relate to the costs of complete hardware systems — including basic essential peripheral devices. Following this type of budget will help you limit your spending to an amount that is necessary to satisfy your real needs. It will help you resist glossy ads and skillful sales pitches urging you to buy the latest components to be 'cool'.

It usually costs a great deal more to buy the latest high-end components. So, you should consider whether their features are of practical benefit to you. The relative percentages listed in Table 2.8 only apply in normal free markets. Recently the market for RAM has been upset by sudden huge price rises. RAM cost about $ 3.50 per gigabyte in mid-2016, but its cost had risen to about $ 13 per gigabyte by early-2018. That's a rise of about 317 %!

As the fourth edition of this book was being prepared, a lawsuit was filed against Samsung, Hynix, and Micron, which collectively control 96 % of the dynamic random access memory (DRAM) market. The lawsuit contends that the three companies colluded to restrict the production and sales of DRAM to artificially increase its price. A short time later, Wu Zhenguo, the leader of China's Anti-monopoly Bureau, commented that the investigation into these three companies was making good progress and had '...yielded massive evidence'.

Table 2.8: Suggested Expenditures for Components and Devices

Components and Peripherals	% of Total Hardware Costs	Notes
Components		
CPU	15	for a recent high-powered CPU
motherboard	19	—
random access memory	9	—
soundcard	0	up to the equivalent of 10 % of total system cost if a soundcard is required
graphic processing unit	0 if integrated	up to the equivalent of 100 % of total system cost for serious game-playing or virtual reality systems
case	10	—
power supply unit	7	—
CPU cooler	0 if using heatsink/fan boxed with CPU	up to the equivalent of 5 % of total system cost for third-party[1] cooler needed for a hard-working or overclocked system
secondary storage devices	8	up to the equivalent of 50 % + of total system cost for servers, for video-editing systems, for SCSI[2] systems, and/or for solid-state drive systems
optical drive	2	up to the equivalent of 6 % of total system costs for Blu-ray device or 15 % for Ultra HD Blu-ray
Components subtotal	**70**	—
Peripheral Devices		
monitor	19	equivalent of 30 % of system hardware costs for CAD, game playing, or video-editing
mouse	2	—
keyboard	4	—
printer	5	—
Peripherals subtotal	30	
Grand Total	**100**	

Notes: 1. A third-party is an independent supplier who is not controlled by the seller of a component or software program. 2. 'SCSI' means 'Small Computer System Interface'.

At this stage, you should be able to write a design philosophy statement for your project. That statement should clearly define the type of system you want to build and how much you intend to spend on it. Such a statement would be handy to share with other DIY computer-builders and to discuss with computer component salespeople. For example, the design philosophy statement for the project featured in this book calls for:

'A well-balanced, easy-to-build, ATX form-factor desktop personal computer suitable for home or small office use, as well as for casual game-playing, that would satisfy a prosumer. A form-factor is the physical standards of a component. 'Prosumer' refers to a person who buys higher-quality components than ordinary consumers with small budgets buy, but lower-standard components than professionals with unrestricted budgets might buy.

'The system should be built with the best value-for-money contemporary components that will provide the highest feasible levels of performance, reliability, and future utility. The sole exception is the power supply unit (PSU) which should be of the uncompromised highest reliability.

'The computer is not intended to be a modeling project. Rather, the system design should be conservative, with no extra money or effort spent on purely decorative features such as RGB-lighted components. 'RGB' is a color model based on red, green, and blue lights. The proportional amounts spent on components should be close to the percentages shown in Table 2.8 and should also be close to the monetary amounts listed in the 'Likely Amount' column in Table 2.6.'

The IT industry is dynamic. Hardware and software advances occur frequently. You might, therefore, be interested in four revolutionary advances that were occurring while the fourth edition of this book was being written — even though the prices of some components incorporating these revolutionary features are beyond a prosumer's budget.

The first advance is with primary memory technology. Primary memory is also called 'main memory'. It is the first external source of memory that CPUs can access. The type of memory currently used as primary memory in personal computers is Dynamic Random Access Memory (DRAM). DRAM stores separate single bits of data in the form of off (0) or on (1) electrical charges within separate tiny capacitors inside integrated circuits. Those bits of DRAM data are volatile. That means that they discharge when the power supply to them is turned off, and the data on them is lost. It is referred to as 'random access' memory because each capacitor (i.e., cell) can be directly assessed by referring to the location of the cell. For that reason, it is also called 'direct access' memory.

Until the late-1900s, the DRAM used in PCs was asynchronous. Asynchronous DRAM was not synchronized with CPU clock speeds or motherboard system bus speeds. So, when a CPU requested data from an asynchronous memory module, the CPU had to wait until the data was made accessible via the system bus. That uncoordinated system worked well enough with slow systems. However, with faster systems, the latency involved in waiting for data to be made available at irregular timings from the RAM became problematic. The term 'latency' refers to the delay between the time when a command is sent and when it is executed.

By 2000, a more advanced type of synchronous DRAM was used in all new PCs. The speed of that synchronous dynamic RAM (SDRAM) is synchronized by internal clock signals from CPUs so that it only sends or receives data on clock pulses. It can accomplish that because memory controllers detect on which clock cycles RAM modules will provide data on their pin interfaces. Memory controllers are circuits that regulate the data flows between CPUs and RAM modules. Memory controllers can be located within motherboard chipsets or CPUs. However, these days, they are usually located within CPUs.

Using synchronized RAM means that CPUs waste less time waiting to access memory from RAM modules, which enables entire systems to run more efficiently. The acronym 'SDRAM' is normally only used to refer to the first generation of synchronous DRAM, which transmitted single words of 16 bits of data per clock cycle. After that time, the shorter term, 'RAM', was used instead by most DIY-computer-builders.

'Word' is not precisely defined term, and therefore causes some confusion. In this book it means 'the fixed unit of data size used by a microprocessor's registers, which is also the width of the system's data path. The number of bits in a word is called the 'word size', or 'word width'.

SDRAM memory modules use only the rising edges of clock signals to transfer data. The next improvement in primary memory technology was the release of Double-Data-Rate Synchronous Dynamic Random Access Memory (DDR SDRAM) or just 'DDR RAM' in 2000. It transmits or receives one word of data during both the rising edges (i.e., starts) and the falling edges (i.e., ends) of clock cycles. That is called 'double pumping'. One clock cycle corresponds to one opening and closing of a transistor gate to allow the transfer of data, which is 1 hertz (Hz). The clock speed of RAM is measured in megahertz (MHz) which is one million hertz.

Because DDR RAM can transfer two words per clock cycle, it has twice the clock speed of non-DDR RAM. For example, a non-DDR SDRAM module with a clock speed of 200 MHz could carry out 200 data transfers per second. However, a DDR module with a clock speed of 200 MHz could effectively operate at 400 MHz because it could carry out 400 data transfers per second. That is why it would be labeled as 'DDR 400', even though its internal clock speed was only 200 MHz.

Before 2003, the original version of Double Data Rate RAM was labeled 'DDR' or 'DDR 1'. Since then, three faster versions of double-rate RAM have been developed. They are DDR 2, DDR 3, and DDR 4. Each of those versions can transfer data about twice as fast as the previous version. Each version also has different connectors with different physical notches that match the different spaces in respective motherboard RAM slots. That form-factor arrangement prevents RAM modules being inserted into incompatible sockets.

A DDR 2 module can carry out double the number of transfers per second that a DDR 1 module can because it operates at twice the clock speed of DDR 1. That is because its memory cells are clocked at 1/4 the speed of the memory bus, which is twice as fast as DDR's memory cells. Since DDR 2's maximum data transfer rate is effectively doubled, a 400 MHz DDR 2 module would be labeled as 'DDR 2-800'.

A DDR 3 module can carry out double the number of transfers per second of a DDR 2 module because its maximum clock speed is double its predecessor's speed of 400 MHz. Its memory modules are clocked at 1/8 the speed of the memory bus. Therefore, an 800 MHz DDR 3 module would be labeled as 'DDR 3-1600' to show that its effective working speed is 1,600 MHz. DDR 3 modules have a 240-pin interface.

DDR 4 RAM transfers eight words per cycle, the same as DDR 3. But it has a standard maximum clock speed of 3,200 MHz, which is twice as fast as DDR 3's maximum clock speed. DDR 4 RAM also requires about 20 % less voltage than DDR memory modules and therefore generates less heat than DDR 3 modules. This means that there is less need to use heat spreaders with DDR 4 modules. DDR 4 RAM is not compatible with earlier types of motherboard RAM slots because it uses a different voltage and has a different form-factor interface of 284 pins.

DDR 4 RAM also supports error-correcting code (ECC). ECC technology can detect and correct the most common types of internal data corruption. For that reason, ECC main memory is used with systems running critical applications where data corruption cannot be risked, such as government, scientific, and financial computing.

Intel's Haswell-E CPUs were the first to support DDR 4 RAM in mid-2014. But, motherboards with chipsets and sockets that supported DDR 4 modules did not become available until 2015. DDR 3 RAM remained the most popular type until about 2016 when AMD's Zen CPUs and APUs provided support for DDR 4. Since then, all new PC motherboards have supported DDR 4. The initialism 'APU' refers to a CPU with an integrated graphics processing unit.

Table 2.9 lists typical specifications of five recent RAM types. But RAM technology progresses rapidly, and some of the latest modules might exceed the typical specifications listed in Table 2.8. For example, Kingston's HyperX dual-channel DDR 3 modules support a clock speed of 2,400 MHz, and some Corsair Vengeance LPX DDR 4 modules support a 3,600 MHz clock speed.

Table 2.9: Typical Specifications of DDR RAM Types

Characteristics	SDRAM	DDR	DDR 2	DDR 3	DDR 4
Internal Speed (MHz)	100-166	133-200	133-200	133-200	133-200
Bus Clock Speed (MHz)[2]	100-166	133-200	400–800	800–1,600	1,600-3,200[5]
Transfer Rate (GB/s)[1]	1.3	3.2	6.4	12.8	25.6
Data Rate (MT/s)[1]	100-166	266-400	530-800	1,060-1,600	2,133-3,200
CAS Latency[3]	2-3	2-3	4-7	5-10	10-16
Max. Module Storage	912 Mb	1 GB	8 GB	32 GB	64 GB
Voltage	3.3	2.5-2.6	1.8	1.2–1.65	1.05–1.2
Performance Index[4]	166/3 ≈ 55.3 ns	200/3 ≈ 66.7 ns	800/7 ≈ 114.3 ns	1,600/10 ≈160.0 ns	3,200/16 ≈ 200 ns

Notes: 1. The speed of modules is also sometimes expressed in mega-transfers per second (MT/s). 2. The maximum approved RAM speeds are set by the Joint Electron Device Engineering Council. Modules with higher speeds, such as DDR 3-2,000, are designed to run at non-standard overclocked speeds. 3. Typical speeds and CAS latencies of DDR 4 RAM modules are 1,600 MHz RAM: CAS 10-12, 1,866 MHz RAM: CAS 12-14, and 2,133 MHz RAM: CAS 14-16. 4. 'Performance index' is explained later in this section. 5. By the time the fourth edition of this book was produced, DDR 4 modules with extra-fast clock speeds of up to 4,000 MHz were available.

The specifications for the next generation of DDR RAM, DDR 5, were published in late-2018. Hynix produced both the first non-error correcting DDR 5 RAM modules and the first error-correcting DDR 5 DIMM modules in late-2018. However, DDR 5 modules won't likely be available to DIY computer builders until 2020. They will be able to run at up to 6,400 MHz and store up to 64 GB per module! Also, their voltage will be reduced to 1.1 V.

The Hybrid Memory Cube Consortium recently announced that a new type of volatile RAM, called 'hybrid v-DRAM', might also be available by that time. It is arranged in 'hybrid memory cubes'. The Consortium says that hybrid v-DRAM modules have capacities of 16 Gb, run at a clock speed of 5,200 Hz and support a bandwidth of 160 GB/s (i.e., about seven times more than DDR 4's bandwidth) while using 70 % less power. If it proves to be affordable, hybrid v-DRAM technology might supplant DDR 5 RAM before it is even released.

However, hybrid v-DRAM will, in turn, have to compete with another emerging memory technology. Intel and Micron have developed a type of memory that can be used as both primary and secondary memory. 'Secondary memory' refers to persistent (i.e., non-volatile) memory that is stored on mass storage devices such as spinning hard drives, SSDs, optical drives, and portable flash (i.e., thumb) drives, but which cannot be directly accessed by central microprocessors.

Intel claims that the new 3D XPoint (pronounced 'three-d cross-point') memory is 1,000 times faster than conventional NAND flash memory and has ten times the memory density of ordinary RAM. NAND flash memory is a type of non-volatile flash memory. Intel also claims that, unlike ordinary flash memory that wears out with use, 3D XPoint memory is non-destructive and has 1/10th the latency of current solid-state drives. These features mean that 3D XPoint memory could take the place of ordinary RAM modules. Alternatively, it could be used in addition to ordinary RAM modules or V-DRAM memory cubes.

3D Xpoint memory costs only about half as much as ordinary DRAM and Intel has already released some SSDs incorporating 3D XPoint technology that they brand as 'Optane'. For example, a 58 GB Optane SSD is available for about $ 130. A 118 GB Optane SSD costs about $ 200. That is about the same cost as a 500 GB NVMe SSD or 32 GB of 2,666 MHz DDR 4 RAM. However, the 905P 1.5 TB Optane version cost about $ 2,200 in 2019.

The real-world transfer speeds of the first generation of Optane SSDs are slower than expected. Their transfer speeds are only about 650 MB/s, which is about the same speed as SATA SSDs.

The second area undergoing a radical advance is secondary memory storage technology. Western Digital, Seagate, and Toshiba recently jointly worked on a new type of Heat-Assisted Magnetic Recording (HAMR) helium-filled spinning hard drive. HAMR technology uses lasers to heat the surfaces of disks, which results in data 'shrinking' and becoming more stable. The lasers also make it easier to alter the magnetic polarity of the 'grains' of data used on HAMR drives.

However, the consortium has not yet been able to fully solve some of the technical problems with HAMR technology, and it remains to be seen if it ever will be produced. So, Western Digital is now developing Microwave-Assisted Magnetic Recording (MAMR) technology for spinning hard drives instead. According to Western Digital, the use of microwaves instead of lasers makes spinning hard drives more reliable. MAMR technology is based on the fact that electrons in magnetized locations spin one way or the other. Microwaves can change the spin-directions of those electrons so that they represent on or off binary digital signals. Western Digital expects to release consumer versions of MAMR secondary storage devices in 2019.

Samsung recently produced another new type of non-volatile secondary storage technology for SSDs called V-NAND technology. Samsung claims that V-NAND technology eliminates the wear issues that affect previous types of SSDs. Samsung's EVO SSDs already use V-NAND technology. Samsung released its V-NAND PM1633a SSD with a 15.36 TB storage capacity as the third edition of this book was being prepared. At the time the fourth edition of this book was published, the PM1633a still cost more than $ 10,000. More recently, Samsung announced a PM1643 model with a 30.7 TB capacity. However, they had not announced its price before this book was finalized. But the smaller-capacity 1 TB EVO V-NAND SATA 3 SSD was priced at about $ 150.

In 2018, Nimbus Data released their 3.5-inch form-factor 3D NAND 100 TB ExaDrive DC100 SSD, which supports a throughput of 500 MB/s. V-NAND and 3D NAND are essentially the same technology. The storage space on this device is so large that Nimbus Data has coined a new informal unit of digital storage space measurement to describe it. They call the unit an 'iPhone'. They say that the ExaDrive DC100 SSD can store 2,000 iPhones worth of data! Moreover, it uses 85 % less power than traditional SSDs. Nimbus Data had not announced the price of their ExaDrive SSDs when the fourth edition of this book was being prepared; however, they will likely be similar to the prices of EVO SSDs.

The third area that has recently been radically reformed is optical secondary storage technology. Optical disc drives use lasers to write and read data. Millenniata's revolutionary Blu-ray M-DISCs with storage capacities of 4.7 GB were released in 2014. Their capacities are not much more than the capacities of ordinary DVD-5 discs. Their great advantage is their longevity — not their storage space. They are guaranteed to last at least 1,000 years! Other optical CDs are not even guaranteed to last a decade. Millenniata achieves that longevity by using lasers to burn permanent holes representing digital data into the data surfaces of their discs. That data layer is made from a stone-like metal composite material.

M-DISCs are readable on most current DVD and Blu-ray devices, and M-DISC swirl logos are imprinted on optical drives that can read them. An example is shown in Figure 2.8. Millenniata markets their M-DISCs as 'M-Disc DVD Archive'. A pack of 15 discs costs about $ 43.

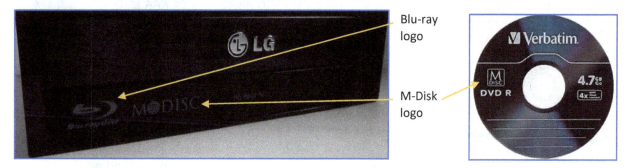

Blu-ray logo

M-Disk logo

<u>Figure 2.8: M-Disc-compatible Optical Disc Drive and Media</u>

The fourth radical advance is with the interfaces between external devices and internal components, and motherboards. Currently, the most common external interface is the Universal Serial Bus (USB). It is a connection specification for cables, connectors, and protocols. USB 1.0 was introduced in 1995 by Intel, Compaq, Microsoft, and IBM, and the first USB devices were released in 1996. The latest version, USB 3.1 (i.e., 'SuperSpeed+ USB' or 'USB 3.1 Gen 2') with a new Type-C connector, has been available since 2013. However, the first devices to use USB 3.1 were not released until-2016. USB 3.1 supports a data rate of 10 Gb/s, compared to USB 3.0's data transfer rate of 5 Gb/s. It is backward-compatible with USB 3.0 and USB 2.0. The next USB version, USB 4.0, will likely be released in 2020.

USB uses a serial transmission protocol. 'Serial transmission' means sending data one-bit-at-a-time over a single thin wire. You might think that serial transmission would be slower than parallel transmission, which uses multiple wires side-by-side simultaneously. However, accurate serial transmissions can be sent faster than parallel transmissions because it is difficult to synchronize the bits of signals that are transmitted on separate parallel wires. Moreover, the longer that parallel cables are, the more likely the data they carry will become misaligned.

Another recent external device-motherboard interface technology is Thunderbolt. It was developed by Intel and Apple to simultaneously transmit PCIe and DisplayPort (DP) signals. Thunderbolt 1 ports have been available on some motherboards since 2012. Thunderbolt 2, with a bandwidth of 20 Gb/s, was released in 2014. It uses the same four transfer channels as in Thunderbolt 1 but uses them bi-directionally to achieve twice the bandwidth. It can support single cinema-quality 4K video monitors. Both Thunderbolt 1 and 2 use Mini DisplayPort ports.

Thunderbolt 3, with a 40 Gb/s bandwidth, was released in mid-2015. It can simultaneously support two 4K monitors running at 60 Hz, while only using half of the power consumed by Thunderbolt 2. Moreover, Thunderbolt 3 cables use the new USB Type-C connector. That means that DC (direct current) power can be transmitted through the same single cables and ports. It also means that USB devices can connect directly to Thunderbolt 3 devices. USB Type-C is just a physical connector form-factor. It is not a specification for data transfer technology. Thunderbolt 3 support was included in Intel's Skylake motherboard chipset in 2015, but the first Thunderbolt 3-certified motherboard was GIGABYTE's GA-X99P-SLI, which was not released until 2016. Table 2.10 lists features of the Thunderbolt versions.

Table 2.10: Thunderbolt Versions

Versions	Years released	Port Types	Max. Transfer Speeds
Thunderbolt 1	2011	Mini DisplayPort	10 Gb/s
Thunderbolt 2	2013	Mini DisplayPort	20 Gb/s
Thunderbolt 3	2015	USB Type-C	40 Gb/s

Currently, the most common interface for connecting internal devices to motherboards is Serial ATA (SATA). It is a computer bus interface that combines SATA software infrastructure with the PCIe interface. SATA was originally used to connect spinning hard disks to motherboards, and, until recently, was also used to connect all SSDs to motherboards. A SATA motherboard socket is shown in Figure 2.9.

The latest version of SATA, SATA Express (i.e., SATA 3.2) was released in late-2014. It supports data transfer speeds of up to 16 Gb/s compared to SATA 3's 6 Gb/s transfer speed. SATA Express is also more efficient (98.5 %) than SATA 3.2 (80 %). That means that only 1.5 % of a SATA 4 signal is overhead; the rest is useful data. SATA Express is abbreviated as 'SATAe'.

As fast as SATA Express is, it is too slow to fully support the latest fast SSDs. Therefore, two faster SSD-motherboard interface technologies, M.2 and U.2, have recently been developed. 'M.2' pronounced as 'M dot two', was originally called Next Generation Form-factor (NGFF). It was released in 2013 for use with internal expansion cards. An example is shown in Figure 2.9. M.2 soon faced competition from another NGFF-derived interface, U.2 (pronounced 'U dot 2'). The U.2 interface was originally called 'SFF-8639'. Four of U.2's advantages are:

1. It supports hot-swapping, whereas M.2 does not. Hot-swapping is the connecting of components without needing to shut down and reboot systems.

2. Its drives are housed in enclosures, whereas M.2 drives are contained on bare circuit boards. The enclosures protect the circuitry on U.2 devices from damage such as scratches and electrostatic discharges.

3. Its connectors are remote to motherboards, whereas M.2 devices are attached on motherboard surfaces. That means that U.2 drives can cool themselves better. It also means that they are also less susceptible to thermal throttling than M.2 devices, which are installed near hot components, such as GPUs.

4. It can be used with larger SSDs than M.2 SSDs that can contain more flash storage space.

Notwithstanding its merits, U.2 connectors have only been provided on a few motherboards, and it seems as if U.2 will soon be completely neglected. There are two reasons for that.

1. The U.2 interface connects directly to the PCIe lanes on motherboards, rather than using a SATA interface. Its maximum throughput is therefore limited to 4 GB/s.

2. U.2 motherboard ports have double-decks, which take up a lot of space. The SSD connectors on U.2 cables are wide and take up yet more space. Examples are shown in Figure 2.9.

M.2 modules come in different physical sizes, and have different keys, which can only fit into matching motherboard connectors. M.2 SSDs are 22 mm wide and 30, 42, 60, 80, or 110 mm long. An M.2 device's dimensions are included in its description. For example, 'M.2 SATA 3.0 2280 SSD' shows that the device is 22 mm wide and 80 mm long. M.2 devices can use SATA, NVMe, or PCIe interfaces. Although adapters that convert PCIe slots into M.2 interfaces are available, it is best to match an M.2 SSD's specifications with your motherboard's specifications.

Because of their small physical sizes, M.2 SSDs can only store moderate amounts of data. Agylstor has overcome that limitation by joining two M.2 SSDs together to form what they call an M.4 NVMe SSD drive, which can hold up to 16 TB of data. Agylstor have not announced if or when they will produce their M.4 SSDs to DIY computer builders.

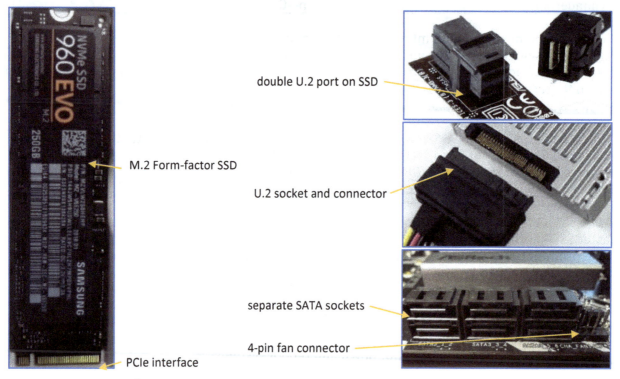

M.2 Form-factor SSD

double U.2 port on SSD

U.2 socket and connector

separate SATA sockets

4-pin fan connector

PCIe interface

Figure 2.9: Internal Device Connectors

Although M.2 may have displaced U.2, its supremacy may not last long. Samsung has already produced Next-generation Small Form Factor (NGSFF) SSDs that combine some of the best features of U.2 and M.2. The Non-Volatile Memory Express (NVMe) standard used on Samsung's NGSFF SSDs was designed especially for solid-state drives. For example, in 2018, Samsung released an 8 TB NVMe NGSFF SSD. It was intended for use in large commercial data servers and was originally priced beyond the budgets of DIY computer builders at this stage. However, the prices of NVMe SSDs have recently nearly reached price parity with SATA SSDs. For example, Samsung's 512 GB 970 M.2 PRO PCIe NVMe SSD costs about $ 230. NVMe is not a physical form-factor. It is a protocol for connecting flash memory to SSDs using the PCIe interface. It is the fastest 2.5" SSD interface available to DIY computer-builders. An example of an NGSFF SSD is shown in Figure 2.10.

512 GB V-NAND chips
NVMe 1.3 protocol and PCIe 4.0 interface

12 GB onboard DRAM (i.e., RAM)

screw holes to enable the device to be screwed to secondary storage device tray

Figure 2.10: NGSFF SSD

Table 2.11 compares the speeds of secondary storage devices that use various interfaces.

Table 2.11: Speeds of Internal Secondary Storage Devices

Device Types[1]	IOPS[1]	Max. Sequential Read / Write Speeds
spinning hard disk	≈ 100[2]	≈ 200 MB/sec.
SATA SSD	99,000 read / 18,000 write	520 MB/s read; 475 MB/s write
M.2 SSD	300,000 read / 110,000 write	2,500 MB/s read; 1,500 MB/s write
U.2 SSD	430,000 read / 230,000 write	2,200 MB/s read; 900 MB/ write
NGSFF SSD	540,000 read / 50,000 write	3,100 MB/ read; 2,000 MB/s write

Notes: 1. 'IOPS' refers to 'input/output operations per second'. IOPS figures are published by storage device manufacturers and do not necessarily relate to real-world performances. 2. '≈' means 'approximately equal to'.

About fifty years ago, Gordon Moore, co-founder of Intel, announced Moore's Law. Moore's Law states that every two years, the integrated circuits used in the IT industry will either double in capacity or halve in cost. That law was reliable until now. However, it no longer applies because we have reached the theoretical limits of transistors. In the future, major advances in IT electronic hardware will come from new technologies — not from improvements to existing integrated circuit-based technology.

An example is quantum computing. The digital computing technology that we currently use is based on binary digits that function like transistors. Each binary digit can only be in one of two states: On (i.e., 1); or Off or (i.e., 0). But quantum computers do not use binary digits. Instead, they use quantum bits called 'qubits'. Qubits are based on tiny particles, such as electrons, that have the property of superposition. Superposition particles can have other values besides '0' or '1'. For instance, qubits can have the values of both '0' and '1' simultaneously!

That means that the outputs from quantum computers can only be given as probabilities — not as absolute values. For instance, with traditional digital computing, the answer to the problem, 'What is 1 + 3?' would be given with a 100 % certainty as '4'. However, with quantum computing, the answer could only be given as a probability such as 'a 0.99999999999 % chance that the answer is 4'. That leads to a fundamental contradiction of our current classical theory of knowledge. Quantum physics and computing suggests that there are no absolute fundamental truths. Rather, there are only alternative relative truths. For example, the answer to the question, 'Do humans exist?' could only ever be that 'Humans might or probably exist'.

Unlike existing binary-based digital computers that can only perform one operation per clock cycle, quantum computers can perform many calculations during each operation. This feature helps make quantum computers millions of times more powerful than the most powerful supercomputers. Indeed, theoretically, one quantum computer could provide as much processing power as all the binary computers currently in the world!

Only the Canadian D-Wave company has yet marketed quantum computers. However, so far, their computers can only solve limited types of problems. A quantum computer that can solve any type of problem has not yet been invented. There are three practical problems with building quantum computers. First, quantum computers need extreme liquid-helium cooling to keep them near absolute zero. Second, they require extensive shielding to protect them from changes in the earth's magnetic field. Third, the qubits they use are so delicate that any slight physical vibration upsets them. For that reason, Microsoft is trying to build a more robust type of qubit, which they call a 'topological qubit'.

You may use a quantum computing simulator, such as Microsoft's recently released LIQUi|>, to learn more about quantum computers. It can run on macOS and Linux distributions as well as on Windows 10. You can access it for free at http://stationq.github.io/Liquid/.

Typically, the latest components are expensive; so, taking advantage of the most recent revolutionary IT advances normally comes with a high cost. But, one recent revolutionary advance, which you might already be using without even realizing it, costs nothing extra at all. That is the replacement of the old Basic Input/Output System (BIOS) with the new Unified Extensible Interface (UEFI). The UEFI is primarily a software program, although it also relies on its own tiny firmware program stored on a ROM BIOS chip. An example is shown in Figure 2.11.

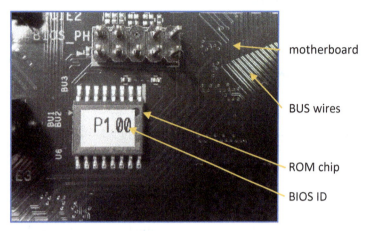

motherboard

BUS wires

ROM chip

BIOS ID

<u>Figure 2.11: ROM BIOS Chip</u>

To distinguish the two types of BIOSs, they were called 'legacy-BIOSs' and 'UEFI-BIOSs' in the third edition of this book. Since then, some component manufacturers have also begun using the term 'UEFI-BIOS', although others still use the generic term 'BIOS' to refer to the UEFI-BIOS. The UEFI-BIOS is explained in detail in Section 6, which is about powering-up your system.

Some people remain bedazzled by the types of advances in information technology described in this section. They perpetually rationalize that they will wait until the latest generation of technology becomes available before they build their computer systems. However, by the time new technology becomes available and affordable, manufacturers are already planning to release the next generation of components. So, people who wait to buy the very latest technology may never get around to building their PCs.

If you would like to practice building a PC before you buy the components for your system, you can use a computer-building game titled *PC Building Simulator*. It is available on Steam at www.PC buildingSIM.COM for $ 20. Steam is a digital rights management, video streaming, and social networking service platform. *PC Building Simulator* provides real-world pricing of components and software, as well as hardware simulations. It also provides typical problem diagnosis and fixing scenarios.

The PC building simulator demonstrates the Fractal Design R6 case that is featured in the project described in this book. It also demonstrates other Fractal cases, as well as cases from other manufacturers. Design-conscious DIY computer builders will particularly like the PC Building simulation game because it shows what systems would look like without having to build them. Three examples of screen dumps from the simulator are provided in Figure 2.12.

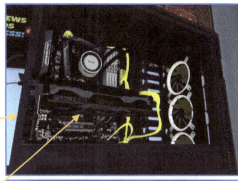

Fractal Design
Meshify C TG Dark
case

Fractal Design R6
Case

ZOTAC GeForce GTX
1080 Ti AMP
Extreme graphic
card

Patriot Viper Ram

Figure 2.12: PC-Building Simulations

A computer once beat me at chess, but it was no match for me at kick boxing.

3. Selecting Components

In this section, you will learn about selecting the hardware components for your PC. Components are available within a range of prices and with various features from different manufacturers. It takes some research to find the ones that best meet your system's technical requirements and are also within your budget. Indeed, researching your system's components will take much more time than the actual physical building of your PC. The amount of information provided in this book about the various components is intended to be enough to satisfy enthusiastic first-time PC builders — but not so much as to be overwhelming.

Comparing the specifications of contemporary components would help you become familiar with their ranges of features and capabilities. That knowledge would allow you to make better-informed decisions about selecting them. For that reason, tables are provided that compare specifications of examples of each of the types of components.

3.1: Selecting the Central Microprocessor Unit

Several components collectively performed the processing in early computers. Nowadays, however, all the central data-processing parts are contained within single silicon microprocessor chips. Computer industry professionals have called those microchips 'central processing units' (CPUs) since the early 1960s. The first central microprocessor unit chip commercially available to personal computer DIY builders was Intel's 4004, which was released in 1971.

The term 'central microprocessor unit' is often shortened to 'microprocessor'. However, that shortened term may be misleading because there are other microprocessors in modern PCs, aside from central microprocessor units. For example, graphic cards, which process graphical data, also contain microprocessors.

A CPU carries out all the instructions given to it by all the installed software programs. Regardless of how much RAM a PC has and how fast its secondary storage devices are, the CPU primarily governs how fast applications will run. Even the performances of motherboards are limited by the power of the CPUs installed on them.

Central microprocessing units and motherboards are like the proverbial chicken and egg. People often disagree about which should be selected first. However, most DIY builders select their CPUs first. That is because CPU features will only work if they are supported by their motherboards. The various CPU models can work with several different motherboards and motherboards have many features, such as their chipsets, that must be considered. So, selecting a CPU first narrows down the amount of research that must be undertaken about motherboards.

Most modern CPUs can work with most modern operating systems. Nevertheless, it is a good idea to check that the CPU you are interested in is certified to work with your intended operating system — particularly if it is a Linux distribution or a UNIX OS. For example, Threadripper CPUs are certified to work with Windows 10 64-bit edition, Ubuntu 64-bit, and Red Hat Enterprise Linux 64-bit OSs. Red Hat Enterprise is a Linux distribution developed for large commercial servers.

There are four basic specifications to consider when selecting a CPU: number of cores, clock speed, data path size, and amount of cache.

Modern CPUs can contain multiple cores. Each core in a multi-core CPU is, in effect, a separate CPU that can carry out its own set of instructions during each clock cycle. You can see evidence of that fact in the MemTest86 report shown in Figure 8.12. However, cores must share supporting hardware such as memory controllers and motherboard buses. That is the reason that doubling the number of cores in a CPU does not double its speed. A dual-core CPU is only about 150 % as fast as a single-core CPU, and a quad-core CPU is only about 125 % fast as a dual-core one.

CPUs can also have dual threads. A thread is a process that is active within a core. Intel uses a proprietary 'hyperthread' technology to enable cores to carry out two sets of instructions at the same time by allowing operating systems to address two virtual cores for each physical core. So, for example, a quad-core CPU with hyperthread technology would effectively operate as eight CPUs. AMD Ryzen CPUs use a similar simultaneous multithreading (SMT) technology to allow multiple threads to issue instructions on each cycle.

These days, most CPUs used by DIY computer-builders have from 2 to 10 cores. At the time the fourth edition of this book was written, low-power computers typically had dual-core CPUs. Mid-range computers typically had dual or quad-core CPUs, while high-powered systems had six or more-core CPUs. CPUs with more than four cores are expensive but provide little practical benefit with most ordinary tasks.

Nevertheless, the two main CPU producers compete to produce ever more expensive CPUs with ever more cores. Intel released the first 10-core PC CPU, the Core i7-6950X Broadwell, while the third edition of this book was being produced in 2016. That CPU also incorporated hyperthreading technology and featured a 128 MB L4 cache. It cost about $ 1,500 at the time. AMD released their Summit Ridge FX CPUs in late-2016 and their 7th generation Zen APUs in early-2017. Both of those CPUs have up to 8 dual-thread cores. More recently, Intel released its Core i9-9980XE CPU in 2019 with 18 cores and a clock speed of 3.0 GHz. It is even more expensive to buy and run. It costs about $ 1,980 and requires at least 165 W of power.

Most recently, Intel demonstrated a 28-core CPU, while AMD released its Ryzen-based Threadripper 2nd Gen 2990WX CPU with 32 cores! Intel will likely release its Cascade Lake AP CPUs with 48 cores in late-2019, whereas AMD's upcoming Epyc CPU will likely have 64 cores! Such powerful CPUs are intended for enterprise servers and large commercial or scientific workstations and the like. They typically provide powerful features such as extra RAM slots, inclusion of large caches, support for dual-motherboard CPU sockets, and support for more PCIe lanes.

Multi-core CPUs are not the same thing as dual-CPUs. Dual physical CPUs attach to separate motherboard slots and buses and have separate memory controllers. That duplication enables systems to work faster than they could with single memory controllers and buses. It also enables dual-CPU systems to continue to function — even if one CPU fails.

Dual-CPU-socket motherboards require extra spaces to accommodate two CPUs. For that reason, they are only available on ATX or larger-form-factor motherboards. Because they contain extra circuitry, dual-CPU systems are expensive and are therefore typically used in commercial or scientific servers. For example, two Intel Core i7 6900K Eight-Core LGA 2011-3 3.2 GHz CPUs would cost about $ 2,200. A suitable motherboard capable of supporting them would cost about $ 350. Populating just eight motherboard RAM slots with 512 GB of HP 805358-256 2,400 MHz ECC Quad Rank DDR 4 modules would cost another $ 7,000! A dual-CPU motherboard is shown in Figure 3.1.1.

2 RAM slots

Intel LGA 2011-3
CPU socket

4 RAM slots

Intel LGA 2011-3
CPU socket

2 RAM slots

Figure 3.1.1: ASUS EEB Power Dual-CPU DDR 4 Motherboard

Windows' default setting allows it to slow down fast CPUs. However, Ryzen CPUs have a Balanced Power option that forces Windows to keep all of their cores available. That, in turn, enables Ryzen's CPU-tunning technologies to function. You can find the Balanced Power setting option in Window's Control Panel. AMD says that using the Balanced Power configuration can increase system performance by up to 21 %. To use it, it is necessary to install an up-to-date AMD driver for your motherboard chipset from https://support.amd.com/en-us/download/chipset?os=Windows+10+-+64.

A CPU's internal clock speed (i.e., its frequency) determines how many cycles of instructions it can execute per second. One cycle per second is one Hertz. The clock speeds of CPUs are usually expressed in gigahertz (GHz). One gigahertz is 1,000,000,000 cycles per second.

In 2000, AMD was the first manufacturer to produce a CPU with a clock speed of 1 GHz. They also produced the first CPU with a clock speed of 5 GHz, the 8-core AMD FX-9590 in 2013. Intel produced their first 5 GHz CPU in 2018. But, these days, most CPUs used by DIY-builders have clock speeds of 3–4 GHz. The downsides of faster processors are that they are more expensive, require more power, and generate more heat. Excessive heat is detrimental to the performances and lifespans of CPUs.

With some software, such as most games, a CPU's clock speed is more important than its number of cores. This is because those programs are designed to use single cores. For those applications, a higher-speed CPU with few cores might be a better choice than a lower-speed CPU with many cores. For that reason, Ryzen and Threadripper CPUs come with the Ryzen Master utility that allows users to configure the number of active CPU cores. It enables game players to switch to single-thread mode with the click of a mouse button to optimize their CPUs to work with game engines designed to run on single-core systems.

On the other hand, with CPU-intensive tasks, such as editing video using programs like Adobe Premiere Pro CC that support multiple cores, using multiple cores is advantageous. That is because such software programs are designed for multitasking. In other words, they are designed to carry out multiple sets of instructions simultaneously using different CPU cores. Some applications designed to use multiple cores can run up to 30 % faster on systems with multi-core CPUs.

For that reason, Threadripper CPUs have a Dynamic Local Mode utility that automatically allows multitasking programs to make use of Threadripper's multiple cores. Most current Linux distributions, including Ubuntu 64-bit and Red Hat 64-bit, as well as Windows 10 64-bit, can take advantage of Dynamic Local Mode. AMD has reported performance increases of up to 47 % with some applications when Dynamic Local Mode is enabled! Microsoft is also developing an EP CPU that is designed to allow CPU cores to work more efficiently. However, it won't likely be available to DIY-builders for some time.

In Section 2, you learned that operating systems are designed to work with CPUs that have different size data paths. You also learned that a data path is the size of the chunks of data that CPUs can move around during each clock cycle. In 1985, the standard size of CPU data paths was increased from 16 to 32 bits. Nowadays, as has also been explained before, CPUs are available that use either 32 or 64-bit data paths. Recall also from Section 2 that 64-bit processors can transmit data much quicker than 34-bit CPUs — all else being equal, and that 64-bit CPUs can make use of larger amounts of RAM than 32-bit processors, which can only address up to 4 GB of memory.

A cache is an intelligent memory location that can be quickly accessed by a CPU. Cache memory is intelligent in the sense that it can identify the data that a CPU will most likely need. The larger a CPU's caches, the faster it can work. Previously, Level-1 (L1) cache referred to cache that was located on CPUs, while Level-2 (L2) cache referred to cache that was on motherboards. However, nowadays, L2 cache usually also resides within CPUs. Moreover, many CPUs now include yet another level of cache, L3 — although it located outside of their cores. The only way to be certain where L2 and L3 caches are physically located is to check a CPU's specifications. The term 'shared cache' refers to a cache that can be used for storing both data and instructions.

You can use this knowledge about cache to interpret some CPU specifications. For instance, you should now be able to interpret the following specifications of Intel's Core i7-4770HQ CPU. It has an L1 cache consisting of 4 separate 32 kB caches for instructions, and four more 32 kB caches for data. It also has an L2 cache consisting of a 256 kB cache for each of its four cores and a shared L3 cache of 6 MB. Therefore, all totaled, it has 6,680 kB ($\approx$ 6.7 MB) of cache. The $\approx$ symbol means 'approximately equal to'. You should also be able to use your understanding of cache to appreciate the huge amount of it on some Threadripper CPUs — 83 MB!

When a CPU looks for some memory in its caches, but cannot find it, it is called a 'cache miss'. Every time a CPU has a cache miss, it has to look in the system's slower primary storage, RAM. If it still can't find the data there, it must then look in the system's much slower mass secondary storage devices, such as spinning hard drives, SSDs, or flash (i.e., thumb) drives.

Some people confuse the idea of a CPU's bandwidth with its clock speed. However, a CPU's clock speed is just the number of cycles it can process per second. One Hertz (Hz) is one clock cycle per second and one MHz is 1,000,000 Hz. A CPU's clock speed usually has no effect on its bandwidth because its bandwidth is more limited by other factors.

There are two easy methods for discovering a CPU's bandwidth. First, you might be able to simply check its specifications. Some manufacturers publish their CPUs' bandwidths. Those published bandwidths depend upon the number of channels used in the system. They also depend upon the system's RAM speed. For example, Intel publishes the Core i7 CPU's bandwidth as '25.6 GB/s'. That quoted 25.6 GB/s bandwidth depends upon using dual-motherboard channels and using RAM with a speed of 1,600 MHz.

The second method is to run a CPU bandwidth testing program. For example, the FPS Review website published a WinRAR report about the bandwidth of the AMD Ryzen 7 2700X CPU. They reported that its measured bandwidth was '35.68 GB/s'. That bandwidth is also dependent upon using two motherboard channels, but working with 2,666 MHz RAM.

You could run a performance test of your own for free CPU by downloading and using Sandra Lite v 30.16. It is available from SiS (Strategic Industry Solutions). It runs continually in the background and provides extensive data about other components, as well as CPUs.

As you just read, a CPU's theoretical bandwidth is dependent upon two main factors that are external to the CPU. They are the number of channels used in the system and the system's RAM speed. The number of channels is a factor because the multi-channel memory controllers in most modern CPUs can utilize multiple 64-bit motherboard data channels, resulting in larger bandwidths between RAM and CPUs.

However, in order to achieve those larger bandwidths, multiple memory modules must be installed into matching banks of motherboard RAM slots and the system motherboard's chipset must support the same number of channels. Although RAM modules do not have multi-channel architectures, RAM speed is also a bandwidth-limiting factor. That is because RAM memory speeds are slower than CPU speeds and therefore RAM can't exchange data as fast as CPUs can.

Because two factors external to CPUs effectively govern their bandwidths, so-called 'CPU bandwidths' actually are parts of overall system bandwidths. In other words, they refer to the maximum speeds at which data can be transferred between CPUs and RAM.

The theoretical memory bandwidth of a system can be calculated by multiplying its RAM's effective clock speed in megahertz, by its memory bus width in bits, and then by the number of channels used in the system. The result must be divided by 8 to convert it to byte-speed.

These days, RAM speeds are usually expressed in terms, such as 'DDR 4 3200'. Recall that those speeds are twice the module's operating speeds because DDR RAM transfers data twice per clock cycle. For example, 1,600 Mhz DDR memory effectively runs at 3,200 MHz. Therefore, we don't need to multiply by '2'.

Sometimes manufacturers also label their modules' speeds with old PC rates. For example, a module's label might state, 'DDR 3 1600 PC 3 12800'. Those PC-rates show the maximum number of megabytes transferred per second on single-channel 64-bit-wide memory buses. For example, 'PC-6400' shows that a module can transfer 6,400 megabytes per second. They reflect the fact that DDR module speeds are doubled. So, we don't need to multiply PC rates by 2 if we use them to calculate a system's bandwidth either.

All modern motherboards that work with DDR RAM have 64-bit memory bus widths. That enables them to transfer eight 8-bit bytes at a time. Multi-channel (i.e., multi-interface) systems can use multiples of those 64-bit bus widths. For example, a dual-channel system would, in effect, have a 128-bit memory bus data width. Similarly, a quad-channel system would have a 256-bit data width. So, we must multiply by the number of functioning channels in a system to calculate its bandwidth.

Single-channel CPUs are common in older, lower-power CPUs. However, more recent multi-channel CPUs have multi-channel memory controllers, which can make use of multiple 64-bit memory data channels. Most current CPUs have dual-channel memory controllers, but some of the latest and most powerful CPUs, such as Intel's i7 Extreme and AMD's Ryzen Threadripper, support quad-channel memory technology.

We could use the bandwidth calculation formula to calculate the bandwidth of the Intel Core i7 microprocessor mentioned previously. Recall that its published bandwidth is 25.6 GB/s. Since it can work with 1,600 MHz RAM, and since it supports 2 memory channels, its bandwidth (i.e., the system bandwidth) would be calculated as: 1,600 MHz RAM frequency X 64-bit memory bus width X 2 channels ÷ 8 bits/byte = 25,600 MB/s. Notice that the result is in MB/s. That is because we used a RAM frequency in megahertz. We can divide it by 1,000 to get 25.6 GB/s.

Other factors, such as the mode a CPU runs in, its number of active cores and threads, and even which BIOS is used, can alter a system's bandwidth. Although these factors usually have only minor effects, sometimes they can be significant. For example, I have seen published Threadripper 1950X CPU-system bandwidth test results ranging from 36.4 GB/s to 64.12 GB/s.

Make sure that the CPU you buy satisfies the technical requirements of the programs that you identified in Table 2.4. For example, to play Ultra HD Blu-ray 4K content, your system would need a CPU that is at least as powerful as Intel's Core i5 or AMD's Ryzen 3 CPUs. Also, if you intend to use your computer for several years, choose a CPU that will be fast enough to run upcoming software — including expected new versions of your system's operating system.

AMD and Intel are the two principal CPU manufacturers. You don't need to worry about the reliability of warranties for boxed CPUs from either of those manufacturers. A third, smaller CPU manufacturer, VIA Technologies, specializes in building small-form-factor Nano and C7 CPUs (and motherboards). The two main CPU manufacturers also produce some low-wattage CPUs for use in small-form-factor systems. For instance, Intel's Intel Atom Processor C3758 draws only 25 watts and therefore only requires a small power supply unit.

Compaq and Nvidia also make CPUs but don't usually sell them to DIY PC builders, and another company, Qualcomm, manufactures low-powered CPUs for laptops, not for desktop PCs. They are branded as Snapdragon CPUs.

Researching the four CPU specifications so far explained in this section might not always be enough to enable you to select the best-value CPU. This is because AMD and Intel use somewhat different CPU-technologies that produce real-world speeds that are different from the speeds suggested by their specifications alone.

You can use websites, such as AnandTech's, to compare test results of various types and models of CPUs. Until 2011 AnandTech used SYSMark's to make those comparisons. 'SYSMark' refers to a 'standardize benchmark test result'. It is a standard developed by BAPCo, the Business Applications Performance Corporation. However, AMD representatives complained that those SYSMarks were misleading. Therefore, AnandTech now uses real-world test results. For example, part of AnandTech's comparison of two CPUs, an AMD Ryzen 3 1300X and an Intel Core i5 7400, is shown in Figure 3.1.2.

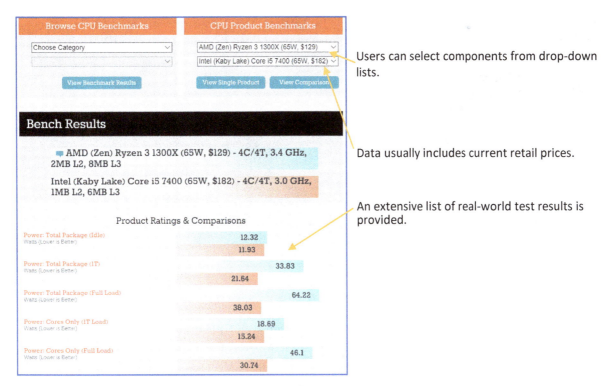

Users can select components from drop-down lists.

Data usually includes current retail prices.

An extensive list of real-world test results is provided.

Figure 3.1.2: AnandTech Benchmark CPUs' Reports

Another website, the UserBenchmark website, also provides comparisons of CPUs. A partial example of a UserBenchmark comparison of two contemporary CPUs is provided in Figure 3.1.3.

retail prices

benchmarks

Figure 3.1.3: UserBenchmark CPU Report

If you only intend using your PC for word-processing, browsing the Internet, occasional photo editing, and other simple tasks, you can save money (and an expansion slot) by choosing a CPU with an integrated graphics processing unit (GPU). They provide adequate levels of performance for most purposes, including casual game playing. For example, AMD's Ryzen 5 2400G APU has a built-in AMD Vega 11 graphics chip, which equals the performance of the Nvidia GT 1030 graphic card shown in Figure 3.1.4.

Some integrated GPUs can even support High-Definition (HD) three-dimensional (3-D) video nowadays. For example, the integrated GPU on the Intel Core i5 APU supports HD 4000, and passive 3-D glasses technology. '3-D' means 'three-dimension'.

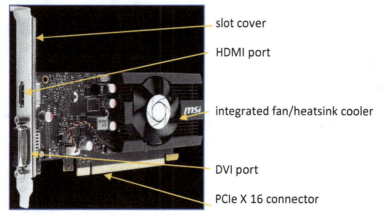

slot cover

HDMI port

integrated fan/heatsink cooler

DVI port

PCIe X 16 connector

Figure 3.1.4: MSI Nvidia GT 1030 Graphic Card

Recall that a central processing unit containing an integrated GPU is called an accelerated processing unit (APU). An APU must be installed on a motherboard that has a monitor port to enable it to send data to a monitor. So, you can see if a motherboard supports integrated video simply by checking if it has a monitor port.

You might only need to install a separate graphics processor unit if you want to play complex games or use virtual reality (VR). Only a few of the most powerful integrated GPUs are yet capable of fully supporting virtual reality (VR). So, if you want to use VR software, you might need to install a GeForce GTX 970 or AMD Radeon R9 290 graphic card or better. Although integrated GPUs usually have three monitor ports that can simultaneously support at least two mid-sized monitors at moderate resolutions, you might also need to install a graphic card if you want to use two large, high-resolution monitors simultaneously.

Buying an APU with integrated graphics would not prevent you from installing a more powerful separate graphics processing unit if your needs change. The separate graphic card, instead of the CPU's integrated graphics unit, would automatically process the system's video data. That would relieve the CPU from doing much work.

AMD released its revolutionary powerful Ryzen CPU architecture in 2017. That new CPU architecture was technically superior to Intel's equivalents and provided more processing power for the price. However, AMD's new Ryzen and Threadripper architecture is so revolutionary that some early users encountered compatibility problems with RAM modules, BIOSs, and motherboard chipsets. A similar situation was experienced when Intel introduced its revolutionary i7 CPUs and X 58 Express chipsets in 2008. That is why I waited for the second-generation Ryzen 2000 CPUs to be produced before selecting a Ryzen CPU for the project featured in this book. I expected, by that stage, the initial compatibility issues would be identified and rectified. That has proven to be the case. An example of a Ryzen 2000-series CPU, released in 2018, is shown in Figure 3.1.5.

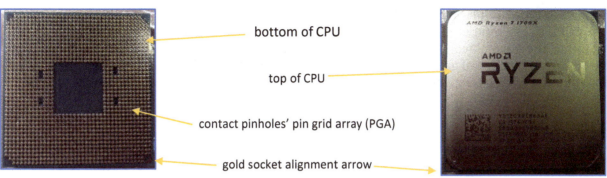

bottom of CPU

top of CPU

contact pinholes' pin grid array (PGA)

gold socket alignment arrow

Figure 3.1.5: AMD Ryzen 2000-series CPU

The first series of Ryzen CPUs were built using 14 nm manufacturing units. However, second-generation Ryzen 2000 series CPUs were built using a 12 nm manufacturing process. 'Nm' is the abbreviation for 'nanometer'. A nanometer is one-billionth of a meter. Human hair has a diameter of about 80,000 nm. The smaller the manufacturing units used in a CPU, the more transistors that can be fitted onto it and the more economical and powerful it can be.

The first Ryzen-1000 CPUs supported DDR4 2,666 MHz memory modules while the following Ryzen-2000 CPUs supported DDR4 2,933 MHz modules. As the fourth edition of this book was being finalized, details about the next 3000-series generation of Ryzen processors started to become available. The upcoming Ryzen 3000-series CPUs, branded as 'Matisse', will automatically support DDR4 3,200 MHz modules. However, their integrated memory controllers will likely be able to be overclocked to support memory speeds up to 4,400 MHz. They will be built using a 7 nm manufacturing process. Moreover, Ryzen 3000-series CPUs are expected to support up to 64 GB memory in dual-channel configurations. However, since 32 GB DDR 4 modules are now available, it is likely that Ryzen 3000 CPUs will be able to support four 32 GB modules, or 128 GB, of main memory, with a BIOS upgrade. Table 3.1.1 lists features of the various Ryzen versions.

Table 3.1.1: Ryzen CPUs

CPU	Architectures	Sockets	Max. Memories Supported	Process Sizes	Release Years
Ryzen 1000	Zen	AM4	DDR4-2666	14 nm	2017
Ryzen 2000	Zen+	AM4	DDR4-2933	12 nm	2018
Ryzen 3000	Zen 2	AM4	DDR4-3200	7 nm	2019

CPUs often come boxed with air-heatsink/fan-type coolers. For instance, Ryzen 2000 series CPUs and Threadripper CPUs can usually be purchased with boxed Cooler Master Wraith Prism RGB air-heatsink/fan coolers. An example is shown in Figure 3.1.7.

However, CPUs are also sometimes supplied without coolers. For example, Intel's Skylake and Broadwell CPUs are not supplied with coolers. That is probably because the type of enthusiastic DIY computer builders who might choose such CPUs are also likely to prefer various high-performance cooling systems that suit their particular needs.

The standard coolers that are boxed with CPUs might not be able to sufficiently cool overclocked CPUs. You could try cooling an overclocked CPU by adding one or two more case fans. But you would then need to closely monitor its temperature. But, if you intend to make extreme overclocking demands on a CPU, you might need to choose a higher-capacity CPU cooler. Indeed, you might need to install a liquid-CPU-cooler instead of a traditional air-heatsink/fan-type unit.

Whatever type of third-party CPU-cooler you might select, make sure that it will be able to keep your CPU's core temperature within its recommended working temperature range. For example, the normal working temperature of an Intel Core i7-700K CPU is 70 ° C, and the normal temperature of an AMD Ryzen 7 1700 CPU is 65 ° C. If a CPU's temperature exceeds its maximum working temperature, it will likely automatically throttle back so that it runs slower and cooler.

People who overclock their CPUs gamble that their CPUs have built-in safety margins. For instance, if a manufacturer specifies that a CPU's frequency is 3.0 GHz, overclockers might hope that it is capable of running at 3.2 GHz. A reasonable expectation from overclocking a CPU is a performance increase of 5-10 %.

Yuri Bubliy (aka '1usmus') developed a DRAM calculator that recommends optimized memory timing sets for particular memory kits for Ryzen CPUs. The latest version in mid-2019 was 1.5.1. Following that calculator's suggestions might allow you to achieve faster memory overclocks with better stability. A screenshot of the calculator is shown in Figure 3.1.6.

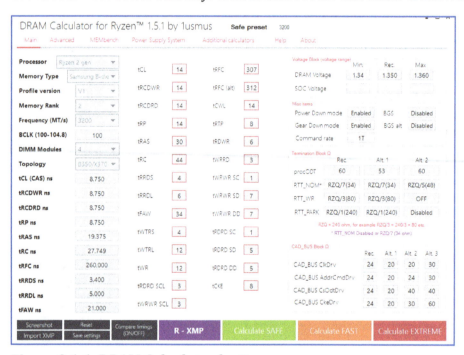

<u>Figure 3.1.6: DRAM Calculator for Ryzen</u>

If a CPU comes with a boxed cooler, but you install a different cooler, the CPU's warranty might be invalidated. Although, in some cases, you can use liquid-coolers, and still retain a CPU's warranty. When the third edition of this book was published, AMD was offering closed-loop liquid-coolers boxed with their top-line FX-8150 CPUs. Intel was doing likewise with their top-line 3960X CPUs. Both companies provided liquid-coolers produced by Asteck. Unfortunately, however, since that time, both companies have stopped providing liquid-cooler options boxed with their top-line CPUs.

There are two types of liquid CPU cooling systems. DIY liquid cooling systems that must be assembled by users are called 'custom liquid-coolers'. Liquid cooling systems that are assembled at their factories are called 'all-in-one' (AIO) coolers. AIO coolers are closed-loop, leak-free systems that require no maintenance. They come with liquid coolant already installed and are almost as easy to install as air-heatsink/fan coolers. Moreover, AIO coolers are compatible with all current ATX motherboards and cases. An example is the Castle AIO CPU-cooler shown in Figure 3.1.7. It costs about $ 90.

Custom liquid-cooling systems can be built to provide more cooling than AIO systems because extra pumps, radiators, and fans can be included. However, building a customized cooling system is more complicated. It requires manually connecting flexible tubes, pumps, radiators, compression fittings, valves, fluid reservoirs, fans, and CPU-cooler blocks. That complexity increases the risk of liquid leaking onto electrified computer components.

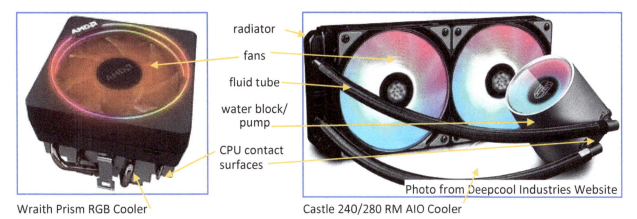

Wraith Prism RGB Cooler   Castle 240/280 RM AIO Cooler

Figure 3.1.7: CPU Coolers

Liquid-coolers with 120 or 140-mm fans are the easiest to install because their fans fit into the standard mounts provided in most cases. Liquid CPU-coolers should come with at least three-year warranties. That indicates that their manufacturers have confidence in their reliability.

The design philosophy statement for the system featured in this book called for selecting the best value-for-money components available. Accordingly, I choose an air tower cooler because they provide the best balance of quietness, reliability, safety, effectiveness, and economy. Liquid-coolers cost about twice as much. For example, the Thermaltake Floe AIO Riing RGB 360 TT Premium Liquid Cooling System costs about $ 200.

More particularly, the best value-for-money air-tower CPU cooling system I could find that was suitable for the Ryzen CPU featured in this book was the Noctua NF-S12 B cooler. It is shown in Figure 3.1.8. This cooler is large and extends 150 mm above a motherboard's surface. Nevertheless, that distance is within the 160 mm distance accommodated by most modern mid-tower ATX cases. It is also narrow enough that it doesn't extend over the RAM slots in ATX-form-factor and larger motherboards. It, therefore, doesn't limit the height of RAM modules. Like all Noctua case fans, it comes with optional speed-limiting power cables, a low noise adapter, and vibration-dampening fittings.

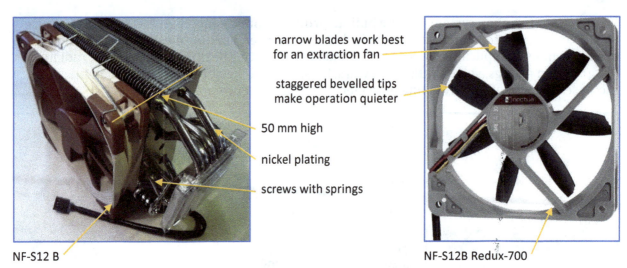

narrow blades work best
for an extraction fan

staggered bevelled tips
make operation quieter

50 mm high

nickel plating

screws with springs

NF-S12 B

NF-S12B Redux-700

Figure 3.1.8: Noctua Fans

Few, if any, liquid CPU-coolers are small enough to fit into small-form-factor cases. Usually, only low-profile air-heatsink/fan units will fit. One example is the Gelid Slim Hero cooler, which costs about $ 38. The Slim Hero fits most Intel Pentium and Core CPUs, as well as AMD Athlon and Phenom CPUs. It is shown in Figure 3.1.9. Noctua's NH-L9i cooler is even more compact. It is just 37 mm high and has a footprint area of only 95 X 95 mm (3.7" X 3.7"). This means that it allows more room for tall RAM modules and graphic cards to be installed onto mini-ITX motherboards. The NH-L9i's fan has high-quality aluminum fins and comes with a low noise adapter that makes it virtually silent with low-power mini-ITX systems. It costs about $ 39. An example is shown in Figure 3.1.9.

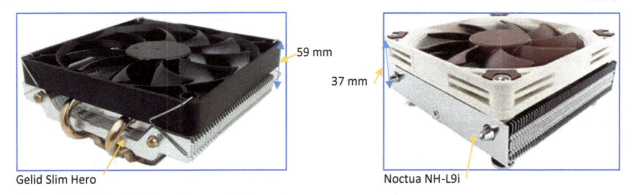

59 mm

37 mm

Gelid Slim Hero

Noctua NH-L9i

Figure 3.1.9: Small form-factor CPU-coolers

Some older CPU-coolers designed to be compatible with AMD AM2, AM2+, AM3, and AM3+ sockets will not fit directly onto the latest AM4-compatible motherboards. However, most manufacturers offer free upgrade kits that enable their coolers to be attached to AMD AM4-socket motherboards. Noctua, have also recently released coolers that directly fit onto the AM4 socket used for AMD's Ryzen processors. Threadripper CPUs are not provided with boxed liquid-coolers, but they do include bracket adapters that fit most liquid-coolers based on Asetek designs.

Whatever CPU cooling system you select, look for one with quiet fans. Fast fans generate more noise than slow fans. Fans that spin at less than 1,200 RPM are particularly quiet. Indeed, fans spinning at less than 1,200 RPM are usually so quiet that they cannot be noticed.

Small fans generate more noise than large fans spinning at the same speeds, all else being equal. One hundred twenty millimeter and one hundred forty-millimeter case fans usually spin slower than smaller fans. Also, fans with sealed ball bearings are quieter and more efficient than fans without sealed ball bearings.

Some liquid-cooler fans are noisier than the fans on air-heatsink coolers. You can reduce the noise from loud liquid-cooler fans by replacing them with quieter ones, such as the Noctua NF-S12 B Redux 120 mm fan mentioned earlier. It is exceptionally quiet, running at only 6.8 dB. It features sealed oil pressure bearings, magnetically-stabilized rotor blades with aerodynamic vortex control notches, and anti-vibration mounts. An extra slow, extra quiet, 700 rpm version, as shown in Figure 3.1.8, is also available. It costs about $ 30 and comes with a 6-year warranty.

If you intend to overclock your CPU, buy one that does not have its multiplier locked. A CPU multiplier sets the ratio between a CPU's internal (i.e., core) clock speed and a system's bus speed (i.e., the external clock speed). CPU multipliers are also called 'clock multipliers'.

The systems of wires that carry data throughout motherboards between components and devices are called 'buses'. Those bus wires are noticeable in Figure 2.12. In the first personal computer motherboards, there was only one type of overall bus wiring system, called the 'system bus'. That bus directly interconnected the central processing unit, RAM, peripheral devices, and external devices. As a result, all components and devices connected to motherboards were forced to run at the same speed as the system bus. The architecture of bus systems has changed greatly since that time.

To eliminate the problem of components and devices having to run at the system bus speed, manufacturers developed bus controllers that separated the CPU, and main memory and cache memory, from peripheral devices and secondary storage devices. That system allowed CPU speeds to increase without being limited by the speeds of other components and devices. That system also allowed expansion cards to exchange data without sending it through the CPU, which facilitated quicker data transfers. However, no industry standard for the new bus system was implemented, and the architectures used on different motherboards produced by different manufacturers varied somewhat.

As a result of the many non-standardized architectural changes, bus terminology has become confused. That situation has been made worse by the fact that some buses are called by different names. Many DIY computer builders now find the situation so confusing that they prefer to think of a motherboard's bus system as a single unit — as it originally was. However, if you feel up to the challenge of learning more about the bus system, you can start with the generalization that, until recently, motherboards had two main types of buses: internal buses and external buses.

Until the 2010s, internal motherboard buses were often called 'main buses' or 'system buses'. They transferred internal memory data between the main memory and the cache, via motherboard chips called Northbridges. Sometimes caches were on motherboards and other times caches were within CPUs. A connection between two different buses is called a bridge. Internal memory is the data stored on chips that can be accessed directly by CPUs — as distinct from secondary memory spaces such as on hard disks, tapes, or optical discs. The prime source of internal memory is main memory (i.e., RAM) although internal memory also includes ROM and flash memory. Northbridge chips contained system memory controllers and were therefore also called 'memory controller hubs'. The term 'front side bus' (i.e., FSB) refers to buses used only on dual independent bus architecture systems to transfer data between CPUs and main memories.

Dual independent bus architecture systems have separate high-speed backside buses for exchanging data between their CPUs and their cache memories. Those backside buses were necessary because old CPUs did not contain any onboard L2 or L3 caches. Backside buses were used to enable CPUs to access caches that were located on motherboard chips. For that reason, backside buses were also called 'cache buses'.

More recently, L1 and L2 caches were contained on CPUs, although they were not at first part of CPU cores. But most recently, L2 and L3 caches have been integrated into CPUs, which made backside buses obsolete.

The previous generation of motherboards also contained another bridge, called the Southbridge, for transferring memory data via external buses between the CPU and in/out devices, such as spinning hard drives, expansion slots, and USB devices. For that reason, the Southbridge chip is sometimes referred to as the 'I/O Controller Hub'. That arrangement avoided the bottleneck that would have otherwise resulted from transmitting data from devices and expansion card slots through slower motherboard system buses. External buses are also called 'expansion buses' or 'I/O buses'. 'I/O' is an acronym for 'input/output'.

In older mainboard designs, the devices handled by the Southbridge were controlled by separate motherboard chips. Combining those chips into the single Southbridge chip saved space and reduced manufacturing costs. The Southbridge was typically connected to the system CPU via an internal bus, the Northbridge, as well as the frontside bus.

A generic bus system based on previous generation legacy architecture would look something like the one shown in Figure 3.1.10. It is just provided to help you understand the origins of the various bus-related terms; not to describe any particular bus system.

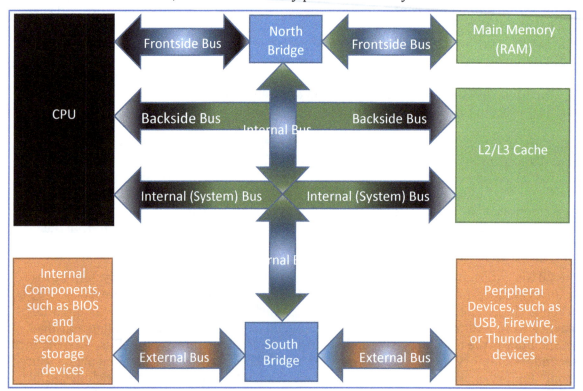

Figure 3.1.10: Generalized Legacy Bus System

The previous frontside bus/Northbridge/internal bus/Southbridge architecture has now been superseded by other technologies. Since about 2011, both Intel and AMD have built memory controllers within their CPUs. These memory controllers still set the speeds of the system buses and are still be called Northbridges, as shown in Figure 3.1.11. What is more, technologies such as AMD's HyperTransport technology, and a similar technology used on Intel CPUs, use multiple virtual channels to enable CPUs to exchange data with RAM modules and motherboard chipsets simultaneously using single physical channels.

HyperTransport technology is a revolutionary new type of peripheral device bus, which was originally called the 'lightning data transport bus'. It provides some major advantages, such as:
- providing separate channels to CPUs so they can send and receive data simultaneously,
- exchanging data with peripherals devices up to 48 times faster than previous buses, and
- allowing dual physical CPUs to be interconnected.

Some manufacturers have also combined the Northbridge and Southbridge into single chips. For example, the Intel Hub Architecture, combines Northbridge and Southbridge functions, as does the AMD EPYC 7000 Series Integrated Server Controller Hub. So, the bus system on a recent CPUs might be more like the diagram in Figure 3.1.11 than the diagram in Figure 3.1.10.

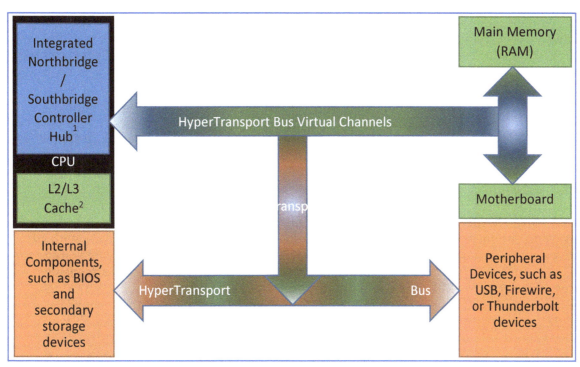

Notes: 1. Such as Intel Hub Architecture and AMD EPYC 7000 Series Integrated Server Controller Hub. 2. Some CPUs now include L4 caches as well. Most likely the L2 cache will be within the core, and the L3 cache will be outside the case.

Figure 3.1.11: Recent Bus System

A motherboard's bus speed governs the effective maximum speed of the system CPU. For instance, a CPU that can run at 3 GHz would waste some of its potential on a motherboard with a maximum system bus speed of only 2.8 GHz. You can use the CPU-Z utility to discover your CPU's multiplier, your CPU's core speed, and your motherboard's bus speed. For example, in Figure 8.1, you can see that the CPU's multiplier of 7 is equal to the CPU's core clock speed of 1,517.15 MHz (≈ 1.52 GHz) divided by the system's bus speed of 216.74 MHz (≈ 0.22 GHz). We can use the same relationship to calculate a CPU's clock speed. For example, the CPU's clock speed would be 216.74 MHz X 7 = 1,517.18 MHz (≈ 1.52 GHz).

The buses explained in this section are used for transferring data from memory locations to and from CPUs. They are therefore called 'data buses'. However, there are three other types of computer buses with different functions. They are not explained in this section. If you want to learn about them, you will need to study:

- address buses, which carry information about the locations of data in memory,
- control buses, which carry signals that control the flow of data from place to place, and
- expansion buses, which carry data between expansion boards.

An unlocked multiplier allows a CPU's frequency to be changed. A locked multiplier forces a CPU to use the multiplier set by the manufacturer. For instance, the multipliers are locked, and cannot be overclocked, on Intel Core i5-4770 CPUs, whereas, the multipliers on all AMD Ryzen and Threadripper CPUs are unlocked. CPU manufacturers sometimes lock their CPU multipliers to prevent dishonest retailers from overclocking them and selling them for the higher prices of faster models.

The smaller a CPU's multiplier is set, the more efficiently a system works. Various methods for changing CPU multiplier settings have been used in the past, including jumpers, DIP switches, CMOS settings, firmware updates, and software utilities. However, these days, the usual way is to use the motherboard's UEFI-BIOS to increase the CPU's frequency.

Increasing a CPU's frequency also allows the speeds of other components, such as the RAM and graphic card, to be increased — providing they can support the higher speeds. If you want to try that, select a small frequency increase of about 0.1 GHz.

If you increase a CPU's multiplier and frequency, you should also increase its core voltage. That would improve the CPU's stability when running at overclocked speeds. Typically, PC builders who overclock their systems increase their CPU core voltages by 1/10 of a volt. You should also be able to do that using your system's UEFI-BIOS. Beware, however, that increasing a CPU's voltage will make it run hotter, which will, in turn, increase the stress on it and shorten its lifespan. Also, overclocking an APU would likely disable its integrated GPU.

CPU and RAM clock speeds are so fast these days that there is little practical need to overclock systems to gain slight speed increases. Moreover, the latest generation of CPUs automatically overclock themselves when under high loads, while keeping themselves within safe voltage and temperature limits. That is called 'boosting'. Boosting can achieve temporary clock speed increases of about 15 %. XFR (eXtended Frequency Range) is the automated overclocking feature built into AMD's Ryzen 5 and 7 CPUs. XFR-enabled CPUs can boost their clock frequencies about 100–200 MHz above normal turbo frequencies depending upon the capability of their coolers. Threadripper CPUs provide a similar built-in automatic Precision Boost Overdrive overclocking option. In 2019 Intel likewise provided their free Intel Performance Maximizer automatic CPU overclocking tool as a free download for Z390 motherboards. Moreover, they now also offer a warranty for the price of $ 19.90 that covers CPUs overclocked by Intel Performance Maximizer.

AMD's Ryzen Master overclocking tool can be used for monitoring Ryzen systems. It reports on real-time CPU temperatures, fan speeds, memory timings, core voltages, and CPU frequencies. A quick-start icon automatically appears on monitors' screens. An example of a Ryzen Master report is shown in Figure 3.1.12.

Figure 3.1.12: Ryzen Master System Report

Other overclocking techniques, aside from automatic boosting, create some risks. For that reason, manufacturers usually withdraw their warranties for manually overclocked components. For instance, the motherboard manufacturer, ASRock, warns:

> *… there is a certain risk involved with overclocking, including adjusting the setting in the BIOS or using third-party overclocking tools. Over-clocking may affect your system stability, or even cause damage to the components and devices of your system. It should be done at your own risk and expense. We are not responsible for possible damage caused by overclocking.*

Similarly, AMD makes it clear in its 2017 Ryzen Overclocking Guide that it:

> *… does not provide support or service for issues or damages related to use of an AMD product outside of the Specifications or outside of factory settings and [the] Recipient assumes any and all liability and risk associated with such usage, including by providing motherboards or other components that facilitate or allow usage outside of the Specifications or factory settings.*

Even using an overclocking utility provided by a CPU's manufacturer presents some risk. For example, AMD provides users of its Ryzen Master overclocking utility with the warning shown in Figure 3.1.13.

AMD RYZEN MASTER   ×

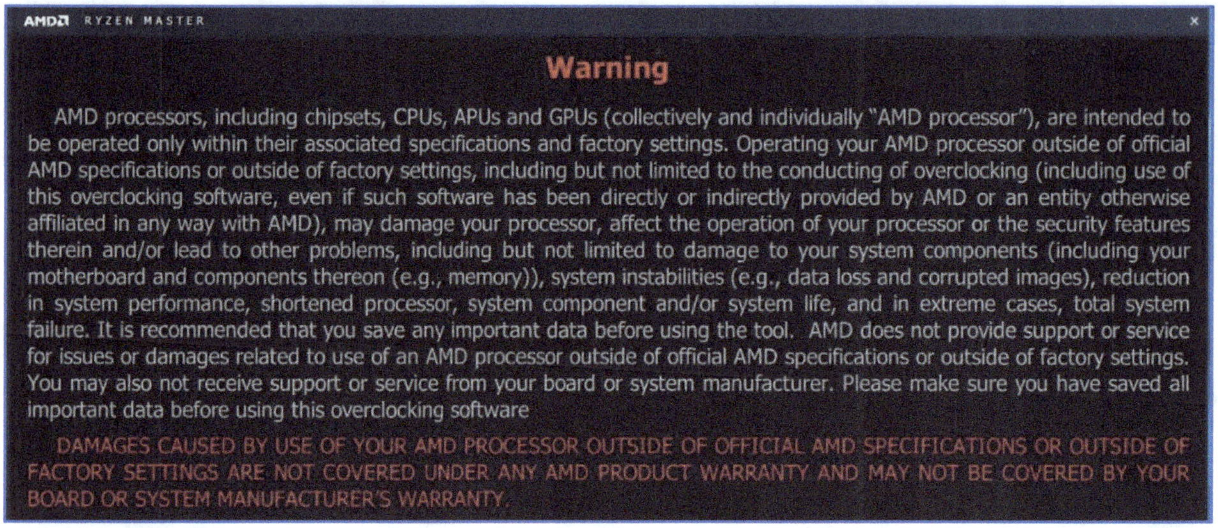

Warning

AMD processors, including chipsets, CPUs, APUs and GPUs (collectively and individually "AMD processor"), are intended to be operated only within their associated specifications and factory settings. Operating your AMD processor outside of official AMD specifications or outside of factory settings, including but not limited to the conducting of overclocking (including use of this overclocking software, even if such software has been directly or indirectly provided by AMD or an entity otherwise affiliated in any way with AMD), may damage your processor, affect the operation of your processor or the security features therein and/or lead to other problems, including but not limited to damage to your system components (including your motherboard and components thereon (e.g., memory)), system instabilities (e.g., data loss and corrupted images), reduction in system performance, shortened processor, system component and/or system life, and in extreme cases, total system failure. It is recommended that you save any important data before using the tool. AMD does not provide support or service for issues or damages related to use of an AMD processor outside of official AMD specifications or outside of factory settings. You may also not receive support or service from your board or system manufacturer. Please make sure you have saved all important data before using this overclocking software

DAMAGES CAUSED BY USE OF YOUR AMD PROCESSOR OUTSIDE OF OFFICIAL AMD SPECIFICATIONS OR OUTSIDE OF FACTORY SETTINGS ARE NOT COVERED UNDER ANY AMD PRODUCT WARRANTY AND MAY NOT BE COVERED BY YOUR BOARD OR SYSTEM MANUFACTURER'S WARRANTY.

Figure 3.1.13: Ryzen Master Overclocking Warning

These days, most people who overclock their CPUs do so because of their interest in IT — not because they need faster systems. Such competitive IT enthusiasts often enter overclocking competitions. For example, Futuremark used to offer prizes of up to $ 3,000 to the winners of its overclocking competitions. However, Futuremark became part of UL in 2014. UL is a global company involved in IT testing and certification.

UL now conducts a new GALAXY Overclocking Contest offering prizes up to $ 5,000. At the time the fourth edition of this book was printed, their champion was K|NGP|N from Taiwan. He overclocked an Intel Core i7-5960X CPU to a turbo core clock speed of 4.8 GHz! ASUSTEK's Republic Of Gamers website also conducts overclocking competitions. ASUS's Republic of Gamers World Record Holder in 2018 was The Stilt, who overclocked an FX-8370 CPU to 8.723 GHz!

Another IT-enthusiasts' organization, Overclock.net, conducted its first overclocking competition called Freezer' Burn in 2018. Their competition has two sections. The ambient section is for systems cooled with normal liquid-coolers, and the extreme section is for systems cooled with liquid nitrogen or dry ice. Its inaugural champions were Noxinite in the ambient section and bigblock990 in the extreme section. G.SKILL also offers large overclocking prizes. For instance, they awarded a $ 10,000 prize to their overclocking champion at Computex in 2018.

Computex is the main international ICT (Information and Communication Technology) trade exhibition. It is held in Taipei, Taiwan. A photo of G.SKILL's 2018 overclocking champion, Daniel Schier (nickname, Dancop) from Germany, is shown in Figure 3.1.14.

If you are interested in overclocking, you should visit the HWBOT website. It provides comprehensive information about competitive overclocking around the world.

Figure 3.1.14: G.SKILL 2018 World Cup Overclocking Champion

These days, it is possible to turn your PC into a computer that is much more powerful than any DIY PC-builder could ever dream of creating merely by overclocking. In 2013 Intel released their Knights Landing co-processors with up to 72 cores. Moreover, each core had four threads — producing the equivalent of 288 single CPUs! Some models of the co-processor had up to 36 GB of memory cache and could process data five times faster than DDR 4 RAM can deliver it. Those co-processors required up to 300 Watts of power. They were called 'co-processors' because they worked under the control of CPUs. An example of the interior of a Knights Landing co-processor is shown in Figure 3.1.15. These co-processors were intended for use in supercomputers, servers, and high-end workstations and were very expensive. Indeed, they were so expensive that there was only a limited market for them, and they were discontinued by 2018. However, you might still be able to find them for sale for about $ 900.

pre-installed water cooler

An air-cooled option with an onboard hard drive is available but limits the processor's memory to 70 % of its potential.

liquid coolant hoses

water cooler hose connectors

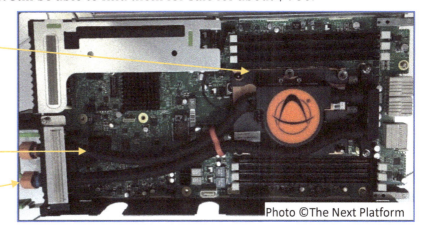

Photo ©The Next Platform

Figure 3.1.15: Knights Landing Co-processor

However, even a Knights Landing Co-processor can't make a desktop PC as powerful as a supercomputer. The term 'supercomputer' is not exactly defined. We can only say that a supercomputer is an exceptionally powerful one that is used to run extremely complex programs, such as nuclear research programs or weather forecasting programs.

Supercomputers usually work on separate aspects of such complex programs simultaneously, which is called 'parallel processing'. The first supercomputer was Cray's CDC 6600. It was built in 1964 and was the size of a small truck. It ran at a speed of 3 megaFLOPS. A megaflop is 1,000,000 floating-point operations a second. Nowadays, that is not considered to be a supercomputer speed.

The term 'floating-point' refers to the process of moving a number's decimal point relative to its significant digits. Moving the positions of decimal points compromises the precision of floating-point numbers but enables them to be used in feasible arithmetic calculations.

When the third edition of this book was produced, the Sunway TaihuLight in China was the fastest supercomputer in the world. It has 40,960 64-bit processors, each with 260 cores, and can reach a speed of 124.5 petaFLOPs! One petaFLOP is equal to one quadrillion floating-point operations per second (FLOPS). In other words, one petaFLOP is equal to 10^{15} floating-point operations per second. A human would have to perform one calculation per second for about 31,688,700 years to perform the same number of calculations.

As the fourth edition of this book was being prepared, the United States Department of Energy's National Laboratory announced that their new supercomputer, named Summit, almost doubled the power of the Sunway TaihuLight. Summit can perform calculations at the rate of 200 petaFLOPs! Even more powerful supercomputers than the Summit are now being developed in China, Japan, and Europe. But the U.S. Department of Energy, with Oak Ridge National Laboratory, have leapfrogged them all by announcing plans for a 1.5 + exaFlop supercomputer named Frontier. One exaflop equals 1,000 petaFLOPS. Frontier will be built on AMD's EPYC CPUs and Radeon's Instinct GPU processors. It will be the size of two basketball courts when it is completed in 2021.

Table 3.1.1 provides a basic checklist to help you select an appropriate CPU.

Table 3.1.2: CPU Selection Checklist

Factors	Suggestions	Your Decisions
AMD or Intel	AMD is usually less expensive	
socket pin type	the same as the motherboard's[1]	
clock speed	meets requirements noted in Table 2.2 plus 10 % for future needs	
data path	64-bit unless 32-bit is needed for some software	
cores	at least 4, but the more, the better	
cache	at least 96 kB L1, 192 kB L2, and 4 MB L3	
RAM	supports DDR 4 with speeds of least 2,200 MHz for Intel CPUs and 2,900 for AMD Ryzen CPUs[2]	
multiplier	unlocked for overclocking	
warranty	at least three years	
cost	about 15 % of system hardware budget	

Note: 1. As long as your CPU's interface matches your motherboard's CPU socket, the CPU will be able to access the system bus. 2. Ryzen CPUs work best with fast RAM.

3.2: Selecting the Motherboard

Motherboards are sometimes called 'mainboards', 'planar boards', or 'system boards'. They are also informally called 'mobos' by DIY computer-builders. They are the most complex components in PCs and control all the operations within systems.

Motherboards contain groups of chips, called 'chipsets', that provide interfaces to CPUs and control the flows of data throughout their systems. 'Chip' is short for 'microchip'. A microchip is a small flat piece of semiconducting material, such as silicon, that an integrated circuit is embedded into. Microchips are normally used to store memory, to provide logic circuits, or to transmit data.

Different motherboard chipsets are compatible with different CPUs. They also support different features. For instance, some chipsets support overclocking; some do not. Some support Scalable-Link Interfacing (SLI) for compatibility with Nvidia (GeForce) graphic card cards or CrossFireX for compatibility with AMD (Radeon) graphic card cards. SLI and CrossFireX technologies link two or more graphic cards together to produce single outputs. They both allow up to four graphic cards to be used together in single computers.

Table 3.2.1 provides an example of different chipsets that are compatible with the same CPU. It lists six Ryzen-compatible chipsets that support different features. The latest of these is the new B450 chipset that provides automatic Ryzen 2000-series support, including eXtended Frequency Range 2 (XFR2) support. It should be available by mid-2019.

XFR is the automated overclocking feature within AMD's Zen CPU architecture, which is used on Ryzen CPUs. XFR can boost a CPU's clock frequency above its advertised turbo frequency depending on the capabilities of the CPU's cooler.

Table 3.2.1: Features of AMD AM4 Ryzen Chipsets

Chipsets	USB 3.1 Gen 2	SATA	PCIe	Overclockable[1]	CrossFireX/SLI
X470[2]	✓	✓	✓	✓	✓
X370	✓	✓	✓	✓	✗
B350	✓	✓	✓	✓	✗
A320	✗	✓	✓	✗	✗
X300	✗	✓	✓	✓	✗
A300	✗	✓	✓	✗	✗

Notes: 1. The multipliers on all AMD AM4-based CPUs are unlocked. 2. X470 chipsets support a 2,999 MHz memory speed, whereas previous Ryzen chipsets support a memory speed of 2,660 MHz, although it might be necessary to change the memory speed in the BIOS to 2,999 MHz.

The five main functions of motherboards are to:
1. manage the flow of instructions between operating systems and hardware devices,
2. provide bus communication wires that enable components, including CPUs, to interconnect,
3. provide expansion slots that allow extra internal components, such as graphics cards, to be attached to add extra capabilities to systems,
4. provide ports that allow peripheral devices to connect to systems, and
5. contain firmware parts of BIOSs that allow computers to boot and enable components to be configured.

Firmware is software that is permanently etched into a hardware device's ROM (read-only memory). It is usually located on small memory chips and provides instructions about how devices should communicate and perform other basic functions. Firmware can only be changed or updated using special programs.

A motherboard's form-factor specifies its size and shape, the arrangement of its mounting holes, its power supply interface, and the placements of its connectors and ports. A motherboard's form-factor, therefore, determines which types of cases it can be installed into. If you are new to computer building, you might think that there is only one motherboard form-factor. However, there are nearly a dozen motherboard form-factors.

The form-factor most commonly used by DIY desktop computer-builders is the Advanced Technology eXtended (ATX) form-factor that was developed by Intel in 1996. Modern ATX motherboards have two power supply sockets. One socket has 20 or 24 pins and provides power to the motherboard. The other socket has 4 or 8 pins and supplies power to the CPU. These sockets are explained in more detail in Section 3.7, which is about power supply units. Figure 3.2.1 shows a modern ATX form-factor motherboard.

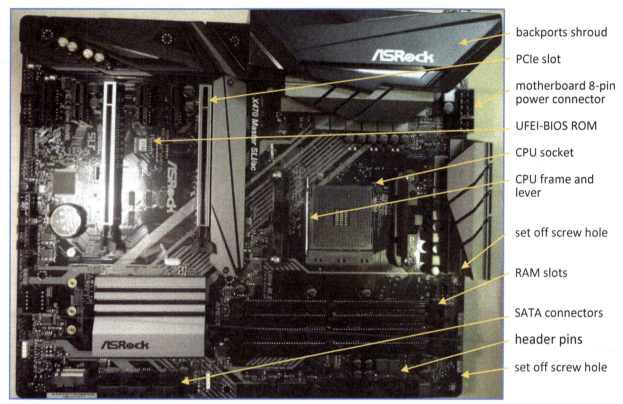

backports shroud

PCIe slot

motherboard 8-pin power connector

UFEI-BIOS ROM

CPU socket

CPU frame and lever

set off screw hole

RAM slots

SATA connectors

header pins

set off screw hole

Figure 3.2.1: ASRock X470 Master SLI/ac ATX Motherboard

Between 1996 and 2007, five smaller-form-factor motherboards were developed that are also used by DIY PC builders. They are the micro-ATX that was released in 1997, the mini-ITX that was released by VIA Technologies in 2001, the mini-ATX that was released in 2005 by AOPEN, the Nano-ITX that was released by VIA Technologies in 2005, and the Pico-ITX that was also released by VIA Technologies in 2007.

The most recent small-form-factor desktop personal computer motherboard, the Next Unit of Computing (NUC) format, was produced by Intel in 2011. NUC computers are usually sold as system kits that users must assemble, although those kits don't normally come with secondary storage devices or RAM modules. Intel was preparing to release its Haydes NUC with a Canyon 8th generation CPU while the fourth edition of this book was being produced. The Hades Canyon CPU incorporates an integrated AMD Radeon Vega GPU capable of supporting virtual reality. That means that the Hades Canyon CPU is an APU. Recall that the initialism 'APU' refers to a CPU with an integrated graphics processing unit.

Currently, the most popular small-form-factor cases are the micro-ATX (24.4 cm X 24.4 cm or 9.6" X 9.6") and the mini-ITX (17 cm X 17 cm or 6.7" X 6.7"). Fractal Design has recently concentrated on designing cases for those two small-form-factors. An example is their modular Define Mini C tower case that accommodates both micro-ATX and mini-ITX systems. It costs about $ 120.

Small-form-factor motherboards, which fit into small-form-factor cases, are just as expensive as larger motherboards. Their prices reflect their features, just as the prices of larger motherboards do. For instance, the well-featured MSI Z370 Gaming Pro Carbon micro-ATX LGA 1151 motherboard costs about $ 190. However, the components used with small-form-factor motherboards are usually more expensive than their ATX form-factor equivalents. Small-form-factor motherboards also provide fewer ports for connecting external devices and fewer bays for internal devices than ATX form-factor, or larger, motherboards. A good source of information about selecting small-form-factor systems is provided at the SFF (Small-form-factor Forum) website.

Four motherboard form-factors larger than the ATX form-factor have also been produced, although two of them are no longer available. Balanced Technology Extended (BTX) motherboards were produced for a short period from 2005-2006 to take advantage of new technologies at the time such as SATA, USB 2.0, and PCIe. But they were not compatible with standard ATX cases, and Intel eventually stopped producing them. The Workstation Technology Extended (WTX) form-factor motherboard, with dimensions of 356 mm X 425 mm (14" X 16.75") was introduced by Intel 1998. It was designed for high-end servers and workstations that included many spinning hard drives and required special WTX power supply units. The term 'workstation' refers to a powerful desktop computer used by a single person for work. The WTX form factor was discontinued in 2008.

The Extended ATX (EATX) motherboard form-factor has a length of 330 mm (13") instead of 244 mm (9.6"). The extra space is typically used to accommodate dual CPUs and extra RAM slots. EATX motherboards are expensive and are typically used in servers. An example is ASUS's S2066 EATX ROG Rampage Vi Extreme DDR4. Although some ATX cases will accommodate EATX motherboards, it would be wise to check their compatibility before purchasing either. ASUS's Z9PE-D8 WS SSI EEB form-factor motherboard is the same size as an EATX form-factor motherboard, 305 mm X 330 mm (12" X 13"). However, it does not have the same mounting holes or I/O connectors as ATX form-factor motherboards. A list of the most common motherboard form-factors and corresponding case sizes is provided in Table 3.5.1.

Recall from Section 3.2 that modern motherboard chipsets have multi-channel memory bus architectures. Multi-channel bus architecture increases the potential data transfer rate between RAM and the memory controllers in CPUs by providing more wires (i.e., channels) of communication between them enabling memory controllers to access two or more RAM modules simultaneously. That arrangement enables data to be transferred more quickly between RAM modules and CPUs. The more channels on a motherboard's bus, the larger its potential data transfer rate and the better a system's performance. In fact, as previously explained, the bandwidth of a system is multiplied by the number of motherboard RAM module channels. That is because each channel in a memory controller can utilize a separate 64-bit stream of data. The chipsets on most modern motherboards support either dual or quad-channel memory bus architectures.

Dual-channel architecture should not be confused with double data rate (DDR) technology. The two technologies are independent of each other. As you learned before, 'DDR' refers to a system that exchanges data twice per DRAM clock cycle — on both on the rising and falling edges of memory bus clock signals. A signal edge is a transition between a low (i.e., 0) and a high (i.e., 1) state. Although the two technologies are independent of each other, most modern motherboards use DDR memory in multi-channel configurations.

The number of usable motherboard channels is governed by a system's memory controller. These days, memory controllers are integrated into CPUs and are therefore usually called 'integrated memory controllers'. However, they are also sometimes called 'memory chip controllers' or 'memory controller units'.

Although a motherboard channel corresponds to one RAM module, RAM, itself, does not have channels. Every RAM module is a separate 64-bit device. So, motherboards can only take advantage of multiple memory channels if their RAM slots are populated in multiples of the motherboard's number of channels. That is because their matching RAM slots are designed to work together as channels. So, dual-channel motherboards are designed to work best with combinations of two modules. On dual-channel motherboards, with two installed RAM modules, memory controllers see the two 64-bit RAM modules as single combined 128-bit channels. Similarly, quad-channel motherboards are designed to work with four RAM modules because they enable four memory modules to be accessed at the same time. So, a memory controller would see four modules installed into four slots on a quad-channel motherboard as a single 256-bit device rather than as four separate 64-bit devices.

That is why using more memory channels increases a system's bandwidth. For example, it would be better to install a kit of two 4 GB modules on a dual-channel motherboard rather than a single eight GB module. That would enable dual-channel access and would double the memory bandwidth. A kit is a set of identical RAM modules that are packaged together and validated to work together on a motherboard channel. Memory modules from the same kits have the same:
- DDR types (for example, DDR 4),
- speeds (for example, 3,200 MHz),
- voltages (for example, 1.2 V is the default voltage for DDR 4 RAM),
- capacities (for example, 1,024 MB),
- number of sides and chips (for example, 2 sides with 4 chips on each side), and
- latencies (for example, 14-14-14-34).

In some situations, the number of modules installed can affect a motherboard's speed. For example, if four slots on a motherboard with a Ryzen-1000-based chipset are populated, the fastest RAM speed it will support is 2,400 MHz. However, if only two slots are populated, the motherboard will support a RAM speed of 3,000 MHz. A similar situation applies to some Intel CPUs and their motherboards. For another example, if a dual-channel motherboard was populated with, say, three modules, they might only run on a single channel and downgrade the system to its single-channel speed. For a third example, if two dual-channel module kits were installed onto a quad-channel memory motherboard, it would likely result in a slight decline in the system's maximum speed. For a fourth example, four modules were installed on a dual-channel motherboard, the system would only run in dual-channel mode because the motherboard could only support two RAM channels.

Dual-channel architecture systems support enough bandwidth for normal desktop applications. Only applications that process huge datasets or complex graphic textures are likely to make full use of quad-channel architecture. Moreover, quad-channel motherboards are more expensive because they have more pins and traces. The systems of copper bus lines on printed circuit boards, such as motherboards, that carry data between components are called 'traces'. More traces require more motherboard layers, which cost more money. That is why Ryzen CPUs and their compatible motherboards, do not support quad-channel DDR 4, whereas the more expensive AMD Threadripper and Intel Haswell-E and Skylake-X CPUs and their motherboards do support quad-channel memory.

RAM motherboard sockets are often color-coded. Matching colors usually indicate that the sockets belong to the same channels — meaning that DIMM pairs should be installed into sockets with the same colors. Although on some motherboards, sockets with the same colors might belong to different channels. Usually, sockets belonging to the same channels are not next to one another. Your motherboard's manual will tell you which pairs of sockets to use for multi-channel configurations.

Some DIY PC builders want to buy kits of dual modules but also want all four motherboard RAM slots to be filled for the sake of appearance. Gigabyte offers fake Aorus DDR 4 modules for these builders. The fake modules can be used to populate empty RAM slots to make it appear that kits of four modules have been installed. The fake modules even have RGB lighting that is synchronized with the lighting on the real modules.

Motherboards provide various interfaces to internal and external devices. Older CD/DVD optical disc drives and ZIP devices used the Enhanced Integrated Drive Electronics (EIDE) interface to connect to motherboards. ZIP disks are like large-capacity floppy disks. Most recent motherboards use the Serial Advanced Technology Attachment (SATA) device interface, which supports higher data transfer rates than the EIDE interface. Each SATA device must be connected to its motherboard via its own dedicated cable. So, it is important to select a motherboard with enough SATA ports to connect to all the devices, such as secondary storage devices, that you want to install. If you have old EIDE devices that you still want to use, you can buy adaptors to connect them to SATA ports.

There are various versions of SATA. Most, if not all, modern motherboards support SATA 3. SATA 3 supports a bandwidth of up to 6 Gb/s. For that reason, it is sometimes called 'SATA 6 GB/s'. SATA doesn't provide power to devices through its 7-pin data cables as USB cables can. That is why SATA secondary storage devices must also use separate 15-pin power cables.

The mini-SATA (mSATA) interface was used on some in small-form-factor motherboards but has now been phased-out. However, another version of SATA, external-SATA (eSATA) is still sometimes used to connect external hard drives to motherboards. eSATA is just a normal SATA connector that is located on the backport of a PC to provide shielding from outside electromagnetic fields. eSATA will likely be phased-out because of the competition from the more popular USB and Thunderbolt external device interfaces.

Although its maximum transmission speed is faster than the transmission speeds of spinning hard disks, SATA 3 is too slow to fully support recent fast SSDs. Partly for that reason, the Serial ATA International Organization recently released the latest SATA connection standard, SATA Express (i.e., SATA 3.2). SATA Express employs a new, wider slot that is usually positioned next to the SATA 3 connectors on motherboards. A SATA Express connector is shown in Figure 5.7.4. SATA Express makes use of PCIe expansion bus architecture and can support a bandwidth of almost 16 Gb/s (i.e., 1.6 GB/s). Only a few motherboards were ever produced with SATA Express interfaces, and it is unlikely that any more will be produced for three reasons.

1. SATA Express connectors take up as much space as 2 ½ SATA 3 slots.

2. No SSDs with SATA Express connectors have been released by the time the fourth edition of this book was printed.

3. SATA Express can only use two PCIe lanes, whereas the competing M.2 interface can use up to four PCIe lanes.

M.2 devices may be either SATA-based or PCIe-based. However, SATA-based M.2 cards can only support the SATA 3 speed of 6 Gb/s whereas PCIe-based M.2 cards can support transmission speeds of up to 23.6 Gb/s. M.2 devices do not require data or power cables, as SATA devices do, because they plug directly into their motherboards' connectors. For those reasons, devices with M.2-PCIe interfaces will likely become the most popular with DIY PC-builders.

M.2 cards are also available in various form-factors (i.e., physical sizes) ranging from 12 mm X 16 mm to 30 X 110 mm. The most common size is 22 mm wide by 80 mm long. An example of an M.2 motherboard socket and expansion card connector is shown in Figure 3.2.2.

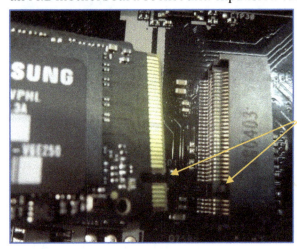

align matching notches

Figure 3.2.2: Connecting M.2 SSD to M.2 Port

M.2 devices are also available with three types of keys that support different capabilities. They are: 'B-key', 'M-key', and 'B & M-key'. Intel SSDs have B and M keys, whereas Samsung SSDs have M keys. The types of keys are labeled near the edge connectors (i.e., the gold fingers) of SSDs. A motherboard's M.2 slot and an M.2 SSD must have the same physical form-factors, use the same keys, and support the same PCIe or SATA interfaces. The types of M.2 keys are compared in Table 3.2.2.

Table 3.2.2: M.2 Keys

Keys	PCIe Interface Lanes	Typical Uses
B	2 lanes, i.e.,10 Gb/s (1,000MB/s)	SATA or PCIe SSDs, USB 2.0, USB 3.0; audio
M	4 lanes, i.e., 20 Gb/s (2,000MB/s)	SATA or PCIe SSDs, and PCIe X 2 SSDs
B & M	2 lanes; i.e.,10 Gb/s (1,000MB/s)	SATA or PCIe SSDs, Wi-Fi/Bluetooth; cellular cards[1]

Note: 1. The term 'cellular card' refers to a 3G card modem that allows computing devices to access the Internet wirelessly through a cellular provider's 3G network. The term '3G' stands for 'Third Generation'. It refers to a set of standards and capacities of cellular technology to transmit data. 3G cards, which usually have built-in antennas, can be found in several forms, including internal PCI cards.

Working through the following seven considerations will ensure that you make a good choice of your motherboard.

1. Make sure that the motherboard is physically compatible with the CPU you select. As mentioned before, the physical interface between a CPU and a motherboard is called a socket. Sockets are specific to CPU brands and models. For instance, AMD used the AM3+ socket from 2011 until it introduced the AM4 socket for its new Ryzen Zen-based CPUs in 2016. Similarly, Intel used the LAG 1150 socket for its CPUs since 2011 but now uses a new LGA 2066 socket with its 2018 Sky Lake, Kaby Lake, and Cascade Lake processors. Socket information is available on CPU and motherboard specification sheets.

2. Check that the motherboard includes a driver for the operating system you want to use. Most modern motherboards include drivers for recent Windows operating systems as well as recent Linux distributions, such as Ubuntu. Nevertheless, if you plan to run a Linux or UNIX operating system, make certain that the motherboard is compatible.

If you intend to use the Ubuntu OS, you could also check the Ubuntu Desktop certified hardware website at www.ubuntu.com/certification/desktop/. As well, you could research online hardware newsgroups to find out how a motherboard/OS combination you are considering has worked in practice.

3. Make sure that the motherboard supports enough of the right kind of random access memory. A decade ago, motherboards only supported 8 GB of DDR 3 RAM. DDR 3 was still the most popular type of RAM at the time the second edition of this book was written. However, from 2015 onwards, manufacturers began providing motherboards that supported the latest DDR 4 RAM standard. Since then, all new ATX motherboards can support at least 32 GB of DDR 4 RAM. Also, select a motherboard with the number of RAM slots you want. Most have four slots. However, some, such as Gigabyte's X299 UD4 LGA 2066 ATX, have 8 RAM slots.

4. Check that the motherboard supports Redundant Array of Independent Disks (RAID). That might save you the cost of installing a RAID controller. RAID is a set of protocols for arranging multiple hard drives into arrays to provide fault tolerance and to increase the speed of data transmission between them. In effect, RAID allows multiple hard drives to operate as single units.

Most recent motherboards automatically support Windows RAID systems. However, if you want to build a Linux-based system, you will likely need to use a RAID configuration based on a device-mapper called 'mdadm'. Mdadm is Linux's RAID management tool, and it is standard in most modern GNU/Linux distributions. Several tutorials about installing it are available online. A good example, *How to install and activate RAID 1 Ubuntu (Server) 14.04 LTS Step-by-Step*, was posted by Martin Slavov in 2015.

Consider how many external USB ports you will need. Most peripheral devices use USB connections, so it is handy to have more, rather than fewer, USB ports. Bear in mind that the transfer capacity of USB is shared among all the USB devices that are connected to a system. So, if several USB peripheral devices are working at the same time, their transfer speeds would be reduced. Select a motherboard that has at least one USB 3.0 port. USB 3.0's data transfer rate of 5 Gb/s is about ten times faster than USB 2.0's rate of 480 MB/s. If you need many USB ports, consider MSI's Prestige X570 Creation motherboard. It provides 11 USB 3.2 ports and 6 USB 2.0 ports! It cost about $ 500 plus tax.

At the time the third edition of this book was prepared, no manufactures produced cases with the new USB 3.1 Type-C front ports. However, ASRock and ASUS offered dual-USB 3.1 front panels that could be installed into cases using 5.25-inch optical device drive bays. These add-on units must connect to SATA Express motherboard ports and require two of the Molex-type PSU power plugs. 'Drive' refers to a mechanism that physically rotates a disk or moves a magnetic tape.

Fractal Design will also soon be offering their optional Connect D1 fitting for some of their cases. It includes a USB 3.1 Type-C connector along with other more usual connectors. However, it was not available for testing as the fourth edition of this book went to print.

Consider how many expansion slots, with which types of interfaces, your motherboard will need. Most expansion cards these days use PCIe connectors; so look for a motherboard with at least three PCIe slots. It is a good idea to reserve a spare PCIe X16 expansion slot in case you want to install an extra expansion card in the future. Your needs might change. For example, you might later decide to install dual graphic cards to run dual monitors.

PCIe X numbers show the number of lanes in cards or slots. For example, 'PCIe X16' means a card or slot has 16 lanes. The bandwidth of a PCIe card or slot increases linearly with its number of lanes. So, for example, an 8-lane PCIe connection supports twice the bandwidth of a 4-lane one. There are four different physical forms of PCIe slots, all of which support full-duplex transmission. So, in theory, any PCIe card can work in any PCIe slot that it can physically fit into. You can see from Figure 3.2.3 how it would be possible to fit PCIe devices with smaller X numbers into slots with higher X numbers, but not the reverse. However, PCIe connections only work at the lower bandwidth of either the card or the slot.

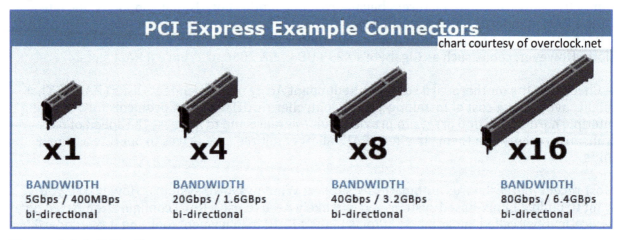

Figure 3.2.3: PCIe Slots

There are currently four different versions of PCIe X16 with lanes that support different transfer rates. Their transfer rates are usually measured in gigatransfers per second (GT/s). They are listed in Table 3.2.3. You can see from that table that a single PCIe 1 lane supports a full-duplex transfer rate of 2.5 GT/s; a PCIe 2 lane supports a full-duplex transfer rate of 5 GT/s, and a PCIe 3 lane supports a transfer rate 8 GT/s. Sending data in both directions simultaneously on a single lane is called 'full-duplex transmission'. A PCIe lane achieves full-duplex transmission by using two wires: one to receive data and the other to send it. The newest available version of PCIe, version 4, which was released in 2017, supports a transfer rate of 16 GT/s.

Table 3.2.3: Performance of PCIe X16 Versions

Measures	PCIe 1	PCIe 2	PCIe 3	PCIe 4
clock speed	2.5 GHz	5.0 GHz,	8.0 GHz	16 GHz
transfer rate per lane	2.5 GT/s	5.0 GT/s	8.0 GT/s	16 GT/s
bandwidth per lane in one direction	250 MB/s	500 MB/s	1 GB/s	2 GB/s
total full-duplex bandwidth per 16 lanes	8 GB/s	16 GB/s	32 GB/s	64 GB/s

Notes: 1. Some of these measurements are rounded-off approximations. 2. A gigatransfer means one billion (1,000,000,000) transfers per second in both the International System of Units and the US short scale. A gigatransfer bandwidth measurement includes bits that are lost as a result of interface and overheads.

A few devices, such as Samsung's GB XP941 M.2 512 GB SSD, which costs about $ 400, already have PCIe 4 interfaces. However, at the time the fourth edition of this book was printed, there were still no motherboards that supported PCIe 4. Motherboards with PCIe 4 slots might become available later in 2019.

However, the PCI-SIG has already announced that the PCIe 5.0 standard, which can support a bandwidth of 31.5 GB/s per lane, will be released in 2019. It might be supported by motherboards as early as 2020. Since PCIe 5.0, will be released so soon afterward PCIe 4.0, motherboard manufacturers might skip PCIe 4. PCI-SIG is an electronics industry consortium that specifies the Peripheral Component Interconnect bus standards.

Data transfer rates are not the same as the 'bandwidths'. 'Bandwidth' is the theoretical maximum speed at which data can be transmitted between devices. It is usually measured in bits or bytes per second. However, data transfer rate (i.e., 'throughput' or 'bitrate') is the speed at which data is actually transmitted. A device's data transfer rate is never as fast as its bandwidth because there are always bottlenecks and overheads that prevent devices from achieving their theoretical maximum speeds.

'Overhead' is the extra data carried by signals to provide routing information, error corrections, and directions for carrying out instructions. Overheads partially account for the relative performances of the different PCIe X 16 versions. For example, PCIe 3's clock speed of 8 GT/s per lane is only 60 % greater than PCIe 2's rate of 5 GT/s per lane, yet it has a bandwidth of 1 GB/s per lane, which is twice PCIe 2's bandwidth of 500 MB/s per lane. That is because PCIe 3 is more efficient and has a smaller overhead than PCIe 2. PCIe 1.0 and 2.0 interfaces lose 20 % of their bandwidths to overheads. According to the Peripheral Component Interconnect Special Interest Group (PCI SIG) PCIe 4 enables a transfer speed of 16 GT/s.

Researching the factors explained so far is about as much as you might want to, or need to, bother with. However, if you are more interested, you might also want to research the following three aspects.

1. The reliability of a motherboard is an important consideration. Faulty motherboard chipsets cannot be replaced. Entire motherboards must be replaced instead. Moreover, replacing a failed motherboard requires disassembling much of a computer and probably reinstalling the operating system and applications as well. So, when you have narrowed the range of motherboards you are considering, you might take the extra step of checking their reputations. You can do that by searching online groups to see what other people say about them and by reading reviews in computer magazines. You can also study online reviews of motherboards, as well as CPUs, graphic cards, cases, and hard drives, at websites such as Motherboards.org.

2. If you intend using a cable or Digital Subscriber Line (DSL) for your Internet connection, your system will need an Ethernet adaptor port that can connect to a network using an Ethernet cable with an RJ-45 connector. You might, therefore, look for a motherboard with an integrated Ethernet adaptor (i.e., controller chip).

Gigabit Ethernet is currently the most common transmission technology used in local area networks. However, 10-Gigabit Ethernet (10 GbE) is also now available. The world's first single-CPU-socket motherboard with integrated 10 GbE support was the GA-6PXSVT produced in 2014. Since then, only a few others, such as ASRock's X99 WS-E/10G motherboard, have been released. Perhaps the most remarkable example is the ASUS X99-E-10G WS motherboard. It was released in 2016 with two 10 GbE ports.

If you can't find a 10-Gigabit Ethernet motherboard, you could install an Ethernet network interface controller card (NIC). However, NICs that support 10-Gigabit Ethernet are expensive. For instance, Intel's X540T1 Ethernet Converged Network Adapter costs about $ 300.

3. If you want to build a SCSI system, it would be convenient to use a motherboard that has a built-in SCSI card. They eliminate most of the bother of setting up SCSI systems. However, SCSI motherboards are more expensive than other motherboards because of the additional cost of including the SCSI controller cards. Adaptec and Super Micro Computer jointly released the first SCSI-enabled motherboards in 2005. But since then, it has been difficult to find motherboards with SCSI controllers.

One SCSI motherboard that was still available at the time the third edition of this book was produced was the ASUS NCL-DS1R1 socket 604 SCSI motherboard, which cost about $ 500. However, I'm not aware of any new SCSI motherboards that were available or planned when the fourth edition of this book was produced.

Nevertheless, Serial Attached SCSI is still being developed and promoted as a fast and reliable interface for use in critical storage systems. The SCSI Trade Association, which was formed in 1996 to promote SCSI, recently announced that fourth-generation SAS products would soon be available. For example, the Association announced that SSDs with a new SAS-4 interface would be available in 2019. The Association said that SAS-4 technology will increase the interface's bandwidth to 3 GB/s; will support 20-bit error correction and will have backward-compatible connectors so that older SCSI drives will be compatible with the latest controllers.

Some motherboards provide extra features. For example, as mentioned before, a few motherboards have dual CPU sockets to allow the installation of two physical CPUs. For another example, some of the latest motherboards have built-in I/O shields. That is a useful design feature because it eliminates the possibility of forgetting to install shields, installing them upside-down, or breaking any of their tabs. It also provides better dust and sound insulation. Other motherboards, such as the ASUS ROG Maximus VIII Formula ATX motherboard, offer both integrated water and air-cooling features. Still others, such as GIGABYTE's GA-Z170X Gaming motherboards, provide certified Thunderbolt 3 support with USB 3 Type-C ports. More special motherboard features that you might want to look for include:
- extra RAM slots or support for extra high-speed RAM,
- extra Ethernet local area network (LAN) sockets, and
- Wi-Fi adaptors that enable wireless transfer to smart devices.

A few mini-ITX small-form-factor motherboards with AM4 sockets that support Ryzen CPUs are also available. They have dedicated 300-series chipsets. One example is the Biostar X370GTN Mini ITX, which costs about $ 120. The mini-ITX form-factor is 17 cm X 17 cm (6.7" X 6.7").

You won't, however, be able to find a new motherboard with an integrated graphics processing unit. Several years ago, some motherboards did have integrated video cards built into their chipsets. However, these days, integrated video cards are only contained in CPUs (i.e., APUs) not motherboards.

A motherboard, costing about $ 125, would be sufficient for a basic system. However, high-end motherboards with powerful integrated graphic cards, integrated wireless networks, and other advanced features, might cost more than four times that amount. But spending four times as much for a motherboard does not necessarily mean that it will be four times as good.

The law of diminishing returns tells us that we might pay a lot more to gain only marginal practical extra benefits. If you research motherboard reviews, you might find an inexpensive motherboard that can perform nearly as well as a more expensive one. PCPartPicker provides a handy online motherboard picker tool, and interloper.com provides a useful motherboard configurator. Examples of specifications of four modern motherboards are provided in Table 3.2.4.

Table 3.2.4: Specifications of four Modern Motherboards

Features	Motherboards			
form-factor	ATX		Micro-ATX	
CPU socket	Coffee Lake (8th Gen)		Intel LAG 1155	
motherboard	ASUS PRIME Z370-A	GIGABYTE GA-970A-D3P	MSI Z77MA-G45	Biostar Hi-Fi H170Z3 Ver. 5.x
power connector	24 and 4/8	24 and 4/8	24 and 4/8	24 and 4/8[1]
RAM slots	4 X 64 Gb DDR 4	4 X 32 Gb DDR 3	4 X 32 Gb DDR 3	2 X 16 Gb DDR 3 2 X 32 Gb DDR 4[2]
memory speed (MHz)	DDR 4 4,133	DDR 3 1,866	DDR 3 2,667	DDR 4 1,866
SATA ports[3]	6 SATA 3	6 SATA 3	2 SATA 3 4 SATA 2	4 SATA 3, 1 SATAe; 1 M.2
multi-channel	2	2	2	4
RAID support	0, 1, 5; 10	0, 1, 5; 10	0, 1, 5; 10	0, 1, 5; 10
USB ports	2 back; 2 front	8 X USB 2.0 back 2 X USB 3.0 back 1 X USB 3.0 front 3 X USB 2.0 front	2 back, 1 front	4 X USB 3.0 port 2 X USB 2.0 port 1 X USB 3.0 header 2 USB 2.0 header
PCI slots	2 X PCIe X16 2 X PCIe X1 1 X PCI	1 X PCIe X16 3 X PCIe X1 2 X PCI	2 X PCIe X16 2 X PCIe X1	1 X PCIe X 16 3.0 1 X PCIe X 1 3.0 2 X PCI
onboard graphics	X[4]	X	X	supports DX12
onboard audio	8-channel HD	7.1-channel HD VIA VT2021	8-channel Realtek ALC892	Double Hi-Fi[5]; sampling rate of 192 Hz/24-bit
system bus (Intel no longer uses a front side bus measurement)	4,800 MT/s Hyper Transport[6]	4,800 MT/s Hyper Transport	100 MHz Hyper Transport	unspecified
chipset	AMD 970 Northbridge AMD 950 Southbridge	AMD 970 Northbridge AMD 950 Southbridge	Intel Z77	Intel H170
FireWire or	2 FireWire	X	X	Thunderbolt 3
SLI or CrossFireX	CrossFireX	CrossFireX	CrossFireX	X

Notes: 1. The 4-pin CPU connector can be used if you do not intend to overclock your system. The 8-pin CPU connector should be used if you intend to overclock. 2. DDR 3 and DDR 4 modules cannot be used together. 3. 'SATA 1' is the first version of SATA. It is also called 'SATA' or 'SATA 150'. Similarly, the second version of SATA is called, SATA II, SATA 300, or SATA 2. The third version of SATA has a similar range of names. 4. 'X' means 'not available'. 5. Biostar uses the term 'Hi-Fi' to refer to a system with its own hardware amplifier, its own PSU power supply, and its own isolated circuitry to reduce noise. 6. HyperTransport is dependent on the ability of the system CPU.

If you intend to overclock your system, ensure that your motherboard will support your intended overclocked speeds. Most motherboards come with overclocking software to allow users to adjust system voltages and clock rates. Table 3.2.5 provides a basic checklist to help you select your motherboard.

Table 3.2.5: Motherboard Selection Checklist

Factors	Suggestions	Your Decisions
supports the operating system	check that motherboard is certified for your intended OS	
CPU socket	matches the CPU's interface	
form-factor	standard ATX is best for most self-build	
RAM	4 DDR 4 slots supporting 32 GB of at least 2,600 Hz for Intel CPUs and 3,200 Hz for Ryzen CPUs	
SATA connectors	at least 5 SATA connectors including at least 3 SATA 3 connectors	
onboard video/audio	onboard, unless higher performance is needed, with at least an HDMI interface[1]	
PCIe X16 slots	2 or more	
USB 3.0 or USB 3.1 ports	at least one front USB 3.0 ports and three rear USB 3.0 ports, and, if possible, at least one USB 3.1 port to accommodate future fast external devices	
FireWire or Thunderbolt port	FireWire might still be needed for some older camcorders, but Thunderbolt will be most common in the future	
motherboard quality	check current reviews	
chipset	supports intended CPU — check features lists and current reviews	
Wi-Fi adaptor	to connect a PC wirelessly to the Internet[2]	
Gigabyte Ethernet port	RJ-45 sockets[3] for each non-portable device requiring an Internet connection	
SLI or CrossFireX[4]	possibly useful for sophisticated gaming, or video-editing	
RAID support[5]	0, 1, 5, and 10	
NVMe-aware UEFI-BIOS[6]	makes system compatible with new technology	
M.2 SSD slot	at least 1 to make system compatible with new SSD technology	
warranty	at least one year, but three years preferred	
cost	about 19 % of total hardware budget	

Notes: 1. Display Port 1.4a interface now supports the fastest transfer speeds and highest resolutions. It can support 8K monitors using USB Type-C or Thunderbolt connectors. USB Type-C is just a physical connector form-factor. It is not a specification for an underlying data transfer technology. 2. Many Wi-Fi systems now support mesh technology. 3. Also called 'Ethernet sockets'. 4. Technologies for allowing two graphic cards to be used together. 5. 'RAID' means 'redundant array of Independent devices'. 6. PCs can't boot from NVMe SSD drives otherwise.

3.3: Selecting RAM Modules

Random access memory (RAM) is a fast, volatile type of primary memory. It is also called 'main memory' or 'system memory'. Primary memory holds data that CPUs need quick temporary access to but can't fit into their memory caches. After the CPU and motherboard, RAM has the greatest effect on the overall speeds of systems.

During the early years of personal computers, primary memory was only available in the form of small chips, called dual in-line packages (DIPs). Those DIP chips were delicate and tricky to install. DIY computer-builders usually had to attach DIP chips by pushing them into awkward little motherboard sockets. Sometimes they even had to solder the chips to their motherboards.

The DIPs were occasionally damaged during either process. Fortunately, modern RAM modules are composed of circuit boards that have multiple dynamic random access memory (DRAM) chips, similar to DIP chips, hardwired onto them. Those RAM modules can be easily inserted into large motherboard slots located near CPU sockets. Those RAM modules are often informally called 'sticks'.

RAM modules are not the same things as memory chips. Unlike RAM modules, memory chips can be integrated into hardware devices such as graphic cards. Memory chips can also hold non-volatile read-only memory (ROM) as well as volatile random access memory.

RAM modules can have dynamic random access memory chips attached on only one of their sides or on both of their sides. Modules with DRAM chips on only one side have single rows of In/Out pins to transmit data through the motherboard RAM sockets. Those modules are called 'single in-line memory modules' (SIMMs). SIMMs can transfer 32-bit blocks of data per clock cycle. A data block is a unit of memory of a specific number of bytes that can be transferred during a clock cycle.

Modern CPUs use 64-bit words — not 32-bit words. So, for a short period, SIMMS were installed in pairs so they could manage 64-bit data blocks and support 64-bit systems. However, these days, SIMMs have been replaced on desktop PCs by other types of modules that support 64-bit data blocks.

These newer RAM modules can handle two 32-bit blocks of data during each clock cycle because they have double rows of In/Out pins. They are therefore called 'double in-line memory modules' (DIMMs). Don't confuse DIMMS with double data rate (DDR) memory. DDR memory doubles the speed of memory transmission between RAM and CPUs by transferring data on both the rising and falling edges of clock signals.

A group of DRAM chips on a DIMM that can manage one 64-bit block of memory data is called a 'rank'. DIMMs can contain more than one rank, but the number of DRAM chips that can manage one rank is not standardized. So, one company might manufacture a DIMM containing a single 64-bit DRAM chip that manages a rank. Another company might manufacture a DIMM containing a set of eight 8-bit DRAM chips that manages a rank. Yet another might manufacture a DIMM containing sixteen 4-bit DRAM chips that manage a rank. All three configurations would be single memory ranks.

DIMMs are available with one, two, or four ranks. Single-rank modules are labeled '1R'. Dual-rank DIMMs are labeled '2R'. Modules with four ranks are called 'quad-rank' modules and are labeled '4R'. Figure 3.3.1 illustrates some typical configurations of one, two, and four-rank DRAM chips on RAM modules.

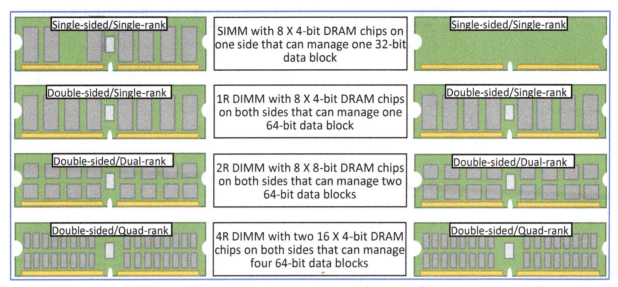

Note: Registered modules have extra ECC error checking chips, which are not shown here. SIMMs only manage 32-bit data blocks, which are half the data width of modern standard 64-bit ranks.

Figure 3.3.1: SIMM and DIMM Configurations

Since one rank can handle 64-bit blocks of data, you might suppose that a DIMM with two ranks could handle data blocks of 128 bits and a DIMM with four ranks could handle 256-bit blocks of data. However, that is not the case. Only one rank on a DIMM can be accessed at a time because there is only one data path between DRAM and CPUs. Memory controllers must therefore use chip selects to select which ranks to use when accessing DIMMs. A chip-select is a control line used to select particular DRAM chips on a DIMMs. Table 3.3.1 list the number of ranks and block sizes available with RAM modules.

Table 3.3.1 Types of RAM Modules

Sides with DRAM Chips	Ranks	Data Blocks (bits)
1 (i.e., single-sided SIMM)	1 (i.e., single)	32
2 (i.e., double-sided DIMM)	1 (i.e., single)	64
2 (i.e., double-sided DIMM)	2 (i.e., dual)	2 X 64
2 (i.e., double-sided DIMM)	4 (i.e., quad)	4 X 64

Single-rank DRAM is faster than dual-rank DRAM, and dual-rank memory is faster than quad rank DRAM. That is because CPUs must access separate ranks on separate successive clock cycles. So, for example, quad rank DRAM requires four clock cycles to access all four of its ranks. You might therefore wonder if it is better to buy DIMMs with more ranks or faster clock speeds. There is little noticeable difference because there is a trade-off between memory speed and memory volume.

However, the best performance is achieved when four ranks are used in each motherboard memory channel in a dual-channel motherboard. You could do that by installing four single-rank DIMMs, or two dual-rank DIMMs. Four dual-rank DIMMs would provide two DIMMs for each channel.

Somewhat different RAM DIMM interfaces are used in small-form-factor motherboards. The RAM modules used in laptops and mini-PCs are called small outline DIMMs (SO-DIMMs). Registered DIMM modules are also slightly different. Registered modules support Error Correction Code (ECC). ECC data blocks require extra 8 bits of data. So, the rank-size of registered RAM is 72 bits, not 64. Registered RAM is explained in more detail later in this section.

The number of modules in a kit is usually the same as the number of motherboard channels they are intended to be operated in. For example, a kit with two modules is intended for a dual-channel system, and a kit with four modules is intended for a quad-channel system. However, motherboards with eight RAM slots are designed to work with two kits of quad-channel modules. Kits of eight modules are therefore comprised of two quad-channel modules. An example is G.SKILL's Dual/Quad DDR 4 4,266 MHz Trident Z RGB kit. That kit costs about $ 770.

The topic of system bandwidths was explained in Section 3.1, starting from the notion of CPU bandwidth. But, since some people confuse the ideas of 'CPU bandwidth' and 'RAM bandwidth', the same topic is explained in this passage — this time starting from the idea of RAM bandwidth.

RAM modules have maximum clock speeds just as CPUs do. However, RAM clock speed is the not same thing as CPU clock speed, even though both speeds can be measured in Megahertz. Moreover, just as CPU bandwidths are actually parts of system bandwidths, so-called 'RAM bandwidths' are also actually parts of system bandwidths. They are both integral parts of overall system bandwidths.

Two terms are commonly confused with 'bandwidth'. They are 'data rate' and 'throughput'. The bandwidth of a channel, such as a RAM module, is the theoretical maximum speed at which it can transfer memory data expressed in megabytes per second. Whereas, data rate (also called 'bit rate' or 'data transfer rate') is the speed at which data is actually transferred.

Some people consider that there is also a distinction between 'data rate' and 'throughput'. However, for most purposes, we can consider them to be the same things. Throughput is usually considered to be the average rate at which data is actually transmitted. There are always system bottlenecks and overheads that cause data rates (i.e., throughputs) to be less than bandwidths.

Understanding RAM memory bandwidths is further complicated by the fact that RAM manufacturers use three speed measurements. In this passage, the three parameters are called 'DDR real clock speed', 'DDR effective speed' and 'PC speed'.

The real clock speed of DDR memory is half of its labeled effective clock speed. That is because DDR technology transfers data twice per clock cycle. For example, a DDR 2400 module has an effective speed of 2,400 MHz, but runs at a real clock speed of 1,200 MHz. You could use the real DDR module speed in the bandwidth calculation formula, but then you would need to multiply it by '2'. Manufacturers typically label their modules with their larger effective clock speeds rather than their smaller real clock speeds.

In Section 3.1 you learned that a module's PC speed shows how many megabytes it can send per second to a motherboard memory bus and then on to the memory controller. For example, 'PC 3200' indicates that a module can send 3,200 MB/s. Although PC-ratings are useful for comparing the performances of modules with different combinations of DDRs and clock speeds, they are not much used these days.

Many people think that the 'PC' stands for 'personal computer'. However, it stands for 'pipeline clock'. A pipeline is used when circuitry is broken into stages. It is a series of linked processing elements in microprocessors that use the outputs of one element as the inputs of the next element. Each element processes part of an instruction and then passes the results on to the next element.

The circuit elements are often logic gates such as 'NAND' or 'NOR' gates that send their outputs to storage registers which temporarily hold the outputs. A 'clock' is a signal that coordinates the signals, usually relative to the bus speed.

A module's PC speed is calculated by multiplying its real DDR clock speed in MHz by its 64-bit data width and then dividing by 8 bits per byte. This calculation converts the module's transfers-per-second speed into its megabytes-per-second speed. For example, the PC speed of a module with a real clock speed of 3,600 MHz would be: 3,600 MHz X 64 bit data width ÷ 8 bits/byte = PC 28800. Similarly, a DDR 4 2,400 MHz RAM module would be labeled 'DDR4-2400' or 'PC-19200'.

The single-digit numbers that often appear after 'DDR' and 'PC', but before any hyphens, refer to the generation of the module's technology. For example, both 'DDR 4' and 'PC 4' refer to fourth-generation technology.

The formula to calculate a system's bandwidth is the same if we start from the notion of a module's bandwidth. We still multiply the module's clock speed in megahertz by the system's memory bus channel width. Remember, all modern PC motherboards have 64-bit memory buses. Then we multiply by the number of streams of data that the system can transfer per clock cycle.

If two modules were installed on a dual-channel motherboard, the system would have two working channels. If four modules were installed on a quad-channel motherboard, the system would have four working channels. Finally, we divide the result by 8 to express the system bandwidth in bytes instead of bits because there are 8 bits in a byte.

For example, we could use the formula for a DDR module with a 1,600 MHz effective clock speed running on a quad-channel system. It would have a bandwidth (i.e., it would be part of system bandwidth) of (1,600 MHz X 64-bit bus width X 4 channels) ÷ 8 bits/byte, which equals 51,200 megabytes. To convert that speed to gigabytes, we would divide it by 1,000 megabytes per gigabyte to arrive at a speed of 51.20 GB/s.

The upcoming DDR 5 6400 RAM will be able to operate at an effective DDR speed of 6,400 MHz (i.e., MT/s)! We can use the bandwidth formula to calculate that it could support a system bandwidth of 6,400 MHz memory speed X 64-bit bus width X 4 channels ÷ 8 bits/byte. That equals 204,800 megabytes per second or 204.8 GB/s!

Motherboard manufactures validate that their RAM module kits will work on particular motherboards at particular memory speeds. They list those speeds in their qualified vendor lists (QVLs). RAM manufacturers also often refer to 'Tested RAM Speeds'. However, 'Tested RAM Speed' is not a scientific measurement. It is just a marketing term used by memory manufacturers to certify that they have tested particular modules at particular speeds.

RAM latencies show the time delays taken by different stages of a module's operation. These latencies are also called 'RAM timings'. Recall that the term 'latency' refers to a delay between the time when a command is sent and when it is completed. The smaller a latency number, the faster an operation. RAM latencies are shown on module stickers and on module datasheets. An example is shown in Figure 3.3.2.

aluminum heat spreader

certified (i.e., tested) bandwidth

CAS latency speed

Voltage

XMP (Extreme Memory Profile) lets users set up profiles in the BIOS that will automatically overclock system RAM.

notch in row of pins to prevent module being inserted into wrong DDR motherboard socket type

curved section of row of double I/O pins

Figure 3.3.2: Memory Module Data

The first latency number is the most important. It is the Column Address Strobe (CAS) latency number. It is sometimes abbreviated as 'tCL', which stands for 'Time CAS Latency'. The CAS latency refers to the time required for a module to find some memory data and make it available on its output pins for a CPU's memory controller to access. The other RAM latency numbers show the times required to perform other tasks that have less influence on the overall speed of the RAM; so, they aren't explained here.

The CAS latency of asynchronous DRAM is usually measured in nanoseconds. Recall that a nanosecond (ns) is one billionth of a second (i.e., 1/1,000,000,000 s). However, the CAS latency of synchronous DRAM is usually measured in clock cycles. For example, a synchronous memory module with a CAS latency of 13 would require 13 clock cycles to deliver data to a CPU's memory controller.

Calculating the overall latencies of modules allows us to compare their effective speeds. The overall latency of synchronous DDRAM equals its clock speed times the number of clock cycles required to deliver data from its memory. For example, the latency of the DDR 4 module in Table 3.2.2 is calculated as 0.75 ns X 18 clock cycles = 13.50 ns. Table 3.3.2 shows the latencies of four different modules with four different DDRs. Those latency values show that faster data transfer rates more than compensate for slower CAS latency speeds.

Table 3.3.2: Latencies of Typical RAM Modules

Data Rates	Module Speeds (MT/s)	Clock Speeds (ns)	CAS Latencies (tCL)	Overall Latencies (ns)
DDR 1	400	5.00	3	15.00
DDR 2	800	2.50	6	15.00
DDR 3	1,600	1.25	11	13.75
DDR 4	2,666	0.75	18	13.50

These days, most desktop PC operating systems have paging systems that allow CPUs to access more memory than is available in the system's RAM. Paging systems accomplish that by using secondary storage devices as temporary primary memory locations. That method is slow because it takes much longer for memory data to be delivered from secondary storage devices to CPUs than it takes for memory data to be delivered from RAM to CPUs.

For that reason, the more RAM installed in a system, the better. However, RAM is expensive, and it would be wasteful to buy more than is necessary. At the time that the first edition of this book was written, 4 GB was the typical amount of RAM installed in desktop PCs. Typically, 4 GB of memory is ample for undertaking simple tasks such as browsing the internet, listening to music, or word processing. However, to play Ultra HD Blu-ray 4K content, or to undertake a moderate amount of photo editing, a system would benefit from 8 GB of RAM. Multitasking, that is, running several programs at once, would also benefit from at least 8 GB of RAM — especially if a virtual machine was used. That is because virtual machines must run two operating systems as well as multiple applications simultaneously. A virtual machine might be used to run a guest OS that can run legacy software (that is, old software that the main installed OS cannot operate).

If you intend doing much video editing or much intensive database work using a fast solid-state drive, your system would probably be able to make good use of 16 GB of RAM. However, installing more than 16 GB of RAM would not usually result in a noticeable performance improvement. It might only be worthwhile installing 32 GB of RAM if you intend to frequently undertake intensive CAD, 3-D modeling, virtual reality, or large-scale video-editing tasks. Refer to Tables 2.3 and 2.4 to check the minimum amount of RAM that your system will need.

Most RAM manufacturers provide online configurators that can show which of their products suit particular factory-built PC systems. However, G.SKILL's configurator does better than that. It also provides RAM recommendations based on motherboard chipsets. Even better, if you are building a Ryzen-based system, Guru 3D's benchmarks can show you how much Ryzen systems can improve with faster memory speeds.

Different RAM manufacturers construct their RAM modules on different dies. A die is a small block of semiconducting material that a circuit is constructed on. At the time the fourth edition of this book was produced, Samsung B-die RAM could run at up to 3,466 MHz. G.SKILL and GeIL are the main suppliers of B-die memory modules. B-Die modules provide the best compatibility with Ryzen processors. Speeds of 3,200 MHz were possible with Hynix M-Die RAM, whereas other die types usually support speeds of up to 2,933 MHz.

Recent UEFI-BIOS updates have enabled more DDR 4 RAM kits to work with Ryzen CPUs. A list of available RAM models with Samsung B-die chips at the time the fourth edition of this book was produced was compiled for the Reddit website by a website user, Wiidesire.

Avoid RAM with clock speeds slower than 2,400 MHz. Such slow memory would limit a faster motherboard memory bus to the slower speed of the RAM. On the other hand, memory faster than 3,200 MHz provides diminishing cost-benefit returns. The sweet spot (i.e., the best value-for-money) for RAM speed used with Ryzen CPUs is probably 2,667 MHz.

However, if you intend using a motherboard with an integrated graphic card, select RAM with the fastest tested speed that your CPU and motherboard will support. But, buying RAM with a faster clock speed than your motherboard memory bus would be a waste of some money — unless you intend to overclock your system. Using RAM with a faster clock speed than a motherboard or CPU won't increase the speed of either the motherboard or CPU. Although motherboard BIOSs can be used to overclock systems, motherboards can't be overclocked.

Overclocking RAM is of little practical value because increasing its frequency automatically also increases its CAS latency. That is because modules with faster clock speeds must have slower CAS latencies to keep their memories stable. However, if you do intend to manually overclock your RAM, buy the fastest available modules with the lowest CAS latencies. Also, look for RAM that can run on the highest voltages. If you manually increase the RAM voltage by 10 % or more, you risk destroying the modules.

Intel's Extreme Memory Profile (XMP) automatic overclocking system allows Intel CPUs to use faster memory modules than their nominal DDR 4 speeds. AMD's Memory Profile (AMP) does likewise. For example, Ryzen CPUs using AMP can support DDR 4 memory with speeds of up to 3,600 MHz. AMD's Ryzen Master utility allows Ryzen or Threadripper users to configure the frequencies of their DDR 4 memories. Figure 3.3.3 shows a module's voltage being configured.

Figure 3.3.3: Configuring RAM Voltage

You will notice from Figure 3.3.3 that a QR code must be used to receive the configuration details. Using a QR code involves different processes depending on whether you use a mobile device or a desktop computer and which operating system you use. To use the code with an Android mobile phone:

1. Open the Android device's Google Play Store. Tap the Google Play Store app icon, which resembles a multicolored triangle.

2. Tap the Google Play search bar at the top of the screen.

3. Type in 'qr code reader'. Press 'Enter' to generate a menu with search results.

4. Select a reader. In this example, I selected QR Code Reader – free by G. Krainz.

5. Tap the INSTALL button on the right side of the screen, and then tap 'ACCEPT' on the next screen. The QR Code Reader app will begin downloading.

7. Tap 'OPEN' on the next screen. Tapping it will open QR Code Reader on your device. The reader will then be able to use the device's camera.

8. Point your Android device's camera at the QR code. Center the QR code in the screen so that it fits between the four brackets in the middle of your device's screen. It will focus on the code and scan it within a few seconds. You will then see the QR code's content displayed below the image.

Single-bit errors might occasionally occur in ordinary RAM. That ordinary type of RAM used to be called 'unbuffered RAM'. However, nowadays it is called 'unregistered RAM', and unregistered dual in-line memory is referred to as 'UDIMM'.

The few errors that might occur in unregistered RAM usually cause only minor annoyances — although they can occasionally cause programs to crash. Nevertheless, even minor nuisances are unacceptable in critical enterprise servers. For that reason, a more expensive type of RAM, called 'registered RAM', was developed.

Registered double in-line memory RAM modules (RDIMMs) use an error-correcting code (ECC) type of memory, which improves a system's data integrity. However, ECC memory can only work in motherboards that are designed to use it.

Recall that registers are the memory storage locations on CPUs that hold volatile data that CPUs must directly access to carry out their processing tasks. The requests for data in unregistered memory systems go directly from memory controllers to main memory modules. However, ECC memory architecture involves loading memory data into extra registers before CPUs can access it. CPUs must send their requests for memory data to those extra registers. The extra registers, in turn, must access the data from the RAM. The extra registers reduce the electrical stresses on CPU memory controllers, which helps keep systems stable.

One trade-off of registered RAM is that it is slower than unregistered RAM. That is because the extra registers must hold data for one extra clock cycle before it can be accessed by CPUs. So, registered RAM runs one clock cycle behind equivalent unregistered RAM. Registered memory is also more expensive because of the cost of its extra ECC circuitry. In fact, registered RAM is about twice as expensive as unregistered RAM. For example, 16 GB of Hynix DDR 4 2,400 MHz ECC RAM cost $ 178 in early-2019. At the same time, 16 GB of Hynix DDR 4 2,400 MHz unregistered RAM cost just $ 93. Since unregistered RAM memory is less error-prone than it used to be, few DIY computer builders bother with it these days.

Nevertheless, if you want to find a motherboard that can use registered RAM, you can search for one on major IT shopping websites. Go to a motherboard section. Then filter the generated list by searching for 'Registered' and 'DDR4', as shown in Figure 3.3.4. You will notice that only a few such motherboards are available and that they are intended for use in enterprise servers.

ASRock's Intel server motherboard

Supermicro's AMD server motherboard

If you select error-correcting (ECC) as well, you will be limited to Supermicro's AMD motherboard.

Filter for 'Registered' and 'DDR4 Standard'.

Figure 3.3.4: Website listing of Motherboards that support Registered RAM

A memory divider controls the ratio of a module's speed to a motherboard's memory bus speed, which is sometimes called a 'DRAM/FSB ratio'. A memory divider is, in turn, managed by a memory controller. Most motherboards enable memory dividers to be changed to support overclocking.

By default, motherboard memory bus speeds and RAM speeds are usually set to a 1:1 ratio. That ratio makes RAM run at the same speed as a motherboard memory bus. Increasing a motherboard's memory bus speed by overclocking it would also increase the RAM speed by the same amount if a memory divider's ratio remains set at 1:1. However, no noticeable performance gains usually result from setting memory ratios greater than 1:1.

It is best to install RAM with the same speed as the system CPU. For instance, Ryzen CPUs do not have 3,000 MHz or 3,400 MHz memory dividers. Therefore, it best to install RAM modules with memory speeds of 3,200 MHz or 3,600 MHz, which Ryzen CPUs memory dividers support. Finding modules with the correct memory speeds that support Ryzen CPUs is easy because many 3,200 MHz and 3,600 MHz modules have recently been validated for chipsets.

RAM might not be able to run at the overclocked speed of a CPU. In that case, you can use a memory divider to increase the speed of RAM relative to that of the motherboard memory bus and CPU. Along with latency timings, memory dividers can be used to overclock memory to higher motherboard bus frequencies. For instance, if a memory bus speed is set to 200 MHz, and the memory divider is set at 2:1, the RAM will be forced to run at 400 MHz.

Motherboard manufacturers usually advise that their motherboards will only support kits of identically-matched modules. Nevertheless, different brands of RAM with the same specifications might sometimes work together on some motherboards. Sometimes, modules with different speeds will even work together. However, in such cases, the motherboards will run all the memory modules at the speeds of the slowest modules. Therefore, it is always best to install kits of identical modules.

It is best to install a kit of at least two RAM modules, rather than a single module with the same total capacity. Then, if one module fails, a system can keep running using the remaining good module. If a PC has only one module, and it fails, the system will not be able to work. Two modules with the same capacity of a single module also have twice the surface area of one module. They will, therefore, run cooler. Moreover, if only one RAM module is installed in a multi-channel motherboard, it would likely operate using a slow single-channel mode.

It is best not to install three modules on dual or quad-channel motherboards. That might cause problems — or even prevent the Power On Self Test (POST) from completing. The POST is explained in Section 6, which is about powering-up your system. Nevertheless, three RAM modules installed in dual or quad-channel motherboards will run in flex mode if the motherboard supports it. Flex mode allows two modules to work together on a dual-channel while allowing the remaining module to work as a separate single channel. Otherwise, on motherboards without flex mode, three modules would likely run in single-channel mode. A kit of four RAM modules installed on either a dual or quad-channel motherboard would work correctly as part of a multi-channel system.

Keeping RAM cool is important because modern RAM modules use automatic thermal throttling that slows them down if they overheat. The simplest method of cooling RAM modules is using passive heatsinks. Passive heatsinks are aluminum coverings. Those coverings provide large surface areas that radiate heat from modules. That cooling helps modules run efficiently and prolongs their lifespans. Passive heatsinks also provide physical protection for the DIMM chips on DRAM modules and protect them somewhat from electrostatic discharges. RAM modules with passive heatsinks are shown in Figures 3.3.2 and 3.3.5.

These days, active heatsink RAM coolers are also available. An example is the inexpensive G.SKILL Turbulence cooler shown in Figure 3.3.5. However, DIY computer builders interested in decorating their systems would be more interested in customizable RGB-equipped active RAM coolers, even though they are more expensive.

An example is the Corsair II Dominator Airflow Platinum RAM cooler, also shown in Figure 3.3.5. It features dual fans with ball bearings and toolless mounting brackets that fit most ATX motherboards. It costs about $ 80.

G.SKILL Turbulence RAM Cooler   passive heatsink   Corsair II RGB RAM Cooler

Figure 3.3.5: RAM Coolers

If you want to install an active RAM cooler, choose one that will leave enough room in your case for you to also install your CPU-cooler. That might only likely to be an issue if you intend to install some over-sized air-heatsink/fan CPU-coolers.

There are many RAM manufacturers. If you buy RAM from any reputable manufacturer that provides a lifetime warranty, you should have no cause for concern. However, buying unbranded RAM, or original equipment manufacturer (OEM) RAM with a dubious warranty, is not wise. Table 3.3.3 provides a basic checklist to help you select the RAM for your PC.

Table 3.3.3: RAM Selection Checklist

Factors	Suggestions	Your Decisions
clock speed	the same as motherboard's bus, but faster is okay	
DDR	4	
total kit capacity	8 GB ordinarily; 16 GB for playing games or VR[1]	
passive heatsink	useful with faster, higher-capacity modules	
active heatsink	for very fast RAM, or decorated systems	
warranty	lifetime[2]	
registered ECC	only for critical business or scientific servers	
cost	about 9 % of the total cost of hardware	

Note: 1. 'VR' means 'virtual reality'. 2. RAM modules are highly-reliable components that can usually be relied upon to last for at least seven years or so.

For a computer to boot (i.e., start working) its BIOS needs data about the size, data width, speed, and voltage of the system's RAM modules. The BIOS uses this data to configure the RAM so that the system can access it. This data is called the 'serial presence detect' (SPD) data. It is stored on tiny electrically erasable programmable read-only memory (EEPROM) chips that are located on RAM modules.

The SPD typically includes a fail-safe speed that might be slower than a RAM's maximum tested speed. It uses that slower speed to avoid possible timing conflicts with motherboards, which might prevent systems from booting.

These days, SPDs are typically programmed to a standard 2,133 MHz. For that reason, you might need to manually configure a faster system RAM speed in your system's BIOS. To check the speed that RAM is running at in Windows 10:

1. Type 'cmd' in the Type here to search dialog box.

2. Click on the Command Prompt icon.

3. Type 'wmic memorychip get speed' in the command prompt line, and then press the enter key, as shown in Figure 3.3.6.

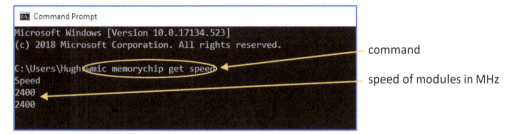

Figure 3.3.6: Checking RAM Speed

You could also use CPU-Z to check your RAM's configuration. To do that, look under the Memory tab, as shown in Figure 3.3.7. Since 'DDR' means 'double data rate', you must double the indicated DRAM frequency speed. For example, the 1,197.1 MHz speed shown in Figure 3.3.7 means that the RAM will be working at 2,394.2 MHz, or approximately 2,400 MHz. I was unable to make the latest standard version of CPU-Z work on my Ryzen 2000-series/Windows 64-bit system. However, following the suggestion of a CPU-Z representative, I was able to make the portable 1.86 version work.

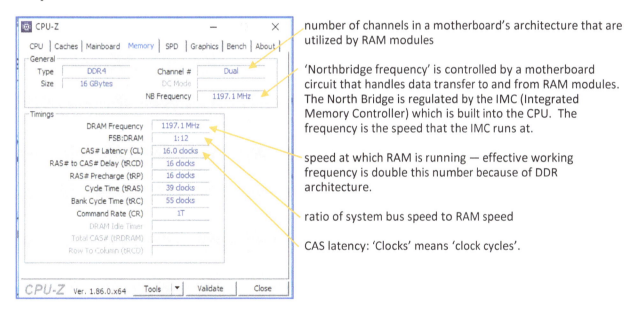

number of channels in a motherboard's architecture that are utilized by RAM modules

'Northbridge frequency' is controlled by a motherboard circuit that handles data transfer to and from RAM modules. The North Bridge is regulated by the IMC (Integrated Memory Controller) which is built into the CPU. The frequency is the speed that the IMC runs at.

speed at which RAM is running — effective working frequency is double this number because of DDR architecture.

ratio of system bus speed to RAM speed

CAS latency: 'Clocks' means 'clock cycles'.

Figure 3.3.7: Checking RAM Configuration in CPU-Z

If you discover that your system's RAM is working slower than its labeled maximum speed, you can access the UEFI-BIOS to adjust the RAM's configuration. To do that: Go to 'Overclock' settings. Then look for 'memory settings' and then 'DRAM Timing Mode'. Finally, look for the DRAM Frequency on the drop-down list, and choose the correct speed for your RAM. If you increase the memory's speed, you might also need to increase its CAS timings so that they correspond with the speeds printed on the module's label.

When you are finished, press the F10 keyboard key to save your settings and then reboot the PC. Your system should restart normally. You can then you can check the RAM's speed using either Windows 10 or CPU-Z to make sure that the new configuration was saved correctly.

3.4: Selecting the Expansion Cards

Expansion cards are circuit boards that can be plugged into motherboard expansion slots to add extra capabilities to systems. The two types of expansion cards most often installed in desktop PCs are soundcards (also called 'audio cards') and graphic cards (also called 'graphic accelerators').

Until the late-1980s, PCs had tiny internal speakers that could only generate simple sounds such as beeps. Soundcards were then developed that could convert more complex digital signals from computers into analog signals that could be played through speakers. Those early soundcards were also designed to reduce some of the interferences that can degrade the quality of sounds generated within computers.

Until recently, the quality of onboard audio (i.e., soundcards integrated within motherboards) was only mediocre. However, these days, many motherboards have integrated soundcards that provide sound-quality that is acceptable for most purposes. Indeed, nowadays, integrated soundcards typically support 7.1-channel High-Definition (HD) surround-sound and other advanced features, such as virtual reality.

In previous sections, you learned that a channel is a wire that can carry data between parts of a computer system. But, in relation to audio, the term 'channel' refers to a separate stream of audio data that can be sounded by a separate speaker. The number after the '.' refers to a subwoofer channel. A subwoofer is a speaker that produces low-pitched audio frequencies known as 'bass'. Five-point-one channel sound is the industry-standard format for movies and CD music and is also used with most games. It can support five main channels, each of which can be sounded by a different speaker, as well as a sixth subwoofer.

If you are discerning about the quality of the music you listen to, or have other sophisticated audio requirements, you might want to buy a separate soundcard with higher specifications than are available from integrated soundcards. For instance, you might want to record high-quality commercial music or play games with special sound effects. But, beware that cheap separate soundcards are not as good as most integrated soundcards. In fact, they use CPUs to do much of the audio processing. High-end soundcards, on the other hand, are likely to support Digital Virtual Disc (DVD) audio, provide extra ports aside from the normal 3.5 mm (1/8") jacks, and provide controls that fit into case front bays. The capacity to accept front audio controls is yet another advantage of cases with front device bays.

The six basic specifications to consider when selecting a soundcard are its bit-depth; its sample rate; its frequency response; its bandwidth; its signal-to-noise ratio (SNR); it's digital-audio-converter (DAC) and its physical interfaces.

Bit-depth is the number of bits of data contained within a sound sample. The greater the bit-depth, the better the sound quality. The first soundcards were low-quality 8-bit soundcards. They are now obsolete. CD-quality 16-bit soundcards, which provide much more accurate sound samples, are now common. Sixteen-bit soundcards are adequate for most games because their audio is limited to 16-bit CD-quality to minimize file sizes. However, some 24-bit soundcards are also available, and there are even a few 32-bit soundcards. Soundcards with such high bit-depths can generate higher-quality sounds than can be reproduced by CD audio players, although Blu-Ray movies can make use such high-quality soundcards to generate high-quality audio. On balance, 24-bit-depth soundcards provide the best value-for-money.

The sample rate (i.e., 'frequency rate') is the number of sound samples produced by a soundcard every second. It is measured in hertz or kilohertz. The greater the sample rate of a soundcard, the higher the quality of the audio it can generate.

Sometimes people confuse 'frequency rate' with 'frequency response'. 'Frequency response' refers to the amplitude (i.e., the volume) of a sound at a particular frequency. For example, we might say that a soundcard can generate a frequency response of 120 decibels (dB) at a frequency of 25 kHz. A decibel is the unit of measurement of the intensity of sounds. Complete silence would be 0 dB, whereas a normal human conversation would be about 60 dB. A frequency response of more than 85 dB can cause hearing loss in humans.

The frequency responses of soundcards are often given in expressions such as '34 Hz-20 kHz +/-3 dB'. That measurement indicates that sounds with sample rates between 34 Hz and 20 kHz will be accurately reproduced within a variation of plus or minus 3 decibels. A frequency response range of three decibels is common in soundcards.

You may recall that the term 'bandwidth' was used earlier to refer to the maximum potential data transfer rate between two devices. However, when we use 'bandwidth' in relation to sound, we refer to the range of frequencies that a device can transmit. For example, human ears can typically hear frequencies in the bandwidth of 20 Hz to 20 kHz (20,000 Hz). Good soundcards should, therefore, produce tones across that bandwidth.

There are many sources of electrical interference inside computer cases. Those noises are called 'background noises' or 'static'. The signal-to-noise (SNR) ratio of a soundcard is a measure of the amount of intended original sound transmitted compared to the amount of interference noise that is also transmitted. The signal-to-noise ratio is measured in decibels. Soundcards with higher signal-to-noise ratios provide better-quality audio. Good soundcards have signal-to-noise ratios of 110 dB or higher. The amounts of undistorted sounds that are produced by soundcards are also sometimes measured as total harmonic distortion + noise (THD+N) in percentages. The closer to 0 % a soundcard's THD+N is, the more accurate the sounds it can generate. Good soundcards have THD+Ns of 0.005 % or less. 'THD' is an initialism meaning 'total harmonic distortion'.

SNRs are not the same as dynamic ranges. 'Dynamic range' is not a scientific term. Rather, it is a vague term sometimes used by manufacturers to refer to soundcards' abilities to project ranges of instrumental and vocal tones. At other times, it is used to refer to the ratio of the quietest sound to the loudest sound that a soundcard can generate. For example, using the second definition, we could say that the dynamic range of human hearing is the difference between the quietest sound we can perceive and the loudest. That range is about 120 dB. The best soundcards can generate dynamic ranges of 109 dB or more.

Sound signals from soundcards must go through digital-analog converters (DACs) that convert digital audio signals to analog signals and then send those signals to headphones or speakers. The abilities of DACs to reproduce original analog sounds vary significantly. To play 16-bit CD-quality sound, a soundcard's DAC must support a sample rate of at least 44.1 kHz. That rate is ample for ordinary purposes. However, to play high-fidelity music from DVDs, a DAC must support a 96 kHz sample rate. The DACs in a few extremely high-quality soundcards support sample rates as high as 192 kHz. These cards can generate high-quality sounds.

The best sound reproduction is provided by some external DACs, such as Chord Electronics' Qutest DAC. It has an extraordinarily low of THD of less than 0.0001 %, but it is expensive. It costs about $ 1,900!

Soundcards must have interfaces with both their motherboard's expansion slots and with the peripheral devices that connect to them. The first soundcards used Industry Standard Architecture (ISA) interfaces that connected with the ISA slots provided on motherboards. At best, the ISA interface supported a 16-bit bus with a speed of 10 MHz.

After the early 2000s, most soundcards connected to motherboards via the superior Peripheral Component Interconnect (PCI) interface. However, some of the most recent powerful soundcards now use the newer PCIe interface.

Soundcards must have one 3.5 mm (1/8") output jack for each pair of speakers (i.e., left and right speakers). However, several other types of ports are also used to connect peripheral audio devices, such as microphones, headphones, and electronic musical instruments to soundcards. These ports include TOSLINK, XLR-M, TRS ¼" (6.3 mm) jack, RCA, Sony/Phillips Digital Interface (S/PDIF), FireWire, and Musical Instrument Digital Interface (MIDI). You must, therefore, select a soundcard with the correct ports to connect with the external devices you want to use. For instance, you might want to use an S/PDIF connector to output audio to a digital amplifier through a coaxial cable. On the other hand, you might need to use a MIDI port if you want to use an electric keyboard, or another digital instrument, to input sounds. MIDI is the standard interface used by musicians to connect musical instruments to PCs.

If you want to record vocal sounds, you will, of course, also need a microphone. However, the tiny microphones in most webcams and headsets are rudimentary and insufficient for recording high-quality sounds. You would therefore need to use a separate high-fidelity microphone to record high-quality sounds.

Since the time that the first edition of this book was written, the best affordable, stand-alone microphone, in my opinion, has been the Blue Yeti. It can record 16-bit sound at 48 kHz and costs about $ 125. But, if you prefer to buy the most expensive microphone instead, you would need to select the Sony C800GPAC Studio Condenser Microphone. It costs about $ 10,000!

Figure 3.4.1 shows a Yeti microphone with some DIY modifications and a DIY desk stand. I used that setup satisfactorily-enough for several years. However, the stand was always somewhat in the way on my desk. Also, the microphone sometimes transmitted a bit of vibration noise. So, while working on the fourth edition of this book, I bought a Blue Compass microphone arm and a cheap microphone vibration dampener. Using them allows me to position the microphone closer to my mouth; frees up some desk space and seems to eliminate the last vestiges of transmitted vibration noises. This new set up is also shown in Figure 3.4.1.

foam to reduce recorded noise

tea strainer pop filter inside foam wrapping

headphones attach using 3.5-inch (1/4") jack

stand made from a cord spindle

rubber vibration insulation

carpet padding to reduce vibration noises

Blue Compass boom arm

microphone vibration dampener

wire is hidden inside arm (i.e., boom)

Figure 3.4.1: DIY Microphone Stand and Blue Compass Boom Arm

If you want to record commercial-quality sounds such as podcasts, digital book readings, music, or the like, you will also need to control background noises. Ideally, you could use a sound-proof booth to accomplish that. However, buying a professionally-designed sound booth constructed from special sound-insulation materials would be expensive.

Figure 3.4.2 shows an effective small DIY alternative. It is constructed from recycled high-density polystyrene slabs. Recycled foam mattress pieces with rippled surfaces are glued to the inside of the booth to reduce sound waves bouncing inside the booth. Styrofoam blocks are also glued to the outside of the booth to reduce other sound waves bouncing around the room outside the booth. This DIY booth is quite effective. It is assembled by simply slotting the panels into the desk's recesses, which takes only a minute or so.

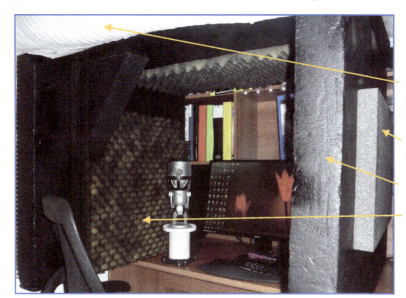

folding back cover made from high-density foam strips glued inside foam bag

medium-density foam blocks on the outside

10 cm high-density polystyrene

soft-density foam with rippled surface

Figure 3.4.2: DIY Recording Sound Booth

High-quality soundcards provide noise-limiting features such as EMI (electromagnetic interference) shielding, as well as digital signal processing systems that remove background noises during silent periods. However, it is not essential to use a soundcard to record high-quality microphone sounds. That is because some headsets with in-built microphones, as well as most stand-alone microphones, such as the Yeti, can connect directly to computers using USB ports. This method avoids the necessity of using DACs to convert digital signals into analog signals. Even some high-quality soundcards are not able to record sounds as good as USB-recorded sounds.

That is not to say that USB-sound is perfect or entirely free of noise. It can be somewhat affected by voltage noise as well as some other sorts of interferences. However, devices such as the AQVOX USB Low-Noise 5V Isolated Linear Power Supply, which costs about $ 135 (plus shipping costs and the cost of a voltage converter — if you live outside Europe) can eliminate those minor problems.

The quality of digital sound is also affected by the file format that it is stored in. Until recently, the most popular audio formats were MP3 and WAV. However, these formats will increasingly be supplanted by a superior format, called the Free Lossless Audio Codec (FLAC). A codec is a combined hardware and software system used to convert analog signals into digital signals and back again.

FLAC is the only digital audio format that can be losslessly compressed. That feature is increasingly important because digital audio distribution services require uploaded files to be in a lossless format. The algorithms used to compress lossy audio formats, such as MP3, discard some data to reduce their file sizes. That data-loss results in encoded audio that is inferior to the original. There are three other reasons for the increasing popularity of FLAC.

1. FLAC produces the highest resolution and the most accurately-formatted digital sound.

2. Ripped FLAC files are only about half the size of WAV files with the same resolutions.

3. FLAC is the only free non-proprietary digital audio codec.

MP3, WAV, and FLAC logos are shown in Figure 3.4.3. Utilities, such as the Free MP3 to FLAC Converter, are available to convert MP3 files to FLAC files. Other utilities, such as FreeFileConvert and Pazera Free Audio Extractor, provide free online services for converting WAV files to FLAC files.

Figure 3.4.3: Audio Format Logos

Of course, you would need speakers, or a headphone set, or both, to be able to hear audio produced from your computer. If you buy external speakers, it is best to select shielded types. Otherwise, their magnets might interfere with your monitor if it is connected with a VGA cable.

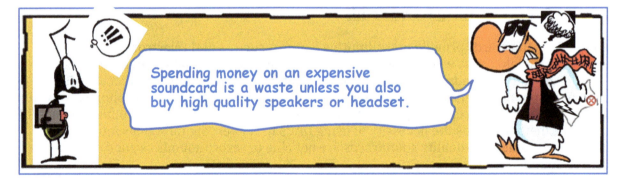

Playing audio on large speakers requires strong amplified sound signals. High-quality soundcards, therefore, have built-in amplifiers. Alternatively, external USB DAC/amplifiers such as the FiiO K1, which costs about $ 45, are also available.

Few new features have recently been developed for soundcards. An exception is the Environmental Audio Extensions (EAX) reverberation engine. Soundcards with EAXs can generate immersive 3-D sounds that seem as if they are coming towards listeners from various directions. Many high-end games use EAXs to generate surround-sound 3-D effects. Examples of PC games that utilize EAX engines are Battlefield 2142, Bioshock, and Mass Effect. But so few new soundcards with other new features are developed these days that Top Ten Reviews stopped reviewing them in 2011. AnandTech did likewise in 2014. Nevertheless, some websites, such as About.com's, still provide occasional soundcard reviews.

One recent outstanding soundcard is the Sound Blaster ZXR. It is expensive, costing about $ 230, but provides impressive features such as a 124 dB SNR, a 600-ohm headphone amplifier, a PCIe connector, as well as a USB cable connector. In fact, it provides so many high-quality features that they can't be fitted into a single soundcard. It, therefore, comes as a system comprised of a main soundcard, a daughter card, and an external audio control module, as shown in Figure 3.4.4. Another interesting, but less-expensive soundcard, produced in the last few years is the Sound BlasterX AE-5. To appeal to contemporary case designers and modelers, it includes inbuilt RGB-lighting that can be synchronized with external RGB lighting. It costs about $ 140.

Sound Blaster ZxR PCIe   Gemini External SC1

Figure 3.4.4: Contemporary Soundcards

These days, there is a third option aside from integrated audio and separate internal soundcards. That option is external sound cards. For instance, Gemini's SC-1 is a USB-powered plug and play external soundcard that enables Windows and MAC systems to use extra outputs as well as to record audio. It costs only $ 50 and is shown in Figure 3.4.4.

Prices for soundcards reflect their qualities and features. For example, ASUS' XONAR DGX 5.1 Channel 24-bit 96 kHz PCIe soundcard costs only about $ 40, whereas RME's AIO HDSPe AIO-PCIe digital audio card soundcard costs about $ 850. Table 3.4.1 compares the specifications of two modern soundcards at different price points.

Table 3.4.1: Features of Soundcards at different Price Points

Features	ASUS Xonar GHX PCIe GX2.5	Sound BlasterX AE-5
price	$ 40	$ 150
output SNR	105 dB	122 dB
frequency response	THD+N[1] at 1kHz <0.0025 %	THD + N: 0.00032 %
sample rate	192 kHz	384 kHz
resolution	24-bit	32-bit
ports	6.3 mm jacks	3 X 3.5 mm jack lines out 1 TOSLINK optical out one 3.5mm headphone jack out one 3.5mm microphone jack in one Intel HD audio front panel
interface type	PCIe	PCIe
3-D sound	yes	yes

Note: 1. 'THD+N' means 'total harmonic distortion + noise'.

Table 3.4.2 provides a soundcard selection checklist.

Table 3.4.2: Soundcard Selection Checklist

Features	Suggestions	Your Decisions
Aboutcom or other review	according to your judgment	
SNR	110+	
frequency response	10 Hz to 90 kHz[1]	
sample rate	96 kHz	
resolution	24-bit	
ports	3.5 mm (1/8") jacks and ports for devices	
slot type	PCI or PCIe	
EAX	for serious game playing	
warranty	one year minimum	
cost	up to 10 % of system costs	

Note: 1. Bandwidth should at least span the 20 kHz–20,000 HZ range that can be detected by human ears.

Processing audio makes only modest demands on systems, whereas processing graphics and video makes much greater demands on them. Displaying virtual reality, undertaking complex CAD work, editing video, and running complex 3-D games, in particular, require considerable processing power. By themselves, CPUs may lack sufficient power to quickly manage such intensive graphic tasks. Specialized microprocessors designed to efficiently process graphics data must be used. The first was the GeForce 256 released by Nvidia in 1999. The term 'graphic card' is often used interchangeably with the term 'video card' and the initialism 'GPU'. However, they are actually different things. A video card is an internal device that is built into a motherboard. It just presents graphic data as it is to a monitor panel screen.

A graphic card is connected to a motherboard via an expansion slot. It helps to control and improve graphic data that is displayed on panels. For instance, a graphic card might generate a picture with a higher resolution than a video card generates, or it might better display fast-moving 3D images. A GPU is a processing chip, which is an essential part of both graphic cards and video cards.

GPUs can be integrated within CPU dies. The term 'Accelerated Processing Unit' (APU) was first used by AMD in 2010 to refer to its CPUs with integrated graphic units. However, the term is now often used as a generic term to refer to any CPU with an integrated GPU. Integrated video units must share the use of systems' relatively slow RAM, which slows down the rendering (i.e., drawing) of screen displays.

The most important specifications of separate graphic cards are their clock speeds, frame rates, bandwidths, amounts, and types of video RAM (VRAM), memory bus speeds, resolutions, motherboard expansion slot types, monitor interface types, and application programming interfaces (APIs).

Different graphic cards operate at different core clock speeds, just as different CPUs do. Medium-quality graphic cards typically operate at clock speeds of about 800 MHz, whereas high-end graphic cards have clock speeds of up to 1,600 MHz.

When the term 'bandwidth' is used to describe a graphic card, it refers to how many bits of data the GPU can process and send to a monitor per clock cycle. For example, we could say that a GPU that can process and transmit a resolution of 1,366 X 768 bits at a frame refresh rate of 30 f/s, would have a bandwidth of 1,366 X 768 bits X 30 f/s, or 31,472,640 b/s (≈ 3.14 MB/s). The higher a GPU's bandwidth, the higher the resolution of video it can transmit without the need for compression.

The effective bandwidths of both graphic cards and monitors are limited by the bandwidths of the ports and cables that connect them. Poor-quality cables of any type can fail to transmit enough bandwidth, which will cause monitors to freeze or flicker.

VGA cables are now considered to be a legacy technology, and even Digital Visual Interface (DVI) cables are becoming outdated. Good-quality DVI cables can only support a bandwidth of 9.9 Gb/s. When the High-Definition Multimedia Interface (HDMI) was first released in 2002, it supported a bandwidth of 3.96 Gb/s. However, the HDMI standard has been progressively increased. Good-quality HDMI 1.4 cables can support a bandwidth of about 10.2 Gb/s, and HDMI 2.0 cables can support about 18 Gb/s. The most recent version of HDMI, 2.1, supports a bandwidth of 48 Gb/s — although it has not yet been used on any devices. Ultra-High-Speed HDMI cables that can transfer 48 Gb/s, however, have just become available. They cost about $ 30 for 2 meters.

The Video Electronics Standards Association (VESA) released DisplayPort v 1.4a standard in 2015. It supports a bandwidth of 32.4 Gb/s and can support the latest high-resolution monitors, including the new 5K monitors with pixel resolutions of 5,120 X 2,880. However, DisplayPort cables can only support a bandwidth of 17.28 Gb/s. To overcome that bottleneck, a few companies have just released DisplayPort 1.4 cables that can support the full 32.4 Gb/s bandwidth. The typical price for a 1-meter DisplayPort 1.4 cable as the fourth edition of this book was being finalized was $ 18.

Thunderbolt 1 and 2 use Apple's Mini DisplayPort ports, which can support data transfer speeds of up to 10 Gb/s and 20 Gb/s respectively. The cables used with these older Thunderbolt versions are passive. Passive cables cannot supply power to devices. They must use a powered chip to boost their performances. Thunderbolt 3, which has been available since 2011, uses active cables with USB Type-C connectors. Active cables can carry their own power. Short, good-quality Thunderbolt 3 cables can support data transfers of up to 40 Gb/s and simultaneously carry up to 100 watts to charge devices. All good-quality USB Type-C cables can work as Thunderbolt 3 cables. Therefore, any USB Type-C device plugged into a Thunderbolt 3 port will function normally.

A graphic card's speed is affected by the amount and type of onboard video RAM (VRAM) it has. Originally, the term 'VRAM' referred to a particular brand of video RAM that was popular in the 1990s. However, nowadays, the term is loosely used to refer to any RAM on any graphic card. Because video-RAM is integrated into graphic microprocessors, video data can be delivered from VRAM to a GPU extremely quickly. You can check your system's VRAM in Windows 10 by:
1. opening window's settings app menu;
2. selecting the system entry, then clicking display on the left sidebar;
3. scrolling down the display box and clicking on 'advanced display settings';
4. on the next menu, selecting the monitor's name; then clicking the Display adapter properties text at the bottom. In the next window, you'll see your system's video RAM details listed next to 'Dedicated Video Memory'. If you see 'AMD Accelerated Processing Unit' or 'Intel HD Graphics' instead, it means that the system is using integrated graphics.

Graphics double data rate (GDDR) VRAM is the type of memory used on most modern graphic cards. It is the same as ordinary VRAM; it just uses a different voltage. Less-powerful graphics cards use GDDR 3 VRAM. However, the latest and most powerful GPUs, available from 2016, use GDDR 5 VRAM, which supports a data rate of up to 14 GB/s. Up to a point, the more GDDR VRAM, the better a graphic card's performance. Graphic cards with less than 2 GB of VRAM can't handle most modern games at fast settings. They are also not recommended for video editing or 3D work. Cards with 2 GB of GDDR 3 VRAM are adequate for most ordinary purposes. Mid-range graphic cards with 3-6 GB of VRAM are OK for casual gaming and moderate video-editing. High-end graphic cards with 8 GB or more VRAM are useful for serious gamer players, who play the latest games at 4K resolutions. Having more VRAM than is actually used will not speed up a graphic card. For instance, there would be no speed difference between 2 GB and 10 GB of VRAM if only 1 GB was being used.

A graphic card's bandwidth is also limited by its memory bus interface. Its memory bus is the pathway to its own internal VRAM. Low-price graphic cards have 128-bit bus-widths. In other words, they can transmit 128 bits per clock cycle on their memory buses. Medium-quality graphic cards have 256-bit memory interfaces. Higher-end graphic cards have up to 512-bit bus interfaces.

APUs do not have access to the large amounts of VRAM that separate graphic cards do. Instead, they must first use the limited cache memory available on CPUs. If that is insufficient, they must use the system's RAM.

A graphic card's resolution is the highest precision it is capable of outputting. The typical standard of resolution displayed by monitors these days is 1,920 X 1,080 pixels. That resolution is satisfactory for most purposes. Nevertheless, recent high-quality graphic cards can deliver resolutions of 3,440 X 1,440 pixels or more.

Each new image that is generated by a graphic card is called a frame. A graphic card's frame rate is the number of frames per second (f/s) that it can output. The higher the frame rate, the fewer the pixels that can be transmitted with each refreshed screen frame. In other words, a graphic card can transmit a higher-resolution image at a lower frame rate and vice versa. You can check your graphic card's frame rate using free utilities such as Fraps 3.5.99 or Bandicam 3.2.4.

Monitors operate at fixed frame rates. However, the frame rates generated by games are not fixed — they fluctuate. These fluctuating frame rates place varying workloads on graphic cards. Monitors must therefore continually make two-way handshakes with their graphic cards to synchronize their frame rates. AMD released its FreeSync 2 technology in 2017 to resolve that frame rate coordination issue. Nvidia also developed a similar GSync technology.

FreeSync 2 also enabled High-Dynamic-Range (HDR) rendering. HDR standards were developed in 2016 by the UHD Alliance, a technology industry group, to ensure that images are lighted as they would with natural light in the real world. To accomplish that, it can dynamically alter the brightness of individual scenes and even individual frames. The HDR also specifies a minimum luminescence of 1,000 nits. A nit is a measure of brightness. One nit equals one candela per square meter. HDR standards also specify HDMI 2.0 as the minimum monitor connection interface. HDR has become such an important feature that AMD recently rebranded 'FreeSync 2' as 'Free Sync 2 HDR'. Only a few AMD Radeon APUs and graphic cards yet support FreeSync 2 HDR. To take advantage of AMD's FreeSync 2 HDR technology, systems require an Adaptive-Sync-compatible monitor, a Thunderbolt or DisplayPort cable (although Free Sync also supports HDMI) and a compatible AMD Catalyst graphics driver.

Most current graphic cards have either PCIe 2 X16 or PCIe 3 X16 interfaces that insert into PCIe motherboard expansion slots. As with soundcards, you can connect a PCIe 2 GPU to a PCIe 3 slot or vice versa. Using PCIe 2 slots is feasible with less-powerful graphic cards that don't need all the bandwidth supported by PCIe 2, let alone all of PCIe 3 X16's bandwidth of 31.5 GB/s. On the other hand, the most powerful graphic cards use more bandwidth than is supported by PCIe 3 X16.

Of course, graphic cards must also interface with monitors. The first monitor video interface standard was Video Graphics Array (VGA). It is an analog display standard that was introduced in 1987 for use with cathode-ray tube monitors, which is susceptible to noise interference. It supports a 640 X 480-pixel resolution at a refresh rate of 60 Hz. Super Video Graphics Array (SVGA) was an improvement that supported an 800 X 600-pixel resolution. That standard is still supported by most LCD monitors. However, LCD monitors must convert analog video signals to digital signals, which results in reduced picture qualities.

Intel introduced the Accelerated Graphic Port (AGP) interface in 1997 to enable faster graphic cards to connect to motherboards. The fastest version was AGP 8X, which supported a transfer speed of 2.1 Gb/s. Since 2008, AGP has been regarded as legacy standard. Motherboards no longer provide AGP slots and cannot accept old AGP graphic cards. Nowadays, graphic cards have faster digital ports. The three most common types are Digital Visual Interface (DVI) ports, High-Definition Multimedia Interface (HDMI) ports, and DisplayPort ports. These ports support the high bandwidths required by most current monitors — although DVI cannot support the bandwidth required by 4K-standard monitors. You can see from Table 3.4.3 that different GPU/port interfaces support a range of frame rates and resolutions. The most common types of monitor ports are listed in Table 5.5.2 and illustrated in Figure 5.5.2.

Table 3.4.3: Resolutions of Monitor/Computer Interfaces

Interface Port Types[1]	Frame Rates (Hz)	Resolutions (pixels)
VGA (XGA)[2]	70	1,024 X 768
DVI	60	2,560 X 1,600
HDMI 1.4[3]	24	3,840 X 2,160 (Ultra HD/consumer 4K)[4]
HDMI 2.03	60	4,096 X 2,160 (cinema-quality 4K)
DisplayPort[5]	60	4,096 X 2,160 + (cinema-quality 4K)+
Thunderbolt 3	120	4,096 X 2,160 (cinema-quality 4K)

Notes: 1. GPUs used in laptops have a different form-factor from the GPUs used in ATX form-factor motherboards. Laptop GPUs use the MXM form-factor. 2. There are many VGA versions. XGA is the version that was introduced by IBM in 1990. 3. There are different versions of HDMI. The most recent, HDMI 2.0, which was released in 2013, supports a bandwidth of 18 Gb/s. 4. '4K resolution' refers to approximately 4,000 horizontal pixels (actually 3,840 pixels on consumer 4K devices). 5. DisplayPort 1.3 was released in 2014 and can support 8K transmissions at 30 Hz. Display Port 1.4, which can support 8K transmissions at 60 Hz, became available in 2017. '8K' refers to a horizontal resolution of approximately 8,000 pixels (actually 7,680 pixels).

AMD recently released a graphics card that incorporates an SSD as well as 2 TB of NAND flash memory! AMD says that the card can run 8K video at up to 90 frames per second. When the fourth edition of this book was produced, that AMD Radeon Pro SSG graphic card cost $ 7,000! It is shown in Figure 3.4.5. AMD also released the Radeon R9 295X2 GPU shown in Figure 3.4.5 while the fourth edition of this book was being prepared. It actually incorporates two of AMD's most powerful graphics processors; has 8 GB of GDDR 5 memory and includes an integrated liquid cooling system. It is much more affordable, costing $1,500. At the same time, Nvidia announced that their next-generation GeForce 20 Volta graphic card would soon be released. Its 16 Gb/s GDDR 6 memory is twice as fast as typical GDDR 5 memory. AMD's upcoming Navi GPUs will likely make use of the same GDDR 6 memory technology.

Pro SSG

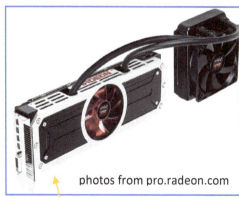

photos from pro.radeon.com

R9 295X2

Figure 3.4.5: Recent Radeon Graphic Cards

As you learned earlier, you can install dual- graphic cards to run dual monitors with high resolutions and high frame rates. However, some recent single-graphic cards, such as AMD's R9 290X and ASUS' ROG STRIX GTX 1080 O8G Gaming, are so powerful that they can run complex games on dual monitors. If you want to run dual monitors from a single graphic card, make sure that it provides two video outlets — each with a large enough bandwidth for your purposes. Dual-monitor systems are easy to set up in Windows 10 because it can natively support two monitors.

Modern high-end graphic cards provide application programming interfaces (APIs). An API is a software-to-software interface that is invisible to users. APIs make it possible for devices, such as secondary storage devices and graphic cards, to transmit data directly to each other without going through operating systems. APIs also provide enhancement features, such as DirectX.

DirectX enables complex 3-D surfaces to be displayed. DirectX 11.1 was built into Windows 8.1. Windows 10 is supplied with DirectX 12, which supports a 20 % faster frame rate than DirectX 11.1's. The other popular API is SGI's OpenGL. Its latest version, in 2018, was 5.0.4.

There are several graphic card manufacturers. However, since 2006, when AMD acquired ATI, the two main graphic card chipset suppliers to all these manufacturers have been AMD and Nvidia. Graphic cards with chipsets from either manufacturer are equally reliable and supported by good warranties. Nevertheless, some users claim that there is a slight advantage in using AMD graphic cards with motherboards with AMD chipsets. Some others claim that Nvidia motherboard chipsets provide a slight advantage when used with Nvidia graphic cards. Still others report that Nvidia sometimes provides better support for cards running on Linux distributions. Table 3.4.4 compares some of the specifications of two modern graphics cards at different price points.

Table 3.4.4: Specifications of two Graphics Cards

Specifications	Radeon HD 5450[1]	Nvidia GeForce GTX 690[2]
interface	PCIe	PCIe 3
core speed	650 MHz	915 MHz
monitor ports	VGA, DVI; HDMI	2 DVI-I, 1 DVI-D; 1 Mini-DisplayPort
API	DirectX 11	DirectX 11
frame rate (f/s)	22.8	84 at 2,560 X 1,600 pixels
pixel-fill-rate (Gp/s)[3]	2.7	65
CrossFireX or SLI	CrossFireX	SLI
VRAM	2 GB DDR 3	4 GB GDDR 5
max resolution	2,560 X 1,600 pixels	5,760 X 1,080 pixels
cost	$ 45	$ 1,000

Notes: 1. The 5450 generates so little heat that some versions are passively cooled. Other versions use a tiny 40 mm fan to cool a small 4.5 cm X 4.5 cm (1.8" X 1.8") heatsink. 2. The GTX 690 has two vapor chamber heatsinks. A center-mounted fan channels air through both heatsinks. The GTX 690 draws 300 watts of power. 3. 'Pixel-fill-rate' is the number of pixels a graphic card can render to a screen per second.

Both AMD and Nvidia offer high-end VR-certified graphic cards that can support virtual reality headsets. You would need an Nvidia GeForce GTX 1060 or an AMD Radeon RX 480 graphic card or better to support the latest hi-resolution VR headsets. Virtual reality headsets also require middleware such as 3DCeption to generate 3-D effects. Middleware is software that integrates other separate programs. A graphic card must be High-Bandwidth Digital Content Protection (HCDP) compliant to play Blu-ray media. A graphic card must also support the new HDR Rec 2020 UltraHD Premium standard to work fully with the latest HD Blu-ray players.

The most powerful graphic cards may consume more electricity than all the other components of a typical system combined! For example, a Radeon R Fury X (which is composed of 4 graphic cards) requires 1,600 W! Such powerful GPUs have their own coolers and typically require their own six-pin PSU connections, which raises their costs.

Until recently, closed-loop liquid-cooling kits were only available for CPUs — not for graphics cards. Then, in 2014 NZXT produced a bracket, called the Kraken G10, that enabled Asetek-based liquid-cooling kits to be installed on most modern graphics cards. An example is shown in Figure 3.4.6. Since that time, dedicated graphic card liquid-coolers have also been produced. The latest model, when the fourth edition of this book was being produced, was the EK-FC1070 GTX Ti ASUS water block. It features a clear acrylic top and RBG lighting. An example is also shown in Figure 3.4.6.

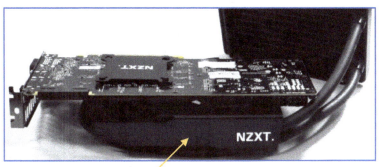
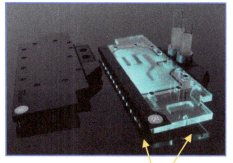

Kraken GPU Cooler Bracket   EK-FC1070 GTX Ti Water block

Figure 3.4.6: Liquid GPU Coolers

There is also another option for installing a graphics card. Razer produces an external graphics enclosure branded the Core X. It contains its own factory-installed 650-watt ATX GPU power supply. The Core X only overrides installed internal GPUs when it is connected to a system. It supports plug and play with most recent Nvidia and AMD PCIe graphics cards and connects to computers using Thunderbolt 3 USB Type-C cables. It works with Windows 10 64-bit OS and is available from Razer's website for $ 299.99. It provides three main benefits. It:
1. locates hot GPUs outside of cases,
2. relieves PSUs from the necessity of providing up to 650 W of power to graphic cards, and
3. frees up a PCIe slot on motherboards.

Modern graphic cards contain integrated frame buffers. Frame buffers temporarily hold those video signals until they are required by a monitor. As previously mentioned, PC builders sometimes overclock their graphic cards as well as their CPUs. Overclocking a graphic card usually involves increasing both its clock frequency and its memory frame buffer speed. Both of those changes force a graphic card to work faster.

Both AMD and Nvidia provide built-in tools to enable their graphic cards to be overclocked. For example, AMD's Ryzen Master utility allows users to configure the frequencies of integrated Radeon Vega graphics cards.

Alternatively, some users manually overclock their graphic cards. To do that, they increase their clock frequency setting sliders in 10 MHz increments until visual anomalies occur or their systems crash. Then they reduce their graphic cards' clock frequencies by 10 MHz. Some users can increase the speed of a graphic card by as much as 200 MHz over its default setting. They then follow a similar procedure to find the graphic card's maximum stable frame buffer speed and set both speeds to the same slowest maximum speed that either will run at.

Increasing a graphic card's voltage will increase its power consumption, increase the stress on it, shorten its lifespan, and probably invalidate its warranty. Nevertheless, some people use third-party utilities, such as MSI's free Afterburner, to configure the voltages sent to their graphic cards and to adjust their working temperatures. Those changes might allow them to overclock their cards even more. They then use the free version of Heaven Bench Mark 4.0 from UNIGINE Corporation to test the overclocked graphic cards to ensure that they are stable.

A few manufacturers produce graphic cards designed to fit into small-form-factor cases. For example, Gigabyte's GTX 1080 mini graphic card has dimensions of H: 37 mm, L: 169 mm, and W: 131 mm. It is expensive though, costing about $ 810.

There are even more graphic card specifications than have been explained here. Instead of comparing all these additional specifications, it is easier, and perhaps more useful, just to review their benchmarks. AnandTech provides an outstanding online service providing such benchmarks. For example, partial AnandTech test results comparing the Nvidia GeForce GTX 560 Ti and AMD Radeon HD 7770 graphic cards are shown in Table 3.4.5. You could also refer to PassMark's graphic card benchmark database to help you evaluate current graphic cards.

Table 3.4.5: AnandTech Test Results for two Graphic cards

SYSMark Tests	Nvidia GeForce GTX 560 Ti	AMD Radeon HD 7770
Total War: Rome 2 -1,920 X 1,080 -High-quality + Med. Shadows. Frames per second — higher is better	45.9	62.6
Synthetic: TessMark, Image Set 4, 64x Tessellation. Frames per second — higher is better	437	539
Synthetic: 3-DMark Vantage Pixel Fill. Gigatexels[1] per second — higher is better	6	3.8

Note: 1. A Gigatexel is 1 billion textured pixels. Texture filtering uses adjacent texels to select pixel colors.

Table 3.4.6 provides a basic GPU selection checklist.

Table 3.4.6: Graphic Card Selection Checklist

Factors	Suggestions	Your Decisions
PassMark G3D Mark[1]	2,000 + (the most powerful are over 21,000)	
dedicated VRAM	2+ GB	
API interface	DirectX 12, or OpenGL 4.6	
PCI interface type	PCIe	
core speed	900 MHz or faster (some are up 7 GHz)	
memory bus width	256-bits (some are up to 512-bits)	
resolution	consumer-4K-format 3,840 X 2,160 or	
frame rate	at least 60 f/s at the desired resolution	
HCDP-compliant	to play Blu-ray media	
warranty	at least three years; preferably lifetime	
cost	5 % of system cost for basic purposes, but equal to the cost of all other components for complex games and VR	

Note: 1. PassMarks are based on many performance test results and are frequently updated.

You could use a TV in place of a computer monitor. That is because most modern TVs have both VGA and HDMI ports, while most graphic cards or video cards have DVI, HDMI, and VGA ports. You could use any common ports to connect a computer's graphic card to a TV. However, it would be best to avoid using the analog VGA-port option if possible. Instead, use the common digital interface, which is likely to be HDMI, with a good-quality HDMI cable.

Short, good-quality HDMI cables, with male connectors on both ends, cost about $ 25. Longer, high-quality HDMI cables are much more expensive. To connect your graphic card or video card to your TV:

1. Plug the graphic card's HDMI cable into the TV's HDMI port.

2. Then, on your TV's menu, select the HDMI port.

3. You might also need to change the monitor's display settings to match your TV's resolution.

4. If you are using Windows 8.1 or 10, press 'Windows' + 'P' on your keyboard and select 'Duplicate' to show your monitor's screen on the TV.

You can also watch analog TV on your computer's monitor. That is feasible because Internet speeds are often so fast these days, that they can transmit digital TV directly to your PC's monitor. However, you might need to install a TV tuner card. The DANY HDTV-1000 TV Device shown in Figure 3.4.7 is one of the few in the market.

VGA port

USB port

Figure 3.4.7: Dany HDTV-1000 TV Tuner

3.5: Selecting the Case

Selecting your computer case is one of the most important steps in your system planning process. Yet, paradoxically, some DIY PC-builders do not use any cases at all. They build completely open PCs. These computer-builders sometimes argue that not using cases makes their systems cooler. However, that argument is usually not correct because it means that there are no case fans to concentrate airflows over hot components. Some DIY computer-builders use liquid component coolers to overcome that problem. Although that strategy may adequately cool components, it still leaves them exposed to dust, foreign objects, and static electricity.

Other DIY computer builders argue that aluminum cases keep components cooler because aluminum is a better conductor of heat than steel is. However, that argument is only correct if all powered components have direct thermal conduction paths to a case's panels. Only a few cases that are specially designed to be passively cooled have that design feature. Otherwise, aluminum cases are no cooler than steel cases.

Steel is normally used for cases because it is denser than aluminum and therefore is less susceptible to scratches and dents. Moreover, because aluminum is only about 30 % as dense as steel, it is more likely to transmit fan and hard drive noises than steel cases transmit. Steel is also cheaper than aluminum.

The first consideration in choosing a case is its form-factor. The form-factor of your motherboard will determine the size of the case you need. Various case sizes can accommodate various form-factor motherboards. Most DIY computer-builders use ATX form-factor cases because there is a greater variety of them to choose from with a greater range of features.

ATX cases also provide more room for expansion cards, RAM module coolers, secondary storage devices, and large CPU and GPU-coolers than smaller-form-factor cases provide. Also, because of their large internal spaces, ATX-sized cases are less likely to overheat.

ATX desktop cases that lay on their sides save some desk space if their systems' monitors are placed on top of them. However, they have limited internal room, can be difficult to cool, and are inconvenient to access. On balance, vertical ATX form-factor cases provide the best balance of providing adequate space for powerful expandable systems without taking up excessive desktop space.

Mini-ITX cases and motherboards have also become popular with some DIY computer-builders since that form-factor was introduced in 2002. Some mini-ITX cases can now even accommodate liquid-coolers, such as the Corsair Hydro H75 liquid cooler, providing that no 3.5-inch secondary storage devices are also installed. ASUS has even recently produced a Ryzen CPU-based system with a mini-ITX X370 motherboard in a mini-ITX case. Cases larger than ATX-size, such as full-ATX tower cases, are only necessary for systems, such as servers, that include many internal devices.

Table 3.5.1 lists the most common case form-factors and corresponding motherboard form-factors. As a general rule, you can install smaller-form-factor motherboards into larger-form-factor cases. For example, you could likely install ATX, micro-ATX, and mini-ITX motherboards, as well as EATX-motherboards, into EATX cases. Similarly, micro-ATX motherboards can be used in most standard ATX cases as well as in mid and full-tower ATX cases. You can see from that table that a standard ATX motherboard will fit into a mid-tower ATX case, a full-tower ATX case, and a tower-server-ATX case, as well as an ATX case. However, some of the other relationships in Table 3.5.1 are only suggestions about the probability of matching case and motherboard form-factors. You would need to research particular cases and motherboards to confirm their particular relationships.

Table 3.5.1: Case and Motherboard Form-factors

Form-factors	Motherboard Sizes	Case Types	Typical Case Heights
SSI MEB[1]	41.1 cm X 33 cm (16.2" X 13")	MAGNUM SMA8	65.4 cm (25.8")
WTX[2]	35.6 cm X 42.5 cm (14" X 6.75")	WTX-Tower-Server	62.5 cm (24.6")
EATX or SSI EEB[3]	305 mm X 330 mm (12" X 13")	EATX	57 cm (22.4")
ATX	30.5 cm X 24.4 cm (12" X 9.6")	ATX-tower-Server.............. full-tower-ATX................... mid-Tower-ATX................. ATX......................................	67 cm (26.4") 52.2 cm (20.6") 46 cm (18.1") 44 cm (17.3")
micro-ATX	24 cm X 24 cm (9.6" X 9.6")	micro-ATX; flex-ATX	40 cm (15.7")
flex-ATX	22.9 cm X 19.1 cm (9" X 7.5")	flex-ATX	40 cm (15.7")
mini-ITX	17 cm X 17 cm (6.7" X 6.7")	mini-ITX; flex-ATX	33 cm (13.0")
mini-ATX	15 cm X 15 cm (5.9" X 5.9")	mini-ITX; flex-ATX	33 cm (13.0")
nano-ITX	12 cm X 12 cm (4.7" X 4.7")	nano-ITX	23 cm (9")
NUC[4]	10.2 cm X 10.2 cm (4" X 4")	NUC	51 mm (2")
pico-ITX	10 cm X 7.2 cm (3.9" X 2.8")	pico-ITX	16.8 cm (6.6")

Notes: 1. Manufacturers don't produce cases especially for this format. It is necessary to adapt a large case such as the MAGNUM SMA8. 2. This form-factor motherboard was designed to accept multiple CPUs. It was discontinued in 2008. 3. SSI EEB form-factor motherboards do not have the same mounting holes or I/O connector area as EATX motherboards. 4. Also called 'Ultra-Compact Form-Factor' (UCFF).

Manufacturers occasionally develop yet more case form-factors. For one example, Fractal Design recently produced their Define Mini C tower case. It is a high-quality, modular, mini-tower-size case designed to work with micro-ATX and mini-ATX systems. For another example, Corsair recently released their aluminum and tempered glass Obsidian 1000D Super-Tower case that is designed to accommodate ATX systems and mini-ITX systems simultaneously.

Most cases have spaces on their right sides through which cables can be routed. They make it easy to arrange internal cables so that air flows are maximized. But, if you chose a case without a right-side space, you might use the trick of routing cables underneath the motherboard in the space created by the set-off screws.

Excessive heat is a serious threat to computer components. If a case's fans are ineffective, the heat generated by the system's PSU, CPU, graphics card, motherboard, secondary storage devices, and expansion cards would soon exceed the system's operational temperature limit. Therefore, make sure that you intelligently position the case fans to maximize airflow. Different fan locations can result in operational temperature differences of more than 10° C!

Inlet and outlet case fans installed near each other are useless. They just move air between them without circulating it throughout the case. At least one case fan should blow cool air into the case from the front, and another should push hot air outside from the back.

It is also a good idea to take advantage of the fact that hot air rises by installing an extraction fan at the top of your case, preferably above the CPU and RAM modules. Also, if you install a passively-cooled PSU, such as the Seagate PSU featured in this book, it is a good idea to position any bottom case fan adjacent to the PSU to help draw more air through it.

Decide on the type of air pressure you want to create inside your case. A positive airflow system pulls more air into a case than it actively pushes out. That imbalance creates a slight high-pressure inside the case, which helps to keep dust out. A balanced airflow system pulls in the same volume of air that it pushes out. Balanced pressure systems typically keep systems a few degrees cooler than positive-pressure systems.

Consider the types of blades you want for your case fans. Wide fan blades are designed to push air and create high pressures. They are sometimes called static blades. They are best used to push air past radiators, secondary storage devices, heatsink fins, or constricted spaces. Indeed, it is essential to use them on liquid-cooler radiators.

Narrow blades generate less pressure but move higher volumes of air more quickly. Therefore, narrow-blade fans are best used to exhaust air from cases. A wide-bladed fan is shown in Figure 3.1.8. A narrow-bladed fan is shown in Figure 3.1.7. Figure 3.5.1 shows the airflow characteristics inside the Fractal Design R6 case system featured in this book.

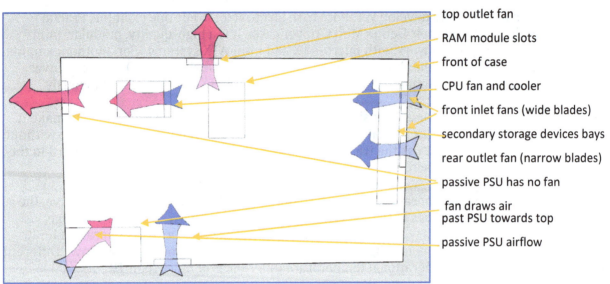

- top outlet fan
- RAM module slots
- front of case
- CPU fan and cooler
- front inlet fans (wide blades)
- secondary storage devices bays
- rear outlet fan (narrow blades)
- passive PSU has no fan
- fan draws air past PSU towards top
- passive PSU airflow

Note: Cool incoming air is shown by light-blue arrows; hot expelled air is shown by dark-red arrows.

Figure 3.5.1: Case Airflow Diagram

Good-quality cases provide many 3 and 4-pin fan connectors. For example, a bank of fan connectors in a Fractal Design R6 case with both three and four-pin connectors case is shown in Figure 3.5.2.

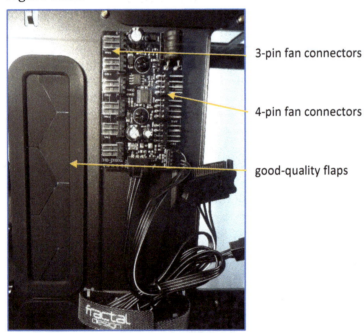

- 3-pin fan connectors
- 4-pin fan connectors
- good-quality flaps

Figure 3.5.2: Fractal Design R6 Case Fan Connector Bank

Check user reviews to discover what the owners of a case you are interested in say about its noise level. These days, the maximum noise level that you should accept from any case fan is 20 dB. Regardless of what materials they are made from, some cases amplify and project fan noises. Also, some cheap factory-installed fans are noisy. To minimize this problem, as explained in Section 5.1, good-quality cases include sound-deadening materials on the insides of their panels. For example, the Fractal Design R6 case featured in this book has sound-dampening material on its top panel as well as on both of its side panels.

In combination with five Noctua case fans, a Noctua CPU-cooler fan, and the Seagate Titanium fanless PSU, the insulation in my Fractal R6 case keeps the computer so quiet that it does not emit any noise that I can detect.

You can buy fan controllers that automatically adjust the speeds of your case fans according to the case's temperature to minimize fan noises. Fan controllers also usually have temperature alarms. The displays for these controller units fit into 5.25-inch optical drive bays on the fronts of cases. Figure 3.5.3 shows a Lamptron fan controller display. This model features a retro valve display without control knobs. Instead, it comes with a remote control for making fan settings. Fan controllers with LED displays and control knobs or buttons are also available. For example, a touch screen NZXT model is also shown in Figure 3.5.3.

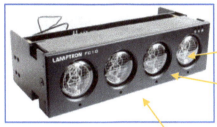

controls up to 5 fans

valve tube displays

no buttons –
controlled with remote
controller

Lamptron FC 10 Fan Controller

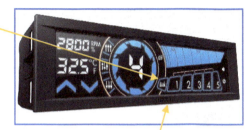

NZXT Sentry Fan Controller

Figure 3.5.3: Fan Controllers

The current trend is for case manufacturers to provide single optical drive bays in their cases. They argue that is because DIY computer-builders are using fewer optical storage devices. Unfortunately, a case with only one optical drive bay will not provide a place to install a fan controller device if the bay is occupied by an optical drive.

Cases with multiple optical disc drive bays present many other useful possibilities. For example, that configuration would accommodate the installation of two optical devices, which could be used to copy files directly from one optical device to another. It could also accommodate other devices that might be installed in optical device drive bays such as card readers and tape drives.

A card reader is an electronic device that can read data from portable memory storage devices. An example is Thermaltakes's Black Extreme 3.0 Plus card reader, which costs about $ 35. Some types of memory card readers can read the magnetic strips and bar codes on credit cards or membership cards. A tape drive storage device uses magnetic tape media. An example is Tandberg's Data LTO-6 HH 2.5 TB Ultrium SAS tape drive, which costs about $ 2,000.

All ATX cases have some ports on their fronts. They usually have at least two USB 2.0 ports, a 3.5 mm headphone jack, a 3.5 mm microphone jack, and a USB 3.0 port. A few cases are now also available with 10 Gb/s USB Type-C connectors on their front panels.

It is easier to build a computer in a well-designed case. A poorly designed case can make what should be a satisfying building experience a difficult one instead. If possible, check the case you are interested in a store before buying it. Consider how easy it would be for you to build and maintain your PC. Pay particular attention to how easy it is to open and close the side panels. Consider whether the drive trays and fan filters would be easy to remove for cleaning. Also, check the chassis' edges. Some cheap cases have sharp edges on their inside panels that can cut your fingers when you work on them. On the other hand, high-quality cases have features that make building a computer convenient.

For example, some of the screws on the Fractal R6 are designed so that they can't fall out of their screw holes, as shown in Figure 3.5.4. Although that is a minor design feature, it prevents the otherwise annoying inevitable dropping and losing of those screws. Other examples of the R6's well-conceived features are its reversable front door, its alternative places for graphics cards and hard disk drives, and its right-side fan hub that can connect up to six mother board-controlled case fans and three PWM fans, as shown in Figure 3.5.2. Yet another example is its release button that enables easy top cover access, as shown in Figure 3.5.4.

SSD

device tray

tray securing screw can't fall out of bracket

top cover secure/release button

Figure 3.5.4: Fractal Case Convenience Features

Standard 3-pin fan connectors have three wires. Their third wires carry signals that are proportional to the fan's speed. If any signal is present, most 3-pin fans run at 100 % of their capacities. Pulse Width Modulation (PWM) fan connectors, which have four pins to connect to four fan wires on PWM fans, have been available since 2003. PWM provides a smarter way to control the speed of fans and pumps by regulating the amount of power sent to them. They constantly cycle on and off — providing either full +12V power or no power. By sending intermittent power impulses, they run motors and pumps more slowly than they would otherwise.

Inexpensive cases only provide a few zip-ties for bundling cables and wires. Well-designed cases come with built-in cable-management features, such as clips, panels, and holes for routing cables and wires. They also provide good-quality rubber flaps that allow wires and cables to be routed between the front and back sides. An example is shown in Figure 5.1.2.

Conservative DIY PC-builders are interested in building systems that are within their budgets and that satisfy their technical needs. They regard additional expenditures of effort or money on fashion to be extravagant wastes. On the other hand, some DIY computer-builders enjoy turning their computers into works of art. A new craft called 'case modeling' has been created by these design enthusiasts. Appendix 5 provides an introduction to case modeling.

Design-conscious builders usually prefer acrylic or glass side panels that reveal the interiors of their cases. Even some conservative DIY builders prefer cases with transparent side panels so that they can monitor whether component LEDs are on and when fans need cleaning. For example, a Fractal R6 with a clear glass side panel is shown in Figure 3.5.5. Tempered glass panels are much less susceptible to scratches than acrylic panels. It is also possible to buy completely transparent cases, such as the transparent acrylic case shown in Figure 3.5.5.

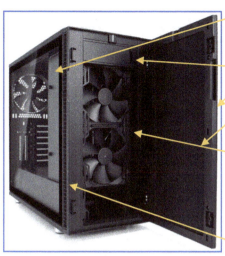

clear glass or acrylic side panel

single optical drive bay

reversible front door

sound-deadening material

dual 120 mm front intake fans

colored coolant in clear tubes

RGB front intake fans

Fractal R6 ATX Mid-tower with transparent side panel

QDIY acrylic

Figure 3.5.5: Transparent Cases

Even if you are a conservative PC-builder, you should give some thought to the appearance of your case. After all, you will see it on your desk for years. Consider if it blends in with the style of your work or play space. These days, you can buy cases that are finished in brushed aluminum or are painted in various colors aside from the standard black. Moreover, there is no reason you couldn't paint your case whatever color you wanted. If you expect to move your computer often, you can even select a case with integrated carrying handles.

Make sure that the number of card slots on the back of the case you select at least equals the number of expansion card slots on your motherboard. If there are more card slots on a motherboard than in the case, the utility of the system will be limited.

Also, select a case with enough secondary storage device drive bays of the correct sizes to satisfy your present needs — plus at least one or two extras to accommodate future possibilities. Until recently, it was common for cases to have plenty of 5.25-inch bays, but few, if any, 3.5-inch bays. Fortunately, inexpensive adapters are available that allow you to install 3.5-inch drives into 5.25-inch bays. An example is shown in Figure 3.5.6.

adapter tray rubber mounting

solid-state disk

screws that attach to the tray

Figure 3.5.6: 3.5-inch SSD Drive Adapter Tray

Table 3.5.2 compares features of two contemporary cases. Cases are complex components these days, and you will notice that both of these cases have many features.

Table 3.5.2: Features of two Cases

Features	Cases	
	be quiet! Dark Base 700 Mid-Tower	Fractal Design Node 304 White
form factor	Mid-tower EATX 519 mm X 241 mm X 544 mm	Mini ITX 250 mm X 210 mm X 374 mm
USB 3.1 Type-C port or USB 3.0 port	1 front USB 3.1	2 front USB 3 ports
color	Black	white
sound insulation	Yes	no
weight	30 lbs.	4.9 kg.
material	steel, front panel – aluminum	steel
installed fans	fluid-dynamic bearings X 3	Silent Series R2 hydraulic bearing fans X 3
maximum radiator size	360 mm	CPU-cooler up to 170 mm (6.7") in some configurations
optical drive bays	0	0
side panels	tempered glass left-side panel	steel with ventilation screens
RGB illumination	controllable lighting strip embedded in exterior frame	none
secondary storage device bays	3.5-inch (89 mm) X 3; 2.5" (69.8 mm) X 12	63.5-inch (89 mm)/2.5" (69.8 mm) X 6
warranty	three years	two years
price	$ 180	$ 90

Computer cases vary greatly in price and quality. You could therefore buy an inexpensive case to save money. On the other hand, because you can keep a case indefinitely, you might decide to invest in an expensive high-quality case. Table 3.5.3 provides a basic case selection checklist.

Table 3.5.3: Case Selection Factors

Factors	Suggestions	Your Decisions
form-factor	standard ATX for most self-build PCs	
front USB 2.0 ports	at least 2	
front USB 3.0 ports	at least 1 (also, a 3.1 port for future devices)	
front headphone jack	should be standard	
front mic jack	should be standard	
storage device drive bays	at least 4; preferably 6+	
optical device bays	2[1]	
boxed PSU	only if you are satisfied with its reliability	
chassis fans	at least two 120 mm in and two out fans	
design aesthetics	to suit your work or play space	
warranty	at least one year	
cost	about 10 % of total hardware budget	

Note: 1. The author's opinion. Most manufacturers provide only one, or even no, optical device bay.

3.6: Selecting the Secondary Storage Devices

Secondary storage is a non-volatile memory. In other words, it is a type of permanent memory that remains intact even after a computer's power is turned off. Secondary storage devices are used to save all types of files and software programs — including operating systems. Five interface types have been used with secondary storage devices over the last decade or so.

1. Advanced Technology Attachment (ATA) was also called 'Integrated Drive Electronics' (IDE) and later 'Parallel ATA' (PATA). IDE was released by Western Digital in 1986. It was revolutionary because it enabled hard drives to use onboard controllers instead of controllers on separate circuit boards. However, it also required the use of wide flat cables that obstructed airflows inside cases. ATA secondary storage devices can only support a maximum transmission speed of 133 MB/s and can only support secondary storage devices with capacities up to 528 MB. ATA also requires drives to be configured as masters or slaves using jumpers. Enhanced Integrated Drive Electronics (EIDE) as its name suggests, is a development from IDE. EIDE devices can support secondary storage devices with up to 137 GB of storage space.

2. Serial Advanced Technology Attachment (SATA) is actually an advanced type of IDE interface. SATA has now replaced the older ATA/EIDE technology on the latest generation of secondary storage devices and motherboards. It does not work with older versions of Windows, such as Windows 98. SATA uses round cables that are smaller than IDE cables, which allow better airflows inside cases. SATA also provides longer effective cable lengths, easier connection to devices, lower power consumption, and reduced electromagnetic interference. SATA 1.0 supported a transfer rate of 150 MGB/s. SATA 2.0 supported a rate of 300 MB/s. Since 2008, SATA 3.0, which supports a 600 MB/s transfer rate has been available. SATA 3.0's transfer rate is faster than 7,200 RPM spinning hard drives can read or write, and most modern motherboards support SATA 3.0. But the potential transfer speeds of the latest types of solid-state hard drives are so fast that even SATA 3's data transfer speed cannot fully support them.

Some of the latest motherboards include support for the most recent version of SATA, SATA Express (also labeled 'SATA 3.2' or 'SATAe'). It works with both SATA and PCIe storage devices and supports transfer speeds of up to 1,600 MB/s. The first storage devices to take advantage of SATA Express were produced in 2014, and the first motherboard that supported SATA Express was ASUS's Z97. The newest version of that motherboard, the Z97-A, includes M.2 support, as well as SATA Express support.

3. Peripheral Component Interconnect (PCI) was first released by Intel in 1992. It originally had a 32-bit bus with a 33 MHz bus clock speed that enabled a maximum data transfer speed of 533 MB/s over a 16 lane connection. PCIe 1 was released in 2005. It supported a one direction bandwidth of 4 GB/s in an X 16 slot. PCIe 2 was released in 2007. It supported 8 GB/s in an X 16 slot. PCIe 3 was released in 2010. It supported 15.7 GB/s in an X 16 slot. PCIe 3 is so fast that only high-end graphics cards can fully take advantage of its transfer speeds.

To get around SATA 3's data transfer speed limitation, some SSD devices were built with their own built-in PCIe expansion card interfaces. An early example was OCZ's 350 240 GB RevoDrive that supported a bandwidth of 1.8 GB/s. That speed is about four times faster than a SATA SSD's interface. However, devices with built-in PCIe expansion cards are expensive. For example, the 960 GB version of OCZ's RevoDrive cost about $ 2,300 and can therefore only be justified in hard-working commercial servers.

PCIe 4 was released in 2017. It supports double the one-direction bandwidth of PCIe 3.0, 31.5 GB/s via an X16 PCIe 4 socket. It can also deliver 300 W of power through the same socket. The Peripheral Component Interconnect Special Interest Group say that they will release PCIe version, 5.0, in 2019. It will support transfer speeds up to 63 GB/s over 16 lanes. What is more, the Group have just announced that PCIe 6, with a 128 GB/s bandwidth, will be released in 2021.

4. The Non-Volatile Memory Express (NVMe) interface was recently developed to allow computers to boot from both PCIe and M.2 SSDs — although PCs can't boot from NVMe SSD drives unless their motherboards have NVMe-aware UEFI-BIOSs. Only a few of the most recent motherboards have NVMe-aware UEFI-BIOSs as well as M.2 slots with PCIe 3 interfaces.

5. Small Computer Interface (SCSI) pronounced 'Scuzzy', was a popular interface that was first released around 1980. The SCSI can be used on PCs, Apple Macs, and Linux-based systems for attaching internal, as well as external devices, whereas the USB and FireWire interfaces can only accept external devices. Another of SCSI's advantages is its ability to daisy-chain devices. That is why the SCSI is often used in servers and video-editing systems where many secondary storage devices must be linked. However, SCSI faces new competition from the Thunderbolt 3 interface, which allows up to six external Thunderbolt devices to be daisy-chained using Thunderbolt 3.0 cables. A daisy-chain is a group of devices connected in a series, one-after-another on a single data cable, without each one needing to be directly attached to the motherboard. Each SCSI device on a daisy-chain has its own address. Data sent to a particular device is passed on by each other device on the daisy-chain until it reaches its intended device.

SCSI spinning hard drives are often used in critical commercial situations because they are more reliable than SATA hard drives. However, they cost as much as 50 % more than SATA drives. Therefore, they are seldom used by DIY computer builders. Spinning hard drives using the latest version of the SCSI, Serial Attached SCSI (SAS) are particularly expensive. For example, Dell's PowerEdge 342-2082 600 GB SAS hard drive costs about $ 330. SCSI tape drive storage devices are even more expensive. For example, the TC-L52AN-EY-C LTO-5 1.5TB SAS tape drive costs about $ 1,400.

Intel released Internet SCSI (iSCSI) in 2003. It is an Internet protocol standard for carrying SCSI commands between devices linked over networks. It supports the Gigabit Ethernet interface and Internet Protocol routers. However, as far as I know, at the time the fourth edition of this book was prepared, motherboards were no longer being produced with integrated SCSI adapters. I could only find a couple of Chinese companies, Shenzhen Huaitai Technology and Shenzhen Hongzhisheng Technology, that were advertising 'checked' used SCSI motherboards. The SCSI Trade Association confirmed during the preparation of the fourth version of this book that SAS is now intended only for enterprise computing and is no longer intended for DIY computer builders.

Nevertheless, you could still set up a SCSI system if you could find an adapter card, such as Adaptec's AHA-2940AU or ATTO Technology's Dual-channel X4 PCIe to Ultra 320 SCSI controller card, which originally cost $ 380. You would also need to ensure that your motherboard supported SCSI controllers. It would only make sense to set up a SCSI system if you had SCSI devices that you wanted to keep using.

Spinning hard disk drives store data on non-portable spinning magnetic disks. That is why they are called 'spinning hard drives'. 'Disk' refers to a magnetic media, whereas 'disc' refers to optical media. The rate at which disks spin is measured in revolutions per minute (RPM). The greater the RPM of a spinning hard drive, the faster a system can boot, start programs, and open files. These days, 7,200-RPM hard drives are the norm. Faster 10,000-RPM drives are also available, but they wear out sooner and are noisier.

The most common size for internal spinning hard drives is 3.5 inches. They fit into the standard caddy trays provided in most computer cases. However, some recent spinning hard drives come in a 2.5-inch form-factor (which is actually 2.75 inches, or 70 mm, wide). These smaller hard drives are most often used in notebooks and in small-form-factor PC systems.

Tape drives are another type of magnetic secondary storage device. Tape drives are removable and are most often used for offline archival storage of large databases and the like. There are two types of tape drives. The Travan type is less expensive but requires a separate controller card. Travan tapes are 8 mm (0.3") wide and 228.6 m (750 feet) long. The digital audio tape (DAT) type is faster; usually uses the SCSI, and costs much more than the Travan type. For example, the 40 GB Quantum TD3100-801 Travan tape drive costs about $ 90, whereas the 36 GB Quantum CD72SH-SSTU DAT 72 Tape Drive costs about $ 500.

Another type of magnetic secondary technology device that also uses portable media is the Removable Disk Technology (RDX) developed by Tandberg Data. RDX drives can be mounted into standard optical drive bays in the fronts of cases. They are available in both standard 2.5" SATA and USB hard drives. A Tandberg Data RDX QuikStor SATA docking station costs about $ 150. The RDX storage medium is as expensive as the docking station. A Tandberg QuikStor 1 TB removable disk drive also costs $ 150. The maximum capacity of RDX drives is 2 TB.

Floppy drives were a popular type of device that used a portable magnetic medium until a decade or so ago. However, their capacity is too small to be of much practical use these days. Also, the data stored on them degrades quickly. In fact, they will only reliably save data for a few years. The surfaces of their disks are prone to grow mold that destroys their data. Moreover, the data transfer speed of floppy drives is only about 1/20th the speed of spinning hard drives. Also, their wide cables take up much space inside cases.

For all these reasons, most PSUs no longer include floppy drive connectors; most cases no longer include front bays especially for floppy drives, and no motherboards have supported them since 2010. Nevertheless, if you want to install an internal floppy drive, you can still purchase them. For example, the SONY MPF 920 internal floppy drive costs about $ 30. However, if you want to use a floppy drive, the best method these days is to connect it to your PC's motherboard as an external device via a USB cable. An example of such an external floppy drive is the Dynex External 3.5-inch 1.44 MB USB floppy disk drive. It costs about $ 35.

Solid-state drives (SSDs) are a faster type of secondary storage device that uses a non-portable media. SSDs use semiconductors to store data and therefore have no moving components. SSDs take up less space than spinning hard drives, do not vibrate or make any noise, use about 1/10 the power of spinning hard drives, and generate less heat. SSDs have been available for about forty years, and, until recently, only used the SATA interface. Figure 3.6.1 illustrates the physical differences between spinning hard drives and solid-state hard drives.

movable arm must find the data on a spinning disk's surface, which is called the 'seek time'

interior of solid-state disk has only circuit chips — no moving parts

Figure 3.6.1: Comparison of Spinning and Solid-state Drives

Until recently, the largest capacity SSDs could only store up to 1 TB of data. However, much larger-capacity SSDs are now available — although they are expensive. For example, the world's first 13 TB SSD was released by Fixstar in 2016 for about $ 13,000! The prices for such large-capacity SSDs have fallen somewhat since then. For instance, soon afterwards, Samsung released a 15.36 TB PM1633a SSD at a price of about $ 10,000.

Nevertheless, large-capacity spinning hard drive storage space remains much cheaper than large-capacity SSD storage space. For example, Seagate's new IronWolf 12 TB spinning hard drive, with 256 MB of cache, costs only $ 400. The IronWolf is more reliable than older types of spinning hard drives. It has a mean-time-between-failure of 1,000,000 hours and comes with a 3-year warranty. For another example, Hitachi released its helium-filled 10 TB spinning hard drive model, the Ultrastar He10, as the fourth edition of this book was being written, it also at a price of about $ 400.

Moderate-sized SSDs are also more expensive than equivalent-capacity spinning hard drives. For instance, Samsung's 850 Evo SSD's prices range from $ 190 for the 250 GB model up to $ 300 for the 1 TB model. Smaller spinning hard drives are much less expensive. For instance, a 2 TB, 3.5-inch SATA internal spinning hard drive costs only about $ 75. That is only about $ 25 more than a 500 MB capacity model. At present, the capacity sweet spot that provides the best value-for-money for spinning hard drives is 3 TB. For example, Seagate's ST3,000DM001 3 TB 64 MB Cache SATA 6.0 3.5-inch internal bare hard drive costs about $ 90. A bare hard drive is one that does not come with a manual, mounting screws, or cables.

So, unless you have a small project budget, buying a 3 TB capacity drive would be a reasonable decision — even if you don't need that much capacity when you build your system. On the other hand, because spinning hard drives are so inexpensive, and are so easy to replace, you could upgrade your system's secondary storage capacity with a large one at a later stage if your project budget is too small at the time you build your PC.

Most SSDs installed by DIY PC-builders are of the standard 2.5-inch form-factor size. However, there are four other SSD form-factors as well. They are listed in Table 3.6.1. The most recent of these form-factors is the M.2. It has only been available since mid-2013. M.2 SSDs are compact and are not enclosed in covers; so, they look similar to ordinary RAM modules without heatsinks. M.2 connectors are now provided on all ATX motherboards. M.2 devices are not hot-pluggable. So, hot-plugging them might damage them and even harm the person plugging them in. For that reason, only install M.2 SSDs when the system power is turned off. M.4 SSDs have been demonstrated but not yet released.

Table 3.6.1: SSD Form-factors

Form-factors	Widths	Lengths
5.25-inch	146 mm (5.75")	203 mm (8.00")
3.5-inch (fits standard hard drive tray)	101 mm (4.00")	146 mm (5.75")
2.5-inch (fits into laptops)	70 mm (2.80")	100 mm (4.00")
1.8-inch (for small mobile devices)	54 mm (2.10")	79 mm (3.10")
M.2	22 mm (0.87")	60, 80; 110 mm (2.4, 3.2; 4.3")
M.4	44 mm (1.74")[1]	80 (3.2")[1]

Note: 1. I have not seen published M.4 dimensions. I have just estimated these dimensions from photos.

Until recently, SSDs had significant failure rates. Those failure rates were a symptom of the type of planar (i.e., 2-D) NAND flash memory cells used on that generation of SSDs. Planer storage cells 'wear-out' and can only be rewritten a limited number of times. You can use BlackBlaze's website to check the failure rate of any type of spinning hard drive or SSD. BlackBlaze is an online backup service company.

As explained in Section 3, a new type of Vertical-NAND (V-NAND) flash memory has just been released by Samsung that overcomes the wear-out problem inherent with planar NAND memory. V-NAND memory cells are stacked in a 3-D arrangement of many layers on top of one another. That arrangement allows V-NAND memory to contain many more memory cells within a given space while using much less power than ordinary planer NAND memory. V-NAND SSDs can also use the NVMe interface.

At the time the fourth edition of this book was written, the best value-for-money V-NAND SSDs had capacities of about 500 GB. For instance, Samsung's 950 PRO M.2 512 GB internal SSD cost about $ 320.

NAND memory is a type of non-volatile flash storage technology. It is called 'NAND' memory because it employs the 'Not AND' type of digital logic gate. Logic gates perform the logical computing functions that are the building blocks of digital integrated circuits. A NAND gate operates as an AND gate followed by a NOT gate. In other words, its logical operation is 'and followed by a negative condition'. So, a NAND gate's output would only be 'false' if both of its inputs were 'true'. Otherwise, its output would be 'false'.

The basic specifications to consider when selecting your system's secondary storage device are its storage capacity, its amount of cache, its speed, the portability of its media, and its price.

You need enough space on your system's secondary storage device/s to hold all the system's applications and data, as well as enough room for performance management. For basic home use, a 250 GB secondary storage device should be ample. However, if you intend to process much video or maintain a large database, you might need 1 TB or more of secondary storage space.

Refer to Tables 2.3 and 2.4 to accurately assess how much secondary memory your system will need. Bear in mind that a spinning hard drive's capacity should be at least double the amount that you expect to use. That is because when a spinning hard drive becomes more than about 60 % full, its performance starts to decline. Similarly, the wear-leveling feature of planar NAND SSDs that spreads the wear-and-tear evenly among the available cells requires that at least 40 % of the device's space should be left empty.

Nowadays, hybrid SSD/spinning hard drives are available. The small SSDs in these hybrid storage devices are best used to store OSs and the most frequently used programs to speed up system boot times. External spinning hard drives and SSDs that connect to motherboards using USB ports are also available. For example, Seagate's 2 TB Backup+ Ultra Slim Portable spinning hard drive costs about $ 85 and Samsung's 500 GB USB 3.0 T1 SSD costs about $ 270. These days, some relocatable external spinning hard drives don't even require physical connections to their motherboards. They use wireless connections instead. An example is Western Digital's My Passport Wireless 250 GB External SSD, which costs about $ 290.

If you plan to use an older version of Windows, such as Windows XP, you will find that it can only access 2.19 TB of secondary storage memory. Using larger secondary storage devices on systems with such older OSs would be a waste of the devices' storage capacities.

Hard drive cache is a type of RAM provided on spinning hard drives. It is also called a 'disk buffer'. It stores data that CPUs most recently use so that it is quickly available to the CPUs the next time they need it. The more cache a spinning hard drive has, the better. These days, spinning hard drives typically have 64 MB of cache, although some have 256 MB or more. However, you probably would not notice any speed difference between a hard drive with 64 MB of cache and one with 256 MB — all else being equal — when running most ordinary applications.

SSDs are faster than spinning hard drives, so they have less need for cache. For that reason, many SSDs have no cache systems. The cache in solid-state drives that do have it is DRAM. It is fast enough to keep pace with SSDs and enables them to manage fast read and write times.

Table 3.6.2 provides a basic checklist to help you select a secondary storage device.

Table 3.6.2: Secondary Storage Device Selection Checklist

Factors	Suggestions	Your Decisions
type	spinning drives are still less expensive; however, SDDs are faster, and V-NAND SSDs are probably at least as reliable as recent spinning hard drives	
storage capacity	at least 250 GB, but double the requirements estimated in Table 2.3	
interface	SATA 6 GB/s, M.2, or possibly NVMe	
cache	128–256 MB for spinning hard drives	
warranty	at least three years	
cost	8 % of system cost for basic use, but up to 45 % of system cost for dual large-capacity RAID hard drives for a server	

Installing two internal secondary storage devices presents some advantages. For instance, you could use one as a backup device in a RAID system. Also, if you are building a Ryzen-based system, such as the one featured in this book, you might be able to take advantage of a recent free secondary storage device technology called 'StoreMI'. Alternatively, you could use separate storage devices with separate cameras when doing multi-camera video-editing.

StoreMI blends two different types of secondary storage media, SSDs and spinning hard drives, into single volumes. A volume is not the same thing as a partition. Partitions are logical divisions of spinning hard disks that are created when disks are formatted. Volumes are sometimes called 'dynamic disks' or 'virtual disks' because they are logical structures that can span multiple physical disks, although they are most often created on single spinning hard disks. Those volumes usually appear as 'C:' drives to operating systems.

StoreMI automatically and intelligently stores the most-actively-used data on the faster media and stores the less-actively used data on the slower media. In that way, it dynamically provides the speed of a fast SSD secondary storage device combined with the capacity of both a fast SSD device and a larger-capacity, but slower, spinning hard drive.

Running StoreMI uses only about 1-2 % of a CPU's capacity. It is compatible with all SATA spinning hard drives and SSDs, including all NVMe SSDs. It is available as a free download from the manufacturers of motherboards with AMD AM4-sockets. At the time the fourth edition of this book was written, StoreMI did not support RAID. However, an AMD representative said that StoreMI would be able to support RAID within a year or so. But there was no promise about when StoreMI might work with UNIX OSs or Linux distributions.

Optical secondary storage devices use lasers to read and write digital data on optical media. They are still useful in modern desktop computers. For instance, your PC will need an optical drive if you want to install a program or driver that is supplied on a CD/DVD. Your PC will also need an optical drive if you want to listen to music or watch movies on CD/DVDs.

There are four types of optical secondary storage media: compact discs (CDs); Digital Video Discs (DVDs); Blu-ray discs (BDs) and ultra-high-definition Blu-ray (Ultra HD Blu-ray) discs. Most optical drives installed in older PCs can only read from and write to CDs and DVDs. Those CD/DVD optical drives were first released in the late-1990s. A common CD can store about 650 MB, whereas a dual-sided, dual-layered DVD-18 disc can hold 17 GB (although DVD-18 it is not supported by either the DVD-RW or DVD+R/W standards).

There is little difference between different brands and models of CD/DVD drives. All new CD/DVD devices connect to motherboards using SATA cables and can write to discs at about the same speeds. The speeds of CD devices are indicated by numbers with Xs after them. These numbers show the number of times faster a device can read or write data compared to the original CD speed of 153.6 kB/s. Nowadays, CD devices with speeds of up to 56X are available, but a more typical CD data transfer rate is 24X, which equals 3,600 kB/s.

DVD device read speeds are about nine times faster than CD device speeds. For example, DVD X1 ≈ CD X9 ≈ 1.4 MB/s. However, DVD devices write speeds are only about three times as fast as CDs. CD/DVD drives are now so inexpensive that there is no reason not to install one — even in low-budget systems — providing your case has an available front optical drive bay to install it into. An internal CD/DVD player costs only about $ 20.

Blu-ray disc (BD) technology, released in 2006, uses blue lasers that can write more data onto discs than the red lasers can. Blu-ray devices can read and write all common CD/DVD standards, including the DVD+-R standard. That hybrid standard supports both the DVD-R and DVD+ standards.

There is more variation in the read and write speeds of Blu-ray devices. Some fast Blu-ray devices, such as the ASUS BW-12B1ST, can write BD-Rs at a speed of X12 and read BD-Rs at a speed of X8. However, a more typical BD write speed is X8. According to the Blu-ray Disc specification, 1X speed is equal to 36 MB/s. Internal Blu-ray players cost about $ 50.

You can also buy external Blu-ray drives with USB interfaces, such as the Buffalo MediaStation 6X BDXL Blu-ray writer, which costs about $ 200. However, such external devices have slower data transfer speeds than internal devices that use SATA connections. Some external optical devices require two USB ports, one for power and the other for data.

The Ultra HD Blu-ray standard was released in 2015. It supports 10-bit color and consumer-4K resolution. Ultra HD Blu-ray discs with transfer speeds of up to 128 Mb/s that can store up to 128 GB are now available. Ultra HD Blu-ray devices should be able to play legacy Blu-ray discs.

The first Ultra HD Blu-ray PC optical drive was Pioneer's UHD BD player released in 2017. Soon afterward, LG released its Ultra HD Blu-ray Playback device. At the time the fourth edition of this book was produced, the Pioneer player cost about $ 150, and the LG player cost about $ 200. Both players are shown in Figure 3.6.2. Wi-Fi Ultra HD external Blu-ray players that cost about $ 310 are also available. Table 3.6.3 provides an optical drive checklist.

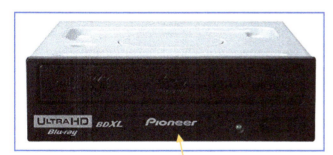

Pioneer Ultra HD Blu-ray Player   LG Ultra HD Blu-ray Player

Figure 3.6.2: Internal UHD Blu-ray Players

Table 3.6.3: Optical Drive Selection Checklist

Factors	Suggestions	Your Decisions
burner utility	included	
CD/DVD, BD, or UHD Blu-ray	include Ultra HD Blu-ray if required; otherwise, CD/DVD is much less expensive	
transfer speed	CD: 24X, DVD: 3X; BD: 6X; 128 Mb/s for UHD BD	
cable/interface	SATA	
warranty	at least two years	
cost	2 % for CD/DVD, 5 % for BD; 15 % for UHD	

Installing two optical drives makes it convenient to copy files directly from one optical disc to another. The terms used to describe the copying of optical files are 'ripping' and 'burning'. 'Ripping' refers to the extracting of data, such as song tracks, from an optical disc and transferring it onto another secondary storage media while changing it some way — usually by converting it to a different file format. 'Burning' refers to the process of copying music or video data from a secondary storage device, other than an optical drive, onto a blank optical disc. This process was originally called 'burning' because the lasers used in optical storage devices could, theoretically, burn objects.

Both processes, ripping and burning, are often used to circumvent the technical and legal restrictions that apply to the copying of files on optical media. Indeed, some people now use the term 'ripping' to refer to 'ripping-off' (in other words, 'stealing') digital intellectual property. It is not always clear whether current copyright regulations prohibit ripping optical discs for making backup copies for private personal use.

Windows 8.1 and 10 both come with their own International Standards Organization (ISO) burning software. To burn a disc using Windows 10, insert a blank writeable CD/DVD into your optical storage device. Next, select 'This PC'. Then, browse to the names of the files or folders you want to burn and drag those names, one-at-a-time, onto the empty optical disc drive icon. As you drag files onto the disc icon, they will automatically be copied to the disc.

However, many people prefer to use specialized utilities for ripping and burning optical disc files. Two popular alternatives are Nero and Ashampoo Burning Studio 2018. Exact Audio Copy is another popular utility used for ripping and burning FLAC files. The Exact Audio Copy website makes it clear that the program is only intended for backing up or converting legally obtained audio files — not for creating illegal copies of copyrighted works.

3.7: Selecting the Power Supply Unit

The power supply unit (PSU) is likely to be the last component you select because you need to choose all other electrical components before you can calculate how much electricity your system requires. Nevertheless, the PSU is a most important component.

A PSU converts 120 V or 240 V mains alternating current power into +3.3 V, +5 V, and +12 V currents and directs them via separate rails to the components that require them. The term 'rail' refers to a particular voltage carried on a separate power circuit. The +3.3 V wires are usually orange; the +5 V wires are usually red, and the + 12 V wires are usually yellow — although not all manufacturers follow that color-coding standard.

A PSU's voltages are generated by its voltage regulator modules (VRMs). A PSU prevents its motherboard from starting until its VRMs can deliver stable supplies of the required voltages on all of its rails. A PSU also delivers a constant 5 V power supply to components, including motherboards, that have standby functions, even when their computers are turned off.

PSUs are probably the components that most often fail. And when they fail, they can ruin other components — including motherboards and CPUs — by delivering variable voltages. The main failure point of PSUs is their fans. If a unit's fan stops, the unit will quickly overheat and fail. That is one of the reasons I chose the fanless Sea Sonic PSU for the system featured in this book. It has no fan that can fail.

Currently, there are two standards for desktop PC PSUs. The first PSU standard was the Advanced Technology (AT) standard. It was developed by IBM and supplied a mere 63 watts. That AT standard was replaced by the Advanced Technology eXtended (ATX) power supply standard in 1995. The ATX standard is still used for desktop computer PSUs — although many changes have been made to it over the years.

Many of these changes occurred in 2000 with the production of the ATX 1.0 standard. Indeed, so many fundamental changes were made that the name of the standard was then changed to 'ATX12V'. Some of the changes included:
• changing the number of motherboard power connector pins from 20 to 24 (although ATX12V power supplies can still work with older ATX systems using 20-pin main power connectors),
• removing the 6-pin auxiliary power cable specification and substituting the SATA power cable standard,
• providing up to 265 watts for CPUs,
• adding a specification for a 75 W 6-pin power connector for expansion cards,
• adding a specification for an 8-pin PCIe connector capable of delivering 150 W, as well as an additional 4-pin +12V connector called a 'P4' connector, and
• supporting 'soft power' switches that enable PCs to go into sleep modes.

Not all subsequent changes to the ATX12V standard have been improvements. For example, the ATX12V 2.3 standard released in 2007 required power supplies to be at least 70 % efficient. However, the most recent version, ATX12V 2.4, released in 2013, reduced the minimum required efficiency standard specification to just 55 %.

The other current PSU standard is the Entry-Level Power Supply 12-volt (EPS12V) specification. It was derived from the ATX form-factor several years ago to provide more powerful and stable power supplies for critical server-based systems and high-power workstations. EPS12V PSUs have 24-pin 12 V motherboard power plugs, (the same as ATX12V v2.x PSUs) and 8-pin 12 V CPU connectors. Their 8-pin EPS12V connectors are actually two combined ATX P4 connectors. They can, therefore, be split into two 4-pin connectors that are compatible with ATX motherboards. Motherboards that support multi-core CPUs use 24-pin motherboard power connectors and 8-pin CPU power connectors.

Some PSU manufacturers certify that their units fully support both ATX12V and EPS12V standards. For example, CORSAIR's CX-M Series CX750M 750W 80 PLUS BRONZE ATX12V & EPS12V semi-modular power supply even proclaims its dual-compatibility in its name. However, most recent high-quality PSUs support both standards. For example, the Seasonic Prime Titanium PSU featured in the build described in this book also supports both standards, although that fact is only mentioned in its documentation — not in its name.

Most recent motherboards should work with either ATX12V or EPS12V PSUs because most current high-end motherboards accept both EPS12V connectors and ATX12V cables. However, some ATX power supplies don't have all the necessary connectors to adequately provide power to EPS motherboards. Adaptor kits are available to enable recent ATX12V power supplies to work with EPS motherboards, although those kits may limit some functions and reduce system performance. Older ATX motherboards might only work with ATX12V PSUs.

Both ATX12V and EPS12V power supply units will have both Molex peripheral power connectors, and SATA power connectors, although some older ATX power supplies will not have SATA connectors.

Make certain that your PSU has enough SATA power cables to power to all the secondary storage devices you intend to install. Most power supplies these days come with at least three SATA cables. A SATA power connector is thin and has 15 pins. If a PSU does not have enough SATA power cables, you can use inexpensive 4-pin male Molex to SATA 3 converters to enable it to power extra SATA devices. See Figure 3.7.1.

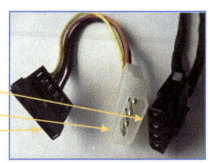

4-pin male Molex connector from PSU

4-hole male Molex connector on converter cable

SATA connector that connects to device

Figure 3.7.1: Molex to SATA Power Cable Converter

You will need enough cables to supply power to all expansion cards and other internal devices. Legacy AGP graphic cards, floppy-drives, some old fan controllers, early spinning hard drives, and some other types of peripheral devices used 4-pin Molex connectors. An example is shown in Figure 3.7.3. Those connectors can still be used to power extra case fans, to provide extra power to some graphic cards, and to power some case lighting systems. You will need one if you intend using an internal floppy drive or any other device with a 4-pin power connector.

Make sure that your PSU's capacity is adequate for your system's needs. Otherwise, if your system is underpowered, the PSU will be liable to shut down when it must work hard. Until recently, the trend was for CPUs to require less power. They typically required only between 45-95 W. However, the most recent high-power CPUs have reversed that trend. They require much more power. For example, some Threadripper models require up to 250 W!

If you are planning to install multiple spinning hard drives and a low-power CPU, you might use the old rule-of-thumb power requirement suggestions provided in Table 3.7.1. However, if you intend to install a powered GPU, you will need to provide additional power. Entry-level graphic cards consume as little as 25 W, but high-end GPUs, such as the Geforce GTX 590 and the Radeon 6990, draw 1,000 watts. Some draw even more! For that reason, Table 3.7.1 also provides some rough power supply requirement suggestions based on different system types.

Table 3.7.1: Typical System Power Supply Requirements

Spinning Hard Drives	Typical System Uses	Watts
2–3	basic gaming, computing; Internet browsing	380–500
4–5	single GPU, or two non-overclocked CPUs	500–650
6–8	large database server with multiple secondary storage devices, and powerful CPU	650–1,200
9+	most powerful CPU, or dual CPUs, with dual graphic cards	1,200–1,600

Tools are available online to help you more accurately estimate your computer's power needs based on the actual components you intend to install. One example is Sea Sonic's an online PSU wattage calculator. Two other online calculators are the eXtreme Power Supply Calculator Lite and the Outerison PSU calculator.

It is a good idea to add 10 % to the estimated power requirements generated from such calculators. Your system will then likely have enough extra power to run additional expansion cards and devices that you might want to install in the future. Moreover, if you are planning to overclock your system, you might need a further 5 % power allowance to meet the extra demands of overclocked components.

You do not have to worry about buying a PSU that supplies too much power. It will not harm your components or waste electricity. For instance, if you buy a 550-watt unit, it does not mean that it will constantly produce 550 watts. If your system only requires 400 watts, that is all the PSU will deliver. Indeed, if you were to often run a PSU near its maximum capacity, it would shorten its lifespan. Moreover, the harder a PSU works; the lower its efficiency; the faster its fans must spin, and the more noise its fans will make.

Most PSU manufacturers now display 80 PLUS ratings on their units. These ratings show how efficient the units are. For example, an 80 PLUS-certified PSU would waste about 20 % of the power it consumes. It would draw 500 W of mains electricity to deliver 400 W to its computer. The wasted 100 W of energy would be released as heat. Some un-rated units fall short of any 80 PLUS-standard. Their efficiencies may be as low as 55 %! That is why you should buy a PSU that has one of the 80 PLUS ratings shown in Table 3.7.2.

Table 3.7.2: Power Supply Efficiency Ratings

80 PLUS Ratings	Minimum Efficiencies at 100 % Load
PLUS	80 %
PLUS Bronze	82 %
PLUS Silver	85 %
PLUS Gold	87%
PLUS Platinum	89 %
PLUS Titanium	90 %

Some PSUs have two fans. Those fans not only cool their PSUs but also help to cool other components. Of course, those fans also consume power and contribute to the noises generated by systems. On the other hand, a few high-end PSUs have no fans. Since they don't have any moving parts, they make no noise and never need any maintenance. They are, however, more expensive than units with fans. Some fanless PSUs rely on massive aluminum heatsinks to keep them cool. However, those large heatsinks don't fit the standard PSU enclosures in ATX cases.

You may recall that the design philosophy statement for the project featured in this book specified the use of the highest-possible-quality PSU. That was because the performance and safety of every other electronic component in the system depends upon the PSU. I also decided to use a fanless PSU to minimize system background noises because I record commercial-quality narrations using a microphone attached to my PC. However, I didn't want to use a fanless PSU with a large heatsink that would not fit into the standard ATX-power unit space available in my Fractal R6 case.

Furthermore, I decided to select a modular PSU because they offer more flexibility than non-modular units. All of their cables are detachable. That means that only the necessary cables may be used without others needlessly taking up space and interfering with the air flows. A semi-modular PSU with a permanently attached motherboard and CPU cables would offer the same advantage.

All these criteria led me to select Sea Sonic's recently released PRIME Titanium Modular fanless 600 W PSU, which is shown in Figure 3.7.2. The Sea Sonic Titanium fanless PSU is manufactured by a large, highly reputable manufacturer that concentrates solely on designing and manufacturing the highest-quality computer power supply units.

It also comes with the excellent documentation and accessories shown in Figure 3.7.2. If you intend running a powerful graphic card and a powerful CPU, you might need to install a more powerful fan-type PSU, such as Sea Sonic's PRIME 1300 W Platinum PSU.

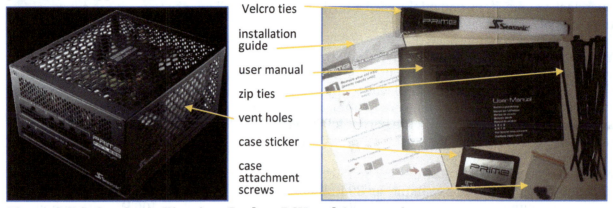

Velcro ties

installation guide

user manual

zip ties

vent holes

case sticker

case attachment screws

Figure 3.7.2: Sea Sonic Titanium Fanless PSU and Accessories

You can see in Figure 3.7.2 that the Sea Sonic Titanium PSU case has many ventilation holes on all its sides. You could take advantage of those ventilation holes by installing the bottom case fan, if you are using one, adjacent to the PSU. That would draw additional airflow through the holes, which would help the unit shed its heat even better. Indeed, that's the configuration used in the project described in this book.

The PRIME Titanium PSU has too many outstanding features to explain here. Perhaps those features can be best be reflected in three statements. The first statement comes from the KitGuru website tester. After extensively testing the unit, he described the PRIME Titanium Modular Fanless 600 W PSU as, '... *a stunning, silent power supply that excels in every possible way. It's expensive, but it ticks every box in my list and delivers clean, stable power... and is my product of the year 2017.*' KitGuru was established in 2010 with the objective of evaluating technology and providing reliable component buying advice. The second statement comes from Sea Sonic themselves. They are so confident about the quality of their fanless PSU that they provide a 12-year warranty for it! I'll confine my own comments about the Prime Titanium PSU to four points.

First, although the 600-watt unit is 80 Plus Titanium-certified, Sea Sonic says that it actually achieves a 96 + % efficiency at 50 % load! This outstanding efficiency means that the unit generates almost no wasted power in the form of heat.

Second, Sea Sonic has kept the dimensions of the unit to a compact: W: 170 mm X L: 150 mm X H: 86 mm. This means that the unit can fit into the standard ATX-size PSU enclosures. Some DIY computer-builders even install it into mini-ITX-sized cases. They do that because small cases are difficult to keep cool since they have little room for air circulation and the PRIME unit produces almost no heat.

Third, the unit incorporates Sea Sonic's Micro Tolerance Load Regulation technology that keeps the output voltage within an exceedingly narrow range of plus or minus 0.5 %. That is ten times better than the industry standard for PSUs recommended by Intel! That feature is significant because the main function of PSUs is to provide stable power supplies at the correct voltages to components. Even slight voltage irregularities can stress sensitive components.

Fourth, the Prime Titanium has Japanese capacitors. Only the best PSUs have these expensive, high-quality Japanese 105C-rated capacitors. The PSUs supplied with cases often have cheaper, less-reliable capacitors. That is another reason it might be wise to replace a power supply unit that comes boxed with a case with a more reliable one.

If you intend installing a modular PSU into a tall case, consider whether you will need any extra-long cables. Standard-length cables might not be able to reach some devices in ATX tower cases, EATX cases, or SSI MEB cases. You can also buy third-party braided cables to use with modular PSUs. Those thin braided cables save even more space inside cases. But avoid buying cheap cables — particularly from manufacturers who don't provide reliable warranties. Poor-quality cables often provide unreliable power transmissions. Unstable power supplies can, in turn, cause system faults and damage components.

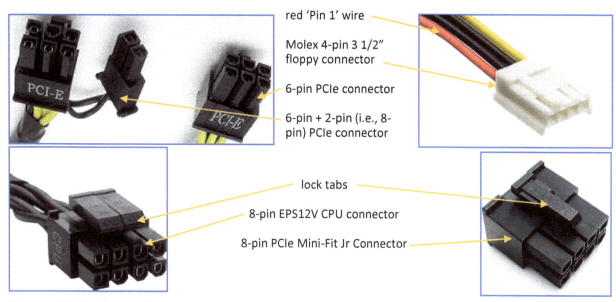

red 'Pin 1' wire

Molex 4-pin 3 1/2" floppy connector

6-pin PCIe connector

6-pin + 2-pin (i.e., 8-pin) PCIe connector

lock tabs

8-pin EPS12V CPU connector

8-pin PCIe Mini-Fit Jr Connector

Figure 3.7.3: Power Connectors

More recent PCIe cards use 6-pin Molex power connectors, but some of the most recent and powerful GPUs have 8-pin Molex Mini-Fit Jr power connectors. These 8-pin connectors can carry up to 300 W. They have locking tabs; so, if one doesn't connect correctly, rotate it 180° so that its tab aligns with its catch.

The Sea Sonic Prime Titanium PSU comes with two such 8-pin PCIe connectors. These 8-pin PCIe high-power card connectors are similar to 8-pin EPS12V CPU power connectors. Although those two connectors are slightly different, they are not color-coded. Therefore, they could be mismatched if you applied sufficient force. Mismatching them could destroy the motherboard, the graphics card, and possibly the power supply as well. They are shown in Figure 3.7.3.

A new type of digital PSU is just becoming available to DIY computer-builders. Those units connect to motherboards via USB connections. Those digital units are more efficient than most analog PSUs. They can also automatically shut themselves down to protect their motherboards if they detect power surges or if they fail.

For example, NZXT and Sea Sonic have just released the E Series semi-digital ATX power supply units. They are 80 PLUS Gold certified; are fully modular; can supply up to 850 W, and are covered by a 10-year warranty. The 850 W model costs about $ 135.
If your system needs an even more powerful digital PSU, you could consider Corsair's recently released AX1600i Digital ATX power supply unit. It is capable of delivering up to 1,600 watts. It costs about $ 350.

If your system needs yet more power, you might consider installing an external PSU as well as an internal unit — although that would involve having a box sitting beside your PC with cables running from it to the PC. It would also involve the cost of buying extra-long cables and making a hole in the case to route the cables through.

If you intend running two linked graphic cards, you might want to check that your PSU is especially-certified to work with CrossFireX and SLI. Some manufacturers provide such certification, which might give you extra peace-of-mind. However, any reliable PSU that delivers enough power should work with dual-GPU systems. Table 3.7.3 provides a basic checklist to help you select a power supply unit.

Table 3.7.3: Power Supply Selection Checklist

Factors	Suggestions	Your Decisions
watts	refer to Table 3.6.1	
80 PLUS rating	silver rating (85 %) or better	
120 V or 240 V	depending on your mains power supply	
modular / non-modular	semi-modular offer good value-for-money and good flexibility	
fan noise	quiet — less than 20 dB (check reviews)	
number of cables	enough for current devices and extras for possible future use	
warranty	at least five years	
cost	7 % of the total system cost	

The discussion about selecting a PSU in this section is limited to ATX form-factor units. However, there are other PSU form-factors as well. For example, Intel introduced the flex-ATX form-factor PSU in 2007. It can deliver up to 270 watts, which is enough for many small-form-factor systems. At the time the fourth edition of this book was written, a few other small-form-factor PSUs were also available. For instance, in 2017 Sea Sonic released their SSP-300SUB 300 W 1U Flex ATX power supply. It is modular and is therefore well-suited to custom cabling configurations. It also features an in-built fan controller that automatically switches the fan off at low loads. It is Bronze-rated and costs $ 55. An example is shown in Figure 3.7.4. A Gold-rated version, the SSP-300SUG, is also available for about $ 67. Another small-form-factor option is the Corsair modular Gold-rated SF 600 W also shown in Figure 3.7.4. It costs about $ 140.

A few large computer manufacturers, such as Dell and Lenovo, produce their own non-ATX12V /non-EPS12V standard power supply units. Their motherboard power connectors might have 6, 8, or even 10 pins. Moreover, the peripheral device power cables used in these systems might come from the motherboards, not directly from the PSUs. If you buy one of these non-standard factory-built systems, you would not be able to choose or replace your PSU.

length: 150 mm

height: 125 mm

width: 100 mm

length: 63 mm

height: 40.6 mm

width: 81.5 mm

Sea Sonic SSP-300 W   Corsair SF600 SFF

Figure 3.7.4: Small-form-factor PSUs

3.8: Selecting the Monitor

Monitors are not PC components. Rather, they are external peripheral devices that are connected to computers. Nevertheless, a discussion about selecting a monitor is included in this book because they are such complex devices that are so integral to the use of PCs. Monitors are like cases in one respect. You can invest in a good-quality monitor that you can reuse with a number of systems, just as you can re-use a good-quality case.

All new monitors these days have liquid crystal display (LCD) or light-emitting diode (LED) panels. The term 'panel' refers to the screen part of a monitor. LCD and LED monitors have now completely replaced the previous generation of monitors that used cathode ray tube (CRT) technology. There are only a few panel manufacturers that all monitor manufacturers buy their panels from them. For example, Acer, AOC, and ASUS all buy their panels from the same manufacturer.

LCD and LED monitors appear to be similar because they both use the same liquid crystal display technology. The difference between them is only how their displays are illuminated. LCD panels are not self-illuminating. Their crystals do not produce any light. Rather, their lights are generated from cold cathode fluorescent backlight lamps. LED panels, on the other hand, use light-emitting diodes. A diode is a solid material that allows electrical current to pass in only one direction and emits light when a current passes through it.

To display pixels on LCD or LED panels, an electrical current is sent from graphic cards to the crystals in each pixel to change their states. LCD and LED monitors do not appear to flicker as CRT monitors do. That is because LCD and LED pixels do not fade to darkness between refreshes. Instead, they glow steadily and, almost instantly, change from one state to the next.

LED monitors are about 20 % more expensive than LCD monitors. However, the extra expense is worth it. That is because LED monitors have nearly twice the lifespans of LCD monitors, provide better pictures, and can be dimmed. Organic Light-Emitting Diode (OLED) monitors are a type of LED monitor that provides better contrast ratios and greater efficiency, although they are even more expensive.

LCD and LED monitors have much smaller desktop footprints than legacy cathode ray tube monitors. Nevertheless, some game players, who play old games designed to run on 640 X 480-pixel monitors, prefer to use CRT monitors. Old CRT panels can become demagnetized. So, it is important to check the display of one that you might be interested in before purchasing it second hand.
The seven most important factors to consider when selecting any type of LCD or LED monitor are its: resolution, refresh rate, response time, contrast ratio, brightness, interfaces, and physical size.

The resolution of a monitor refers to the number of pixels it is capable of displaying. Resolution is measured by the number of pixels a monitor can display across its width by the number of pixels it can display vertically. The higher the resolution, the sharper the image. A resolution of about 1,280 X 800 is satisfactory for most ordinary purposes. However, most computer-aided design (CAD) users, graphic artists, and serious game-players prefer resolutions of at least 1,600 X 1,200 pixels.

The highest resolution that most current high-end monitors can display is 3,840 X 2,160 pixels, which is called a 'consumer 4K' or 'Ultra HD' resolution. The term '4K' nominally refers to a horizontal resolution of 4,000 pixels. However, in 2012, the movie industry's Digital Cinema Initiatives group released a 4K display standard resolution of 4,096 X 2,160 pixels (or 4 times the resolution of full-High-Definition [HD] video).

A few of the latest high-end monitors can display as many as 5,120 X 2,880 pixels — although they are built by joining two 2,560 X 2,880 panels together. Some manufacturers are even developing 8K-resolution screens, and Dell has already released their UP3218K 8K monitor. In this context, '8K' refers to a resolution of 7,680 pixels X 4,320 pixels. It would require four HDMI cables or two DisplayPort 1.2 cables to fully support an 8K-resolution on a medium-sized monitor! Table 3.8.1 lists the most common contemporary monitor resolution standards.

Table 3.8.1: Common Panel Resolution Standards

Common Names	Pixels	Devices
720p; High Definition (HD)	1,280 X 720	TVs
1080p; Full HD	1,920 X 1,080	TVs; monitors
Widescreen Ultra Extended Graphics Array (WUXGA)	1,920 X 1,200	monitors; projectors
2K	2,048 X 1,080	projectors
consumer 4K; Ultra-High Definition (Ultra HD)	3,840 X 2,160	monitors; TVs
cinema 4K	4,096 X 2,160	projectors
consumer 8K	7,680 X 4,320	monitors; future TVs

Resolution is related to pixel pitch. 'Pixel pitch' is the distance between pixels. The smaller the pixel pitch, the less the distance between pixels. The smaller the pixel pitch, the closer you can sit to a monitor and still see a sharp image on its screen. A pixel pitch of 0.285 mm is fine for most ordinary purposes on screens up to 21". Even a poor pixel pitch of 0.311 mm or so is usually satisfactory on a large screen.

Don't confuse 'pixel pitch' with 'pixel rate'. The pixel rate (i.e., fill rate) is the speed at which pixels can be rendered from a GPU and sent to a monitor via memory. It is measured in megapixels per second (MP/s) or gigapixels per second (GP/s).

As mentioned before, monitors' resolutions are limited by the bandwidths of their ports and cables. Good-quality high-speed HDMI 1.4 cables should work well enough with the latest DisplayPort 2.0 standard. However, to display cinema-quality 4K-resolution video, a monitor would need to be connected to a graphic card with a DisplayPort 1.2 cable or an HDMI 2.0 cable, or better. The bandwidth of DVI cables can only support a maximum resolution of 2,560 X 1,600 pixels at a refresh rate of 60 Hz.

Human eyes can only distinguish separate images when they are presented at a rate of 25 or fewer per second. If a sequence of images is presented any faster, our brains perceive them as movement, rather than as separate still images. Actually, the situation is more complex than that because our brains don't always construct entirely new images.
Instead, our brains construct a stream of consciousness that smooths out insignificant differences between separate sequential images while concentrating on any significant differences between images.

A separate image composed of entirely new pixels sent by a graphic card and received by a monitor is called a 'frame'. The speed at which a monitor can display new frames is called its 'frame rate'. Frame rate is measured in frames per second (f/s). 'Frame rate' is not the same thing as 'refresh rate'.

A refresh rate tells us how many times per second a monitor can refresh the images on its screen — including repeating the drawing of identical frames. The more often a screen is refreshed, the smoother the images of moving objects will appear on it. Refresh rate is usually measured in hertz (Hz). Most people prefer a refresh rate of at least 60 Hz to avoid experiencing lag when viewing fast-action 2-D video. That is why high-quality 2-D games support refresh rates of at least 60 Hz. That is also why a 60 Hz refresh rate was traditionally used with LCD monitors.

However, to display 3-D satisfactorily, a refresh rate of 120 Hz is required. That doubling of the 2-D refresh rate is necessary to provide alternating images with 60 Hz refresh rates for each of our eyes. Some panel manufacturers are now producing expensive consumer 4K panels that can run at 120 Hz.

Some people are more sensitive to refresh rates and find that 60 Hz monitors strain their eyes when fast-moving objects are displayed. A refresh rate of 72 Hz is considered to be flicker-free for everyone — even for people whose eyes are sensitive to refresh rates. Therefore, some panel manufacturers now produce monitors with refresh rates of 144 Hz. They can generate flicker-free 3-D images. Refresh rates that are any faster sometimes cause visual artifacts if they are not supported by monitors' pixel response times. Artifacts are minor digitally-created distortions within images.

You may better understand the difference between frame rates and refresh rates by considering a film movie projector. A projector's film might be advanced from one frame to the next one 24 times per second. So, its frame rate would be 24 f/s. However, each frame might be illuminated and projected three times before the next new frame is advanced. In that case, we would say that the movie projector has a refresh rate of (3 X 24 f/s) or, 72 Hz. Likewise, we could say that a monitor with a 120 Hz refresh rate and a 24 f/s frame rate and would repeat each frame at the rate of 120 Hz ÷ 24 f/s, or 5 frames every 24th of a second.

There are two TV frame rate standards. Until recently, the National Television System Committee (NTSC) standard frame rate of 30 f/s with a refresh rate of 60 Hz was used in North America and in part of South America. It required that one new frame every 1/30 th of a second was displayed, which was refreshed twice before the next new frame was displayed. The NTSC standard has recently been replaced by a digital format, which still uses a frame rate of 30 f/s.

Most other countries used the Phase Alternating Line (PAL) standard of 25 f/s at 50 Hz (or, in other words, one completely new frame every 25th of a second, which is refreshed twice before the next new frame is shown). The new digital format used in these countries still uses that 25 frames per second rate. The traditional NTSC and PAL video playback standards are still used in some devices such as older VCRs, analog camcorders, and DVD players.

The term 'lag' refers to the latency between the time a signal is input to a monitor from a peripheral device such as a keyboard, joystick, or mouse, and when that input is displayed on the screen. It also refers to the slow response of monitors to the frames they receive from GPUs. A 60 Hz monitor's lag time might be as much as the equivalent of 4 frames. TVs typically have greater lags than computer monitors.
So, if you intend to play games using a TV as your display device, select a TV with a 'Game Mode' option. That option bypasses some unnecessary image processing and thereby decreases lag.

Monitors cannot govern the frame rates generated by graphic cards. That is because, monitors have only tiny amounts of memory that is used to store their brightness, contrast, and other settings. So, if a graphic card's frame rate is faster than a monitor's frame rate, the monitor will not be able to entirely display all the frames delivered to it. The monitor's display will be laggy, and screen tearing may occur. Screen tearing occurs when data from two or more frames are displayed at the same time.

Most modern 3-D games provide an optional feature, called Vertical Synchronization (VSync) that can solve the problem of screen-tearing. It does that by synchronizing graphic card frame rates with monitor frame rates. VSync forces graphic cards to render and send new frames only when monitors are ready to redraw their screens. The problem with that process is that it might limit a graphic card's frame rate and cause lags before frames can be sent to monitors.

To overcome that problem, Nvidia and AMD developed technologies respectively branded 'G-Sync' and 'FreeSync'. G-Sync was released in 2014 and FreeSync was released in 2015. They both eliminated the input lag caused by V-Sync and prevented screen tearing by using adaptive sync technology. That technology automatically synchronizes graphic card frame rates and monitor refresh rates, whenever necessary.

However, the FreeSync and G-Sync technologies only work with monitors and GPUs that support them. G-Sync technology is contained on chips within monitors, whereas FreeSync uses graphic cards in combination with the Adaptive-Sync standard, which is part of the DisplayPort standard, to manage monitors' refresh rates. Moreover, neither G-Sync nor FreeSync can circumvent cable and port bandwidth interface limitations. An example of screen tearing and FreeSync is shown in Figure 3.8.1.

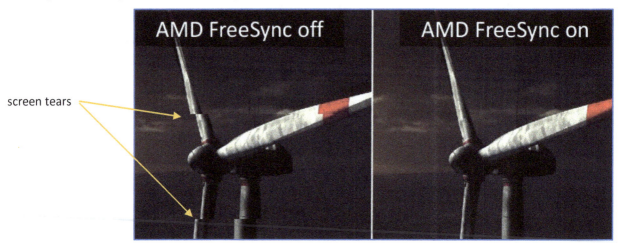

Figure 3.8.1: FreeSync Monitor Screen

G-Sync and FreeSynce were both originally designed to run via DisplayPort because it supported a higher bandwidth than either DVI or HDMI. But these days, FreeSync also works with HDMI providing the system monitor supports 'FreeSync over HDMI'. That means that the monitor supports a refresh rate of 120+Hz using the HDMI. G-Sync doesn't work with the HDMI.

FreeSync is free to use, and more monitors support FreeSync than support G-Sync. In 2017, AMD released the second generation of FreeSync. It provided many improvements, including support for HDR (high-dynamic-range) displays. As the fourth edition of this book was being finalized, Nvidia announced that its new video GTX 1000 and RTX 2000 cards would also work with FreeSync.

Even though the pixels in LCD monitors do not fade in and out of brightness, they, nevertheless, have response times. Their response times refer to how fast their pixels react to electrical currents. More particularly, their response times are the times required for their liquid crystal pixels to go from black to white and then return to black again. The smaller the response time, the less the blurring effect of fast-moving objects on screens. On LCD screens with slow response times, faint streaks following fast-moving images might be noticeable.

A response time of 8 milliseconds (ms) or more is likely to appear laggy when fast-moving images are displayed. A response time of 5 ms is satisfactory for watching most videos. Nevertheless, some enthusiastic game-players prefer monitors with exceptionally fast response times — times as low as 1 ms.

Until recently, monitors with extremely fast response times of 2 ms or less were likely to be twisted nematic (TN) types. TN panels use a type of LCD that is made of nematic liquid crystals that are confined between two plates of polarized glass. That is the same type of technology used in watches and calculators. It has three disadvantages: a narrow viewing angle, a low level of brightness, and an inaccurate color reproduction. But now even non-TN monitors have 1 ms response times. An example is the ASUS PB277Q monitor mentioned earlier.

The static contrast ratio is the difference between the brightest white and the darkest black that a monitor can reproduce. It is sometimes called the 'true contrast ratio'. The higher a monitor's static contrast ratio, the more accurate its display. Although some LCD monitors have static contrast ratios of up to 3,000:1, a more typical static contrast ratio is 1,000:1. This ratio is satisfactory for most purposes. Do not confuse static contrast ratios with dynamic contrast ratios. They may be as high as 7,000,000:1. However, dynamic contrast ratios are non-standardized specifications used by manufacturers and can be misleading.

Brightness is a measurement of the amount of light output by a monitor. It is technically called 'luminance' and is usually measured in candelas per meter squared (cd/m^2). Normally, the recommended brightness of a monitor is 120 cd/m^2. However, more brightness is required to make screen images visible in rooms with a lot of ambient light. So, it is a good idea to choose a monitor with a maximum brightness of at least 250 cd/m^2. That much luminance would be ample, even in a room with a great deal of ambient light. Such intense brightness need not cause eyestrain in less-bright rooms because users can reduce the brightness of monitors.

Be sure that at least one of your motherboard's integrated GPU ports, or one of your GPU card's ports, are compatible with your monitor's cable interface. Most LCD monitors still have both analog and digital connectors even though VGA is now a legacy analog standard. Until recently, DVI was also a popular computer/monitor digital interface. However, it is now often omitted from GPUs and is seldom provided with laptops. Instead, the High-Definition Multimedia Interface (HDMI) which is a superset of DVI that uses its own cables, has become more popular. The HDMI can transmit high-quality audio and video simultaneously.

HDMI 1.4b was the industry standard in 2011. It supports a 120 Hz refresh rate with a resolution of up to 4,096 X 2,160 and 1,080i pixel displays. The 'i' in the '1,080i' specification means that a screen's display is interlaced. That means that only every second row is refreshed each time a screen is refreshed.
Version 1.4b of HDMI was superseded by version 2.0, which can support a 4K display at 60 Hz. Even more recently, HDMI version 2.1 was released in 2018. It almost triples the bandwidth of version 2.0.

DisplayPort is another popular digital video interface. It was introduced in 2008 and is now included on most high-end monitors. Apple's Mini DisplayPort connector is compatible with DisplayPort standards. That means that DisplayPort can be used to interconnect DisplayPort and Thunderbolt 1 and 2 devices.

The most recent computer/monitor interface is Thunderbolt. The latest version of Thunderbolt, Thunderbolt 3, uses the USB Type-C cable. It supports a throughput of up to 40 Gb/s. That is double the speed of Thunderbolt 2 and DisplayPort 1.2, and four times the bandwidth of USB 3.0. A bandwidth of 40 GB/s per second can support two 4K monitors running at 60 Hz.

Thunderbolt 3 can also support up to six daisy-chained Thunderbolt 3 devices. That means that users can plug and play (PnP) external devices directly to their computers. A few monitors with Thunderbolt 3 ports, such as the BenQ 32-inch 4K Thunderbolt 3 monitor, were becoming available when the fourth edition of this books was produced.

Thunderbolt 3 cables can work as regular USB-C cables, and vice versa. However, a device's port must have a Thunderbolt 3 chip to take advantage of the potential extra speed. Otherwise, a USB-C cable plugged into a non-Thunderbolt-3-capable USB-C port will only work at the slower 10 Gb/s speed of USB 3.1. A lightning bolt symbol next to a USB-C port signifies that it is Thunderbolt 3-capable.

You should select a monitor with a screen size suited to the tasks you intend to undertake. Fifteen-inch monitors were standard a decade or so ago, but now most desktop screens are at least 19". Of course, larger monitors are more expensive — particularly when they exceed 27" — and they also take up more desk space. Monitors larger than 27" are only worthwhile for serious game-playing, CAD work, movie watching, or split-screen work.

Using split screens is simple with Windows OS. Just press the Windows key on your keyboard as you also press a left or a right arrow key to split a screen. If there is no Windows key on your keyboard, you can usually use the Ctrl plus the Esc keys instead. The minimum Windows split-screen resolution is 1,024 X 768 pixels. Figure 3.8.2 shows a 27" monitor in split-screen mode.

It is also possible to split frames over multiple screens. In 2009, AMD released a technology branded 'Eyefinity 1.0' that works with AMD CrossFire technology to allow Windows 10 and Linux distributions to use up to six physical monitors as single virtual monitors. An example is shown in Figure 3.8.2.

Split Screen   EyeFinity Multi-screen

Figure 3.8.2: Windows 10 Split Screen and EyeFinity Multi-screen Display

Originally, using Eyefinity 1.0 required monitors with DisplayPort or Mini DisplayPort (i.e., Thunderbolt 1/2) cables and connections. However, Eyefinity 2.0, which was released in 2012, enabled Eyefinity 2.0-compatible graphic cards to support high-resolution 4K displays via single DisplayPort 1.2 or HDMI 1.4a ports. It also increased the total resolution displayed on all monitors to 16,000 X 1,080-pixels. Eyefinity 3.0, released in 2014, even allowed different resolutions to be displayed on different monitors.

Microsoft is currently promoting another application branded 'Actual Multiple Monitors' that can also be used to display frames on multiple monitors. It costs $ 25. However, the basic version of another product, DisplayFusion, will do the same thing for free. The number of monitors that can be supported by DisplayFusion is only limited by the capacity of a system's graphic card and the number of monitor output connectors. An example is shown in Figure 3.8.3.

Figure 3.8.3: DisplayFusion Multi-Screen Display

The most careful monitor shoppers research three additional monitor specifications: a screen's surface type, a stand's ergonomics, and the manufacturer's defective pixel policy.

Most workplace screens have anti-glare coatings. The films over those screens reduce the glare from windows and room lights. Unfortunately, those films also mute colors slightly. For that reason, many home users prefer glossy screens. Images on glossy screens appear sharper and display colors better in low-light conditions. The glossy coatings on monitors are sometimes described as 'crystal' surfaces.

You can assess which type of surface would work best in a particular spot by holding a piece of flat glass where your monitor's screen would be positioned. If you see reflections or glare off the glass, it is probably best to buy a monitor with an anti-glare coated screen.

The term 'ergonomics' refers to the relationship between humans and the tools they use. There are four possible monitor stand ergonomic adjustments: height, tilt, swivel, and pivot. Most monitor stands provide only tilt adjustments. However, the ability to adjust a monitor's height, in particular, can make a significant difference to its ergonomics. Remarkably, the ASUS PB27Q monitor used with the build featured in this book enables all four ergonomic adjustments.

LCD or LED screens often have dead pixels that look like tiny black spots. They also often have bright pixels that remain permanently lit, which look like tiny bright spots. One or two dead or bright pixels, providing they are not in the central area of a screen, are usually considered to be acceptable. Nevertheless, manufacturers of some high-end monitors provide zero-defective-pixel guarantees — although those guarantees usually only apply to bright pixels — not to dead pixels. Most monitor manufacturers will only exchange other models for free if they exceed a minimum number of defective pixels. Some manufacturers might also accept the return of monitors with fewer faulty pixels for a restocking fee of about 15 % of the price of the monitors.

Monitors with built-in speakers are convenient because they free users from needing to wear headphones. However, many monitors do not include built-in speakers these days because including speakers raises their prices. I was therefore pleased that the ASUS PB277Q monitor included a useful speaker.

Over the last few years, other features have been added to some monitors. These include:
- support for the Windows touch user interface,
- inclusion of USB 3.0 ports,
- inclusion of Thunderbolt 3 ports, and
- use of In-Plane Switching (IPS) to improve viewing angles and color reproduction, or Samsung's Plane to Line Switching (PLS) which provides viewing angles as wide as IPS monitors, while providing higher brightness and lower power consumption.

There are still more monitor specifications. However, they would only be relevant to particular applications. For one example, a monitor must be 4K-capable, High-Bandwidth Digital Content Protection (HCDP) compliant and have at least an HDMI 2.0 port to play Ultra HD Blu-ray files. For another example, professional photographers, filmmakers, and designers might require higher levels of color accuracy on their monitor screens than normal users would. Therefore, they might prefer monitors, such as ASUS's ProArt PA27AC, that are sRGB, Rec 709, and HDR-10 certified.

The sRGB color-space is the default international standard for describing the reds, greens, and blues incorporated within colors. That data is used to consistently describe colors that are transmitted between devices and platforms such as computer screens, printers, and web browsers.

Rec 709 is the open industry standard color-space for HDTVs. HDR (High dynamic range) technology expands the range of contrasts and colors so that images appear to have more depth. Ordinary HDR sets contrast and color standards by sending static metadata to monitors at the beginnings of games or movies. HDR-10-certified technology uses dynamic metadata that continually adjusts contrasts and colors throughout games or movies.

Most recent monitors provide blue light features intended to ease the strain on users' eyes. However, excessive exposure to blue light presents its own health risks, including disrupted sleep and eye retina damage. Wearing ordinary eyeglasses provides some blue light protection; however, wearing special blue light filtering glasses provides about three times as much protection.

Third-party blue light filter applications are also available. Also, some operating systems have recently included blue light filter features. For example, in 2017 Windows 10 included a blue light feature called 'Night light'. To turn on Windows 10's Night light feature:

1. Open the settings menu by entering 'settings' in the Windows 10's search box.

2. On the pop-up Settings screen, click on 'Settings'.

3. On the next Windows Settings screen, select 'System'.

4. Select 'Display' from the left-hand menu.

5. Toggle the Night light switch on; then click the X on the top right of the screen to exit.

Table 3.8.2 lists the specifications of two monitors at two different price points, and Table 3.8.3 provides a checklist to help you select your own monitor.

Table 3.8.2: Comparison of Monitor Specifications

Feature	ViewSonic TD2220 Full HD	Dell U3014 IPS
diagonal size	22 inches	30 inches
connection interface	DVI-D (1) USB 2.0 type-A (2) VGA (1) 3.5 mm audio in (1)	DVI (1) HDMI (1) DisplayPort (1) Mini DisplayPort (1) USB
glossy or matte screen	X[1]	light matte
native resolution[2]	1,920 X 1,080 pixels	2,560 X 1,600 pixels
touch screen	2-point	X
power consumption	26 watts (typical)	60 watts
vertical refresh rate	76 Hz	60 Hz
pixel pitch	X	0.252 mm
response time	5 ms	6 ms
static image contrast ratio	1,000:1	1,000:1
brightness	200 cd/m^2	350 cd/m^2
integrated webcam	X	X
stand adjustments	tilt 5°–20°	swivel, pivot, tilt; height
IPS or PLS technology	X	IPS
speakers	2 X 2 watts	X
manufacturer's warranty	three years	three years
approximate retail cost	$ 280	$ 1,100

Note: 1. 'X' means 'not provided'. 2. 'Native resolution' means that each pixel output by a graphics card has its own corresponding pixel on a monitor.

Table 3.8.3: Monitor Selection Checklist

Features	Suggestions	Your Decisions
diagonal size	21.5" for ordinary purposes	
connection	HDMI, DisplayPort, or USB Type-C	
glossy or matte	personal preference	
native resolution	at least 1,920 X 1,080 pixels	
ergonomics	tilt (essential); height, tilt, and pivot (desirable)	
touch screen	needed for Windows touch screen option	
power consumption	the less, the better — an 18.5" LED typically uses about 17 W in power-saving mode	
pixel pitch	0.285, or smaller	
refresh rate	at least 60 Hz; 75 Hz preferred if sensitive to refresh rates, and 2 X 60 Hz (120 Hz) desirable for virtual reality projection	
speakers	possibly stereo with at least 1 W/channel	
response time	5 ms or less	
image contrast ratio	static 1,000:1 or more	
brightness	250 cd/m^2 or more	
IPS or PLS	PLS is less expensive	
blue light control	if used more than 1 hour per day	
warranty	two years+ with defective pixel provision	
cost	19 %, but 30 % of all hardware cost for CAD, or video-editing, or 50 % for serious gaming	

As mentioned at the start of this section, a discussion about selecting a monitor doesn't belong in this book. That is because monitors are external peripheral devices — not components that can be built into computers. The two other types of peripheral devices that would likely be attached to every DIY personal desktop computer are mice and keyboards.

No substantial discussion about them is provided in this book because they are not nearly as complex as monitors. Nevertheless, they are no less vital parts of the human/computer interface. Therefore, you should consider their ergonomic features no less than you should consider the ergonomics of your monitor. Although ergonomic mice and keyboards are usually more expensive, they will improve your computing comfort and productivity. An Adesso ergonomic mouse and a Microsoft Sculpt ergonomic keyboard are shown in Figure 3.8.4.

vertical mouse orientation positions hand in neutral 'handshake' position

keyboard positions wrist in natural straight alignment

Figure 3.8.4: Ergonomic Mouse and Keyboard

Until recently, rubber-domed keyboards with membrane switches were most common. However, nowadays, most people prefer keyboards with mechanical switches. They prefer the tactile 'bumps' and audible 'clicks' made by mechanical keys.

Mechanical keys might also reduce word-processing errors because users are more certain when they have pressed keys and are therefore less likely to double-type characters to make sure that they have pressed keys. Mechanical switch keyboards are also more durable. They have high-quality switches made from moving as well as non-moving parts. Some mechanical keyboards have extra features. For example, SteelSeries have recently developed RGB mechanical keyboards branded Apex Pros that can be individually adjusted. SteelSeries say that those keyboards are also eight times faster than traditional mechanical keys. They are expensive however, costing up to $ 210, and they are not ergonomically designed.

Similarly, mice that use optical sensors are becoming more popular than mice that use laser sensors. Optical mice use light-emitting diodes (LEDs) whereas laser mice use infrared laser diodes. Although laser mice are faster, they are less accurate at high speeds than optical mice. Optical mice also tend to be less expensive.

A computer programmer was drowning in the ocean. People heard him call 'F1, F1!', but no one understood.

4. Buying Components and Organizing Work

You can use some smart shopping strategies to buy the best components for your PC at the best prices. You can start by using online services to make technical comparisons of components. Some useful websites are the AnandTech website mentioned previously, the hardOCP website, Tom's Hardware website, and the Passmark website. You can also use online component selection tools, called configurators, to help you choose components that meet your requirements.

The UserBenchmark website mentioned in an earlier section also provides an excellent service for selecting most components. However, it does not include information about cases and peripheral devices, such as monitors. It can, however, be configured to show the prices of components in various currencies, as shown in Figure 4.1. You can even use it to test your current system, as also shown in Figure 4.1.

component price lists   systems benchmarks

Figure 4.1: UserBenchmark Website Screens

If you want to install a new component after you have built your PC, you can also use the free Crucial System Scanner from www.crucial.com/. It will analyze your system's hardware and provide a list of compatible upgrades.

Of course, you will not be able to interpret the information provided by such websites, configurators, or scanners unless you understand the relevant technical jargon. Only then will you be able to make intelligent, well-informed decisions about your components.

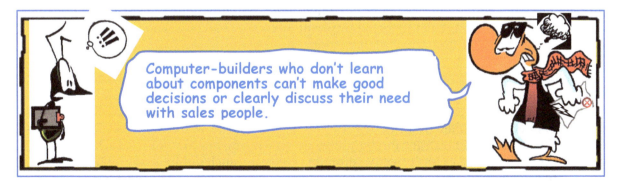

Computer-builders who don't learn about components can't make good decisions or clearly discuss their need with sales people.

After you have made a shortlist of your system's components based on their technical merits, you should compare their prices from various suppliers. PCPartPicker provides current retail prices of components (as well as useful component benchmarks). Current retail prices of components in America are also provided by Pricewatch. Component prices in European countries are listed by Kelkoo. You can also visit major online shops, such as Newegg and eBay, to compare prices.

Avoid buying the latest models of components unless necessary. You will pay a premium for them if you do. You might be able to find slightly older components, with satisfactory specifications, for as little as 50 % of the cost of the latest models. Also, look for promotional specials where you can make significant savings.

Don't overlook local computer shops. You might find better deals there than at big online stores. You will also be able to take your components immediately if they are in stock. Moreover, you are more likely to have your questions answered in a local shop because salespeople at large online stores do not usually have the time to explain technical details, such as the compatibilities between various components. If you encounter a pushy salesperson in either type of store, who is paid by commission, it would probably be better to shop elsewhere.

If a component that you want is not available in your country, you might be able to buy it through a freight-forwarding service. These services will order and receive components from foreign countries and then ship them to buyers. Until recently, DIY computer builders often used those freight-forwarding services to avoid paying sales taxes. Since it is now a legal requirement in most countries to pay sales taxes on components purchased on the Internet, buying components through freight-forwarding services is no longer inexpensive, especially if shoppers have to also pay extra bank or credit card fees.

Weigh-up the pros and cons of buying either Original Equipment Manufacturer (OEM) or boxed components. As mentioned previously, you may be able to save some money by buying OEM components. In particular, OEM CPUs are sometimes significantly cheaper. However, the risk might not be worth the money you save. Warranties on OEM components are likely to be limited, or even nonexistent, and the components usually don't include manuals or software. What is more, sometimes inferior or overclocked components are sold as OEM components.

Boxed versions of CPUs sometimes include compatible coolers. Such boxed coolers are reliable for normal (i.e., non-overclocked) purposes. However, if you buy an OEM CPU, you will have to buy a separate aftermarket heatsink for it. But that might be an advantage. You could spend the money you save by purchasing the OEM CPU to buy a superior-quality cooler.

Another way to save money is to buy components that have been opened and then returned to retailers. The components might have been returned because the buyers made mistakes in ordering them or because the sellers made mistakes in shipping them. These items will be marked as 'New – Opened Box' or 'Reboxed'. That is one reason that sellers expect customers to return components with their packaging, documentation, barcodes, and stickers undamaged. That enables sellers to conveniently resell the components. A barcode is an optical label containing data about the item to which it is attached

You should make sure that any reboxed components you buy carry the same warranties as the original unopened items. Nowadays, secondary storage devices and power supply units should have warranties of at least five years. Never buy components from suppliers that do not allow faulty or incorrectly-supplied items to be returned or that charge 'restocking' fees for doing so. Moreover, beware of extra charges for 'handling' or 'credit card surcharges'. Also, beware of companies that charge extra for 'priority shipping'. Refusing such dubious optional charges is a good way to save money.

You might also be able to save money by purchasing refurbished components. Refurbished components are components that have been returned because they were faulty but have been repaired by the manufacturer. For example, CPUs with pins that have been straightened by a specialist pin repairer might be sold as 'refurbished'. Even major manufacturers sometimes discount factory-refurbished components. Refurbished secondary storage devices sometimes cost less than half of their normal retail prices.

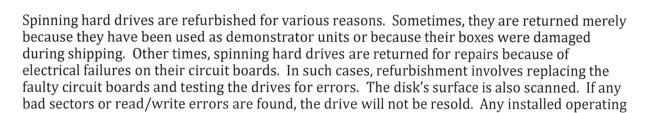

Spinning hard drives are refurbished for various reasons. Sometimes, they are returned merely because they have been used as demonstrator units or because their boxes were damaged during shipping. Other times, spinning hard drives are returned for repairs because of electrical failures on their circuit boards. In such cases, refurbishment involves replacing the faulty circuit boards and testing the drives for errors. The disk's surface is also scanned. If any bad sectors or read/write errors are found, the drive will not be resold. Any installed operating system should also be removed, and the hard drive should be wiped clean.

Manufacturer-refurbished secondary storage devices are sometimes referred to as 'recertified drives'. These devices come with manufacturer warranties, although the warranties may not be for as long as normal warranties. A 90-day warranty is typical for manufacturer-refurbished spinning hard drives, although some sellers may extend their warranties to a year.

Seller-refurbished storage devices are different from manufacturer-refurbished ones. Although seller-refurbished storage devices are usually tested, they are not usually certified to be error-free. For that reason, avoid buying refurbished storage devices from sellers who do not provide reasonable return policies. The latest generation of SSDs is more durable than spinning hard disk drives, and the chance of receiving a faulty seller-refurbished SSD is slight.

You can search for refurbished components on most of the major online retail websites. But take care to buy from a reliable seller. Some online resellers sell fake components as 'refurbished' components. They may also post fake positive product reviews on their websites. Therefore, buy through a reliable seller, such as eBay, that provides a complain-and-return option if a component doesn't match its listing details. PayPal provides a similar dispute resolution service. PayPal even provides buyer refunds itself in some cases.

Sales representatives in some unscrupulous online stores sometimes tell customers that components are in stock — even when they are not in stock. Customers only discover, after they pay for the components, that the supplier does not deliver them on time — and that they won't give refunds to enable the customers to buy the components elsewhere. You can protect yourself from this problem by arranging to pay for components when you collect them in person from a shop, if possible. Otherwise, if you can't pay when you collect your components, the best you can do is check a company's refund policy and reputation in online reviews and forums.

You can also save some money by buying bare hard drives. As mentioned in Section 3.6, a bare secondary storage device is one that is supplied without cables or other extras that would be included in a retail boxed package.

Another cost-saving strategy is to buy components during major on-line sales such as Black Friday, Cyber Monday, End of Financial Year, and Christmas. You can usually save at least 10-15 % at these times — and even more on superseded stock. Retailers actually increase their profit margins during these sales because of the greater efficiencies from selling higher volumes of stock.

A good strategy for buying monitors is to inspect the model you are interested in while it is working at a shop. If it has no defective pixels, ask to take that same monitor — not another boxed one — home with you. If the sales representative tells you that is unnecessary, reply that you will agree to take another boxed monitor, providing he or she gives you a written note saying that the store will exchange it for the display monitor if you discover that the one you buy has any dead or bright pixels. You could use Table 4.1 to help you keep track of suppliers and their respective prices of your components.

Table 4.1: Hardware Components and Peripheral Device Prices

Components and Devices	Supplier 1 Name: _____	Supplier 2 Name: _____	Supplier 3 Name: _____
audio card			
case			
graphics card			
spinning hard drive			
keyboard			
primary memory (RAM)			
monitor			
motherboard			
mouse			
M.2 storage device			
optical drive			
power supply unit (PSU)			
central processor unit (CPU)			
solid-state drive			
soundcard			
other _____			
other _____			
other _____			
other _____			

If you buy components from an online retailer, keep their website's checkout screen open until you receive an email from them containing the order number and purchase details. Also, archive your online invoices. You might require them if you ever need to contact suppliers. Register your products online as soon as you can. That will activate their warranties and ensure that you receive any driver updates.

Check the packaging of your parts before you leave a shop with them, or as soon as they are delivered. If you find any boxes that have been opened, crushed, punctured or show signs of water or fire damage, notify the seller. Ask them if they want you to open the box to check the contents yourself, or if they want you to return it to them.

As mentioned before, leave all stickers and barcodes in place, and keep all printed instructions and packaging materials in original condition in case you need to return a component. Also, keep the case and monitor boxes and their foam padding. That packaging provides ideal protection for your computer and monitor if you ever have to move them.

Most countries have some sort of legal methods for dealing with companies that supply incorrect or faulty goods. For example, in China, World Consumer Rights Day (known as *San Yao Wu*) occurs every March 15. On that day, the unethical business practices of companies are condemned in a special TV broadcast. The consequences are so great that even large information technology companies such as Apple and Nikon have issued public apologies and recalled products.

China has also recently strengthened its consumer protection laws. Now, Chinese retailers must accept all goods for return within seven days of purchase unless a customer has previously agreed otherwise. In the case of online purchases, consumers are not even required to provide any reasons for returns. Western countries typically have government consumer affairs departments where consumers can check the histories of companies and lodge complaints about unfair trading practices.

Organizing a suitable workspace for your computer-building project is important. You need enough clear, clean space to be able to lay-out your case and motherboard, as well as your tools. A large desk or a kitchen table would be adequate.

You also need good lighting to be able to see clearly inside the case. A desk lamp with a flexible neck would serve the purpose. Avoid working on carpet (unless it is anti-static carpet) if possible, because of the risk of static electricity. Your workspace will also need to be within reach of two available mains power outlets.

You will need most, or all of, the tools shown in Figure 4.2. You might also need some small zip-ties, a notepad and pen or pencil, as well as any CD/DVDs containing device drivers. If you are installing a Threadripper CPU or an Intel LGA CPU, you will also need a Torx screwdriver.

Using antistatic gloves is optional. But if you intend to work often with computers, you might want to buy a good pair of antistatic gloves, such as the Zoheyoner ones shown in Figure 4.2. You will also need the user guides for the components — particularly the guides for the CPU, the motherboard, and the case, as shown in Figure 4.3.

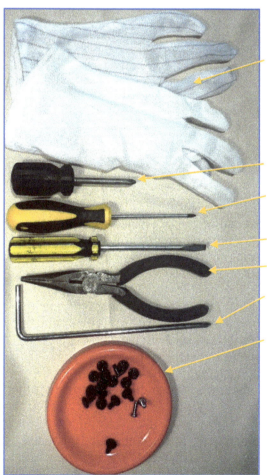
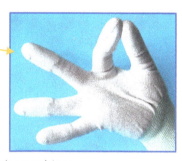

Zoheyoner pu-coated anti-static glove

cheap disposable anti-static gloves

medium-sized (# 2) Phillips head screwdriver

small-sized (# 0) Phillips head screwdriver required to remove M.2 SSD cover

flat-headed screwdriver

small long nose pliers or a 5 mm (0.2") nut driver

special extension Phillips head screwdriver (provided by Noctua to tighten retention screws)

a small container such as a clean ashtray or bowl (magnetized containers are available that hold screws better and prevent them from being knocked out of the container)

profile of end of Torx screwdriver for installing Threadripper or Intel LGA CPUs — they are supplied with the Threadripper CPUs

Figure 4.2: Computer Building Tools

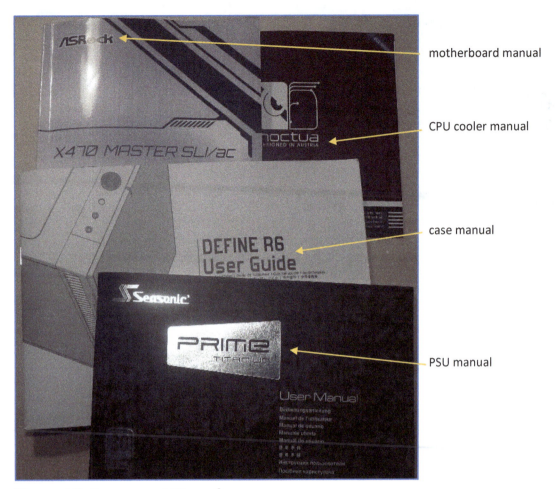

motherboard manual

CPU cooler manual

case manual

PSU manual

Figure 4.3: Component Manuals

If you intend reusing any old components, you could use a can of compressed air to clean the dust and debris off them. However, you could instead use a normal vacuum to clean them just as well. However, take care to use a soft bristle brush attachment and avoid any metal-to-metal contact between the vacuum's nozzle and the components.

Using an electric screwdriver presents something of a risk. It is easy to lose control of one and scratch a motherboard with it, or for it to fling a screw onto a motherboard. Moreover, electric screwdrivers can over-tighten fragile screws. Using a magnetized screwdriver, however, is a good idea. They make it easier to hold screws in position and to retrieve the screws that inevitably fall into hard-to-reach places in cases. The magnetic fields generated by these screwdrivers are not strong enough to damage any storage media — providing that any contact is only brief.

Before you start building, you should be aware of static electricity. Static electricity is caused by an imbalance of electric charges in two materials. It is what gives you a spark when you walk across a carpeted floor on a dry day and then touch something metal, such as a door handle. Such a tiny spark is much stronger than one that could ruin some computer components. A static electrical discharge from your body can be thousands of volts, whereas a static discharge as low as 30 volts can damage some computer components.

For many decades, the metal used to manufacture most computer cases has been SECC (Steel, Electroplated, Cold-rolled, Coil). Unfortunately, SECC is prone to generating electrostatic charges. You should, therefore, consider taking enough of the following twelve precautions to protect your components from static electricity short-circuits. A short-circuit occurs when an electrical current travels along an unintended path.

1. As mentioned before, do not work on a carpeted floor (particularly if it has acrylic in it) unless the carpet is an anti-static carpet.

2. If possible, build your computer on a day when the humidity is high — not when the air is dry. Dry air is more likely to promote the build-up of static electricity. If you intend to work on computers regularly, and you live in an area with low humidity, you might even consider buying an anti-static ionizer.

3. Keep your arms bare below your elbows. That way, your clothing cannot accidentally touch components and conduct sparks to them. Also, do not wear a tie or necklace that might dangle onto a motherboard and conduct static electricity.

4. If you have long hair, use a hair net or hat to keep your hair away from components. Even a single strand of hair can conduct a static electricity charge.

5. Do not wear leather shoes or synthetic or wool socks — especially when standing on carpet. They are prone to generating static. In fact, from an electrostatic management point-of-view, it would be best not to wear anything on your feet at all. But, on the other hand, from a health and safety point-of-view, you should wear enclosed footwear. You can buy anti-static shoe covers that look like baggy slippers if you need to wear leather shoes or work on ordinary carpet while working on computers.

6. Do not wear synthetic clothing such as a polyester shirt. Synthetic clothing is more likely to generate static electricity. If you intend to work regularly with computer parts, you might even consider buying a special anti-static shirt that includes its own static grounding cord.

7. Wear anti-static gloves. This does not mean wearing ordinary rubber or latex gloves. Rubber gloves will help prevent electricity from electrocuting you, but they will not prevent static electricity from leaving your body. On the contrary, they may even cause it. Anti-static gloves also help keep contaminants, such as the natural oils from your fingertips, off components.

8. Never lay an electrified motherboard on a metal, or even a wooden table. Wood is also an electrical conductor and can create a short-circuit. Instead, place your computer case and components on an anti-static desk mat, as shown in Figure 4.4. It would provide some static protection — while also protecting your tabletop from scratches.

If you don't have an anti-static mat, you can use an anti-static spray to temporarily reduce the static on your work surface. You can make your own anti-static spray by mixing one-part fabric softener with ten parts of water. Lightly spray the mixture onto the tabletop and the floor under the table. You can also cut your motherboard's anti-static bag open along two sides; lay it with the outside facing down and use it as a clean anti-static surface to lay your motherboard on when you are working on it.

Some people say to lay motherboards (and any other components that come in anti-static bags) on the tops of their bags. However, my A+ Microcomputer Certification instructor cautioned against that. He said that the charges on the outsides of anti-static bags might be different from the charges on their inside surfaces. If so, laying a motherboard, or any other component, on the outside of its bag, might create a condition for a static discharge.

I have no evidence to confirm that advice. However, the surface of the material that antistatic bags are made of is liable to attract static charges. So, it is conceivable that the outsides of these bags might develop different electrostatic charges than the charges on their insides. You can buy anti-static bags from some computer component suppliers. You can use these bags to store electronic components that you want to remove from your computer for a long time.

9. Plug the PSU into the mains power outlet. That will provide an electrical grounding path to drain static electricity from the case via the cable's grounding prong. Any leaking static electrical current can then be carried away to the earth along the grounding pathway. Some people argue, from a health and safety point-of-view, that it is a safer practice to disconnect a PSU's power plug from the mains socket to avoid any possible chance of electrocution. But that would mean that you would also eliminate the grounding pathway from the PSU. If you do not turn a PSU switch on while you are working inside a computer case, no electricity should flow from the mains supply through the PSU to the motherboard — or to you.

10. Use components that provide their own electrostatic discharge protections. Fortunately, most recent components are not as susceptible to static as previous generations of components were. For example, Gigabyte's recent Ultra Durable 4 Classic motherboards feature anti-surge integrated circuits that help protect other components, as well as the motherboard, from power surges. Those motherboards use new types of microchips that are more resistance to electrostatic discharges than previous generations of microchips were.

11. Wear an anti-static wrist strap, as shown in Figure 4.4. There are two strategies for using these wrist straps. One is to short (i.e., connect) yourself to a ground to drain static electricity from your body. The other strategy is to short yourself to the case to equalize the charges between yourself and the case. Both strategies have their merits. However, wrist straps are most often used to equalize the electrical charges between a wearer and a computer case.

One end of an anti-static wrist strap is made of an elastic band that should be fitted snugly around your wrist. The other end is an alligator clip that must be connected to a bare metal portion of a computer's chassis. Since most cases are painted inside as well as outside, you might have to attach the clip to a screw that is screwed into the case's chassis to make a good electrical connection to it.

You might wonder why you can't just use a length of bare copper wire shown in Figure 4.4. After all, it would drain static electricity perfectly well. The reason is that anti-static straps have 1-Meg ohm resistors built into them. These resistors are designed to stop electrical surges from traveling up the strap and electrocuting you. If you only intend to use a wrist strap a few times, you could save a little money by purchasing a cheap disposable type, such as the 3M type shown in Figure 4.4.

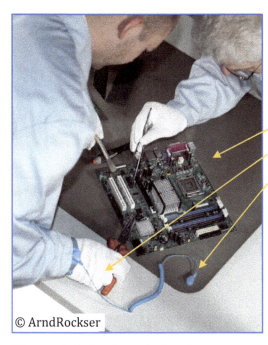

disposable 3M
wrist strap

anti-static mat

anti-static gloves

anti-static wrist
strap

bare copper wire with no safety
resistor

© ArndRockser

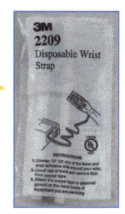

Figure 4.4: Anti-static Devices

12. Touch a bare part of the computer case, such as a screw head, with your bare arm immediately before you touch any components inside a case. That is a good practice even if you use an anti-static wristband and/or anti-static gloves. (The strap connections might be loose, or the gloves might have a tiny, unnoticed hole.) If you only touch a painted part of the case, the paint might act as enough of an insulator to prevent the equalization of the static charges between you and the case. That is why it is best to touch some bare metal, such as a screw, on the case near the PSU.

There is no need to follow all these twelve precautions. Experienced DIY-computer builders and computer technicians routinely ignore some of them. However, you should follow enough of these guidelines to eliminate the risk of damaging your components. If you damage a component by exposing it to static electricity, you cannot reasonably expect its retailer or manufacturer to refund your money.

As well as taking precautions to manage static electricity, take care not to damage components in other ways. Remove any jewelry from your fingers or wrists. It can scratch delicate components. Always handle electronic components by their non-conducting (i.e., non-metallic) edges. Never touch the pins on component connectors. That would leave oil from your fingers on the metallic surfaces, which might cause corrosion in the long term. Don't eat, smoke, or drink while building your PC. That would likely spread contaminants onto your computer's components. Such contamination might cause contact failures in the future. What is more, fluids spilled onto a charged motherboard could cause short-circuits, or even electrocution.

Qualified technicians use ohmmeters to check the capacitors in computers. However, unless you are qualified, never use an ohmmeter on any component circuit boards. An ohmmeter is an electrical instrument that measures electrical resistance, that is, the opposition to an electric current.

I think computer viruses should count as life.
I think it says something about human nature
that the only form of life we have created so far is
purely destructive.
We've created life in our own image.
~ Stephen Hawking ~

5. Building the Computer

Building a desktop personal computer the first time requires patience and preparation. The better prepared you are, the more satisfying the project will be. A good way to prepare is to familiarize yourself with the documentation for individual components before you start. It can become confusing and frustrating if you put-off reading documentation until you are building.

Building your first PC might take you quite a bit of time. But, don't worry about working too slowly and don't panic if you become confused. If you become confused, just take a break and perhaps re-read the relevant documentation before you start again. Problem-solving is a normal part of the building process. If you remain calm, the build will be an interesting and rewarding learning experience — even if you do run into a few minor problems along the way.

In this book, instructions are given to install the CPU and its cooler, as well as the RAM and M.2 SSD before installing the motherboard. That is because it is easier to work on motherboards while they are outside their cases. Indeed, it might even be essential to install a large tower CPU cooler, such as the Noctua NH-U12S SE-AM4, before installing the motherboard. Alternatively, you could install most components onto the motherboard after it has been installed in the case. That method has the advantage of requiring less handling of the motherboard.

5.1: Preparing the Case

The first task is to prepare the case so that the other components can be attached to it. If the case is lockable, undo the locks on its side panels. You will also likely need to unscrew two thumbscrews on the backs of each side panel. Then remove both the left and right side panels. You might need to slide them backwards along rails or slots in the case's chassis. However, high-quality cases might have better systems for attaching their side panels. For example, the side panels on the Fractal R6 have knobs that positively locate in catches in the chassis, as shown in Figure 5.1.1.

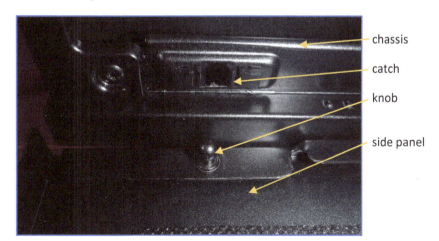

chassis

catch

knob

side panel

Figure 5.1.1: Side Panel Catches on Fractal R6 Case

Remove the packaged screws, printed instructions, and any other accessories. Then, familiarize yourself with the case's interior. Note where the secondary storage device drive bays are. Check whether the power supply space is at the top or the bottom. Some cases, such as Corsair's Carbide Clear 600C Inverse ATX Full-Tower Case, provide their PSU enclosures at their tops. That arrangement has the advantage of preventing the heat from PSUs from rising over other components. Plan where the case fans will be installed and figure-out where any liquid-cooler radiators will be installed. Also, give some preliminary thought to where the various power and data cables will be routed.

Notice the wires and cables coming from the front of the case similar to those shown in Figures 5.1.2 and 5.4.3. The thin wires are used to connect things such as the case's speaker, the secondary storage device's lights, and the power switch. Usually, there is also at least one pre-installed fan at the front of the case with a thin power wire coming from it. The other thicker cables coming from the front of the case connect to USB ports (and possibly to some other ports as well) on the motherboard. An example is shown in Figure 5.4.4.

If your case comes with an installed non-modular power supply, you will see it mounted at the rear. You will also see several thick cables coming out of it. These cables are used to supply power to the secondary storage devices, motherboard, CPU, and possibly internal speakers and other internal powered devices. You can't connect these cables until you have installed the motherboard and devices. It might even be necessary to temporarily remove the pre-installed PSUs in some cases to make room to install the motherboard. The right-side interior of the Fractal R6 case used in the build featured in this book is shown in Figure 5.1.2.

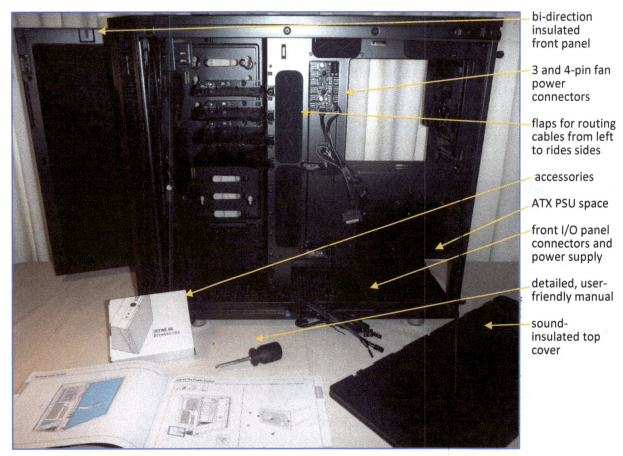

bi-direction insulated front panel

3 and 4-pin fan power connectors

flaps for routing cables from left to rides sides

accessories

ATX PSU space

front I/O panel connectors and power supply

detailed, user-friendly manual

sound-insulated top cover

Figure 5.1.2: Interior of Fractal Define R6 ATX Case

Every case will have some unique design features. High-quality cases will have features that make building and maintaining a desktop PC easy. For example, the Fractal R6 has a sound-insulated top panel that can be easily removed to allow fans or a radiator to be installed at the top. It is necessary to use something like a flat-headed screwdriver to pry the top cover and the filter apart. It also has a catch that secures and releases the top panel, as shown in Figure 5.1.3.

top of chassis

top panel release catch

Figure 5.1.3: Fractal R6 Case Feature

Most motherboards come with I/O faceplates that must be installed. These thin metal shields fit around the I/O ports on the backs of the motherboards. Their purposes are to prevent dust entering cases and to help control the air flows inside cases. However, a few cases come with I/O faceplates already installed. It is best to remove such factory-installed faceplates and use the faceplate supplied with the motherboard instead. The motherboard faceplate is more likely to match the configuration of the ports on the motherboard.

If your motherboard has the type of faceplate that must be manually installed, this is the stage to install it. If you miss this step or get it wrong, you will be sorry. In that event, you will likely have to remove the motherboard to correctly fit the faceplate into the case later on.

If your motherboard has a removable I/O faceplate, you will see a rectangular hole in the back of the case's chassis that the I/O faceplate fits into as shown in Figure 5.1.4. Don't install the faceplate into that hole upside down. The faceplate might be difficult to insert. Nevertheless, don't force it because it is made of flimsy metal that can easily bend. Instead, gently press its corners until it clicks into its place, as shown in Figure 5.1.4.

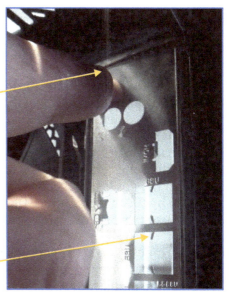

Press corners of faceplate into position from inside of the case.

back of case's chassis

bendable tabs[1]

Note: 1. If these tiny tabs block any of their port openings, you can gently bend them out of the way.

Figure 5.1.4: Aligning and Attaching I/O Faceplate

Some recent high-end motherboards have more substantial integrated I/O faceplates. An example is the ASUS Zenith Extream shown in Figure 5.1.5. The types of faceplates on such motherboards provide physical protection as well as static electricity protection for the motherboard. Of course, if your motherboard has an integrated I/O faceplate, do not attempt to remove it.

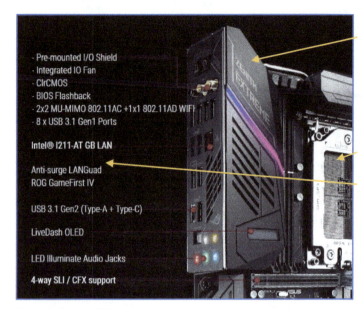

Integrated I/O faceplate

- Pre-mounted I/O Shield
- Integrated IO Fan
- ClrCMOS
- BIOS Flashback
- 2x2 MU-MIMO 802.11AC +1x1 802.11AD WIFI
- 8 x USB 3.1 Gen1 Ports

Intel® I211-AT GB LAN

AMD TR4 Socket for Ryzen Threadripper CPUs

Anti-surge LANGuad
ROG GameFirst IV

Built-in anti-surge guard

USB 3.1 Gen2 (Type-A + Type-C)

LiveDash OLED

LED Illuminate Audio Jacks

4-way SLI / CFX support

Graphic from ASUS website

Figure 5.1.5: ASUS ROG Zenith Extreme Motherboard Integrated I/O Faceplate

Next, take the motherboard out if its box. Locate the circular holes in the motherboard. These holes are for the screws that will fasten the motherboard to the case's chassis. ATX form-factor motherboards have nine such screw holes. Hold the motherboard inside the case to see where its holes align with the screw holes on the case's chassis.

Most people take the motherboard out of its anti-static package to do this. However, it is safer to leave it inside its transparent packaging. That way, there will be less risk of scratching the motherboard or causing a static electrical discharge to it. You should be able to see through its transparent anti-static package well enough to align the screw holes and mark them on the chassis with a felt tip pen. However, if you prefer to take the motherboard out of its packaging, connect your anti-static wrist strap or put on your anti-static gloves first.

Leave the motherboard inside its anti-static bag and lay it on a flat surface. Find the set-off screws. They have exterior male threads on one end that screw into a case's chassis. On their other ends, they have interior female threads that serve as the attachment points for the motherboard's attachment screws later-on. These set-off screws should be included with the motherboard. Make sure that you use the set-off screws that come with your motherboard. If you use other ones, they might be too short and cause the motherboard to short-circuit to the case when the power is turned on. In some cases, the set-off screws might already be screwed into place by the manufacturer. On some other motherboards, plastic spacers that snap into place are used instead of set-off screws.

It is important to screw the set-off screws through the motherboard into the correct holes in the case's chassis. If you screw one into a wrong hole, it could create a short-circuit. So, double-check that the motherboard's screw holes align with the set-off screws you have inserted. You can do that by laying the motherboard on top of a piece of paper and using a pencil to mark the nine mounting holes on the paper.

Then line up the marks on the paper with the corresponding set-off screws and press the paper down until the screws puncture the paper. Every puncture hole should correspond with a pen or pencil mark. Also, check that the motherboard's external connectors align with the holes in the I/O faceplate.

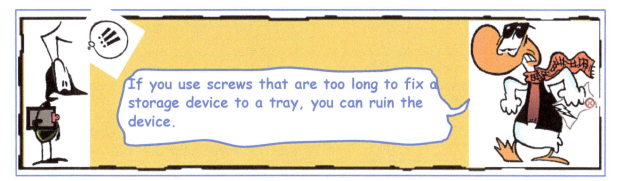

> If you use screws that are too long to fix a storage device to a tray, you can ruin the device.

Be careful when screwing-in the set-off screws. They might not seem to fit at first because paint often clogs the threads in case screw holes. Do not try to force the screws — particularly with an electric nut driver. You would then risk cross-threading them into their screw holes. There would be no simple way to repair that damage. It is better to take your time and gently work each screw back-and-forth, clockwise and then counterclockwise, by hand — making sure it is aligned with its hole — until it gradually and smoothly enters its hole. You could then finish screwing them in with your needle nose pliers — although it would be easier to use a 5 mm (0.2") nut driver. But do not over-tighten the set-off screws. The case's chassis SECC metal is thin. You could easily damage it if you use too much force. A screwed set-off screw is shown in Figure 5.1.6. All the screwed-in set-off screws in an ATX case are also shown in Figure 5.1.6.

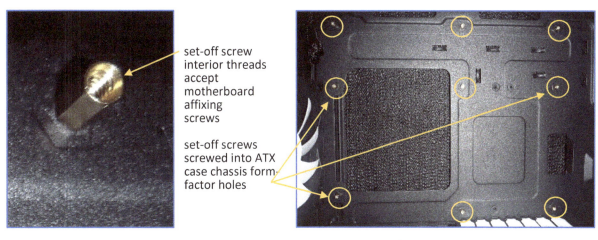

set-off screw interior threads accept motherboard affixing screws

set-off screws screwed into ATX case chassis form-factor holes

<u>Figure 5.1.6: Set-off Screws</u>

Some DIY computer-builders are concerned that the set-off screws will work loose if they move their computers around a lot. That is unlikely. Nevertheless, if you are concerned, you could use a product such as Loctite 222 to secure them in place. Such products stop screws from vibrating loose. But they have low breakaway torques so that screws can be manually removed if necessary.

Pick out the nine screws you will use later to affix the motherboard to the set-off screws. Test them in the set-off screws to make sure they have the correct thread type and are of the correct length. At this point, you could fix the motherboard to the case's chassis, but, as mentioned before, in these instructions we will leave that step until later.

If your case does not have factory-installed sound-deadening material, you can buy such materials from third-party suppliers. Those materials come in the form of mats with self-adhesive backings that you can stick onto your case's panels. An example is SilverStone's 4 mm (0.16") Silent Foam, which costs about $ 20. Some thicker types of acoustic matting are up to 20 mm (3/4") thick. Using such thick mats could cause you to run out of space, particularly if you intend using a small form-factor case or installing a large CPU-cooler.

In the previous edition of this book, I described how I fashioned a DIY noise-reducing system for my previous less-expensive Fractal case by sticking matting onto the insides of its side panels. That experiment made only a modest difference. A fan grill on the side of the case let some fan noise escape — even though noise-reducing material was installed.

Next, install any case fans that aren't already installed. Make certain that you don't install them backwards. If you do, the airflow in the case will not work correctly; the CPU will overheat, and the computer might shut itself off. You will likely see an arrow on top of a fan's shroud pointing in the direction that the air should flow.

If the shroud doesn't have an arrow, check which side of the fan the cable is attached to is. That is the backside of an inlet fan — the side the air is pushed out of. Also, the fan guard will be positioned on the front (i.e., inlet) side of the fan.

The Fractal R6 case provides numerous standard 120 mm fan attachment spaces at the rear, top, bottom and front of its chassis. With the project featured in this book, I decided to take advantage of those spaces to install a Noctua inlet fan at the bottom of the case next to the Sea Sonic fanless PSU as shown in Figure 5.1.7. I also installed an extra Noctua extraction fan at the top of the case above the CPU and RAM.

You might need to use self-tapping screws to attach some extra case fans. Self-tapping screws have sharp cutting ends that allow them to screw into tight pre-drilled holes. Noctua provides these self-tapping screws with its fans. An example is shown in Figure 5.1.7.

self-tapping screw with Noctua fan

bottom of case chassis

Noctua fan attachment self-tapping screw
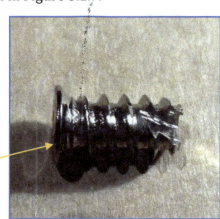

Figure 5.1.7: Attaching Fan to Case Chassis with Self-tapping Screw

You can connect case fans to their own power supplies via 4-pin Molex connectors directly from the PSU. However, it is preferable to connect case fans to the motherboard's power connectors rather than directly to the power supply unit. That will allow the UEFI-BIOS or the legacy-BIOS to report on the performance of the fans and permit you to control their speeds. Figure 3.5.2 shows the bank of both 3 and 4-pin fan connectors provided in the Fractal R6 case.

5.2: Installing the CPU

If you haven't already done so, put on your anti-static wrist strap and/or your anti-static gloves to prevent damaging the CPU or motherboard. Then take the CPU out of its box and verify that you have received the correct model. There are numerous CPU models; so there is a slight chance that an incorrect model might have been put into the box at the factory. In particular, check that the motherboard and CPU use the same socket interface.

Examine the CPU carefully. But, since it is a fragile component, handle it carefully. Hold it only by its edges — not by its top or bottom surfaces. Even if you merely touch the gold connectors on a CPU, the oil left from your finger will eventually damage its contacts. If it is an AMD CPU, check the pins on its underside as shown in Figure 5.2.1. Make sure that the pins are straight and undamaged, but do not touch them. If the CPU is an Intel LAG CPU, you will see that there are female pinholes on its bottom side instead of pins.

It is possible to straighten a bent pin on a CPU or a motherboard CPU socket using something like a plastic credit card — providing the pin hasn't been bent too badly. However, if you do try to straighten one, and you damage it, the supplier will not likely give you a refund. So, it is best not to attempt to straighten bent pins without prior authorization from the supplier. Otherwise, return the CPU or motherboard for repair or replacement. AMD doesn't repair broken CPU pins, but they should replace a CPU if it was shipped with a bent pin.

If you have an anti-static desk mat, lay the motherboard on it while you install the CPU, CPU-cooler, RAM, and M.2 SSD, if you are installing one. If you do not have an anti-static mat, you can cut the motherboard's anti-static bag along two sides and lay it with its outside facing down on the tabletop. You can then use it as a clean anti-static surface to lay the motherboard on.

As previously mentioned, installing the CPU, the CPU-cooler, M.2 SSD, and the RAM before mounting the motherboard in the case is the sequence recommended in this book. This method makes it easier to ensure that they have been properly secured. It also makes it less likely that you will damage the motherboard by accidentally bumping it with a component or screwdriver.

The terms 'heatsink' and 'cooler' are often loosely used to mean the same thing. However, they are different things. A heatsink is a block of aluminum or copper that is attached to a powered component. It has no moving parts and only passively draws heat from a component and radiates it elsewhere. Examples of passive heatsinks are shown in Figures 5.2.2 and 5.2.8. A cooler is a heatsink with moving parts, such as an air-fan or fluid-pump, that actively disperses heat from a powered component.

At one time, Intel soldered cooler heatsinks to their CPUs to maximize the heat transfer between them. However, these days, thermal pastes are used for that purpose with all CPU-coolers. These thermal pastes are often applied to cooler contact surfaces at their factories.

However, such factory-applied thermal pastes typically contain waxes and oils that melt when a heatsink warms up. Those liquefied materials then flow into the microscopic pits in heatsink contact surfaces and CPU contact surfaces. Those waxes and oils don't conduct heat well and are difficult to remove from pits. For that reason, it is best to remove most factory-applied thermal pastes. To do that, you must first remove the plastic sheet that likely covers the thermal paste. It is only used to protect the thermal paste before the cooler is installed. If a CPU's contact surface and its cooler's heatsink contact surface do not have thermal materials on them, cleaning them is not essential. Nevertheless, it is a useful precaution, especially if you happen to touch a CPU's contact surface or cooler's contact surface with your bare fingers.

You would also need to clean the old thermal paste off a CPU heatsink's contact surface if you replaced a CPU. You should also replace a cooler's thermal paste if it no longer keeps a CPU cool enough. It is easier to remove an old CPU-cooler if you run your computer for a while beforehand. That would warm the thermal paste and make it easier to detach the heatsink from the CPU.

Many people use isopropyl alcohol (i.e., acetone or rubbing alcohol) to clean CPU and heatsink contact surfaces. It works reasonably well; however, it leaves a residue on contact surfaces. Moreover, isopropyl alcohol fumes are dangerous to breathe. For those reasons, I don't recommend using isopropyl alcohol. I don't recommend using petroleum-based cleaners, such as WD-40, or automotive degreasers either. They contain oils that are engineered not to evaporate. Those oils would flood the microscopic pits in a CPU's and a heatsink's metal contact surfaces. That would reduce the effectiveness of any thermal compound applied on them.

It is preferable to use a specialized product, such as ArctiClean 1 Thermal Material Remover, to clean the contact surfaces. It dissolves any existing thermal grease from the contact surfaces (including their pits). You could use a clean tissue or cotton bud to apply the cleaning fluid as shown in Figures 5.2.1 and 5.2.2. The cleaning fluid and dissolved grease can then be removed with a cotton bud or tissue paper, as shown in Figure 5.2.2.

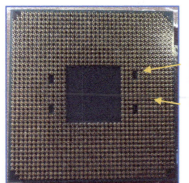

ArctiClean 1 fluid

pins arranged in pin-grid-array (PGA)

CPU bottom

cleaning CPU top contact surface

Figure 5.2.1: AMD Ryzen CPU

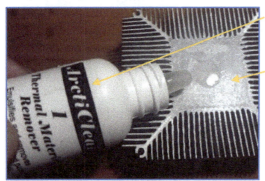

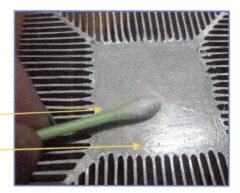

ArctiClean 1 Thermal Material Remover

heatsink

cotton bud

dissolved old paste

Figure 5.2.2: Removing Thermal Paste

To thoroughly remove thermal paste, clean it off the contact surfaces two or three times. It is even better to follow-up with a treatment of ArctiClean 2 Thermal Surface Purifier. It is formulated to remove remaining traces of citrus and petroleum-based oils. It also leaves a film that reduces the corrosion that would otherwise occur on the copper or aluminum contact surfaces of CPUs and heatsinks. That helps to preserve the metal-to-metal contact and the thermal transfer capacity of the interface.

Don't use materials such as tissue paper or cotton buds to finally wipe the contact surfaces. Such materials might leave lint or other particles. Instead, use a soft, clean cloth that doesn't leave any lint behind. The type of cloth used to clean eyeglasses is ideal, as shown in Figure 5.2.3. If you don't have an eyeglass cleaning cloth, you could use coffee filter paper instead. Then, let the surfaces dry for at least five minutes to evaporate any remaining ArctiClean cleaning fluid (or as much isopropyl alcohol as possible if you use isopropyl alcohol instead). If you need to clean thermal paste off pins or out of pinholes, you would need to use a delicate tool such as a plastic toothpick.

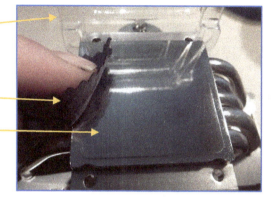

cooler protective cover

eyeglass cleaning cloth

wiping heatsink contact surface

Figure 5.2.3: Cleaning Contact Surfaces

Specific installation instructions will be provided with your CPU. But the following generic instructions might also help you with the process:

1. Unlatch the CPU's socket by pulling its lever up. Intel Haswell CPUs also have metal frames that must also be tilted open, whereas AMD CPU frames do not.

2. Remove the plastic cover that protects the motherboard's CPU socket. Save that socket cover. If you ever need to return the motherboard, the supplier might not accept it without its CPU socket cover in place.

3. Find the corner of the CPU with a gold triangle printed on it. Then, find the matching corner on the motherboard's socket. Align the two gold triangles, as shown in Figure 5.2.4. Some CPUs, such as Intel's Haswell CPUs, also have notches that must be aligned with protrusions on the motherboard's socket.

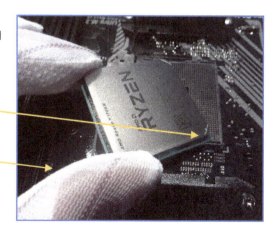

CPU attachment lever raised

pin holes on AMD motherboard CPU socket

CPU alignment gold arrows

anti-static glove

Figure 5.2.4: Installing AMD AM+ CPU

Before the mid-1990s, it was necessary to apply considerable pressure to secure some CPUs into their sockets. Motherboards were sometimes ruined by that operation when the pressure applied to them caused them to flex enough to crack their bus wires. Fortunately, modern CPUs require zero insertion force (ZIF). That means that they should simply drop into their sockets without any force being applied. You might only need to gently wiggle them slightly. If a CPU does not slip into place, remove and reseat it, making certain that the gold triangles are aligned.

4. When the CPU is inserted, lower the attachment lever back down to lock it into place, as shown in Figure 5.2.5.

5. If you are installing a third-party cooler, you may have to remove the affixed cooler brackets and install other brackets for the cooler, as shown in Figure 5.2.6.

lowering attachment cam to secure CPU in the socket

bracket

bracket screw

Figure 5.2.5: Securing CPU

Figure 5.2.6: Removing Cooler Brackets

Installing a Threadripper CPU requires some extra steps. You would need to use a Torx screwdriver to loosen three bracket screws. You would then need to put the CPU into a sled. Next, you would need to open the bracket and click the CPU, with its sled, into the bracket, as shown in Figure 5.2.7. You would then need to close the bracket containing the sled and CPU and fasten it with the Torx screws. Don't lose the Torx screws as they are difficult to replace. If necessary, you could try substituting a Philips head 6-32 T20 screw from a hardware store.

bracket

CPU sled

CPU

motherboard CPU socket

Torx screw

Photo from AMD video Article: *CPU-Install-TR*

Figure 5.2.7: Installing Threadripper CPU

After you install the CPU, you need to install its cooler. Never turn a computer on without a cooler properly mounted on its CPU. A high-powered CPU can be ruined in a few seconds without proper cooling. It is easier to install a CPU-cooler before a motherboard is installed in a case. However, it is best to install a liquid-cooler after you have connected all the case fans and installed the PSU, RAM, and expansion cards. Otherwise, the cooler's waterblock and tubes would likely to get in your way. Coolers are installed slightly differently on AMD and Intel CPUs. Nevertheless, they all are secured by CPU socket retention frames with some sort of latching mechanisms.

Aftermarket third-party CPU coolers of various sizes come with instructions for screwing their frames onto various motherboards. For example, Noctua has produced a customized version of their air-tower cooler to work with the AMD Threadripper/Epyc TR4/SP3 socket. The NH-U14S TR4-SP3 cooler matches the huge contact surfaces of Threadripper/Epyc CPUs. Its copper contact surface is more than double the size of the standard model's contact surface! It costs about $ 80. An example is shown in Figure 5.2.8. You might need to remove the socket retention screws holding the CPU socket retention frames to use most third-party coolers. See Figure 5.2.9. It is a good precaution to check that using an aftermarket third-party cooler, instead of one that might be boxed with a CPU, won't void a CPU's warranty.

third-party cooler frame

cooler frame screw hole in the motherboard

spring-loaded screws

70 X 56 mm contact surface

Figure 5.2.8: Noctua NH-U14S TR4-SP3 Cooler   **Figure 5.2.9: Attaching Cooler Frame**

Next, select a high-quality thermal paste. Using a high-quality thermal paste is especially important if you are installing a powerful CPU, and/or if you intend overclocking your system. The most highly-rated thermal compounds are Arctic MX-4, Arctic Silver 5, MasterGel Maker Nano, Noctua NT-H1, and Thermal Grizzly.

High-quality thermal pastes have high conductivity rates. Conductivity rates are measured in 'Watts per meter-Kelvin' (W/mK). That measurement specifies the rate of heat transfer between materials. The higher the W/mK value of a material, the faster it can transfer heat. The stock factory-applied thermal pastes on CPU heatsinks typically have conductivity rates of about 2.0 W/mK. High-quality thermal compounds have much higher conductivity rates. For example, the conductivity rate of MX-4 is about 8.5 W/mK. Correctly applying a high-quality thermal paste might reduce the working temperature of a CPU by 10 ° Celsius compared to its temperature if a poor-quality thermal compound is used that has not been carefully applied!

High-quality thermal pastes are not expensive. A 3.5-gram syringe of Arctic MX-4 thermal paste, which contains enough paste to cover about a dozen CPU contact surfaces, costs about $ 7. Noctua even supply their NT-H1 paste for free with their fans. Arctic MX-4 and NT-H1 paste dispensers are shown in Figure 5.2.10. I prefer Arctic MX-4 for three reasons.

1. Some other compounds, such as Arctic Silver 5, contain silver particles to maximize the heat transfer between CPUs and heatsinks. However, silver also conducts electricity. So, if any silver-containing compound leaks from between a CPU and its heatsink, it could create a short circuit to the motherboard. Two high-quality pastes that do not contain silver or other electricity-conducting particles are Arctic MX-4 and Noctua NT-H1.

2. The viscosity (i.e., thicknesses) of Arctic MX-4 paste is about the same as toothpaste. That is just right for easy application. On the other hand, some other pastes, such as Arctic Silver 5, are sometimes too thick to spread evenly. You could seal a paste dispenser containing paste that is too thick in a watertight bag and warm it to about 49 °C (120 ° Fahrenheit) to improve its viscosity, although even then it might not spread evenly.

3. The manufacturers of Arctic MX-4 assure users that it will last at least for at least eight years! That is longer than the typical lifespans of CPUs or GPUs. That means that the thermal paste would never have to be reapplied during the lifespans of those components.

drop about the size of a small pea

notice 8-year warranty

high-compounds

quality thermal applying thermal paste

Figure 5.2.10: Using High-quality Thermal Paste

The next step is optional. It involves tinting the contact surfaces of the CPU and the heatsink. The purpose of tinting is to thoroughly fill the microscopic pits on the contact surfaces with thermal paste. To tint a contact surface, squeeze a small drop of paste (about the size of a cooked grain of rice) onto the center of the surface as shown in Figure 5.2.10. Spread the compound and rub it thoroughly into the surface. But do not use a bare finger to do that. That would contaminate the material. Also, do not use a metal implement that might scratch the surface. Instead, you could use a stiff, clean, flexible piece of plastic with a flat surface, such as a credit card. Alternatively, you could use your finger covered with some clean plastic wrap.

When you are finished rubbing the compound, wipe it off the contact surfaces. You should then see a slight film of material remaining on the surface. Check to make sure that no contaminants, such as lint, are left on the contact surface. Then let the film of material dry for about five minutes.

Whether or not you tint the contact surfaces, you must next apply the thermal paste. Put a drop of thermal paste about the size of a large grain of cooked rice onto the middle of the CPU's contact surface. If you apply any more paste than that on most CPUs, it might be squeezed out onto your motherboard when you fastened the heatsink into place later on. That could eventually damage the motherboard. Larger processors, such as Intel's Extreme CPUs and AMD's Threadripper processors, require more thermal paste. Two drops of paste are advised for Extreme CPUs and three drops for Threadripper processors.

Many DIY computer builders spread the paste evenly around on the contact surfaces of their CPUs. If you do spread the paste before mating the surfaces, use a plastic-covered finger or a piece of soft plastic, as explained previously. Many other people don't spread the drops of thermal compound. Instead, they rely on the compression between the CPU and heatsink surfaces to spread the paste evenly in oval patterns. Indeed, that is the method recommended by the manufacturers of Arctic Silver 5 for use with Ryzen CPUs.

To most effectively use the non-manual spreading method, you must understand the heating characteristic of your CPU. Most of a CPU's heat is generated from its cores. The heat from these cores travels directly to the top of the CPU. It is, therefore, more important to ensure a good thermal contact directly above the cores than it is to have a CPU's contact surface evenly covered with compound from edge-to-edge. You can find out the best pattern for applying paste to your particular CPU at the Arctic Silver website at www.arcticsilver.com/intel_application_method.html#.

Gently place the cooler's heatsink squarely onto the CPU's contact surface. Try to align the heatsink correctly the first time. Otherwise, if you slide it around too much, you might spread the thermal paste unevenly. Then, gently twist the heatsink clockwise about 2 or 3 ° and then back counterclockwise about 2 or 3 °. That slight motion will spread the paste evenly and sufficiently.

Then, hook the heatsink's arms over the tabs on the CPU's socket frame. If you are installing a heatsink onto an Intel Haswell CPU, you will also need to insert four posts at each corner into their corresponding holes on the CPU frame and press down on the top of each post until it clicks. You then need to twist the top of the posts so that they lock into place. If you are installing an AMD heatsink, you only need to push down a single large lever (called a cam) until it is parallel with the top of the CPU, as shown in Figure 5.2.5. You have to apply firm pressure to lower the cam so that you can lock the frame over the heatsink. But, if you try to press the lever further than parallel with the top of the CPU, you could damage the motherboard or the heatsink's frame. The pressure on the heatsink will spread the thermal paste evenly.

Hook the two latches on the sides onto the motherboard's pegs. Usually, these are small square tabs sticking out on each side of the socket retention frame. It might be necessary to use your needle nose pliers or flat-headed screwdriver to push down the latch on the second side that you attach.

Connect the cooler's fan power-wire to the motherboard. Don't connect it directly to the PSU. Your motherboard's manual will show you where to connect it. The connector will also likely be labeled 'CPU Cooler' on the motherboard itself, as shown in Figure 5.2.11. You might find that the connectors on the cooler's fan power wire have a different number of pinholes than the number of pins on the header it connects to. That should not be a problem because female fan cable connectors can fit onto both 3 and 4-pin male connectors.

Originally, fans with three-pin connectors could also connect to 4-pin connectors, although they would continually run at full speeds. These days, however, most good-quality ATX motherboards provide both 3 and 4-pin power headers. The three-pin fan connectors support the ability to use ordinary variable voltage speed controls. The four-pin fan connectors support pulse-width modulation technology. Pulse-width modulation technology is a high-efficiency speed control technology that enables motherboards to control fan speeds by intermittingly sending variable current pulses to them.

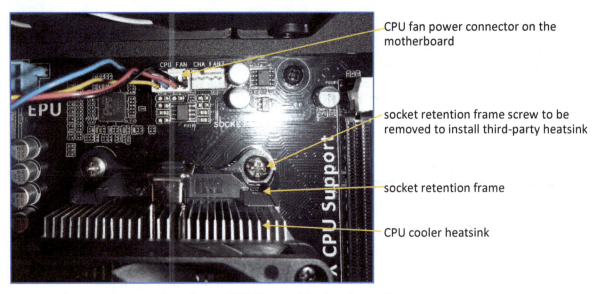

CPU fan power connector on the motherboard

socket retention frame screw to be removed to install third-party heatsink

socket retention frame

CPU cooler heatsink

Figure 5.2.11: Connection from CPU Fan to Motherboard

Liquid CPU-coolers usually come with mounting brackets for both Intel and AMD CPU sockets. The pumps on most liquid-cooler systems are connected to their radiators with factory-sealed tubes, which minimizes the possibility for leaks. Those pumps should be installed in positions that enable them to be gravity fed from the system's reservoir. The best configuration is to mount liquid-cooler radiators at the fronts of cases when installing graphic cards with their own fans and to mount radiators at the tops of their cases for graphic cards without fans. Each liquid-cooled component should have a 120 mm radiator space on the case.

Well-designed cases, such as the Fractal R6 case, offer a variety of spaces for liquid-cooler radiators to be mounted. Those options enable users to install liquid-coolers in positions that don't require excessive bending of tubes. Bending tubes in tight angles puts lateral pressures on tube joints. Those pressures might eventually cause liquid coolant to leak from tube seals onto a system's electronic components.

5.3: Installing the RAM Modules

It is easier to install RAM modules onto a motherboard before installing the motherboard into its case. However, new motherboards are usually packed within foam packing materials around their sides, as shown in Figure 5.3.1. If you press the RAM modules into their slots without first removing that packing foam, the motherboard will flex, which might break its bus wires. So, remove the packing foam and lay the motherboard on a flat, smooth anti-static surface. Then, installing RAM is a simple four-step procedure.

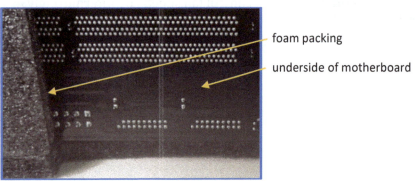

foam packing

underside of motherboard

Figure 5.3.1: Foam Motherboard Packing

1. Check that you have the correct number and type of RAM modules to install onto your motherboard. Then, touch a grounded metal object or use a grounded antistatic wrist strap to drain any electrostatic charge from your body. Also, put on your anti-static gloves if you have them. If you are replacing already installed modules, remove them by pressing down on the tabs at the ends of their sockets.

2. Select the RAM slots on your motherboard to install the modules into. Recall from Section 2.3 that motherboard RAM sockets are usually color-coded or labeled to show which ones should be populated together to work as channels. For example, matching sockets might be colored blue or labelled '0' or '1'. Check your motherboard's manual to confirm which sockets to populate.

3. Remove the first new RAM module from its packaging. Only handle it by its corners or by its heatsink cover. Never touch the exposed integrated circuit contacts (i.e., pins) on a module. If you touch the contacts on a RAM module, you will likely deposit oil and other contaminants from your fingers. That could lead to a contact failure in the future. If you accidentally touch the pins, you should clean them — just as you would clean a CPU's heatsink contact surfaces. Notice that one end of the module will have more pins than the other, and there will be a notch between the two sections of pins, as shown in Figure 3.3.2.

4. Line up the notch in the RAM module with the tab in the motherboard slot. That will ensure that you insert the module the correct way. Then press the RAM module into position. That might require a bit of pressure. But do not apply a great deal of force. As mentioned before, delicate bus wires are built into fiberglass motherboards. If the motherboard flexes — even a small amount — those bus wires can crack, which would ruin the motherboard. Excessive pressure could also damage the RAM slot.

If you rock a module by applying more pressure on one end and then the other, it will gradually slide into its slot. Indeed, the curved rows of pins on DDR 4 modules are designed to assist that rocking installation motion and reduce the physical stresses on the modules while they are being installed. A slot's retaining tab (i.e., clip) will snap into position when a module is fully inserted, and you should then hear the tab make a 'click' sound. Repeat steps 3 and 4 to install any other modules.

5.4: Installing the Motherboard

After the RAM is installed, you can install the motherboard into the case, if you aren't also installing an M.2 SSD. If you are installing an M.2 SSD, you will find instructions in Section 5.7.

Some people do not install their motherboards until after they have performed initial boot tests on them. The boot test is explained in Section 6, which is about powering up your system. Booting a motherboard before it is installed has the advantage of making it easier to replace the motherboard in the unlikely event that it is faulty. However, that is not the sequence outlined in the book for two main reasons.

1. It takes more time to do an initial boot test before the motherboard is installed. That is because, after completing an initial boot-up, it is necessary to disconnect the motherboard from the power supply, the boot secondary storage device, and the monitor. Then the motherboard must be installed in the case and reconnected to everything.

2. It is more dangerous for the motherboard, and possibly for the builder. Objects (including people) can accidentally contact electrically charged motherboards outside their cases.

Double-check that you have installed the In/Out faceplate correctly on the back of the case. Also, if the case came with an installed PSU, check whether you have to remove it, if you haven't already done so, to make room to insert the motherboard.

Modern motherboards do not have all the jumpers that had to be manually set to configure previous generations of motherboards. For example, in the past, it was necessary to use jumpers to set CPU voltages as well as bus speeds.

Nowadays, most system configuration is done within the UEFI-BIOS, and you may not have to set any jumpers. Nevertheless, check your motherboard's manual to find out if any jumpers do need to be set. For instance, some motherboards that use Intel CPUs might still have jumpers to allow the motherboards to be configured from the UEFI-BIOS. Also, some motherboards have jumpers for setting their real-time clocks. A real-time clock is an electrical clock within an integrated circuit that keeps track of the time.

A jumper is a connector with two pins that can be used to close an electrical circuit so that electricity can flow to a section of a circuit board. Jumpers are often used to configure hardware devices. When a jumper connects two pins, it is called a closed jumper. An example is shown in Figure 5.4.1. When a jumper is off or covers only one pin, it is called an open jumper. Before changing the jumpers on your motherboard (or any other device) switch off the mains power supply to the PSU.

It is a good idea to lay the computer case on its right-side with its open left-side facing up. In this position, you can use gravity to help position the motherboard. If your motherboard does not have an integrated faceplate, check that the motherboard's I/O ports align correctly with their respective I/O faceplate holes before you continue.

The motherboard needs to sit about 6 mm (1/4") away from the case's chassis so that it does not touch the case. That would create an electrical short-circuit. Separating the motherboard from the chassis is the function of the set-off screws that you inserted when you prepared the case. Position the motherboard on top of those set-off screws.

Sometimes, it is difficult to get the motherboard port and the I/O faceplate hole to line up perfectly so that the motherboard's mounting holes align with the set-off screws. That is usually caused by pressure from the I/O faceplate. In that event, you have to push the motherboard more firmly against the faceplate to position it correctly. Then, collect the nine screws that came with the case which fit into the set-off screws. Screw them firmly into the set-off screws to fix the motherboard in place. However, do not screw them too tightly. If you over-tighten these screws, you risk cracking the motherboard.

Also, be careful not to allow your screwdriver to slip onto the motherboard. That could ruin the motherboard. A good technique is to use one hand to keep the screwdriver aligned with the screw while the other hand turns the screwdriver, as shown in Figure 5.4.2. If you drop a screw inside the case, retrieve it immediately. If overlooked, a stray screw could cause a short-circuit later-on when the power is turned on.

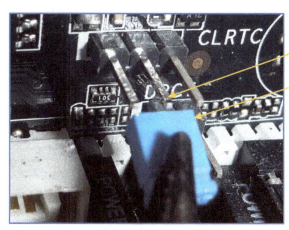

Figure 5.4.1: Closing a Jumper

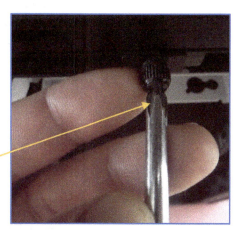

pins

jumper

Phillips head
screwdriver

Figure 5.4.2: Safe Screwdriver Technique

Now connect the wires that come from the front of the case. The small connectors on the ends of these wires have one or two pinholes that plug into the pin header on the motherboard. Those connectors are one of the few types of connectors in a computer that can be connected the wrong way. However, doing so will not cause any damage. It will just mean that a connection will not work until the connectors are correctly aligned. The thin wires connect the light-emitting diode (LED) lights and the switches from the front of the case to the motherboard. They will be labeled 'POWER LED', 'RESET SW', 'H.D.D LED', and so on. There will likely be matching labels on the motherboard's 8-pin header.

These connections differ somewhat from motherboard to motherboard, so check your motherboard's manual to see exactly how its wires should be connected. Your motherboard might also have a small internal speaker that plugs into the 8-pin header. If so, it will also be mentioned in your motherboard's manual. However, many motherboards do not have onboard speakers. In that event, systems must rely on internal speakers that are attached to cases instead. In either event, the UEFI-BIOS or legacy-BIOS uses an internal speaker to make the 'Beep' noises sent from the when a system starts up. You will need to refer to the motherboard's or the case's documentation to determine where your system's internal speaker is located.

The connectors on one pair of thin wires from the front of the case will have positive (+) and a negative (-) pinholes. See Figure 5.4.3. They should be connected to corresponding positive and negative pins on the motherboard's header. You will also find some thicker cables coming from the front of the case. They will have labels such as 'USB', or '1394'. Connect these cables to their respective ports on the motherboard with the corresponding labels, as shown in Figure 5.4.4. You can't confuse USB 2.0 and USB 3.0 cables because their connectors are different. USB 3.0 cable plugs also have tabs that need to be aligned with the notches on their corresponding motherboard sockets. You might also find cables with USB Type-C connectors on the latest motherboards.

You will also find a cable with two plugs on its end labeled 'AC'97' and 'HD AUDIO'. They are used to connect front panel headphone/microphone ports to the motherboard. The AC'97 connection is used with older systems that only support a single pair of stereo speakers. These types of speakers can be switched on and off through a standard switching stereo jack socket. The newer HD AUDIO connection shown in Figure 5.4.3 can support up to eight speakers (i.e., 7.1 audio).

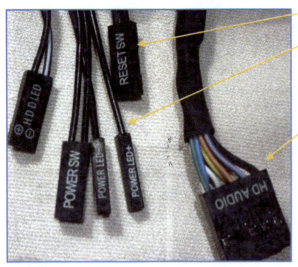

label on wires

negative and positive LED wires

HD AUDIO plugs

USB plug

Figure 5.4.3: USB Motherboard Connection

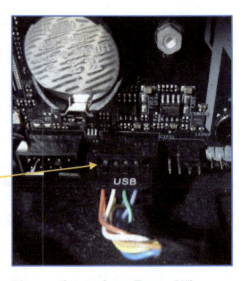

Figure 5.4.4: Case Front Wires

As you connect these various wires and cables, consider where best to route them. Cable management differs from case-to-case, and you will have to work out the best method for your particular case. If you have questions about organizing the cables in your PC, you could post them at Reddit's cable management forum at www.reddit.com/r/CableManagement.

5.5: Installing the Expansion Cards

There are a few types of expansion card slots that allow expansion circuit boards to be installed onto motherboards, although some of them are obsolete. You should be aware of the four most common expansion card interfaces in recent usage.

1. The Peripheral Component Interconnect (PCI) interface was introduced in 1992 and, until recently, was a commonly-used expansion card interface. It was used for modems, network cards, soundcards, and some older graphic cards. Standard 32-bit PCI, with a 33 MHz bus speed, supports a transfer rate of 266 MB/s. The PCI interface is still used on some expansion cards, such as soundcards, that do not require high bandwidths. However, some motherboard chipsets no longer support PCI.

2. The Accelerated Graphic Port (AGP) interface was introduced in 1997 and is a motherboard connector slot — not a port — notwithstanding its name. The term 'port' usually refers to a motherboard connector for an external device, such as a webcam, whereas 'slot' usually refers to an internal expansion card connector. AGP was used only with graphic cards and was a significant improvement over the PCI interface. The transfer rate of the latest version of AGP 3, is 2.1 GB/s. However, it is now considered a legacy interface, and since 2008 has almost entirely been superseded.

3. The Peripheral Component Interconnect Express (PCIe) interface was released in 2003 and is now used with most types of expansion cards. The abbreviations 'PCI-E' and 'PCIE' are often used instead of 'PCIe'. However, 'PCIe' is the official abbreviation used by the PCI Special Interest Group of companies. PCIe is used as an interface for graphic cards in particular because of its fast bandwidth. In the third edition of this book, I suggested that PCIe Version 4.0 X 16, which became available in 2017 and which supports a bandwidth of 31.5 GB/s, would soon be incorporated in motherboards and GPUs. However, when the fourth edition was produced in 2019, no motherboards or graphic cards had yet incorporated it.

When it is eventually incorporated into motherboards and GPUs, PCIe 4 will provide backward compatibility so that PCIe 1, 2, and 3 cards will be able to operate in PCIe 4 slots. Even though PCIe 4 has not yet been used in components, the PCI-SIG has already announced the specification for PCIe 5.0. Its bandwidth will likely be increased to 64 GB/s. The PCIe versions are summarized in Table 5.5.1.

Table 5.5.1: PCIe Versions

Versions	PCIe 1	PCIe 2	PCIe 3	PCIe 4	PCIe 5
Transfer Rate[1]	2.5 GT/s	5.0 GT/s	8.0 GT/s	16 GT/s	32 GT/s
Bandwidth[2]	4 GB/s	8 GB/s	16 GB/s	32 GB/s	64 GB/s

Notes: 1. 'Gigatransfers per second' (GT/s) is an informal measurement referring to the number of operations transferring digital data that occur per second via a data transfer channel. 1 GT/s means 10,000,000,000 transfers per second. 2. Total bandwidth on 16 lanes in each direction.

Of course, expansion cards, such as graphic cards, also have ports that allow them to connect to external peripheral devices such as monitors and speakers. So, you also need to be aware of the most common contemporary types of ports. Three of them: Digital Video Interface (DVI), VGA (video graphics array), and HDMI (High-Definition Multimedia Interface) are shown in Figure 5.5.1.

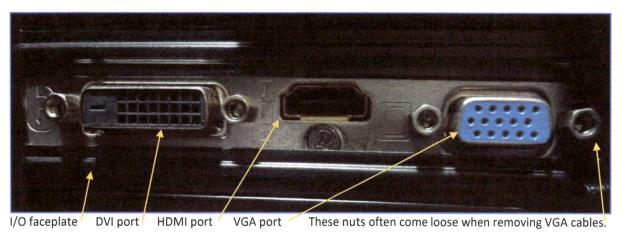

I/O faceplate   DVI port   HDMI port   VGA port   These nuts often come loose when removing VGA cables.

Figure 5.5.1: Common Contemporary Video Ports

More types of commonly used ports are listed in Table 5.8.1, and four of them are shown in Figure 5.8.2. The cable connectors on the four most commonly used of these ports are shown in Figure 5.5.2. It may be worth your while to learn something about three of those types of ports in particular. They are USB, FireWire, and Thunderbolt.

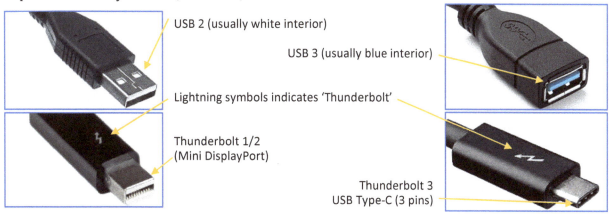

USB 2 (usually white interior)

USB 3 (usually blue interior)

Lightning symbols indicates 'Thunderbolt'

Thunderbolt 1/2 (Mini DisplayPort)

Thunderbolt 3 USB Type-C (3 pins)

Figure 5.5.2: External Port Connectors

1. Universal Serial Bus (USB) ports are used to connect most peripheral devices such as mice, printers, webcams, and joysticks to PCs. They are easy to use because all modern operating systems support USB. USB 1.0, with a data transfer speed (i.e., throughput) of 12 Mb/s, was released in 1996. USB 2.0, with a transfer speed of 480 Mb/s, was released in 2000. USB 3.0, with a transfer speed of 4 Gb/s, was released in 2008. USB 3.0 ports are usually internally colored blue and are backward compatible with USB 2.0 connectors.

The Certified USB Group released the latest USB standard, USB 3.1, in 2014. That standard supports a data rate of 10 Gb/s and is compatible with Thunderbolt. It uses the new USB Type-C physical connector shown in Figure 5.5.2, but it is also backward-compatible with USB 3.0 and USB 2.0.

2. FireWire (IEEE 1394) ports were popular in the mid-1990s. They were used with some high-end digital audio and video equipment and with soundcards and a few other types of cards. FireWire meets plug and play (PnP) standards. That means that when you connect a new FireWire device to a PC, the operating system will automatically detect it.

FireWire 6400 is the same thing as FireWire 1394a and supports a data transfer speed of 400 MB/s. FireWire 6800 is the same thing as FireWire 1394b and supports a transfer speed of 800 MB/s. Firewire speeds of up to 3,200 MB/s were eventually developed. Nevertheless, Intel withdrew support for FireWire in favor of USB 2.0, and the last FireWire-equipped Macs were produced in 2012. FireWire is now a legacy technology that is still only supported by Thunderbolt adapter cables and external hubs.

3. Thunderbolt 1 ports, with bus speeds of 8,000 MHz and transfer rates of 10 Gb/s using Mini DisplayPort connections, have been provided on some PC motherboards since 2002. The first was MSI's Z77A-GD80 motherboard. The Thunderbolt interface can transmit both electrical and optical signals and carry both data and audio-visual signals.

A newer version, Thunderbolt 2.0, with a bandwidth of 20 Gb/s, can support a transfer rate of up to 1,500 MB/s. It can support the 4K cinema-quality video standard with a fill rate of 15 gigapixels per second. Thunderbolt 1 and 2 ports are relatively expensive and have not been widely used, however, ASUS released a Thunderbolt 2.0 EX II Expansion Card, which costs about $ 170, in 2012.

The latest version of Thunderbolt ports is version 3. It accepts the new, less expensive, USB Type-C plug, which can support DisplayPort, USB 3.1, and PCIe transmissions. Thunderbolt 3 ports also double the bandwidth of Thunderbolt 2 ports to 40 Gb/s. For these reasons, it will likely become more popular than Thunderbolt 1 or 2.

Numerous other types of ports that are used with different connectors may be located on motherboards. In fact, about forty different types of ports and slots are used on personal computers. To try to make it easier to identify them, manufacturers have standardized the colors of some of them. Several of these ports and their respective colors are listed in Table 5.5.2.

Table 5.5.2: Common Motherboard Port Colors

Port Types	Colors
audio ports (jacks)	blue, green, black, orange; pink
optical S/PDIF audio out	orange
High-Definition Multimedia Interface (HDMI)	cream or black
Digital Visual Interface (DVI)	white
Thunderbolt 1 and 2 (Mini DisplayPort)	gray – with a lightning symbol
Ethernet LAN (local area network)	black
FireWire (IEEE 1394)[1]	gray
Musical Instrument Digital Interface (MIDI)	gold
PS/2 keyboard[1]	purple
PS/2 mouse[1]	green
SCSI (small computer systems interface)[1]	black
TOSLINK (Toshiba optical link)	black
TV video-out	black
USB 2.0	black
USB 3.0	mid blue
USB 3.1	teal blue
VGA (video graphics array)[1]	dark blue

Note: 1. This type of port is more-or-less regarded as a legacy standard these days.

To install a new expansion card:

1. Uninstall any drivers that might affect the new expansion card because problems often arise from driver conflicts. To do that: open Window's Device Manager; expand the Display Adapters section; right-click on the current display adapter and click 'Uninstall'. Then follow the prompts to remove the driver.

2. Turn the computer's PSU off, but leave it plugged into the mains socket. Ground yourself and/or put on your anti-static gloves.

3. Graphic cards work best in particular PCIe slots on most motherboards — usually the top slots. So, check your motherboard's manual to see if there is a preferred graphic card slot. Also, check that the card's interface type corresponds to the type of motherboard slot that it will be installed into. Then remove the card from its packaging.

4. If you are replacing on old card remove it from its slot. Most recent cards have tabs at the ends of their slots that must be pressed to release the cards. Then hold the new card by its edges and position it over the top of its intended motherboard slot. If the card has a fan on it, you will likely need to leave the adjacent motherboard PCIe slot empty to make room for the fan.

If you accidentally touch the card's pins or notice dirt or lint on them, clean them following the instructions provided earlier for cleaning CPU contact surfaces. Identify and remove the slot cover or covers that must be removed from the back of the case to expose the card's port.

5. Position the card over the top of the slot, as shown in Figure 5.5.3. You might then need to open a latch on the end of the slot. Then press the card down to lock it into place. You might need to use a slight rocking motion to ease the card into its slot.

slot cover

expansion card

PCIe connector pins

PCIe motherboard expansion card slot

Figure 5.5.3: Installing Expansion Card

6. Check that the card is fully inserted into its slot. Replace the screw that you removed from the slot cover to secure the card to the back of the case. But make sure the card is inserted completely before securing the slot cover screw. If the bracket holding the card does not sit flush with the case's chassis when you screw it into place, the card is not seated properly. If the graphics card is two panels wide, you will need to secure it with two screws — one for each slot.

Cover any empty slot openings at the back of your case with their slot covers to help contain fan noises and reduce the ingress of dust. Although screwing slot covers in place is the most common method of affixing slot covers, some case manufacturers provide slot covers with latches or other types of toolless attachment methods instead.

7. Connect a power supply cable to the card if it requires its own power supply. Usually, this requires using a cable with a 6-pin connector from the PSU. Making these connections might require a bit of force. It might take even more force to unplug them. It is best to carefully wiggle them gradually apart. Otherwise, you might break these plugs by pulling them too hard.

8. Integrated video cards are enabled by default. So, if you install a separate graphic card, you might need to disable the integrated GPU. To do that, find the Integrated Peripherals page in the UEFI-BIOS or legacy-BIOS. Then, disable the integrated video.

5.6: Installing the Power Supply Unit

Many experienced DIY-builders install their power supply units (PSUs) after they have prepared their cases, but before they install any other devices. That strategy makes the task a little easier because it provides more room to wrangle the unit's cables into positions. Others prefer to install their PSUs after they have installed all other components because they can then see where to route the cables to the various devices. However, all agree that it is best to install a PSU before installing a liquid-cooling system. Otherwise, the cooler's tubes and hardware would not leave enough room to position the power cables. In any case, before you begin to install the PSU, keep four points in mind:

1. Never try to repair a PSU. If you think its fuse needs to be replaced, take it to a technician. There are highly-charged capacitors inside PSUs. Capacitors are tiny containers that hold electricity. They can remain charged with dangerous levels of electricity for years after they have been disconnected from a mains power supply. PSUs use that stored electricity to temporarily top-up the mains supply if it drops too low.

2. Always turn off a power supply unit, using the switch at its back, before connecting a mains power cord to it.

3. Never plug a PSU into the mains power unless it is connected to a motherboard.

4. Always turn off the mains power to a PSU when you work inside a case.

Take the PSU out of its box. If it has a voltage switch, switch it to 120 V or 240 V depending on the mains voltage used in your country. If you are installing a PSU with modular cables, attach the correct cables to the PSU. It is much easier to attach the cables to a modular PSU before installing the PSU into the case. As you can see from Figure 5.6.1, it might even be impossible to connect cables to the unit after it is installed. Align the PSU with the large rectangular opening on the back of the case's chassis. That space for the PSU is at the bottom of most cases.

If the PSU has only one fan, mount the unit with the fan facing the back of the case. If the PSU has two fans, the second fan will probably be on its bottom. Avoid touching the motherboard with the PSU when positioning it so that you don't damage the motherboard. When you position the unit correctly, you will notice that four holes on its back line up with four corresponding screw holes in the case's chassis. The four matching screws should come either with the case or with the power supply unit. Use those screws to affix the PSU into its place, as shown in Figure 5.6.1.

The best method for affixing the screws is to screw them all in by hand only about halfway to start with. That ensures that they are all properly aligned before you tighten them up. Good-quality cases, such as the Fractal R6, also include small sliding brackets or rubber pads to help support the bottoms of their PSUs.

attachment screws

cables from inside the back of PSU

Figure 5.6.1: PSU Installation

Now, connect the PSU to the motherboard and the CPU. Use the two largest cables from the PSU to make those connections. Those two cables have been the standard connectors for supplying power to ATX motherboards and CPUs since 2004. One of these large cables will have a 20 or 24-pin plug, and the other will have a 4 or 8-pin plug. Plug them into the big 20 or 24-pin socket and the smaller 4 or 8-pin socket on the motherboard as shown in Figures 5.6.2. Make sure that you align their locking tabs with the corresponding catches. It might require a bit of force to push these plugs completely in. Push them in until you hear their locking tabs click.

locking tab on motherboard power cable plug

Figure 5.6.2: Motherboard PSU Connection

Plug the female connectors from any fans that have not already been connected to male motherboard fan pin connectors. A variety of Molex power cables and connectors are used to provide electricity to internal devices such as extra case fans and expansion cards. However, only the 8981-type with four pins, which was commonly used to power spinning hard drives and optical drives, is usually called a Molex connector. If your PSU does not have enough SATA power connectors for all your devices, you can use a Molex cable with a Molex/SATA adapter, as shown in Figure 3.7.1.

5.7: Installing Secondary Storage Devices

Most new secondary storage devices installed these days by DIY computer builders are SATA devices. For that reason, instructions for installing SATA devices are provided here. If you are a first-time computer builder, it is unlikely that you would choose to build a SCSI system. However, if you want to install a traditional SCSI system, instructions are provided in Appendix 4. It is even less likely that you would include old IDE (PATA) storage devices in a new system. Therefore, instructions for doing that, which were included in previous versions of this book, have been removed from this edition.

There are three methods for installing secondary storage devices. Usually, you must pull-out trays, put devices into their trays, screw the devices into their trays, and then slide the trays back into their bays. However, with other cases, you just slide the drives into their bays and then screw them in place. With still other cases, you don't use any screws. You just slide the devices into their bays, and they snap into place.

The most common method is using slide-out trays with screws. To install a SATA secondary storage device into that type of tray:

1. Select the tray you want to place the device into. It's a good idea to position the drive adjacent to a front case fan. That way, the device will gain maximum benefit from the fan's cooling effect. If you are installing multiple secondary storage devices, and your case has enough bays, it is a good idea to leave empty bays between the devices. It is even better to remove any unused trays or cages. That helps keep them cool and allows more airflow between them into the case.

2. Remove the device from its anti-static packaging and slide it into its tray. Spinning hard disk drives are fragile, so do not drop or shake them. The device's power and data connectors should face the interior of the case. If the drive is a 3.5-inch size, align the four screw holes on the device with the four screw holes on its tray. The screws will need to go through grommets on the tray before they enter the device. That is shown in Figure 5.7.1.

Until recently, cases typically did not come with enough trays for 2.5" devices such as SSDs. You can use tray-adaptors in such cases to secure devices to trays, as shown in Figure 5.7.2. However, these days, the trays in most cases have optional screw holes to fit 2.5" devices, as shown in Figure 5.7.3.

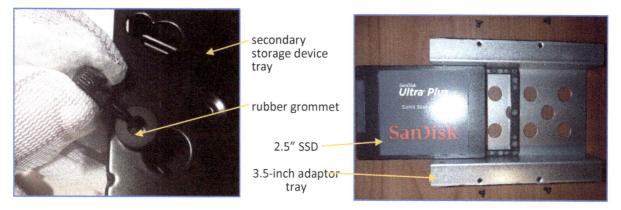

Figure 5.7.1: Storage Device Tray Screw   **Figure 5.7.2: SSD Device Tray Adaptor**

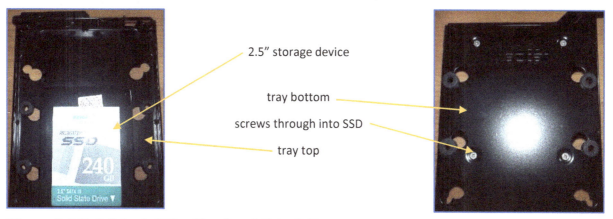

Figure 5.7.3: 2.5-inch SSD affixed to 3.5-inch Tray

3. Screw the device into the tray using the four screws that came with the device. Use those screws — not ones supplied with the motherboard. That is because the screws that come with the device might be shorter. If you use longer screws, you risk penetrating and destroying the device. Then, slide the tray back into its bay in the case.

4. Attach the SATA data cable to the storage device and the motherboard. The cable should come with either the motherboard or with the storage device, depending on whether you bought a boxed retail version, an OEM version, or a bare device.

SATA device data cables are narrow and don't have a standard color. However, they are most often colored black, red, or yellow. Even some glow-in-the-dark SATA cables are now available. The connectors on these cables are easy to install. They are L-shaped, have seven pins, and can only fit one way into device connectors. Since SATA devices have their own dedicated cables, there is usually no need to set any jumpers on them.

SATA Express data connectors are somewhat different from SATA 3.0 data connectors. The SATA Express interface is 1.6 times faster than PCIe 3.0's 12 Gb/s speed and supports a data transfer speed of 16 GB/s on 16 lanes. The two SATA 3.0 ports that form a SATA Express port can be used separately to plug-in two separate SATA 3.0 peripheral devices as shown in Figure 5.7.4.

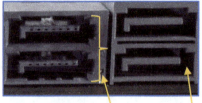

Align optical device front with front of the case.

Align screw holes in case with holes in device tray.

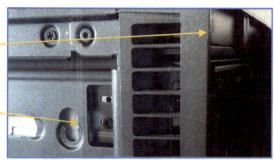

1 SATA Express port   2 SATA ports

Figure 5.7.4: SATA Ports   **Figure 5.7.5: Attaching Optical Device**

5. Next, find a power supply cable with a female connector that matches the SATA device's male connector. The female connector will be a wide, black, L-shaped plug with 15 pins. Plug it into the corresponding socket on the device. Modern UEFIs automatically detect secondary storage devices, so there is no need to configure them manually as there was with legacy-BIOSs.

To install an optical storage device, you must remove the case's front panel. To remove the front panel, you might first have to remove a bezel which surrounds it. The bezel may, in turn, be held in place by tabs that you need to push. Do not pry the panel or bezel too hard though. These days, cases are typically constructed of thin metal and brittle plastic that can easily bend or break. You will also need to remove the panels on both sides of the case so that you can screw-in the screws on both sides of the optical device's tray.

Then, notice the small panels on the front of your case that can be removed. These panels are usually located near the top of the case. Push out the panel covering the bay you want to install your optical drive into. It usually looks best to install optical drives into the top-most bays.

If your case has rails to accept optical drives, you will need to install the rails. You might also need the depth of the rails to match the size of the optical device. Remove the new device from its packaging. Then slide the optical device into its tray.

Check its positioning to make sure that the device will align with the front bezel when the device is installed, as shown in Figure 5.7.5. Then screw it into place. You can connect an optical device to a 4-pin Molex power supply cable. Next, attach the optical device to the motherboard using a SATA data cable the same way you attached the secondary storage device's data cable.

Some older systems have audio cables that link the optical drives to sound cards or motherboard audio connectors. Those cables were required because older optical drives used a direct connection between the drive and the audio adapter to transmit analog audio to the system. Newer optical drives support digital audio, which is communicated directly over the ATA connection to the bus.

CD/DVD drives are standardized these days; so, it is not necessary to install drivers for them. They should be recognized during the POST. The operating system should also automatically detect them when they are connected to USB ports, and the system is powered-up. However, you might need to install drivers for some BD or Ultra HD Blu-ray players. If the device comes with its driver on a CD/DVD, you will need to install the driver. The disc might also contain DVD playing and burning utilities. If the operating system does not recognize the device, turn the machine off and check its jumpers, if it has any, and check the cable connections before trying it again.

Older motherboards had 'CD_IN' connectors. However, by the late-1990s, most CD-ROM drives could transmit digital data directly through motherboard buses. If you still want to use an old IDE CD/DVD device, you would need to attach its data cable to either the system's audio card or to the motherboard. Alternatively, you could buy an adapter to connect an IDE device to a motherboard SATA connector. However, you could buy a new SATA optical device for about the same cost.

Modern optical devices have audio ports that can connect them to peripheral sound systems. These connections are usually made with TOSLINK fiber-optic cables and ports that can carry high-quality digital audio stream signals. Sony/Philips Digital Interconnect Format (S/PDIF) optical cables can also use those TOSLINK connectors. To install an optical cable to a peripheral sound system:

1. Turn the power off on both the optical device and the external sound system.

2. Remove the plastic caps from both ends of the optical cable.

3. Connect the cable to the optical device's Optical Out port. This port might be labeled 'Digital' or 'S/PDIF'. You can use either end of the cable because have the same connectors.

4. Insert the other end of the cable into the Optical In port on the external audio device. You can leave any other unused audio cables attached to the optical device if you want.

5. When you power-up the system later on, turn on the power to the optical device. If you are using an external sound system, turn it on as well. If necessary, configure the device and sound system as instructed in their manuals. Then test the optical device.

Unfortunately, Windows 10 does not include a free media player you could use to do that, although you can buy one from Microsoft. Alternatively, you could download a free player, such as the VLC media player. It supports many file formats including DVD, Blu-ray, and FLAC, as well as podcasts. It has also recently been updated to support Windows 10.

Installing an M.2 card is straight-forward. However, configuring it using a UFEI-BIOS might require more attention. It is easier to install an M.2 secondary storage device before you install the motherboard into your case. To install and configure an M.2 SSD:

1. Locate the M.2 connector on the motherboard. It should be labeled. It should also be identified in your motherboard's manual. An example is shown in Figure 5.7.6. If the M.2 drive slot is covered by a heat spreader, you will need to remove the heat spreader with a flat-head screwdriver. Then check that the motherboard M.2 space and the M.2 SSD are of the same physical form-factor and that the motherboard M.2 socket uses the same keying system as the SSD.

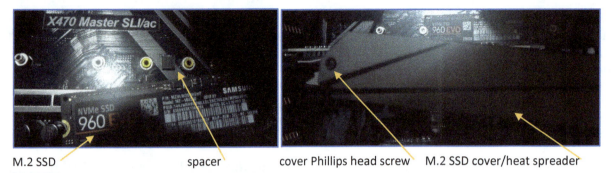

M.2 SSD   spacer   cover Phillips head screw   M.2 SSD cover/heat spreader

Figure 5.7.6: M.2 Motherboard Connector and Heatspreader

2. Remove the screw from the M.2 card's retention screw hole.

3. If the slot has a heat spreader/cover, peel the film off the cover before you screw it in place.

4. Handle the SSD only by the edges, just as you would handle a RAM module. Align the M.2 SSD's pins with the motherboard's socket and insert it. Motherboard M.2 connector slots are aligned parallel to the top of the motherboard. That is unlike other motherboard slots, such as PCIe slots, that are aligned at right-angles to the tops of their motherboards.

5. There will be a spacer on top of the screw hole. That spacer holds the card away from the motherboard's surface. It serves the same function as the stand-off screws used to separate motherboards from their cases' chassis. The M.2 slot will likely be covered by an expansion card if you install one later. For that reason, make certain that you have installed the M.2 device correctly before proceeding. You will need to apply slight pressure to hold the device down. Use the screw removed in step 2 to secure the M.2 SSD.

6. When you power up your system later on, you might find that an M.2 card will not be automatically recognized by the UEFI-BIOS. In that case, you will need to set it up in the UEFI-BIOS manually. To do that:
    6.1. Reboot the computer and rapidly press the UEFI-BIOS access key, usually 'F2'.
    6.1. Go to the Advanced section of the UEFI-BIOS.
    6.2. Select the Onboard devices or Storage Configuration tab.
    6.3. Select the PCI Express Bandwidth option.
    6.4. Select the M.2 mode.

When you have installed the secondary storage devices, you will likely be finished making connections inside the case. You can then use zip-ties to bundle and tidy the various cables. The best approach is to secure the CPU and motherboard power cables first. Next, secure the power and cables to the secondary storage devices. Finally, secure the fan cables and other smaller cables.

Make sure that none of the cables or wires are tightly twisted or bent. Also, make sure they don't obstruct the airflow, interfere with fans, or touch any circuitry on the motherboard or expansion cards. If your case provides space under its right-side panel, use that space for routing most of the cables. For example, a Fractal R6 case, in which most of the cables have been routed through the ample space provided on its right side, is shown in Figure 5.7.7.

Figure 5.7.7: Right-side Case Cable Space

5.8: Connecting External Peripheral Devices

Lastly, you need to connect the basic essential external peripheral devices. In most cases, this will involve connecting a monitor, a keyboard, a mouse, and possibly a microphone and speakers.

First, connect the monitor cable to the video port on the back of the computer. If your motherboard has integrated onboard video, this port will be located on the motherboard's I/O faceplate on the back of the case. This faceplate is shown in Figure 5.5.1. However, if you installed a separate GPU, the monitor port will be on the card's interface located lower down the back of the case.

If you are going to disconnect and reconnect a VGA monitor cable often, it might be worthwhile using a product such as Loctite 222 to secure its set-off screws to the card. Otherwise, these set-off screws are likely to unscrew whenever you unscrew the screws that attach their cables.

A symbol is provided beside each jack port on the fronts of cases that shows its purpose. Jacks on the backs of cases are usually color-coded and labeled on the I/O faceplates. Green jacks are for connecting speakers. Pink jacks are for connecting microphones. Blue jacks are for connecting CD players or cassette tapes. These jacks are shown in Figure 5.8.1.

If you want to use an old device, such as a camcorder, that uses a FireWire port, you will have to use a 1394 port, as shown in Figure 5.8.1. If you want to use high-quality audio devices, you will likely need to connect them to a Sony/Philips Digital InterFace (S/PDIF). This audio connection is typically used in high-fidelity home theatre systems. It is available with two types of cables, coaxial cables, and optical cables — but it only works over short distances with either type of cable. As mentioned in the previous section, the optical cable is usually labeled 'Toslink' or 'S/PDIF IN' and is colored gray or black. The coaxial connector is usually colored orange and might be labeled 'Coaxial' or 'Digital In'. Examples are shown in Figure 5.8.1.

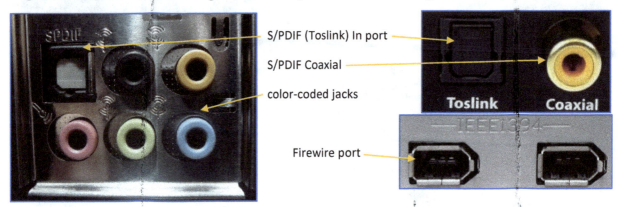

Figure 5.8.1: External Jacks and Ports

Mice and keyboards only require small bandwidths. It is therefore a good idea to plug them into slower USB 2 ports. Reserve any USB 3 or USB 3.1 ports for devices such as flash drives that can make better use of their greater bandwidths.

Tran asked the Buddhist monk, 'Where do the characters go when I delete them on my PC?' The monk replied, 'If a character has lived rightly, and its karma is good, it will be reincarnated as a different, higher character. Those funny characters above the numbers on your keyboard will become numbers, numbers will become letters, and lower-case letters will become upper-case letters'.

6. Powering-up

Starting a computer seems like a simple action, but it actually is a complex process. To understand this process, you need to understand the functions of whichever basic input/output system (BIOS) is used. In particular, you need to understand how the BIOS runs the Power On Self Test (POST) and loads the OS.

It is not essential to learn about this procedure. You might be satisfied to simply know that when a computer is turned on, the CPU reads some instructions. It then carries out those instructions to load the operating system. In case you do want to learn how a computer starts, the following explanation consisting of ten steps is provided.

1. Before the on/off button is pressed, the motherboard circuitry that monitors the power button receives a steady supply of +5-volt DC (direct current) power from the PSU. That current enables the motherboard to begin what is called a 'cold boot' when its power button is pressed.

2. During a cold boot, when the case's power button is pressed, a green wire on the motherboard is momentarily shorted. That signals the power supply unit to start, and its fan begins spinning. At this stage, the CPU is prevented from initializing by a timer chip which continually resets it. It contains an oscillator that produces a constant electrical wave as well as a timer that pulses at precise intervals. Initialization is the process of making a component or device ready for operation. For example, a keyboard must be initialized to make it ready to accept keystrokes. For another example, initializing a secondary storage device involves starting its driver. The timer chip prevents the system from running under unstable power conditions. A timer chip is shown in Figure 6.1

As soon as the PSU starts, it checks that it can produce adequate, stable voltages for the motherboard and CPU. If so, it sends a +5 volt 'power good' signal to the motherboard through a grey ATX 'Power Good Line'. In that case, the motherboard then signals the PSU to start sending various voltages to itself and the CPU.

3. The motherboard then initializes the firmware on its chipset. Firmware is non-volatile instructions or data that are pre-programmed onto read-only memory (ROM) locations, such as ROM chips. After 1975, when the modern system for starting computers was introduced, the powering-up firmware was stored on BIOS chips.

The BIOS remained basically the same for the next thirty years. By that time, its outdated technical limitations could not support many modern computer features. For example, it is only a 16-bit system, which can only access up to 1 MB of memory. For that reason, in 2005, Intel produced a new advanced 64-bit-capable input/output interface system, called the Extensible Firmware Interface (EFI). It was adopted as the IT industry standard instead of the old BIOS and was renamed the Unified Extensible Firmware Interface (UEFI). UEFI is pronounced in various ways, but 'you-fee' is the easiest pronunciation.

A major difference between the UEFI and the old BIOS is that the UEFI is not only stored as a piece of firmware on a ROM chip, as the old BIOS is. The UEFI also includes a programmable software interface between users and their systems. That interface is stored on secondary storage devices, just as any other software program is. The UEFI stores its system-initialization information on secondary storage devices in .efi files. Those files are stored within EFI system partitions (ESPs) located on the second sector of the boot device.

However, UEFI systems also must access their own ROM BIOS chips to start their computers. These firmware chips are called 'UEFI-BIOS' ROM chips in this book to distinguish them from old legacy-BIOS ROM chips. Because the UEFI is software that works in tandem with ROM firmware, you could think of it as a hybrid software/ROM firmware system. Most motherboards built since 2009 have UEFI-BIOS chips installed on them, and all new motherboards since late-2012 have UEFI-BIOSs. Windows 8 or 10 OSs boot using UEFI by default.

Both UEFI-BIOS and legacy-BIOS ROM chips may be soldered onto motherboards. In that case, if they become faulty, they cannot be replaced, and entire motherboards must be replaced. Alternatively, motherboards may have removable UEFI-BIOS or legacy-BIOS ROM chips that are secured in their sockets by spring leaves. That type of ROM chip can be removed and replaced if necessary. A UEFI BIOS chip is shown in Figure 6.1.

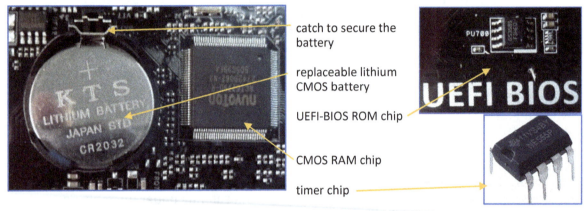

catch to secure the battery

replaceable lithium CMOS battery

UEFI-BIOS ROM chip

CMOS RAM chip

timer chip

Figure 6.1: UEFI-BIOS Chip, Motherboard Battery, CMOS Chip, and Timer Chip

4. When the motherboard receives a 'power good' signal from the PSU (in step 2) it signals the timer chip to stop resetting the CPU. That allows the motherboard to start initializing the CPU. If more than one CPU is installed on a motherboard, or if a single CPU has multiple CPU cores, only one CPU core is chosen to run the bootstrap process.

If the CPU cannot be initialized, the system will remain dead, although the case fans should spin. If the motherboard can start initializing the CPU, it will load default values into the CPU's registers. Recall that a register is a tiny storage place on a CPU that holds instructions or data, which the CPU can quickly access.

The motherboard will then set the CPU's instruction pointer to the address of the input/output system. The motherboard can send this address to the CPU because it stores it in a memory map within its chipset (which it initialized in step 3). An instruction pointer is a command telling a CPU where to look for its next instruction.

5. The CPU follows the instruction pointer and starts reading the BIOS's instructions. This reading process was traditionally called 'bootstrapping'. In the case of a UEFI, it loads its UEFI boot program into memory and executes it. The UEFI boot process then continues the same as the legacy-BIOS system does.

6. The initialized BIOS copies the contents of the CPU's register containing the instructions for starting the computer, as well as any required drivers, into a protected area of the RAM, where it can be accessed by the CPU.

The first instruction tells the CPU to run the initial POST routines. The POST resides on the UEFI-BIOS or legacy-BIOS ROM chip. The POST first checks for the presence of the essential hardware it will need:
- a motherboard bus and battery,
- a CPU (which the motherboard has already started initializing in step 4),
- a sufficient amount of RAM,
- a secondary storage device,
- a monitor and GPU, and
- a complementary metal-oxide-semiconductor (CMOS) RAM chip.

7. The UEFI-BIOS or the legacy-BIOS then reads some essential information from the CMOS RAM chip into its memory. The CMOS contains a tiny amount of RAM (either 64 or 128 bytes) where it holds essential data, such as:
- the time and date,
- security passwords for accessing the computer, and
- the boot sequence, that is, the order of secondary storage devices where the UEFI-BIOS or legacy-BIOS must look for the operating system.

The CMOS is RAM; so, it is volatile. That means that its memory is not saved if its power supply is turned off. It overcomes this problem by never allowing its power to be turned off. It draws a continual power supply from a lithium battery located on the motherboard (or sometimes within the CMOS chip itself). That is why, if you replace a motherboard, you must reset the data in the CMOS. That is also why you can reset a BIOS by removing the CMOS battery and then re-attach it to the motherboard. A UEFI-BIOS ROM chip, system battery, and CMOS chip are shown in Figure 6.1.

8. Recall from Section 3 that to boot a BIOS needs data about the size, data width, speed, and voltage of the system's RAM modules. The BIOS uses that data to configure the RAM so that the system can access it. This data is called the 'serial presence detect' (SPD) data. It is stored on tiny electrically erasable programmable read-only memory (EEPROM) chips that are located on RAM modules.

If the POST runs into any problems at this stage, it can only use beep codes to indicate them because a monitor has not yet been made operational. However, if the POST finds that all essential devices, including the CPU, RAM, and motherboard's bus are operational, it ensures that they are completely initialized. It then passes control to the GPU, which initializes its own video BIOS. The GPU then returns control to the legacy-BIOS or the UEFI-BIOS.

The BIOS then displays the OS's logo on the monitor's screen. After this point, any POST failures can be shown by error messages on the monitor's screen. In any event, the results of the preliminary POST checks are displayed on the UEFI-BIOS' or legacy-BIOS' start-up screen.

In the event of a warm boot, the UEFI-BIOS or the legacy-BIOS will skip the remaining POST routines. A warm boot involves restarting a computer using only the operating system — not by turning the motherboard's power on. In case of a cold boot, the POST will continue to run its remaining routines. Those routines manage the settings for the secondary storage devices and the system clock. They also enable the OS to interface with installed hardware devices, such as the keyboard.

9. After the POST has successfully initialized the essential system hardware and the CMOS data has been copied, the UEFI-BIOS or the legacy-BIOS starts searching for an operating system. It does that by looking for the bootable device, which is usually a spinning hard drive or SSD. If the UEFI-BIOS or the legacy-BIOS doesn't detect a functional boot device, it will halt the boot process and display an error message such as, 'Non-System Disk'.

Spinning hard drives store data on physical discs that must be organized into partitions. A partition is a fixed-size section of a disk that can be recognized by an operating system. Tables containing data about the locations of these partitions called 'partition tables' must be maintained so that operating systems can locate various partitions. SSDs are memory chips — not physical disks; therefore, they don't need to be partitioned (although they can be).

There are two types of partition tables. The Master Boot Record (MBR) type of partition table was first used with the IBM PC DOS 2.0 OS in 1983. It places boot sectors that contain boot loaders at the beginnings of spinning hard discs. Boot loaders provide information about where partitions start and end so that operating systems can locate them. MBRs also contain the bootstrap code. To differentiate the UEFI file allocation table (FAT) file partition system from the traditional FAT system, a new type of partition system file type was invented. That new table system was called a GUID Partition Table (GPT). The GPT is used by the UEFI to store the same information that an MBR does.

When you install a new spinning hard disk on a Windows 10 system, users are asked if they want to configure it as an MBR partition table or as a GPT. Only 64-bit versions of Windows can boot from a GPT, and they can only do that on systems running under a UEFI-BIOS. Linux distributions have built-in support for GPTs and Apple OSs also use GPTs nowadays.

The surfaces of spinning hard drives, floppy disks, and some other types of storage medium are organized into specifically-sized divisions that can store fixed amounts of data. These divisions are called 'sectors'. A sector is the smallest logical unit that can be accessed on a spinning hard drive. The sectors on spinning hard disks are often formatted by default to 512 bytes. When a BIOS locates a boot disk on a spinning hard drive, it looks at its first sector. This sector contains the master boot record. The surfaces of SSDs are divided into blocks called 'frames' that can be addressed using their logical block addresses.

10. If a partition table is corrupted, a BIOS will display a message such as 'Invalid partition table'. Otherwise, if nothing is wrong with the partition table, a legacy-BIOS or UEFI will start the bootstrap sequence by reading the bootloader code, which is contained in the MBR or GPT, into memory and passing control to the OS's boot loader. The bootstrap code contains a small set of instructions that starts the process of loading the operating system. If a problem occurs with the loading the of OS, the BIOS will display a message such as 'Error loading operating system' or 'Missing operating system'.

The most recent versions of Windows use a bootloader called 'Bootmgr' to read the boot configuration data and to display the operating system selection menu. As soon as the Bootmgr bootloader in a Windows system takes control, it loads essential file system drivers and looks for an operating system. When it finds an OS, it loads the OS's kernel and gives control to the kernel, which displays its logo on the monitor. A kernel is a central part of an operating system that boots directly after the BIOS and loads itself into a protected area of RAM so that it can't be overwritten. The main function of kernels is to allow hardware components to receive instructions. UNIX-like systems and Linux distributions, such as Ubuntu, use the Grand Unified Bootloader (GRUB) instead to do the same thing. At this point, the entire system, including the CPU, is ready to operate under the control of the OS.

When a UEFI system starts to operate, it can start other applications depending on how it was configured. That means that a UEFI can load and run programs stored on secondary storage devices that provide extra functions. For example, it could run a program to provide more detailed system information, or it could run extra hardware diagnostic utilities.

Some people do not distinguish between the UEFI and the legacy-BIOS. They refer to them both as 'BIOSs'. There are probably two reasons for that. Firstly, many older computer users are only familiar with the 'BIOS' acronym. So, they still habitually use it to refer to all the functions that the legacy-BIOS undertook. Secondly, some UEFI implementations look like legacy-BIOS interfaces. Even some UEFIs that don't look like legacy-BIOSs by default have optional legacy-BIOS compatibility modes. A UEFI with a legacy-BIOS interface may cause some people to assume that the UEFI is the same thing as a legacy-BIOS.

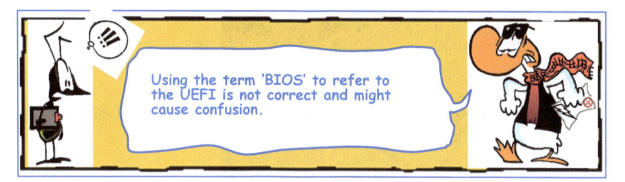

However, the UEFI is a more complex and powerful system than the legacy-BIOS. Indeed, it is so radical that no operating system yet takes full advantage of all its potential. Linux distributions support the UEFI, and some Linux distributions, such as Ubuntu, take advantage of several of its features, including its secure boot feature. However, Windows 10 makes more use of the UEFI than any other operating system at present. Six important advantages that the UEFI has over the legacy-BIOS are:

1. As previously mentioned, the legacy-BIOS is limited to 16-bit processes and can only address 1 MB of memory. However, the UEFI can function in 32-bit as well as 64-bit modes. It can also address all the memory installed in a system — as well as its own small disk storage space. This small storage space can be in a reserved area of onboard flash storage or on the EFI system partition on a spinning hard disk or SSD. Moreover, the UEFI can take advantage of multi-core processors, whereas the legacy-BIOS cannot.

2. The legacy-BIOS' MBR is limited to 4 partitions per disk, and the MBR disk size is limited to 2.2 TB. However, the UEFI's GUID partition table can access at least 128 partitions and access hard disks as large as 9.4 ZB (zettabytes). The UEFI can work with GPT-formatted disks as well as with UEFI File Allocation Table (FAT) 32 partitions.

3. The legacy-BIOS does not have UEFI's Secure Boot security feature. Secure Boot works by requiring digital signatures from boot loaders. That feature allows only authentic drivers and services to load when a computer boots. That prevents some malware programs from being loaded when a computer starts up. Some Linux distributions, such as Ubuntu, support secure booting. However, if you are building a UNIX-based system, make certain that the UEFI-BIOS on the motherboard you choose has a Linux boot loader.

4. The GPT stores cyclic redundancy check (CRC) values. It uses those values to detect corrupted data and to recover uncorrupted copies of data from backup locations.

5. UEFI systems boot faster than legacy-BIOS systems. This is because the UEFI can take advantage of modern hardware features such as multi-threading, fast SSD speeds, and Window's Hybrid Boot Technology. Hybrid Boot Technology suspends an OS's kernel in hibernation and stores data about the current state of a system and memory in a file.

When a system is cold-botted, the kernel's session is restored from the hibernation file, which reduces the system startup time. Hybrid Boot Technology works with both spinning hard drives and SSDs. The hardware initialization processes are also quicker with the UEFI.

6. The UEFI supports a graphical interface and mice, but the legacy-BIOS does not. A graphical UEFI interface is shown in Figure 6.2.

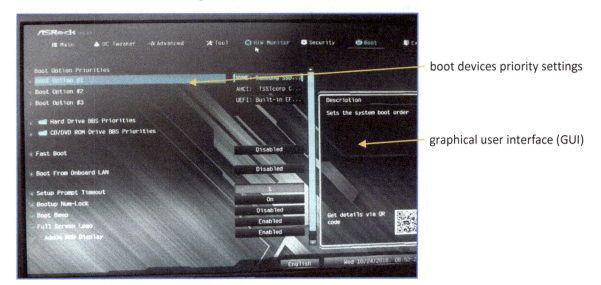

boot devices priority settings

graphical user interface (GUI)

Figure 6.2: UEFI-BIOS Settings

Flashing was sometimes necessary to update legacy-BIOS flash memories to make them compatible with newer versions of operating systems. Flash memory is a type of non-volatile memory used on chips that remains intact when the power is turned off. The code stored in the flash memory of legacy-BIOS ROM chips had to be updated by using special flashing programs provided by the chips' manufacturers.

Because the UEFI is firmware that is stored on a secondary storage device, it does not need to be updated by flashing. Instead, it can be updated by simply downloading updates from its manufacturer's website. Firmware is software that controls hardware devices. It is installed on a ROM memory chip or a secondary storage device. You can check for available system firmware updates using the UEFI Firmware Update Platform within recent versions of Windows.

Nevertheless, a UEFI-BIOS chip can also be updated by flashing it — just as a legacy-BIOS can be flashed. A detailed set of instructions for flashing a UEFI-BIOS has been posted by the MSI NB FAE Team at Micro-Star International at www.msi.com/files/pdf/win8_UEFI_BIOS_Update_auto_en.pdf. But you should only attempt to flash a UEFI-BIOS if it is necessary because your system has become unstable — and if you have sufficient technical knowledge. Flashing a UEFI-BIOS chip's memory requires that all its data is erased. That can result in an unbootable computer if the chip is not then successfully flashed.

As mentioned before, some computer-builders undertake two power-up boot tests. They first undertake a partial boot test before installing their motherboards into their cases. Those partial boot tests only check four conditions:
1. whether the power supply is working correctly,
2. whether the motherboard contains a UEFI-BIOS or a legacy-BIOS chip, as well as a CMOS chip,
3. whether the CPU is functional, and
4. whether at least one functioning RAM module is installed.

As also previously explained, the procedure recommended in this book is to finish building your entire system before running a full boot test. The additional elements that are necessary for a full UEFI-BIOS or legacy-BIOS boot test to succeed are:
- a functional keyboard and mouse,
- a monitor connected to a video-out port with a correct cable, and
- an integrated video card, or an installed graphic expansion card.

Keep the left side panel of the case off when you cold boot your computer the first time. That will make it easier for you to:
- check that all the fans are functioning properly,
- check the motherboard LEDs to assess which elements are working, and
- troubleshoot, if necessary.

To power-up your computer:

1. Make sure that the CPU's cooler fan is connected properly to the motherboard. Otherwise, you risk overheating and damaging the CPU.

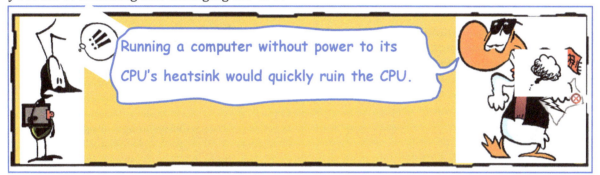

2. If the PSU has a manual switch, check, once again, that it is set correctly to either 110 or 220 volts depending on the mains voltage used in your country. Although, these days, most units have no such switches. They either only work with the mains voltages of the countries in which they are sold, or they automatically switch themselves to the correct voltage.

3. Plug the PSU's cable into the mains power supply socket. As explained previously, it is also a good practice to plug it into a surge protector. It would be a pity for a power surge to destroy your new motherboard with before it ever started. If the green LED Protected light on a surge protector fails to turn on, it is no longer functional and should be replaced.

4. Check that the keyboard, mouse, and monitor are connected properly.

5. Turn the PSU switch on. If the computer briefly seems to come to life when you turn on the PSU switch but then shuts down, don't be alarmed. That is a normal temporary process when a PSU sends power to a motherboard, but the motherboard doesn't then immediately instruct it to continue.

6. Turn the monitor on.

7. Press the power On/Off button on the front of the computer case. The system should then start. Nevertheless, listen for the UEFI-BIOS's or the legacy-BIOS' startup 'Beep'. A single beep from most systems indicates that the POST is complete. In other words, it signals that 'The essential components and connections are functioning correctly, and the UEFI-BIOS or the legacy-BIOS is ready'. The UEFI-BIOS or the legacy-BIOS will then continue to run a full boot test.

If the system doesn't start and you don't hear any beep, it's probably because the power connection to the computer's speaker is faulty, or because the motherboard's power supply connection is not secure.

If you don't hear a single beep, but a series of beeps instead, it is probably a signal that the UEFI-BIOS or legacy-BIOS found a fatal error. A fatal error is a condition, usually caused by a faulty hardware component, that halts the boot process. A computer cannot usually recover from a fatal error until the faulty component is fixed or replaced. A RAM module that is faulty or not seated properly in its slot is a common cause of fatal POST errors.

As mentioned before, UEFI-BIOSs and legacy-BIOSs may also display error messages on monitors. Usually, you must check your motherboard's manual to interpret the beep codes or monitor error messages from your computer's UEFI-BIOS or legacy-BIOS. However, generic diagnostic message decoding cards are also available. For example, BIOSMAN produces a debugging P.O.S.T. card that can display and describe all AMI, Award, and Phoenix BIOS POST codes. It also has four LEDs that show if a motherboard is receiving correct supplies of various voltages from its PSU. It connects to motherboards via their PCI slots.

If you intend to work frequently with computers, buying such a diagnostic decoding card might be a worthwhile investment. Examples of two basic decoding models, which cost less than $ 10.00, are shown in Figure 6.3.

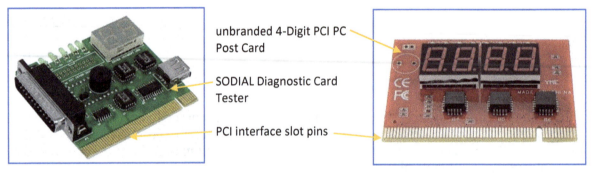

unbranded 4-Digit PCI PC Post Card

SODIAL Diagnostic Card Tester

PCI interface slot pins

Figure 6.3: BIOS Message Decoding Cards

When the POST is completed, three to six other things should happen:

1. The case fans should start spinning.

2. The fans on any expansion cards that have them should start spinning.

3. The CPU cooler's fans should start spinning.

4. Any installed spinning hard disks should start spinning.

5. LEDs should light up on the front of the case.

6. The motherboard's Power On LED should light up. This LED is often located next to the power sockets on motherboards, although Power On LEDs have recently been used as feature lights anywhere on motherboards.

If none of these responses occur, it is likely that the case's power On/Off button has not been connected. In that event, you can press the direct key button on the motherboard, if it has one, to turn the computer on and directly access the UEFI-BIOS or the legacy-BIOS. However, you will still need to correctly connect the On/Off button's wire to the motherboard to turn the power on to the other components. When the On/Off button is working, you can put the side panel back on the case and attach any screws to the back of the case to secure the panel in place.

Of course, if you are building a new system, it will not have an installed operating system, and you will need to install one. If you want to reuse a secondary storage device to hold the OS, it is best to prepare it for a clean installation by formating it.

Instructions for installing a Windows 10 ISO from an optical drive are provided in Appendix 7. An ISO image of a program is an exact downloadable copy of the program, including its entire file system. Instructions for installing Windows 10 from an optical device are provided here. You will need to enter the UEFI-BIOS or the legacy-BIOS and configure the optical secondary storage device as the boot device.

Depending on your system's UEFI-BIOS or legacy-BIOS, you need to keep tapping a particular key or keys after you turn on your computer to access the BIOS. You can usually wait until the monitor's light comes on before you start tapping. Usually, the UEFI-BIOS or legacy-BIOS will display a screen message such as, 'Press DEL to enter Setup' to tell you what key or keys to press. You may also check the motherboard's manual to find out how to access its UEFI-BIOS or legacy-BIOS.

You can then follow the instructions in your motherboard's manual to change the first boot-up device. Typically, the instructions involve selecting 'Boot' from the BIOS's main menu and then choosing the device you want to use as the first boot option from the devices listed in the Boot Option Priorities menu as shown in Figure 6.3. Then, when you next do a cold boot, the UEFI or legacy-BIOS should automatically find the boot loader on that device and load the OS.

After you select an optical storage device as the boot device, insert the OS's CD/DVD into the optical drive; then do a cold boot. The latest versions of Windows should then automatically start the OS installation process. You only need to follow the screen prompts to complete the installation. If the OS doesn't load, do another cold boot. The UEFI-BIOS or legacy-BIOS will then, again, check the boot sequence that you set to determine which drive to boot from. If the OS still does not boot from the optical disk, check that the OS disc was inserted correctly and that it is not dirty or scratched.

If Windows still does not boot, and you installed multiple secondary storage devices, your system might be configured to boot from the wrong device. In that case, go again to the Boot page of the UEFI-BIOS or legacy-BIOS and make certain that the secondary storage device that the operating system is installed on is specified as the first priority boot device.

After the OS install itself, you should not have to make any other UEFI-BIOS or legacy-BIOS settings. Indeed, some motherboard manufacturers caution DIY builders to use only the default settings. Nevertheless, after you have everything else working properly, you can follow the instructions in the motherboard's manual to set the system's date and time and to make any other necessary changes. You should also, update your motherboard's UEFI-BIOS's ROM firmware to the latest version.

Next, you must ensure that the drivers for the devices installed on your system are installed. If your Ethernet, Mesh, or other Wi-Fi internet connection works out-of-the-box, Windows will be able to automatically access the Internet. Windows should then detect and configure most device drivers when it installs itself the first time. It should also automatically update the drivers for most devices.

However, if Windows does not install a device's driver, you will have to install it yourself. If you don't have the driver on a CD/DVD, you should be able to download it from its manufacturer's website. In either case, make sure that all device drivers are updated after you install them. You should then also run a Windows update to apply any security patches and updates. The simplest way to do that s to use Windows 10's update tool by:
1. clicking Windows' Start button,
2. clicking 'Settings', then 'Update and Security'; then 'Windows Updates',
3. clicking 'Check for updates', and
4. Selecting 'Download and install now'.

If Windows fails to run properly from an optical disc, boot it again from the optical drive and select 'Repair your computer'. Then, under the 'Advanced options', select 'Automatic Repair'. Windows might then be able to repair any problems to itself.

If you are certain that your system's OS is correctly installed on a secondary storage device, and that the device is selected as the boot device, but the OS freezes when it attempts to run, it is most likely that some of its files were not copied correctly. In that case, reinstall the OS. If Windows still does not run, it is likely that there is a problem with a hardware component — most likely a defective boot device. In that case, you could try troubleshooting the hard drive, which is discussed in the next section, *Section 7: Troubleshooting.*

If you would like to check every step of the boot process in real-time, you can edit Window's registry so that it will report on each step every time the system cold boots. Instructions for doing that are provided in the next section.

Question: What is the biggest lie in the world?

Answer: 'I have read and agree to the software terms & conditions.'

7. Troubleshooting

There is a logical cause of every hardware problem. It will always be a bad connection, a faulty driver, or a faulty component. Although it sometimes might not seem like it, there is a positive side to troubleshooting: you will learn more about computers by solving problems with them. If you follow a logical sequence of problem diagnosis, you will eventually discover the cause of any problem.

However, diagnosing the cause of intermittent system shutdowns might be complicated if your system is connected to an uninterruptible power supply (UPS). A UPS is a backup battery that a motherboard can access if it does not receive power from its PSU. Don't confuse a UPS with a surge protector. As explained later in this section, surge protectors are devices that are designed to self-destruct to prevent power surges from being transmitted to computer components. UPS batteries usually provide about five minute's worth of power. That is enough time to save work in progress and to shut down a system without it crashing. If your system has a UPS, disconnect it until you have made your fault-diagnosis.

If your computer does not immediately power-up, don't be too concerned. But, if you smell burning, see smoke, or notice that a circuit breaker has blown in your building, the PSU may be faulty, or its plug might be insecurely connected to the mains socket. An insecure connection can cause a PSU's cable to overheat, which can ruin the PSU. Whatever the cause of the overheating, pull the PSU's plug out from the mains electricity socket immediately. Then watch the unit for a few minutes in case it catches fire.

The most tried-and-true diagnosing strategy is the 'known-good bootstrap' method. That method involves swapping a component that does not appear to be working correctly for another one that you know is good. If the known-good component works, then it is likely that the removed component is faulty. That strategy only works when you check one component at a time. Otherwise, you cannot be certain what component is causing the problem.

If you think that your system is not receiving power after you press the On/Off button on the front of the case, check the motherboard to see if its LEDs are on; if the case fans are running, and if any spinning hard drives are making noises. If you don't detect these signs, try the following five remedies.

1. Check to make sure the PSU's power cord is plugged securely into the mains power socket and make sure that the PSU's switch is on. Also, if your PSU has an On/Off light, check it to see if the unit is operating.

2. If your system is plugged into a surge protector or power board that has a switch, make sure that it is switched on.

3. Plug the PSU into a different mains outlet and/or surge protector.

4. Remove the front cover of the case and check that the On/Off button is contacting its switch.

5. If the system still does not receive power, the power supply unit is likely faulty. In that case, use the known-good bootstrap method. In other words, exchange the PSU for another one that you know works to confirm the diagnosis.

An ATX 20-pin PSU connector would likely have a grey or green Power On wire connected to pin 14. It would also likely have an orange or grey Power Good wire connected to pin 8. An EPS 24-pin PSU connectors would likely have a grey or green Power On wire connected to pin 16. It would likely have an orange or grey Power Good wire connected to pin 8. However, these wire colors are not strictly standardized.

If the PSU's fan is spinning, but the system does not start, it might be because the grey Power Good wire is not securely connected to the ATX header on the motherboard. However, if the PSU's fan starts spinning but then stops spinning, or doesn't spin at all, it may be because the green Power On wire to the motherboard is not securely connected. A qualified computer repair technician should know how to short these wires to test if they are working. If you are certain that you can identify the green Power On wire, you could also try briefly grounding it to some bare metal on the case's chassis. If the computer then starts, the fault is likely with the case's On/Off button.

If you suspect that a peripheral device, such as a network cable or USB device, might be preventing your system from starting, disconnect every peripheral device except the monitor. If the PC then starts, you can confirm that one of the devices is causing the problem. Then reconnect the peripheral devices one-at-a-time to identify which one is causing the problem.

If you notice that your computer is receiving power, its fans are running, and its motherboard's LEDs are on, but nothing is displayed on the monitor:

1. Check the monitor's power light. Usually, an orange light shows that the monitor is receiving power but that there is no video signal. A green or white light means that both the power supply and video signal are OK. If neither light is on, check that the monitor's power cord is plugged securely into the mains power socket and the monitor's port. If that doesn't solve the problem, the monitor's power cable might be faulty. Try replacing it with a known-good one.

2. If the monitor's power light is on, but it is not receiving a data signal, turn the monitor's switch off and disconnect the data cable from the monitor to the computer. Reconnect the cable and turn the monitor on. If its lights remain on, but it still does not display a test signal, the monitor might be faulty. However, it is more likely that its data cable is faulty; so, try replacing it with a known-good one.

3. If you installed a graphics card, check that the video-out cable is connected to the graphic card's port — not to the motherboard's video-out port, if it has one.

4. If the monitor still does not work, or displays an irregular or distorted image, there is likely a problem with the graphic card. In that case, remove, and then reinstall the graphic card — making sure that it is connected properly in its slot. If that doesn't work, try swapping the graphic card for one that you know works, and then reconnecting the monitor's cable to it.

5. If you installed a graphic card, and the monitor doesn't work, try using the motherboard's integrated video system instead, if it has one. To do this, you might first need to enable the onboard video in the UEFI-BIOS or the legacy-BIOS. Then, to connect the integrated graphic card:

    5.1. Turn the computer power supply off.

    5.2. Remove the graphic card.

    5.3. Connect the graphic card to the motherboard's video-out port.

    5.4. Turn the power supply on again.

6. If the monitor's power light remains off, and you still do not see anything on the screen, it is likely that the monitor is faulty. In that case, try using a different known-good monitor to confirm the diagnosis.

If a UEFI-BIOS or legacy-BIOS beep code (or error message on a monitor's screen) suggests a problem with the RAM:

1. Turn the PSU power off. Inspect the RAM module pins and make sure that they are clean. Then, ensure that they are seated correctly by reinserting them so that their contacts with the motherboard slots are good. You could also try installing them in other RAM slots.

2. If you have installed two or more modules, try removing them one-at-a-time to identify the problem module. It is extremely unlikely that more than one module would be faulty at the same time.

If you can't hear any sounds from internal or external speakers:

1. Check that the speakers are connected securely to the correct port or jacks — most likely stereo jacks — not mono jacks.

2. Check that any speakers with switches are turned on.

3. Check that the mute toggle is not turned off on the sound mixer.

4. If you are using a recent Windows OS, check its control panel to make sure that any necessary audio drivers have been correctly installed. Then, try turning the computer off for a few minutes and then back on.

5. If you have installed a soundcard, check that it is compatible with your system and then use its software to make sure that the audio is turned on.

6. If you have installed a soundcard, try removing and then reinstalling it.

7. If your system uses integrated audio, check to make sure that it is enabled in the UEFI-BIOS or the legacy-BIOS.

8. If the speakers still don't work, it is possible that the soundcard is faulty. Replace it with a known-good one to confirm the diagnosis.

If a wired keyboard will not function:

1. Check that the keyboard cable is securely plugged into the correct port.

2. If the keyboard connects via a USB interface, as it most likely does, make sure that 'USB keyboard' is enabled in the UEFI-BIOS or the legacy-BIOS.

3. Press the On button at the front of your case again to restart the system. That will give the system another chance to detect the keyboard.

If a wireless mouse or keyboard does not work:

1. Make sure that the mouse or keyboard is turned on. You might need to slide On/Off switches on their bottoms to turn them on.

2. If either device has an indicator light that doesn't illuminate, check to make sure that its batteries are charged and installed the correct way around.

3. Check that the battery compartment cover on the device is closed properly. Otherwise, it's On/Off switches may not function.

4. Try removing and remounting the device's USB dongle — making sure that it is fully inserted into a working USB port. A dongle is a small USB device that allows an external device to make a wireless broadband connection to a computer. Also, try inserting the device's dongle into a different USB port. Keyboard and mouse dongles are shown in Figure 7.1.

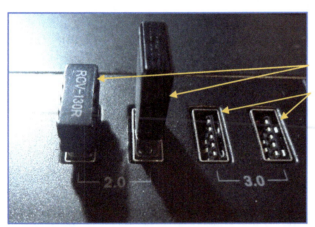
dongles

USB 3.0 ports

<u>Figure 7.1: Dongles and USB Ports</u>

5. Some receiver dongles have reset buttons. In that case, try pushing and holding the button until the dongle's light flashes.

6. Check that nothing is blocking the receiver dongle from receiving signals from the mouse or keyboard.

7. If a driver was supplied with the mouse or keyboard, reinstall a corruption-free copy of it.

8. Some wireless keyboards, such as some HP keyboards, are perplexing to set-up. You might have to press a key on them to connect them. You might also need to push a button on their bottoms until the lights on their dongles stop flashing.

If your motherboard is not working and its LED power-on lights are not on:

1. Check that the 20 or 24-pin power cable is securely connected to the motherboard.

2. Check that the motherboard's voltage settings are set correctly in the UEFI-BIOS or legacy-BIOS.

3. Check that the system bus speeds are set correctly. You could use CPU-Z to do that, as explained in Section 8.

4. If the motherboard doesn't pass the POST, it might be because it's BIOS doesn't recognize the CPU. If that is the case, check the motherboard's website for an updated BIOS. If a UEFI-BIOS or legacy-BIOS doesn't detect a working bootable secondary storage device, the boot process will stop, and some sort of 'Disc Boot Failure' error message will be displayed on the monitor's screen.

If any other secondary storage device, such as an optical device, is not working, its icon will not be displayed in Window's My Computer screen. In that case, the device might be faulty. However, it is more likely that either its data cable or power cable is not connected properly or is faulty. If the device is listed in My Computer, it probably is not faulty and might only need to be configured correctly. So, if a secondary storage drive is not working:

1. First, check that its data and power cables are securely and correctly connected.

2. If it still doesn't work, go to Window's Device Manager and uninstall the device. Then turn the computer off and disconnect the device's power and data cables. Then reconnect them and reboot the system. Windows might then detect the device and list it in Device Manager.

3. If the device still does not work, try changing its cables for known-good ones. There is a fair chance that a cable might be faulty. HDMI and DisplayPort cables are most prone to being faulty.

4. If a secondary storage device still does not work after you confirm that the cables are functional, and you reboot the system, try installing an updated driver for the device.

5. If it still doesn't work, it is probably faulty. That would not be surprising because older spinning hard drives have failure rates of about 1.5–2.5 % depending on their manufacturer. Older, non-V-NAND SSDs also have significant failure rates. So, as a last resort, try swapping a non-functioning storage device for a known-good one.

CPUs are highly-reliable and seldom cause boot-up problems. Nevertheless, they can fail if they overheat or receive variable or insufficient power supplies. If your computer only shuts down when you run a software application, it is likely that the program has corrupted files. In that case, uninstall and then reinstall the software program. However, if your computer shuts off randomly when you run various programs, your system likely has a hardware problem that overheats the CPU. If your CPU does not work at all:

1. Make sure that its PSU power cable is connected correctly and securely attached to the motherboard.

2. If there is any chance that the PSU might not be providing enough stable power, try using a known-good PSU that produces sufficient power.

3. Remove the CPU from its motherboard socket. You will likely first need to remove the CPU's cooler to accomplish that. If the CPU has pins, check that they are all straight and clean. If the socket has pins, make sure that they are straight and clean. Then re-seat the CPU into its motherboard socket. If you also detach a CPU's cooler, you will need to apply new thermal paste between the CPU and the cooler's heatsink when you reattach the cooler.

4. If all else fails, try replacing the CPU with a known-good one that it matches the motherboard's socket type. In that case, a CPU-cooler will have to be installed with the CPU.

If your CPU only works intermittently:

1. Make sure that its cooler's fan is running properly.

2. Check that the case fans are not installed backwards and are running correctly.

3. Enter the UEFI-BIOS or the legacy-BIOS and inspect the Hardware Monitor screen. Look at the temperature readings for the motherboard, the CPU, and the voltage regulator module (VRM) to see if they exceed the manufacturers' recommendations. A VRM senses a CPU's voltage requirement and ensures it receives the correct voltage. An example of a UEFI-BIOS component temperature report is shown in Figure 7.2.

Figure 7.2: UEFI BIOS Temperature Report

4. If you find that a CPU is overheating while its cooler's fan is spinning, you could try renewing the thermal paste between the heatsink and CPU. Poor-quality thermal pastes dry out and lose their effectiveness over time.

5. If the problem remains, you might need to replace the CPU's cooler. Whenever you install a new CPU cooler, you must clean the old thermal transfer grease off the CPU's contact surface and apply a new coat.

It can be difficult to diagnose a failed Ethernet port if you are using an Ethernet adapter that is built into a motherboard. That is because you can't try swapping the adapter for another one. However, it is possible to install an Ethernet network interface card (NIC) and run it at the same time as an integrated Ethernet adapter. That would provide connection redundancy and could confirm a faulty integrated adapter.

You can also use Window's Device Manager to check if a network driver is working correctly. If you find that a NIC is not working correctly, try installing a new driver for it before you go to the bother of installing a new network interface card.

You might be able to reduce the noise from a noisy case fan or CPU-cooler fan that does not have sealed bearings simply by oiling it. To do that:

1. Turn the PSU's power switch off.

2. Disconnect the power cable from the fan.

3. Use a Phillips head screwdriver to remove the fan's mounting screws.

4. Peel off the sticker on the back of the fan, as shown in Figure 7.3.

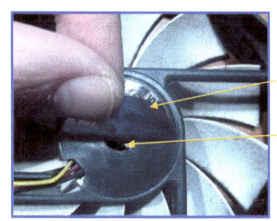

peel off sticker

remove exposed plug

Figure 7.3: Oiling Noisy Fan

5. Pull-out the rubber plug covering the lubrication hole under the sticker.

6. Squeeze a single tiny drop of sewing machine oil into the hole.

7. Replace the plug and sticker and reinstall the fan back onto the case or the heatsink.

Appendix 8 summarizes the troubleshooting suggestions presented in this section in flowchart form. If you cannot confirm whether a component is working correctly after troubleshooting following those suggestions, you have four remaining options.

1. You can ask the person you bought a problem component from for advice. If you bought the component from a local shop, ask the proprietor if they will help you debug the problem. They will likely charge you for their time if it turns out that the component was not defective and did not work because you installed it incorrectly. However, if it turns out that they sold you a faulty component, they should help you obtain a replacement for no charge.

2. You can check the Frequently Asked Questions (FAQs) provided at a component manufacturer's website. You might also be able to use email or telephone support services provided by a component manufacturer.

3. You can ask a more experienced local computer builder to help you, if you know one.

4. You can search the Internet or post your question on a computer-building forum such as Reddit's website at www.reddit.com/r/buildpc or iFixit's website at ifixit.com.

Once your computer is working correctly, you should minimize the need for troubleshooting in the future. Although such problem-prevention is beyond the scope of troubleshooting, some suggestions for avoiding problems are provided in the remainder of this section.

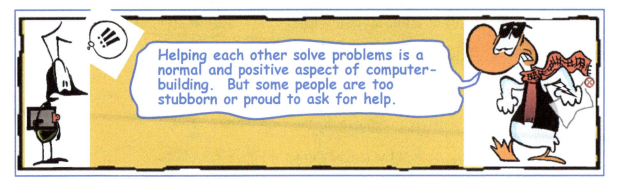

The most likely, and most serious, sort of trouble you are likely to experience is losing files because of file corruption, hardware failures, power spikes, and infection by viruses or malware. The term 'malware' means 'malicious software'. It is software that is created to disrupt computer operations or gain unauthorized access to data. The preventative measures against these risks presented in the remainder of this section are:
- defragmenting disks,
- physical cleaning,
- power spike and surge protection,
- virus and malware prevention, and
- file copying.

Periodically defragmenting spinning hard drives is more-or-less essential for keeping them running efficiently. When large files become broken over several locations, it takes longer for applications to join them together and read them. Badly broken files can even cause system crashes. Defragmenting involves reorganizing the contents of a mass secondary storage device into contiguous locations. 'Contiguous' means 'adjoining each other in sequential order'.

Windows 10 includes a Disk Defragmenter utility and automatically runs scheduled defragmentation of both spinning hard drives and SSDs. You can set the schedule or perform a defragmentation at any time. To do that:

1. Type 'defrag' in the Cortana taskbar.
2. Click on 'Defragment and Optimize Drives'.
3. On the pop-up Optimise Drives box, select the spinning hard drive and then click 'Optimize'.

Some third-party defragmenter utilities provide additional features. For example, Piriform's free Defraggler 2.22 utility provides the ability to move the largest files to the ends of drives, which speeds up system performance. Although there is no need to defragment SSDs, Defraggler also allows you to optimize them by wiping the spaces on them that are marked for deletion. An example of a Defragger report os shown in Figure 7.4.

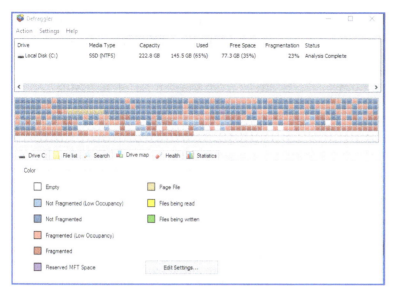

Figure 7.4: Piriform Defraggler

Basic routine physical cleaning helps minimize some other system risks. Dust that accumulates on components can act as insulation and cause overheating. It can also develop into a dielectric material with its own static electrical charge that can adversely affect components. Moreover, it can attract moisture, which, in turn, can lead to rust. As well, it is highly flammable and, no doubt has caused fires in computers.

Dust accumulates where air movements are concentrated, such as on fans. So, clean all fans and fan filters at least every six months. Don't overlook any GPU fans and PSU fans. You won't notice the dust underneath fans unless you inspect them. Figure 7.5 shows the unnoticed dirt that accumulated underneath a CPU's cooler fan when it was neglected for too long. Dust does not only collect near fans. For example, the dust shown in Figure 7.5 had gathered on the chassis of my computer, which sat in a clean room on a clean desk. This computer had been cleaned internally about two months previously.

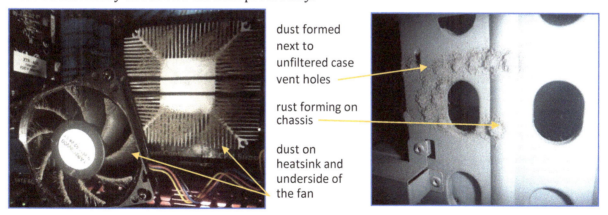

Figure 7.5: Dust on CPU Heatsink, Fan, and Case Chassis

Most cases are not supplied with dust filters on inlet fan grills that do not have fans attached to them. However, you can buy standard-sized 120 mm and 140 mm dust filters to cover them. These extra filters help to contain fan noises, as well as to keep out dust and debris. If you want to install large 200 mm case fans, you will need to look for an ATX case that has extra-large fan housings.

If you use compressed air to remove dust, hold the can upright so that drops of liquid from it don't drip onto your computer's circuitry. However, it is cheaper and simpler to use an ordinary vacuum to remove dust from fans, grills, filters, and components. Just remember to use a soft brush attachment to avoid any metal-to-metal contact between the vacuum and the case or components. Also, point the vacuum's exhaust away from the computer so that it doesn't blow dust back inside the computer.

There are two types of electrical fluctuations that can damage computer components, spikes and surges. Manufacturers and insurance companies would not likely accept claims for damages to components unless you protected them from both spikes and surges.

Power spikes are high voltages — 5,000 volts or more. They usually last only a few milliseconds. Aside from destroying components, power spikes are liable to destroy data on secondary storage devices. Power surges are much smaller voltage increases — only about 10 to 35 % above normal voltages. However, they usually last longer — typically from a few milliseconds to a few minutes. Surges are often caused by erratic power supplies from generators. They are also sometimes caused by electrical appliances.

The circuit breakers in buildings are the main defense against spikes. Circuit breakers act like fuses. They are designed to 'trip' to interrupt excessive electrical currents. A fuse is a thin piece of wire that melts and breaks if too much current flows through it. Unlike fuses, circuit breakers can function more than once.

The circuit breakers in buildings have high clamping voltages. 'Clamping voltage' refers to the maximum voltage that can pass through a circuit breaker before it stops further electricity from passing through. The high clamping voltages on circuit breakers in buildings are designed to prevent large spikes that could electrocute people — but they are not designed to intercept minor surges that would only damage delicate electronic components.

Sometimes components fail for no apparent reason. Often the reason is that they were subjected to such minor power surges. Even minor voltage increases that you might not be aware of can weaken components and cause them to fail. For example, excess voltage running through a motherboard's bus wires might only, at first, generate enough heat to weaken them. However, such repeated minor excessive voltages could eventually ruin the wires.

The defense against minor surges is provided by surge protectors. Surge protectors limit excess voltages by using metal oxide varistors to short excess voltages to mains power socket grounding wires. That is why insurance companies encourage the use of these devices. For example, the Insurance Council of Australia recommends using surge protectors: *... to minimize the effects of power surges, on all 'big ticket' items in the home including ... computers.*

The amount of protection provided by surge protectors is measured in joules (J). Surge protectors can only absorb a limited number of joules in their lifetimes before they fail. For example, if a surge protector is rated at 500 J, it could provide protection from five 100-joule surges or one 500-joule surge. So, the more joules of protection provided by a surge protector, the better. Cheap surge protectors are rated at around 75 to 400 joules. Better-quality protectors are rated up to 600 joules; the best-quality protectors have even higher joule ratings.

It takes some time for surge protectors to respond to power surges. Surge protector manufacturers measure the response times of their surge protectors in nanoseconds. Recall that one nanosecond (ns) is one billionth (1/1,000,000,000) of a second. Although it takes even the best surge protectors at least one ns to respond, they can still provide protection because electrical surges don't reach their peaks instantly either.

Surges take a few microseconds to reach their maximum voltages. The delays before reaching the peaks of power surges result from the nature of alternating current (ac). The direction of the flow of alternating current reverses at regular intervals. It occurs in the form of waves that rise and fall. The delay caused by the wave structure of ac gives fast surge protectors enough time to suppress the most damaging maximum portions of surges.

Mediocre surge protectors only monitor the peaks of alternating current waves, as illustrated in Figure 7.6. Only the best surge protectors monitor and condition the entire ac waves coming from mains power wall sockets. In other words, they smooth-out the normal tiny fluctuations of electricity that occur on ac waves.

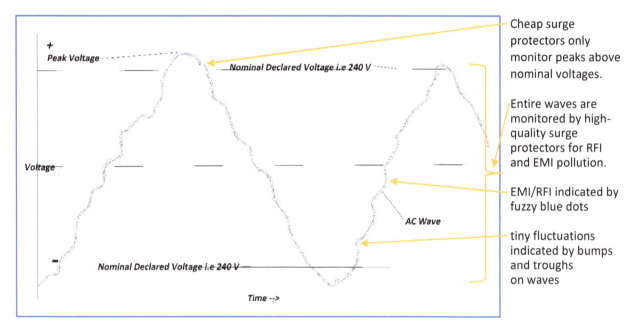

Figure 7.6: Alternating Current

Most surge protectors have LEDs that show if they are still functional. However, those LEDs don't show how many joules of protection the surge protectors have left. Therefore, if your home or workplace experiences an electrical overload strong enough to interrupt its power supply, it's a sensible precaution to replace your surge protector — just to be on the safe side — even if its LED is still on.

Recall that the design philosophy for the project described in the book was to select the best value-for-money components that would provide the highest feasible levels of performance and reliability. With that philosophy in mind, I chose the Australian-manufactured Thor SmartProtect surge protector for the project described in this book. An example is shown in Figure 7.7. The SmartProtect retails for about $ 85. Its full list of features is too long to explain here. However, six of its most noteworthy features are:

1. It has a fast response time of 1 ns. The response times of cheaper surge protectors are so slow by comparison that they are often not revealed by their manufacturers.

2. It has a very high joule-rating. Thor rate their SmartProtect surge protector at 3,637 J! However, the joule capacities of surge protectors are rated in different ways. According to the Underwriters Laboratories 1449-standard rating method, the Thor SmartProtect device has a rating of 846 J. Underwriters Laboratories is an independent global safety science company that develops and publishes standards for safety equipment.

3. It has a resettable 10-amp circuit breaker. Only the best surge protectors have such in-built resettable circuit breakers. These circuit breakers help protect the surge protectors, as well as the devices connected to them, from moderate sustained power overloads.

4. It filters EMI (electromagnetic interference) and RFI (radio frequency interference) pollution from incoming electricity flows. Those types of pollutions can interfere with computer software and hardware but are not filtered by ordinary surge protectors.

5. It has a low 275 V clamping voltage, whereas cheap surge protectors typically have clamping voltages of 400 V or more.

6. It comes with a six-year warranty. If the number of joules is ever used up on a SmartProtect, or if it becomes damaged, Thor will replace the unit free of charge. What is more, Thor's warranty even extends to the equipment connected to the device!

reset button

RJ45 plug[1]

functional
earth path LED

Notes: 1. RJ45 modular connectors are used for Ethernet and other data links on computers. The plug on the Thor SmartProtect stops surges passing through from a modem/router to a PC.

Figure 7.7: Thor SmartProtect Surge Protector/Line Conditioner

Table 7.1 provides a checklist you could use to select your system's surge protector.

Table 7.1: Surge Protector Checklist

Features	Suggestions	Your Decisions
enough outlets	at least 4	
circuit breaker	built-in	
fast response time	less than two ns	
protection level	600 + 1449-standard J	
long power cord	at least 1 m	
clamping voltage	< 300 V[1]	
power filtering	EMI and RFI pollution	
warranty	at least one year for device and attached equipment	

Note: 1. '<' means 'less than'. It is an informal mathematical symbol that has been used for over 450 years.

Power supply units cannot take the place of surge protectors. As you learned earlier, PSUs are primarily designed to regulate very slight fluctuations of mains power voltages and supply the stable voltages required by computer components. Instead, good surge protectors enable PSUs to perform their functions better by smoothing out the larger fluctuations in currents before they reach the PSUs.

Power supply units that are not protected by good surge protectors are liable to be damaged by surges — although they might continue to work to some degree. For example, they might only lose their capacity to accurately detect voltage surges. For that reason, using a PSU that has not been protected by a surge protector and has suffered a power surge is risky.

Some level of electrical protection is also provided by components themselves. For instance, all recent good-quality motherboards are designed to lessen the chances of being damaged by static or voltage surges. They have power chokes to moderate electrical currents within them. A power choke is a coil of insulated wire that blocks excessive high-frequency alternating currents within electrical circuits. As mentioned before, some motherboards also have built-in I/O protective faceplates that help shield them from static electricity.
`

None of the protections explained in this section can reliably protect computer components from lightning strikes. Lightning bolts can exceed 4,000,000,000 J! Whenever a thunderstorm occurs near your computer, the only reliable spike protection is to turn off your computer and unplug its PSU from the mains power socket. Even the best surge protectors, such as the Thor SmartProtect, cannot block lightning bolts. Lightning bolts can travel kilometers through the sky; destroy building circuit breakers and jump across the tiny gaps in surge protectors. Even so, the Thor company will honor the warranty on its SmartProtect device — even if it is affected by a lightning strike!

Using a combination of a reliable real-time, up-to-date virus-checker; a specialized malware detection program; a hack-checking program, and an anti-logger utility provides a practical, comprehensive protection system against viruses and malware. Most computer users are familiar with virus-detection programs, and already have favorites, so they aren't discussed here. I will, however, mention that Windows 10 comes with a basic built-in antivirus utility called Windows Defender. I will also mention that basic versions of some virus checkers are available at no cost. Two examples are Bitdefender Antivirus Free and Avast Free Antivirus. S However, such free programs typically display pop-up ads.

Most virus checking programs include some malware detection features. However, a specialized malware detection tool is likely to detect more malware. Malwarebytes is the only tool I know of that specializes in the detection and removal of malware. A basic version is available for free. Figure 7.8 shows the comprehensive set of Malwarebytes' routines.

You can also use a tool such as HackCheck to see if your files might have been hacked and if any of your private data, such as your passwords, might have been stolen. HackCheck costs about $ 50. A HackCheck report screen is shown in Figure 7.8. Alternatively, you could use Hasso-Plattner-Institute's free online Identity Leak Checker service to check for hacked accounts.

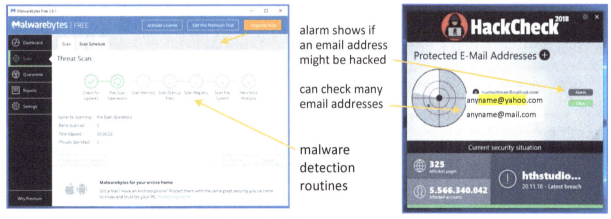

Figure 7.8: Malwarebytes and HackCheck Screens

You could also use a tool such as KeyScrambler to encrypt the keywords you type. That would make it harder for keylogging malware to extract the text that you type. But, most such tools don't detect keylogging malware programs. So, they only function defensively, not proactively.

However, another tool, ANTILogger, can proactively detect malware that can copy your keystrokes. It costs about $ 30 per year.

Sometimes, you might want to allow other people to directly access files on your secondary storage devices — even though that would ordinarily present security risks. For instance, if you want to give access to files on your USB flash drive, you can use Windows 10's Sharing utility. To do that:

1. Open This PC.

2. Right-click on the name of the drive you want someone else to access.

3. Select 'Give Access to' and click on 'Advanced sharing...'

4. On the next screen, click on the Advanced Sharing... box.

5. Click on 'Add' and then give the folder a Share name and set the maximum number of simultaneous users.

6. Click on the Permissions button.

7. On the next Permissions for screen, assign Share Permissions to Everyone. Then, in the Permissions for Everyone box, select 'Full Control'.

8. Click the Apply button; then click the OK button. Finally, click the Close button.

If your files are lost or damaged, you face the problem of trying to recover them. Instructions for using five different methods of maintaining recoverable files are provided in this book. You could use any number of these methods at the same time. These methods are:
1. using Windows File History to automatically save copies of files,
2. using RAID to automatically save copies of files,
3. automatically backing-up files onto internal and/or external secondary storage devices,
4. using Cloud backup, and
5. using machine-readable hardcopy backups.

Using Windows File History allows you to make incremental backups of your files. Incremental backing-up involves saving only the changes made to files since the last time they were backed-up. That method saves a great deal of storage space. File History only works with documents that are saved from selected Windows folders, such as Documents. File History also only saves files to external storage devices such as flash (i.e., thumb) drives.

Using flash drives as backup devices is feasible these days because large-capacity models have recently become available. For example, Kingston released its DataTraveler Ultimate GT in 2017 with 2 TB of storage space. It has a USB 3.1 interface that supports a transfer speed of 200 MB/s. However, it costs about $1,400! A more affordable, smaller capacity example is the SanDisk 64 GB Ultra CZ800 USB 3.1 flash drive. You might be able to find one on sale for about $ 30. Both of these flash drives are shown in Figure 7.9.

To use a USB flash storage drive as a File History storage device, you must ensure that it is not write-protected. Write-protection (i.e., read-only status) prevents new data from being written to a secondary storage device. You can only read data already stored on a write-protected device. Removing write-protection can be difficult with some flash drives.

Figure 7.9: Large-capacity Flash Drives

Start by checking the device to see if it has a physical switch that allows users to write-protect it. If your device has such a switch, switch it to unprotect the device. If your device does not have a physical switch, but you find that it is write-protected, you could try using Windows 10's DiskPart utility to remove its write-protection. To do that:

1. Press the Windows key at the same time as the R key on your keyboard. In the pop-up Run dialog box, type 'diskpart' if it is not already entered. Then press the Enter key or click on the OK button.

2. In the pop-up User Account Control screen, click on the Yes button.

3. In the Windows system DiskPart command prompt dialog box that appears, enter the following three commands, one-by-one, and press the Enter key after each. These commands are shown in Figure 7.10. The commands are:
    3.1. 'list disk' (this will list all the installed disks),
    3.2. 'select disk n' (where 'n' is the number of USB flash drive), and
    3.3. 'attributes disk clear readonly' (this will change the USB drive's property so that it is no longer read-only).

If a 'Disk attributes cleared successfully.' message appears, the write-protection should have been successfully removed from the storage device. In that case, type 'exit' and press the Enter key to exit the command prompt screen. Then check that you can save files to the USB device.

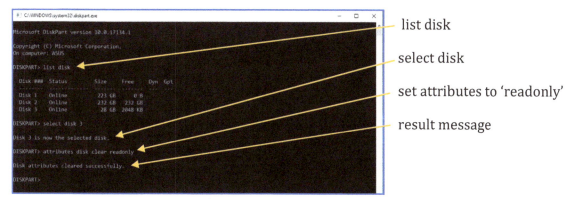

Figure 7.10: Windows 10 DiskPart Command Prompt Screen

If a 'Disk attributes cleared successfully.' message does not appear, or you find that you cannot save files to the USB device, you will need to try another method of removing the USB flash drive's write-protection.

You could try removing the device's write-protection by formatting it using Window's formatting utility. Formatting a storage device deletes all the data on a storage device; so, copy any files on the USB device that you want to keep before you format it. To do that:

1. Select 'This PC' from the list of options on the left of the Windows screen.

2. On the pop-up This PC screen, right-click on the name of the USB backup flash drive and then click on 'Format'. Select whichever file system format you prefer. Then click on 'Format...' from the pop-up menu. Then, in the pop-up Format box, select 'Quick Format', and then click the Start button.

3. In the next pop-up Format box, which warns that formatting will erase all data, click the OK button. A message saying, 'Format Complete.' should then show that the device has become completely blank — just as when it was brand new.

4. Click the OK button. You can then check that the USB flash drive is empty by closing the pop-up Format box and double-clicking on the drive's name in the This PC screen. Then click the X Close button on the top-right corner of the screen to close the screen that shows that the flash drive is empty. You will then be able to use the USB flash drive as the location for saving backup copies of files.

If Windows formatting utility fails to work, you might need to use a special utility to access the USB device. AOMEI Partition Assistant Standard is a free utility that might enable you to do that. To use AOMEI Partition Assistant Standard:

1. Download it from https://www.aomeitech.com/pa/standard.html. The latest version, when the fourth edition of this book was printed, was 7.5.1. Then install and launch it.

2. Right-click on the name of the USB flash drive and select 'Format Partition' as shown in Figure 7.11.

3. In the pop-up Format Partition screen that appears, name the USB drive and initialize the file system type. A file system organizes a drive so that files can be stored and located on it. Windows supports three file systems. NTFS is the default Windows file system. It supports modern features such as file security permissions, a change journal that can be used to recover systems from crashes, shadow copies for backups, and encryption. It also allows users to store files larger than 4 GB. Windows 10 also supports the exFAT file system, which was introduced in 2006. It is optimized for flash drives, but lacks some of NTFS's features.

In 2012, Microsoft released a new file system called Resilient File System (ReFS). It was designed to overcome limitations of NTFS and is part of Windows 10. ReFS is most useful with large data files, such as the files used by photographers, video editors, and server managers because it provides support for larger volumes and file sizes. It also provides additional security features such as fault tolerance, data corruption resiliency, and disk scrubbing (i.e., error correction).

However, you can't use ReFS on boot drives or on removable drives, such as USB flash drives. Moreover, there is no way to convert ReFS-formated drives to other file systems. So, the only practical use of ReFS is with Storage Spaces two-way mirror systems.

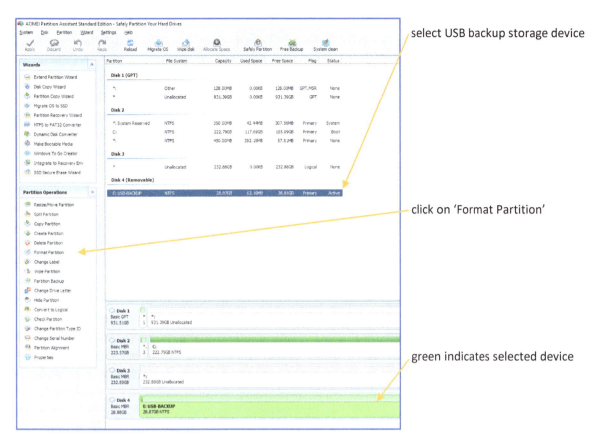

select USB backup storage device

click on 'Format Partition'

green indicates selected device

Figure 7.11: Selecting Device to Format in AOMEI Partition Assistant

Next, select the cluster size. A cluster is a logical unit of file storage space on a spinning hard disk that can be managed by an operating system. Clusters that contain files are listed in a hard disk's file allocation table. Most operating systems set their cluster sizes to either 4,096 or 8,192 bytes by default. The default cluster size of '4' means '4,096' bytes, which is the default cluster size used by Windows 10. Then click the OK button.

4. Click 'Apply' to confirm that you want to format the device. If the device has no damaged or bad sectors, it should then be formatted and be writeable. The USB flash drive should then be accessible to Windows 10. To confirm that, you could again format the flash drive — this time using Windows 10.

Some flash drives are particularly resistant to having their write-protection removed. If a message saying that the device could not be formatted because it is write-protected still appears, you might try a more 'hands-on' technique that involves changing some registry settings. That method is explained in Appendix 7. However, it would probably be simpler just to use a different USB flash drive.

When you have a USB device that is not write-protected, you can enable File History. To do that:

1. Open the Windows 10 Control Panel.

2. In the pop-up All Control Panel Items screen, click the File History icon, as shown in Figure 7.12– A.

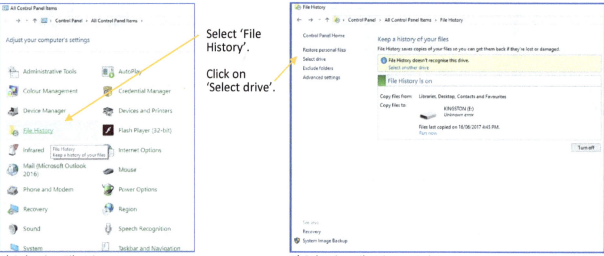

A) Selecting File History   B) Selecting File History Drive

Figure 7.12: File History Screens

3. Now select the names of the folders that you want to have backed up. The instructions that appear on the screen are illogical and confusing. They say you must 'add' folders by 'removing' them. That means that you must exclude the folders that you don't want to be backed up. So, click on 'Exclude folders'. Then select those excluded folders and click the Remove button. Then save the changes.

4. Select the external device as the file storage location. In this example, select the flash drive. To do that, click 'Select drive', as shown in Figure 7.12–B.

5. Give the device (i.e., 'volume') a name and then click on 'Add network location'. A volume is a logical drive storage area, not a physical one. So, a volume might be the same as one disk, or only part of a disk, or even more than one disk. The device should then be listed on the Select Drive screen. Click on the device's name, and then click the OK button.

6. Then click the next OK button at the bottom of the screen. You will see a File History screen that confirms that File History is on and that it is copying your selected files for the first time.

7. Go to Advanced Settings to configure how long you want files to be saved, as shown in Figure 7.13–A. Then click 'Save changes'. When File History has completed its routine, it will display a screen like the one shown in Figure 7.13–B. Windows will continue to make File History files even if the external storage device is disconnected. As soon as the device is reconnected, Windows will automatically save those files to the device.

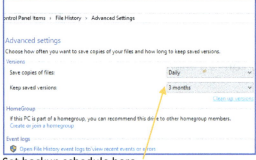

Set backup schedule here.

A) Backup Scheduling Screen

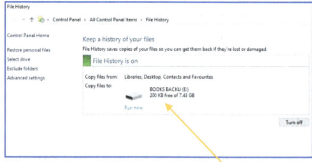

This device is nearly filled by backup files.

B) Backup completion screen

Figure 7.13: File History Backup Screens

You can restore previous versions of backed up files. To do that:

1. Navigate to the flash drive's name.

2. Right-click on the FileHistory folder icon.

3. Click 'Restore Previous Versions' on the pop-up box.

4. Click 'OK' on the FileHistory Properties box.

Sometimes FileHistory can be problematic to set up. If you find FileHistory to be too troublesome, you could download and use a third-party backup utility that is easier to set up such as EasyBackup 2019 (9.08). To use it, simply click on 'Continue Backup' as shown in Figure 7.14–A. Then insert an NTFF-formatted USB backup device. Click on the gear icon, as shown in Figure 7.14–B, to select which folders you want to backup. The backing up process will start automatically, but the process will take a long time if many large folders are backed up. A 'finished' notice will then appear, as shown in Figure 7.13–C. Automatic backups can be scheduled by selecting 'Create manual backup' on the Welcome to EasyBackup screen.

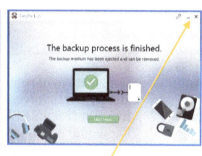

A) Click 'Continue Backup'.   B) Click on gear icon.   C) Click 'X' to close.

Figure 7.14: Using EasyBackup

You can also protect your files to some degree by setting up a RAID system. You may recall that RAID stands for 'Redundant Array of Independent Disks'. RAID is referred to as 'RAID' in Windows 8.1, whereas Windows 10 uses the term 'Storage Spaces' to refer to the same thing. RAID's main value is in providing protection from secondary storage device failures. One type of RAID, RAID 1, is called a 'mirroring system' because it writes exact copies of all files stored on one drive onto another drive simultaneously. That arrangement allows RAID 1 systems to continue to operate as long as at least one of their secondary storage devices remains functional.

You can use either internal spinning hard drives or solid-state drives as RAID secondary storage spaces (i.e., backup devices). In either case, the device used for saving the copies of files must be newly-formatted and must be of equal or larger size than the secondary storage drive containing the original files. You can use storage devices with Serial-Attached SCSI (SAS), SATA, PCIe, M.2, U.2, or USB interfaces. To set up a Windows 10 Storage Spaces system:

1. Click the Windows 10 Start icon and then click on 'Settings'.

2. Enter 'storage' into the Find a setting dialog box and then select 'Manage Storage Spaces' from the options presented.

3. On the Storage Spaces screen, click on 'Create a new pool and storage space'.

4. On the pop-up User Account Control screen, click the Yes button to allow the app to make changes to your PC.

5. Select the drive or drives you want to use as the backup storage space. You can group two or more drives to form a combined storage pool. Pay attention to the warning that any files on the drive or drives that you select as the storage pool will be deleted. Then click 'Create pool'.

6. On the Create a storage space screen, assign a name and a drive letter to the storage device.

7. Choose the type of file-duplication system you want to set up. To only use one drive as a backup device, set up a simple system with no resiliency. A two-way mirror system would make two additional copies of files and would require two extra storage devices to serve as backup devices.

RAID/StorageSpaces systems are normally used to store copies of files on internal storage devices. So, if a computer configured with a RAID system was stolen or destroyed, the backup files would be lost with it. One way to avoid that risk is to regularly back files up onto an external secondary storage device (perhaps using File History) and store the backup device at a different location. Then, if disaster strikes a computer, the files could be retrieved from the external device. However, neither File History nor RAID/Storage Spaces provide any file recovery option if a file becomes infected by a virus because the infected file would automatically be saved to both storage locations.

Another option, instead of removing external storage devices, is to remove the storage media. One way of doing that involves using Inateck's withdrawable HDD enclosure. It converts a 9.5 mm (3.7") or 7 mm (2.5") SATA spinning hard drive or SSD into a portable secondary storage medium. That would be a good use for a redundant spinning hard drive or SSD.

The Inateck device supports hot-swap and plug and play, and costs only about $ 15. It uses a USB 3.1 transfer interface that supports a maximum transfer speed of 10 Gb/s. It is shown in Figure 7.15. Another similar option is Simplecom's SE325 spinning hard drive enclosure. It costs about $ 50. It is also shown in Figure 7.15. If you decide to use either of these devices, buy a caddy for it that is the right size for the storage device you intend to use.

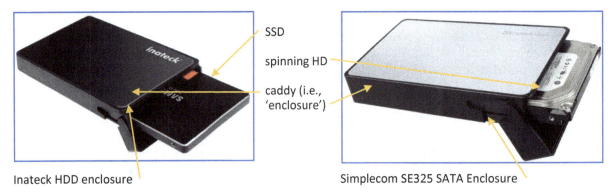

Inateck HDD enclosure
Simplecom SE325 SATA Enclosure

Figure 7.15: External Storage Device Enclosures

To install one of these devices:

1. Remove any brackets or screws from the secondary storage device so that it can fit into its caddy.

2. Check the caddy to see where the USB connector is positioned. Then open the caddy and slide the storage device into it so that the USB connectors align.

3. Use the USB cable included with the caddy to attach the enclosure to your PC. There is no need to provide power cables from PSUs to USB removable storage devices because USB devices can be powered directly from their host motherboards.

4. Check that the new device's name is automatically listed in Windows File Explorer. If so, the device should be ready to use. If its name isn't listed in Windows Explorer, search the Start menu for 'Disk Management'. Then look for an unnamed disk with unallocated space or without a drive letter assigned to it. Right-click on its name and then format it. You should then be able to use it like any hard drive.

External storage devices and media also have practical limitations. Unless users remember to store their portable devices or media in remote locations every time they leave their computers, the files on their portable devices or media are just as vulnerable as they would be on any other secondary storage devices.

These days, there is a convenient solution to that problem. That is backing-up files to the Cloud. The Cloud is a physical network of many large server-computers located in warehouses around the world that stores and processes data. Redundant copies of files are often stored on more than one of those servers. Using the Cloud effectively temporarily reduces a user's computer to a dumb terminal. A dumb terminal consists primarily of a monitor and a keyboard that does not rely upon its own CPU or secondary storage device for processing and storing data.

A good Cloud backup service should:
- encrypt files so that they cannot be read by anyone else,
- save multiple versions of backed-up files, so that if one becomes corrupted, it can be retrieved from a previous version,
- allow users to select which files they want to be backed-up from anywhere on their systems,
- allow users to make automatic scheduled backups of files, and
- provide an adequate storage size limit.

One Cloud backup service that more-or-less satisfies all of these qualities is IDrive. The basic free version allows users to backup 5 GB of data. Microsoft OneDrive Basic offers 5 GB of storage space for free on its OneDrive Cloud system. If you open a Google Account, you can also use 15 GB of Google's Cloud Drive storage for free. You could backup 25 GB by storing your files over all three of these Cloud backup services. However, using free Cloud backup services involves three risks.

1. There is no guarantee that the service will remain in operation.

2. There is no guarantee that users will always be able to access the service on the Internet.

3. There is no guarantee that data stored on a Cloud server won't be illegally accessed — or even claimed by the corporation that stores it.

Another backup option, which avoids those risks, involves using a machine-readable hardcopy medium to store copies of files. One such system is PaperDisk. PaperDisk is a commercial technology that encodes digital data as patterns that can be printed onto paper pages. One megabyte of compressed data (equivalent to 4 MB of text) can be printed on an A4 21.6 cm X 27.9 cm (8.5" by 11") piece of paper. PaperDisk hardcopy files can be returned to their digital formats simply by using an ordinary scanner or digital camera. An example of a PaperDisk file is provided in Figure 7.16.

Another similar program — but which is free — is PaperBack. It enables users to backup files onto machine-readable paper in the form of oversized bitmaps that look like Quick Response (QR) codes. A QR code is a type of machine-readable two-dimensional barcode. A barcode is an optical image that contains data about an item. You can save up to 5 Mb of uncompressed PaperBack data on a single A4-sized sheet of paper. An example is shown in Figure 7.16.

PaperDisk

PaperBack

Figure 7.16: Hardcopy File Backups

My final two suggestions for maintaining your system are controversial. The first involves cleaning your system's registry. A registry is an operating system's database. It stores application and hardware configuration settings, operating system settings, user passwords, and data that enables applications to exchange information. Registries have been part of Windows since Windows 3.1 was released in 1992. Since that time, registry settings have been automatically read into Windows system memories every time they boot.

Over time, registries accumulate thousands of outdated settings and other 'junk' such as leftover details from web browsers and redundant information about software and hardware that have been removed. When a registry becomes too overloaded with such junk data, its performance might decline. Sometimes, registry junk can also cause problems for software applications. For example, Microsoft Outlook issues are often caused by misconfigured system files. Bloated registries also waste secondary storage space. Moreover, some parts of registries are cached in systems' RAM, where they waste yet more space. For example, Abelssoft's WashAndGo utility found 4,045 MB of garbage in the system cache on my computer, as shown in Figure 7.17, even though I frequently clean the registry.

cache space reclaimed from a system with a recently cleaned registry

Figure 7.17: Cache Garbage

Microsoft provides a basic registry Disk Clean-up tool within Windows 10. It can remove much registry junk. To use Windows 10's Disk Clean-up utility:

1. Type 'disk clean-up' into the Windows Type here to search box.

2. Select the drive that Windows is installed on, which is usually C):. The C drive is usually selected by default.

3. Click the View Files button. Disk clean-up will then display a list of files for you to consider deleting. Select the types of files you want to delete in the Files to delete: list, as shown in Figure 7.18.

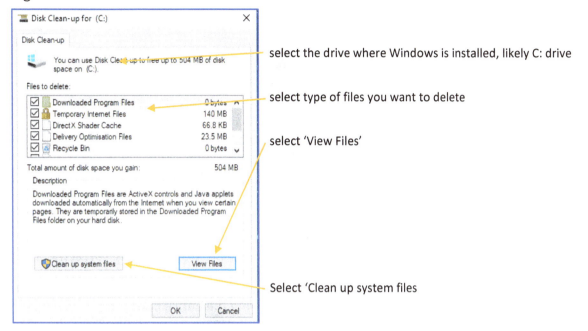

Figure 7.18: Using Windows Clean-up

4. Then click the Clean up system files button.

Many people routinely use third-party registry cleaning utilities instead of, or in addition to, Windows' Disk Clean-up tool. They do that to more thoroughly remove the junk from their systems' registries. Microsoft does not endorse the use of those third-party registry cleaners because there is a small risk that they might accidentally remove essential settings for programs or hardware components. A system might then become unbootable.

That risk was greater with early versions of Windows. However, the registry has been made more stable and resistant to such potential problems with each new version of Windows. Nevertheless, it is important to update third-party registry cleaners whenever Windows 10 is updated so that they work correctly with the updated Windows OS.

If you decide to use a third-party registry cleaner, select a reliable one that has been thoroughly tried-and-tested with your operating system. I have used both CCleaner and WinOptimizer with recent versions of Windows for years without encountering any problems. More recently, I have also used Abelssoft's WashAndGo without experiencing problems. A similar registry optimizer for Ubuntu is Stacer.

If you decide to use a third-party registry cleaner, it would also be a wise practice to make backup copies of your system's registry every time you clean it. As shown in Figure 7.19—A, WinOptimizer 2018 automatically creates such backup copies, whereas, as shown in Figure 7.19—B, you need to manually direct CCleaner to make backup copies. You could use a backup copy of a registry to re-create it using either utility if you ever encountered any problems.

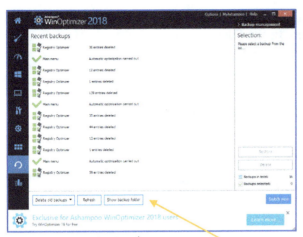
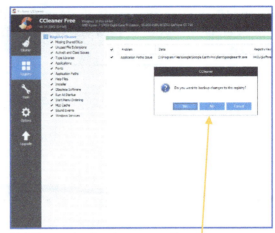

A) WinOptimizer backup/restore options   B) CCleaner backup/restore options

Figure 7.19: Third-party Registry Back-ups

Do not edit any registry data unless you have expert knowledge about the process. Otherwise, as mentioned before, you might prevent applications or hardware from working correctly. You might even prevent the system from booting. However, if you want to practice a harmless change to the Windows 10 registry, notwithstanding my warning, you could alter your system's boot screen so that it shows exactly what is happening during the entire boot process. That is called 'verbose boot'. Verbose boot presents the detailed information that is automatically presented to users of some Linux distributions when they boot their systems. Many Linux users are 'power users' who are interested in such technical details.

Start by examining your system's registry. To do that in Windows 10:

1. Type 'regedit' into Window's Cortana Type here to search dialog box.

2. Then click on the Regedit Run App in the pop-up Windows search result screen. A pop-up User Account Control box might appear. If so, click on 'Yes'. Microsoft calls the registry folders you will then see in the pop-up Registry Editor box 'keys'.

3. Double-click on a key (i.e., folder). For this exercise, select the HKEY_LOCAL_MACHINE key on the Registry Editor screen, as shown in Figure 7.20—step 1. You will then begin to see that the registry is organized into a tree-like structure of keys.

4. Before editing any Windows 10 Registry key, back it up. That is important because it is not possible to correct mistaken registry changes. To do that, select 'File' from the main menu, as shown in Figure 7.20—step 2 and then select 'Export...' from the next pop-up menu.

5. Give the backup key a logical name such as 'HKEY_LOCAL_MACHINE Backup', as shown in Figure 7.20—step 3. Also select 'Registration Files (*.reg)' as the Save as type:, as shown in Figure 7.20—step 4.

6. Select 'Selected branch' (i.e., the key you want to backup) if it is not already selected, as shown in Figure 7.20—step 5. Also, check that 'HKEY_LOCAL_MACHINE' is in the dialog box.

7. Click the Save button, as shown in Figure 7.20—step 6. That will create a backup .reg file that will contain the settings in the HKEY_LOCAL_MACHINE key. It might take a minute or so to save. You could use that key to restore the previous registry settings simply by double-clicking its .reg file name.

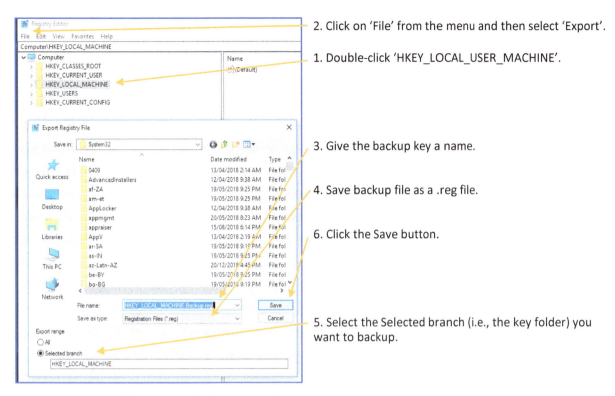

2. Click on 'File' from the menu and then select 'Export'.

1. Double-click 'HKEY_LOCAL_USER_MACHINE'.

3. Give the backup key a name.

4. Save backup file as a .reg file.

6. Click the Save button.

5. Select the Selected branch (i.e., the key folder) you want to backup.

Figure 7.20: Backing up Windows Registry Key

8. Windows will not display verbose boot messages if a VerboseStatus DWORD exists and has a value of '0'. So, next check to see if DWORD with a value of '0' is present. 'DWORD' is a Microsoft term that means 'double word', a data space that can hold a 32-bit number. 'DWORD' is a carryover term from the days when central microprocessors used 16-bit-sized words. To check for DWORD, browse the Registry Editor key structure to find the HKEY_LOCAL_MACHINE\SOFTWARE\Microsoft\Windows\CurrentVersion\Policies\System by clicking on each key in turn, as shown in Figure 7.21—step 1.

9. Right-click the System registry key. Look for a key named VerboseStatus DWORD in the list of key names. If it is not present, click 'New' from the pop-up menu and click on 'DWORD (32-bit) Value' from the next pop-up menu.

10. Now, make a new DWORD (32-bit) Value. In the New Value #1 dialog box with the blue shading, give it the name 'VerboseStatus' as shown in Figure 7.21—step 2. Then, click on 'Edit' in the main menu. Next, click on 'New', and then double-click on the name of the new key DWORD value. Then press 'ENTER'.

11. Assign the number value '1' to the DWORD value, as shown in Figure 7.21— step 3.

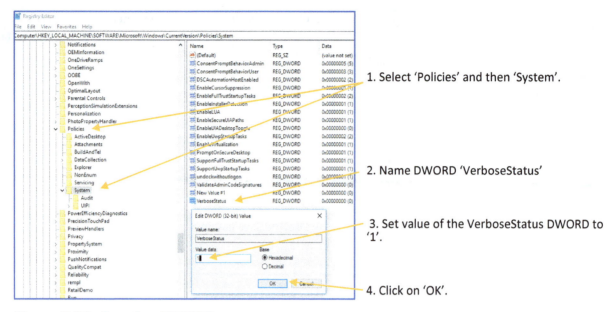

1. Select 'Policies' and then 'System'.

2. Name DWORD 'VerboseStatus'

3. Set value of the VerboseStatus DWORD to '1'.

4. Click on 'OK'.

Figure 7.21: Creating DWORD

12. Click on 'OK', as shown in Figure 7.21—step 4 and then exit the registry editor.

Now, close any programs that might be running and cold boot your Windows 10 system. That means shutting the power supply to the system off and then turning the power back on. Then, as your system boots, you will see a lot of technical details about its boot process. If you decide that you don't want to see all that information whenever you cold boot your system, simply change the value of DWORD to '0'.

A computer makes it possible to make more mistakes more quickly than any other invention in human history — with the possible exceptions of alcohol and cars.

8: Checking Components

After your system seems to be operating correctly, you should check that every component is correct and fully free from defects. An incorrect model of a component might have been supplied to you, or a component might be partially defective, but still work well enough to enable your system to boot-up.

Start by checking that you have received and installed the correct components. You could download the CPU-Z freeware utility to check basic details about the motherboard, CPU, and RAM. Remember, however, whenever you download freeware, there is a chance of simultaneously downloading malware. Therefore, always run a malware removal program, such as Malwarebytes Free, immediately after downloading freeware.

The CPU-Z utility will check the:
- CPU's name and number, core processes, voltage, clock speed, and cache details;
- motherboard's vendor, model, serial number, and chipset;
- RAM's vendor, serial number, and timings, and
- UEFI-BIOS's or legacy-BIOS' model and version.

However, CPU-Z does not report on secondary storage devices such as spinning hard drives, SSDs, or optical drives. An example of a CPU-Z 1.89 report is shown in Figure 8.1. Earlier versions are likely to incorrectly report that Ryzen CPUs have only one core and one thread. CPU-Z offers the option of creating an account where you can save the screen dumps of your system checks for future reference. A screen dump is a copy of an image on a monitor's screen.

Figure 8.1: CPU-Z Reports

Piriform's free Speccy utility can also provide basic hardware identification details as well as a report of the working temperatures of all powered components. An example of a Speccy report is shown in Figure 8.2.

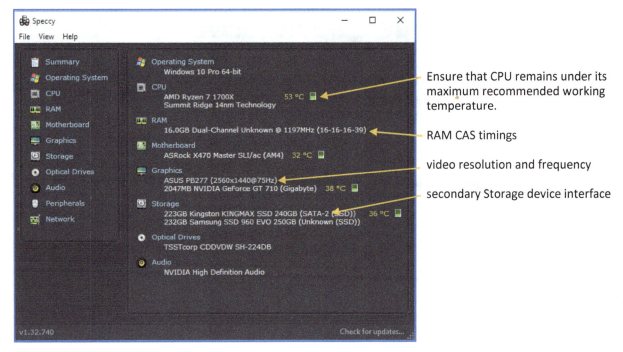

Figure 8.2 Speccy System Report

Next, you might use your operating system's device management utility to make a basic check of whether various hardware devices seem to be working properly. For example, to use Windows 10's Device Manager to do that:

1. Open Window's Control Panel.

2. Select 'Hardware and Sound'.

3. Select 'Devices and Printers', as shown in Figure 8.3—step 1; then select 'Device Manager', as shown in Figure 8.3—step 2.

4. On the pop-up Device Manager screen, double-click the icon of the type of device you want to check. In the example shown in Figure 8.3—step 3 'DVD/CD-ROM drives' was selected.

5. Then, double-click on the name of the drive you want to check. The device's status data will then be displayed, as shown in Figure 8.3—step 4.

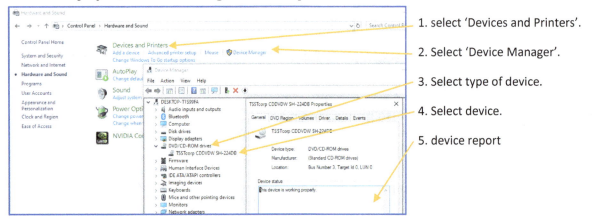

Figure 8.3: Windows 10 Device Manager Report

You will notice from the Device Manager report that no details are provided — only a status report showing whether a device appears to be functioning properly, as shown in Figure 8.3—step 5. Therefore, your next step should be to carry out more thorough tests of the secondary storage devices and RAM. You could start by using Windows 10's Check Disk (chkdsk) utility to check your computer's secondary storage devices in greater detail. To do that:

1. Select 'This PC' from the Windows Desktop.

2. Right-click on the icon of the drive you want to check. In this instance, Local Disk (C:) was selected, as shown in Figure 8.4—step 1.

3. Then click on 'Properties' on the next pop-up box.

4. Click on the Tools tab in the Properties pop-up-up box that appears.

5. Click the Check button under 'Error checking' as shown in Figure 8.4—step 2.

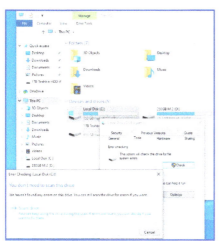

1. Double-click name of device

2. Select 'Check'.

3. Check Disk report

Figure 8.4: Windows 10 Check Disk

6. If no errors are found, a 'You don't need to scan this drive' message will appear in the next pop-up box. Nevertheless, you may click on the Scan and repair box. You will then see a pop-up Error Checking box that confirms that the disk was scanned and mentions if any errors were found. You may then click 'Show Details'. Then, click on the General tab on the pop-up box to see what Check Disk has to report about your hard disk. An example is shown in Figure 8.4—step 3.

Some secondary storage device manufacturers provide online tools that can more thoroughly check their products than the Windows Check Disk does. One such tool, which works with most systems and most secondary storage devices, is Seagate's SeaTools for Windows.

It automatically detects both spinning hard drives and SSDs, and Seagate claims that it works with any SATA, USB, 1394 (FireWire), ATA (PATA/IDE), or SCSI secondary storage device. Moreover, Seagate assures users that the test will not compromise any data on any secondary storage device. They are so confident about the thoroughness and safety of their SeaTools 1.4.0.6 tool that they say, 'If the drive passes SeaTools for Windows, your troubleshooting can move to other areas'. An example of a SeaTools report screen is shown in Figure 8.5.

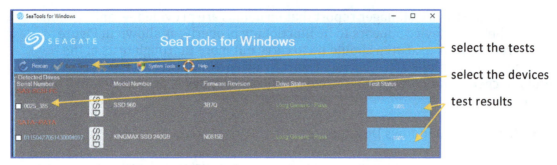

select the tests

select the devices

test results

Figure 8.5: SeaTools Report Screen

If you're using a Windows 8.1 or 10 OS, you can use Window's Memory Diagnostic Tool to make a basic check of your system's RAM. To run it:

1. Hold down the Windows and the R keys simultaneously. In the blank Open: dialog box on the Run pop-up-up screen that appears, enter 'mdschd' and then click the OK button.

2. On the Windows Memory Diagnostic pop-up-up screen that next appears, select 'Restart now and check for problems'. The program will then begin and run its routine for several minutes. During that time, it will display a message on the monitor showing if it finds any problems. When it is finished, it will automatically restart the system. After a few moments, a small box will pop-up momentarily also telling you whether any errors have been found. An example is shown in Figure 8.6.

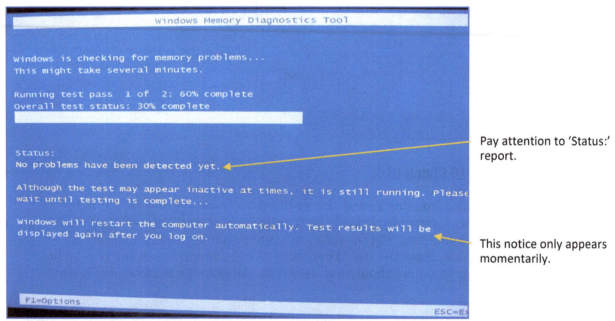

Pay attention to 'Status:' report.

This notice only appears momentarily.

Figure 8.6: Windows Memory Diagnostic Tool Report

Ideally, you should check the RAM even more thoroughly. That is because the POST does not check all of it. The POST only checks that there is enough memory available to boot the system. Neither the Task Manager nor the Memory Diagnostic Tool check all of a system's RAM either. That is because the operating system, as well as any programs that are loaded, use some of the random access memory, which then cannot be checked. The Memory Diagnostic tool only checks the first 4 GB. You must use a specialized RAM-testing utility to thoroughly check all of your system's RAM.

The tool used to do that is MemTest86. It runs outside of operating systems and thereby gives more accurate results. That is one reason that most RAM manufacturers recommend using MemTest to test their modules. MemTest86 was even integrated into some BIOSs to allow users to run it by simply pressing keyboard keys during the boot process. The latest version of MemTest86, when the fourth edition of this book was prepared, was 8.1. It supports booting from UEFI-BIOSs and works with DDR 4 RAM. Indeed, the most recent versions of MemTest86 will only work with UEFI-BIOSs; so, the first step is to make sure that your system is configured to boot from a UEFI-BIOS, which it probably is. A version for Linux/Mac systems is also available. The following instructions explain how to run MemTest86 from an external USB flash device on a PC running on Windows 10 OS with a UEFI BIOS.

First, enter the UEFI BIOS and configure a USB flash drive (i.e., thumb drive) as the system's first boot device. That is necessary because MemTest86 will boot from the USB flash device that it will be installed on. An example is shown in Figure 8.7.

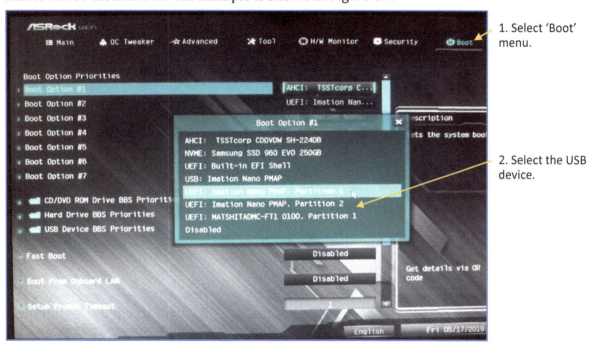

Figure 8.7: Configuring USB Flash Drive as Boot Device

Next, prepare the USB flash drive but don't use an old SanDisk flash device if possible. Old SanDisks contain embedded U3 partitions. Those partitions are difficult to detect or reformat, and they prevent systems from booting from them. U3 partitions were used to automatically launch applications from USB drives by causing OSs to see USB devices as CD/DVDs inserted into optical drives.

SanDisk phased out U3 technology in 2010 and now recommends removing U3 partitions from their storage devices. You could try using the instructions for doing that provided by Sandisk at https://kb.sandisk.com/app/answers/detail/a_id/5358/~/u3-launchpad-end-of-life-notice. I don't know of any certain up-to-date way to remove SanDisk U3 partitions from USB flash drives running on Linux distributions. However, you could try using Sourceforge's u3_tool, which worked with some devices a few years ago.

When you have a USB storage device, other than an old SanDisk flash device with U3 partitions that are not removed, format it using Windows 10's Disk Management. Leave the formatted device inserted in its USB port. Then, to use MemTest86:

1. Download MemTest86 from the PassMark Software website at https://www.memtest86.com/download.htm. Don't download it from the MemTest.org website because it provides out-of-date versions. Select the USB version, not the .iso version, which is for optical devices. To do that, simply click on the Download MemTest86 Free button, as shown in Figure 8.8.

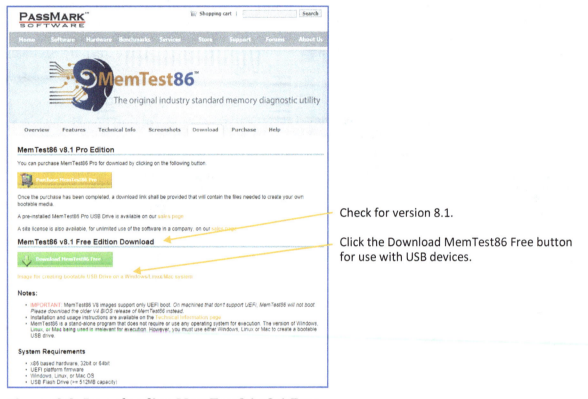

Check for version 8.1.

Click the Download MemTest86 Free button for use with USB devices.

Figure 8.8: Downloading MemTest86 v8.1 Free

2. When the 'What do you want to do with memetest86-usb-zip (8.5 MB)?' message appears at the bottom of the screen, as shown in Figure 8.9, click the 'Save' button. Accept the default file name of 'memtest86.usb-zip', as shown in Figure 8.9. When a message saying 'memetest86-USB-zip finished downloading.' appears at the bottom the screen, click the Open button.

3. An Express Zip Free Version screen will probably appear next. Certify that you will use Express Zip for non-commercial purposes by clicking the appropriate box.

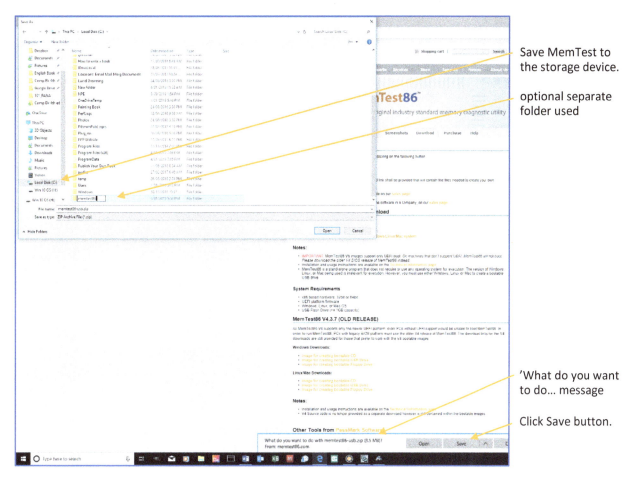

Save MemTest to the storage device.

optional separate folder used

'What do you want to do... message

Click Save button.

Figure 8.9: Saving MemTest 86 V8.1 Free

4. Right-click on the 'imageUSB.exe' file name. That is the name of the file you will need to run later on. On the next pop-up menu, select 'Extract' and on the following pop-up menu, select 'Extract All'. In the Extract Options menu, accept the default file location, which will likely be in the Downloads folder. Alternatively, you could browse and select another location on your computer to store the MemTest files. Then click the Extract button.

5. On the next MemTest86-usb screen, double-click on the 'imageUSB.exe' file name.

6. In the next pop-up User Account Control screen, click on the Yes button to allow PassMark to make changes to the USB device.

7. On the next image USB by PassMark Software screen:
    7.1. As shown in Figure 8.10—step 1, select the name of the USB flash drive that you want the system to boot from.
    7.2. As shown in Figure 8.10—step 2, select 'Write image to USB drive'.
    7.3. As shown in Figure 8.10—step 3, make sure that the name of the saved memtest86-usb.img image file is displayed in the dialog box. If it is not displayed, click the Browse button; look for the memtest-usb.img file name, and select it.
    7.4. As shown in Figure 8.10—step 4, click the Write button.

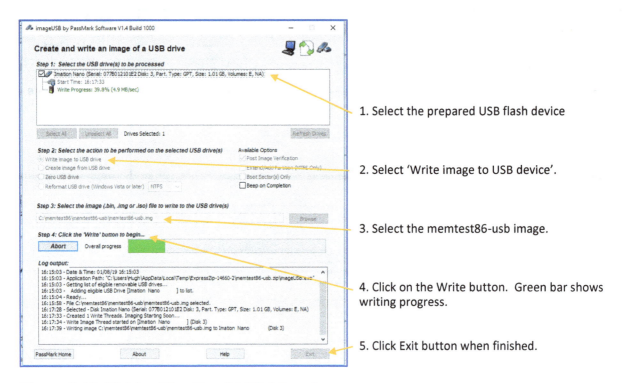

1. Select the prepared USB flash device

2. Select 'Write image to USB device'.

3. Select the memtest86-usb image.

4. Click on the Write button. Green bar shows writing progress.

5. Click Exit button when finished.

Figure 8.10: Writing MemTest 86 V8.1 Free Image

8. Then, in the pop-up image USB Confirmation/Verification screen, click the Yes button. Also, click the Yes button on the next warning screen, as shown in Figure 8.11, to confirm that you want to write the file to the USB device.

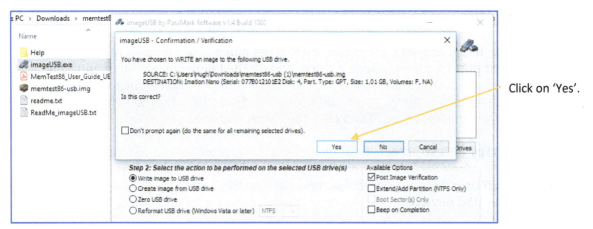

Click on 'Yes'.

Figure 8.11: Confirming MemTest 86 V8.1 Free Image Writing

9. In the next pop-up image USB FINAL WARNING screen, click the Yes button.

10. When the write is completed, click the Exit button on the imageUSB screen. Then close all other screens and leave the flash drive in its USB port.

11. Then, restart your computer. MemTest86 should run automatically from the USB flash drive. If memtest86 does not run, try disconnecting other devices, such as printers, that are connected to your computer by USB ports. Those devices might be consuming too much power or causing a conflict.

You could also try switching the USB flash drive to another USB port on the back of your PC that is directly connected to the motherboard, instead of a USB port on the front of the case. That is because the UEFI-BIOSs on some motherboards might only check the first few USB ports when running MemTest86.

The time required for a complete pass of MemTest86 depends on the CPU's speed and the memory's speed and size. By default, MemTest86 will make four passes of its thirteen tests. That could take several hours if you have a lot of RAM and a slow CPU. In the example shown in Figure 8.12, it took about 35 minutes just to complete the first pass. You can press the 'Esc' keyboard key at any time to end the test. It should be sufficient to run two passes of all thirteen tests to detect any intermittent errors.

Don't remove any RAM modules while the test is running. That could give you an electric shock and also damage the modules. MemTest will display a test result screen that will show the progress of its tests. An example is shown in Figure 8.12. If MemTest86+ detects errors with the RAM, it will highlight them as separate red lines at the bottom of the screen.

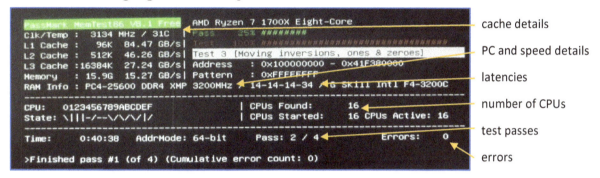

Figure 8.12: MemTest86 V8.1 Free Tests Progress Report

You can refer to the Troubleshooting Instructions in the MemTest86 User Manual that is automatically downloaded to your computer when you save MemTest to interpret any memory errors. If MemTest reports a faulty module, it would be wise to replace it, even if it hasn't yet caused a problem. Otherwise, the module would likely cause a problem in the future. You can also press any key to see MemTest86's main menu, as shown in Figure 8.13. From that menu, you could save a copy of the test report and then exit MemTest86. Change your boot device priority in the UEFI BIOS back to the spinning hard drive or SSD and reboot your PC.

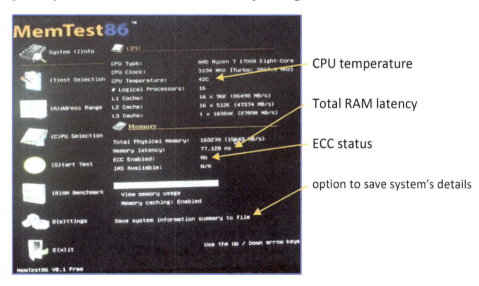

Figure 8.13: MemTest86 V8.1 Test

You might also want to check that your system's CPU and RAM are sufficient. You could do that by running Task Manager in Windows 10. Task Manager will report basic information about the loads on the CPU and RAM. To do that, open all the applications that use a lot of memory that you are likely to run simultaneously. Then:

1. Hold down the Ctrl, Alt, and Delete keys on your keyboard simultaneously.

2. Click on 'Task Manager' on the blue screen that appears. You will then see a pop-up Task Manager screen. It will list the applications that are running.

3. Click on the More Details toggle at the bottom of the pop-up screen. Another screen, similar to that shown in Figure 8.14, will then appear. If you notice that the system is using more than 85 % of your system's RAM, you should consider adding main memory. Also, if Task Manager shows that your CPU is working at more than 85 % of its capacity, you might consider upgrading it.

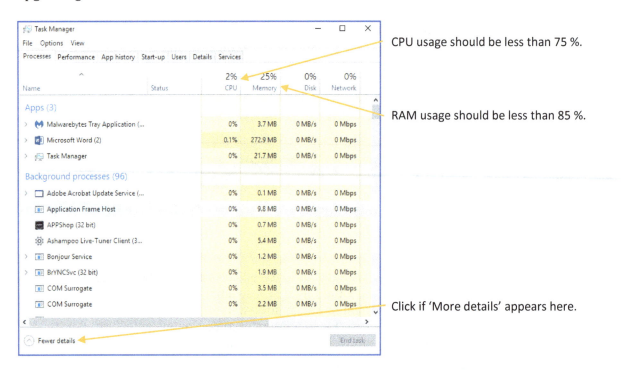

Figure 8.14: Windows 10's Task Manager RAM and CPU Check Report

Once you have confirmed that your system's components are running correctly, you should stress-test them. That involves running a utility program that puts the components under maximum loads for extended periods. The nature of computer components is that, if they are going to fail, they will most likely do so sooner rather than later. Stress-testing components allows you to identify faulty ones within their warranty periods.

Several stress-testing utilities are available. One that offers a free 30-day trial and provides comprehensive reports about entire systems is AIDA64. Another that also offers a free 30-day trial is PassMark's BurnInTest 9.0. It works with both Windows and Linux-based OSs. BurnInTest tests the CPU, spinning hard drives, SSDs, RAM, optical drives (CD/DVDs and BDs), soundcards, graphic cards, VRAMs, network ports, and printers. An optional professional version can also test microphones, webcams, batteries, tape drives, and ports. An example of PassMark 9.0's BurnInTest report is provided in Figure 8.15.

It is a good idea to stress-test the temperature stability of the CPU and RAM for longer times than AIDA64, or BurnInTest test do — especially if you have overclocked your system. You could use Prime95 do that. It is a free utility that intensely stresses the CPU, RAM, and PSU to the point where the CPU, in particular, might overheat. For that reason, only use Prime95 if you have installed a high-quality liquid-cooler. PC-builders who overclock their systems sometimes run Prime95 for twenty-four hours and components might overheat during that time otherwise. Versions of Prime95 are available for Linux distributions, as well as for Windows.

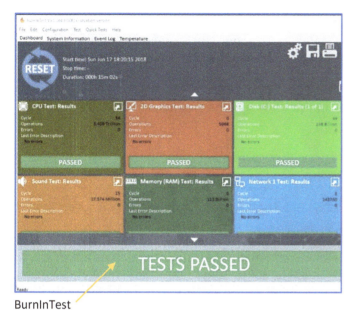

BurnInTest

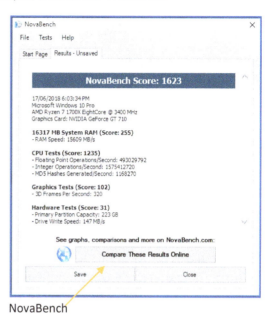

NovaBench

Figure 8.15: Stress-tests Results Screens

If you use Ubuntu, you could use Ubuntu Live Disk to check your system's performance; identify compatibility issues and diagnose and fix many system problems. Unfortunately, using Ubuntu Live Disk is complex and might be too troublesome if you are a first-time PC builder. But, if you feel up to the challenge, you could use the instructions posted online titled *Benchmark PC Hardware To Diagnose System Issues With Ubuntu Live Disk* written by Usman Javaid.

After you have stress-tested your components, it is a good idea to benchmark them. A benchmark is a record of the findings of a standard testing utility that assess the performance of components or systems. Using a benchmark allows you to compare performance results at different times. That can help you test the effectiveness of new components and diagnose the reasons for declining levels of system performance. The idea is to save copies of your system's benchmark results so that you can compare them.

As previously mentioned, you can only use the free versions of most stress-testing utilities to generate benchmarks for thirty days. However, NovaBench 3.0.4 is a free benchmarking tool for CPUs, RAM modules, and GPUs that you can use for a long as you want. It only takes a few minutes to run, and its results are straightforward to interpret. An example is shown in Figure 8.15.

If benchmarking shows that your CPU is not performing as well as you expect, you might try changing its power settings. Windows 10's default power plan setting is 'Balanced'. However, a high-performance setting is also available. Selecting the High-Performance option might increase your CPU's performance by allowing it to run at higher clock speeds for longer, although it would then also consume more power. To change the CPU's power setting in Windows 10:

1. Open the Windows 10 Control Panel. Then, in the View by: options, select either 'Small icons' or 'Large icons'.

2. Then click the Power Options icon and next click 'Create a power plan' in the Power options box.

3. On the next pop-up Create a Power Plan box, select 'High Performance'. Then click the Next button and finally, click the Create button.

As explained earlier in this book, non-V-NAND SSDs and older spinning hard drives are prone to failures. It is therefore worthwhile using a specialized tool to benchmark their read and write speeds. You can use the free CrystalDiskMark benchmark utility to do that. To use the latest version of CrystalDiskMark, 6.0.1:

1. Select the number of times you want the test to run, as shown in Figure 8.16. If you only run one test, the result might be misleading, particularly if the drive is part of a storage area network (SAN) because some activity might occur on the SAN. A SAN is a network that enables storage devices to communicate with other computer systems as well as with each other. Three test runs should be sufficient.

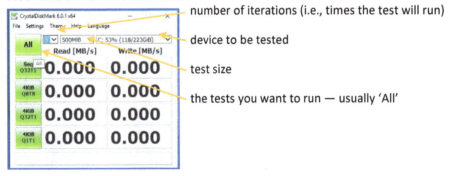

Figure 8.16: CrystalDiskMark Preparation Screen

2. Select the test size. The default size is 1 GiB. One GiB = 1,073,741,824 bytes. That size might be too large for low-speed USB-connected external storage devices. In that case, choose a smaller test size of about 500 MiB. That would reduce the likelihood of the CPU using cache memory, which would result in misleading fast results.

3. Choose the storage drive that you want to test.

4. Click the All button to start all the benchmark tests. Otherwise, choose whichever tests you want to run. The four available CrystalDiskMark benchmark tests are:

1. Seq Q32T1: Sequential (Block Size=128 KiB) Read/Write with multi Queues & Threads. This test is like performing long sequential operations such as backups.

2. 4K Q32T1: Random 4 KiB Read/Write with multi Queues & Threads. This test is like performing many tiny random operations at the same time.

3. Seq: Sequential (Block Size=1 MB) Read/Write with a single thread. This test is like performing large random operations one-at-a-time.

4. 4K: Random 4 KiB Read Write with single Queue & Thread. This test is like performing random tiny operations one-at-a-time.

An example CyrstalDiskMark report is shown in Figure 8.17.

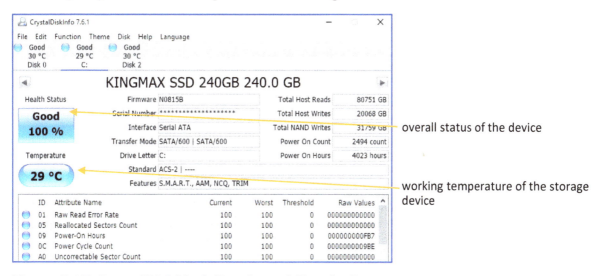

Figure 8.17: CrystalDiskMark Benchmark Results Report

A doctor, an engineer, and a programmer were discussing which is the oldest profession. 'Surely medicine is the oldest profession', the doctor said. 'After all, God took a rib from Adam and created Eve'. The engineer interrupted, 'But before that, He engineered the heavens and the earth from chaos'. Finally, the programmer settled the matter by asking, 'But who do you think created chaos?'

9. Giving Something Back

If you have researched any of your computer components on websites or in IT magazines, as recommended in this book, you have probably taken advantage of reviews posted by other DIY computer builders. If you find that you have a noteworthy experience with any of your own components, you might consider giving something back to the PC-building community. You might post your own review about a component or experience. For example, you might even post a review of this book.

Most people who read such reviews are keen to learn as much as possible, so you don't need to worry about writing too much or including too many details. The language used in such personal reviews is usually casual and includes the use of first-person pronouns to refer to yourself, such as 'I', 'me', and 'my'. That style of language would be considered egotistical and immature in more formal academic or business reports.

You should strive to present accurate and balanced information to the people who read your critiques — just as you would expect to read accurate and balanced information in reviews written by other people. It is also important to be fair when writing your reviews because they may affect people's livelihoods and careers. Moreover, if you post biased or inaccurate reviews, you will damage your own reputation — and even risk legal responses.

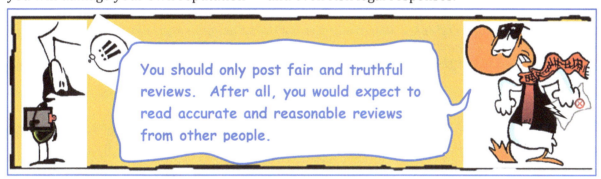

You should only post fair and truthful reviews. After all, you would expect to read accurate and reasonable reviews from other people.

For these reasons, it is a good idea to send draft copies of your reviews of components or software to their respective manufacturers or distributors. That would give them a fair chance to point out any errors you may have made or to ask you to put your comments in a more balanced light. If no one from a company replies to you about your draft review within a week or so, it implies that they cannot find anything to complain about, or that they do not care. A company representative could hardly reasonably complain later on that your review was unfair if they didn't bother to point out any contentious matters when they had the chance.

On the other hand, you might encounter a product representative who will be anxious to try to prevent you from saying anything at all. For instance, some years ago, I emailed the developer of a database program to query an apparent error in his program. His immediate response was to threaten me with legal action for bringing his software into disrepute.

Since I had only mentioned the problem to him, I could only conclude that he was afraid that my query might adversely affect his opinion about his own software? If anyone had brought his software, and his business, into disrepute, it was he for first making a programming error — and then for threatening anyone who mentioned it. Although that story might seem ridiculous, it does raise an important fact-of-life. Posting a review of a component does not place you above the normal laws of slander and libel.

I am not a lawyer, and this is not legal advice. However, in most democratic countries, the principle of freedom-of-speech guarantees the rights of people to post reviews of products or services. But, with that freedom comes responsibility. For example, in America, you can be sued for damages if you make false statements about products or services, and those statements cause harm to someone.

A forum is supposed to be a public meeting place where anyone may freely and openly report their experiences and share their opinions. Sometimes you might notice incorrect information posted in forums. It is part of the ethos of forums for their users to point-out these errors when they do see them. For example, I pointed-out some misinformation about the Blue Yeti microphone in the following forum posting.

'The Blue Yeti has a deserved reputation as being an excellent affordable 16-bit desk microphone. Nevertheless, I have noticed three negative myths in various posts about the Yeti that should be corrected. (However, with a name such as 'Yeti', I suppose that it was inevitable that it would attract some myths.)

'First myth: The Yeti does not work with Windows 8.1 or 10. In fact, the Yeti is a Plug and Play device; is immediately detected by Windows 8.1 or 10 and works perfectly well with them. Indeed, all versions of Windows from XP to 10 are listed as part of the system requirements for the Yeti.

'Second myth: The Yeti does not work with the Dragon Naturally Speaking voice diction program. In fact, the Yeti can work with Dragon in the same manner as any other microphone. Indeed, I have found the Yeti to be much more accurate with either Dragon 12.5 or 13.0 than the Andrea NC-185VM USB headset microphone that was supplied by Nuance with Dragon when I purchased it.

'Third myth: There is no warranty with the Yeti. In fact, the Yeti comes with a 2-year manufacturer's warranty. The following is copied from the Yeti's manual: 'Blue Microphones warrants its hardware product against defects in materials and workmanship for a period of TWO (2) YEARS from the date of original retail purchase, provided the purchase was made from an authorized Blue Microphones dealer. This warranty is void if the equipment is altered, misused, mishandled, maladjusted, suffers excessive wear.' In addition, reliable retailers usually provide their own warranties and return policies.

'It seems a strange thing to say about any product, but, in some respects, I found the Yeti to be too good. It is so sensitive that it needs to be completely isolated from any extraneous sounds and vibrations. For example, I tried using the Yeti's one-directional cardioid function, turning the gain setting down, and wrapping it in a thick foam pillow — leaving only a tiny hole, the size of a coin, for sound to enter. I then held the Yeti close in front of my face, thinking that my head would block any stray noises from entering the hole. However, the Yeti picked up and even seemed to amplify, noises that I wasn't even conscious of. Quiet computer fans sounded like industrial machinery through the headset speakers plugged into the Yeti. Other normal, minor noises such as moving the computer mouse or my chair squeaking were recorded loud and clear. The Yeti even recorded the noise of someone closing a door in an adjacent apartment building — even though the windows in my room were closed!

'For that reason, making commercial-quality podcasts or recordings using the Yeti would likely require using a sound-insulated room or booth. Fortunately, the Yeti's extreme sensitivity does not interfere with its utility or accuracy when using it with Dragon Dictate voice dictation.'

Most component manufacturers host online forums about their products. However, many of these forums are censored. In other words, the forum moderators stop forum users from posting fair and truthful comments about their products if they don't like what the forum users might write. For example, Audio-Technica blocked the following comments I submitted for one of their forums about one of their headsets.

'I bought an Audio-Technica PBHS1 headset to use with a Windows 8.1 PC via a USB port. I wanted to use it to record podcasts, and for voice dictation work with Dragon Naturally Speaking (DNS) 12.5 voice dictation software.

'Both I, and the technician from the shop where I bought the headset, tried unsuccessfully for weeks to get the headset to work via a USB port and with DNS. We tried connecting the headset to a USB port via an XLR-M to USB cable. Both the cable and headset worked correctly when tested separately, but they would not work when interconnected to a USB port. The USB port worked fine with other devices — including other headsets. We also tried using an XLR-USB pre-amp — as suggested by Audio-Technica. In addition, we tried using various audio software programs. However, the headset still would not work when connected to a USB port.

'We were able to get the headset to work by connecting it to the computer's soundcard via a 1/4" to 1/8" jack adaptor. Windows Sound Recorder would then record sounds from the mic. However, using a soundcard defeats the advantage of using a USB port (which eliminates soundcard noise interference and other noise issues). That, in turn, negates the advantage of having such a high-quality microphone as in the PBHS1 headset. We were not able to record any speech through the headset mic with Dragon Dictate even using the soundcard method.

'While trying the headset, I noticed that it felt heavy after wearing it for some time. That is only to be expected, given its solid construction and was not an issue for me. However, I also found that the earpieces made my ears sore after wearing the headset for a while — which was something of an issue. I think that was a result of not enough padding being used in the earpieces. (No, I don't have big ears!)

'Ultimately, neither the technician nor I could think of any more ways to try to get the headset to work, and he refunded my money. I doubt that he will ever sell another Audio-Technica PBHS1 headset to a customer to use with a PC USB port or with Dragon Naturally Speaking.

'That is a pity because the PBHS1 headset is high-quality hardware that was designed especially for voice recording — which is exactly what I wanted to use it for. Sportscasters and musicians do satisfactorily use this headset. However, I can only presume that they do not use it by connecting it to a PC USB port.'

It seemed to me that those comments were entirely fair and accurate and would be of interest to other people who might be interested in the PBHS1 headset. The only reason given by Audio-Technica for rejecting my review was that '... the review breached their guidelines'. Their forum's guidelines are copied in Appendix 9. I could not see how my review had breached any of these guidelines; so I queried Audio-Technica's excuse for blocking my review with the following email message.

'I read your forum's guidelines carefully before I wrote my comments — and again after receiving notice of your rejection of my comments. I cannot see how my comments, in any way, breached any of your guidelines. I would, therefore, be grateful if you could point-out how my comments breached any guideline.'

However, no one from Audio-Technica would answer my query or justify their rejection of my comments. If a forum administrator discovers mistakes in a contributor's comments, they should point them out for the benefit of everyone — rather than just censoring them.

I was motivated to buy the PBHS1 headset after reading an excellent posting about it from Allan Tépper, Director of TecnoTur LLC. I therefore emailed him suggesting that he update the information in his blog about the headset. He replied, suggesting that using a Shure X2U XLR-to-USB Signal Adapter might enable the headset to work correctly via a USB port, but made no suggestions about getting it to work with Dragon Dictate. However, by that time, I had bought other headphones; so, I can't confirm whether his advice was correct or not. Unfortunately, potential buyers of the PBHS1 headset, visiting the Audio-Technica forum, would not have access to Allan's potential solution because of the forum administrator's blocking of a free and open discussion.

If a forum administrator blocks your participation in a forum without a justifiable and transparent reason, you will know that it is not an open forum where information and opinions may be freely exchanged. In that case, the best response is to post your review in another forum that is open and not manipulated. When you do so, it is a good idea to also warn people about the censored forum, as I have done here.

Murphy's first three Laws of Computing are: 1. When you finally get to the point where you really understand your computer, it's probably obsolete. 2. For every action there is an equal and opposite malfunction. 3. If at first you do not succeed, blame your computer.

Glindex

Now, how can I find what I am looking for?

A

adapter card	a circuit board that plugs into a motherboard socket to provide a system with extra functions, such as the ability to process audio or video data — also called an 'expansion card'	**112**
API	application programming interface, a software-to-software interface that is invisible to users that allows devices to send data directly to each other without the intervention of an OS	**100**
APU	1. Accelerated Processing Unit, a combination CPU and GPU on a single central microprocessor chip; 2. Audio Processing Unit, an expansion card that only processes audio data	**54; 97**
architecture	the overall construction of a computer system, component or software program	**27**
asynchronous	a type of DRAM whose clock speed is not synchronized with CPU clock speeds or motherboard system bus speeds	**36**
ATX	Advanced Technology eXtended, the most common standard form-factor of PC motherboards since 1995; also a PSU form-factor	**68; 119**

B

bandwidth	1. the theoretical maximum speed that data can be transmitted between devices; 2. the range of frequencies generated by a signal measured in kilohertz (kHz)	**51, 81, 91; 97**
BD	Blue-Ray disc, a digital optical disc data storage format that superseded the DVD format	**117**
benchmark	the findings of a utility program that runs standard tests to assess the performance of components or systems	**221**
binary system	a system of measurement that uses units which are multiples of 1,024 (which are powers of 2)	**14; 43**
BIOS	Basic Input/Output System, the firmware that provides basic low-level operating control of computers	**44; 175**
bit-depth	the number of bits of data in a sound sample — the higher the bit-depth resolution, the better the sound quality	**90**
boosting	the ability of CPUs to automatically overclock themselves when under high loads, while keeping themselves within safe voltage and temperature limits	**62**
boot	loading an operating system to start a computer	**88; 175**

| bus | a wire circuit that electronic signals can travel along; also called or 'data path' | **59, 69; 189** |
| byte | a data unit of eight binary digits used to represent a character such as a letter, number or punctuation mark | **17** |

C

cache	a small, fast memory location on a CPU, RAM module, hard disk, or another component	**50; 115**
CAS latency	Column Access Strobe latency, the time in clock cycles required to access a column of memory on a RAM chip	**83**
case modeling	the art and craft of designing and building custom-made computers	**108; 243**
cache miss	the occurrence of a CPU not being able to find memory within its cache	**50**
CD	compact disc, an optical disc media originally developed for storing digital audio, but which is now used for storing any type of digital data	**116**
channel	1. a distinct stream of audio data that can be sounded on a separate speaker; 2. a bus wire that carries data	**69; 89**
chassis	the frame of a computer case that various components, such as motherboards and case fans, are mounted onto	**108, 142; 147**
chipset	a collection of integrated electronic circuits attached to a motherboard that manages the data flow between a CPU, RAM and peripheral devices	**66**
clock speed	the operational speed of a RAM module, CPU, or another microprocessor — usually expressed in gigahertz	**37, 49, 81; 97**
Cloud	many interconnected remote real-time computers that host services which appear to be provided by a single server	**205**
CMOS	Complementary Metal Oxide Semiconductor, a tiny amount of permanent RAM located on a chip that holds data, such as the system time and date	**177**
codec	a hardware and software system used to convert analog signals into digital signals and back again	**31; 94**
configurator	a software sales tool that enables shoppers to choose components that meet their technical requirements	**84; 135**
core	a central microprocessor processing unit that is capable of reading instructions and functioning on its own, but only one core in a CPU can communicate with outside components	**48**
CPU	central processing unit, the main processing unit within a PC, which is located on a microprocessor chip	**47**

D

| DAC | Digital-Analog Converter, a device that converts digital data into analog signals | **91** |
| daisy-chain | a method of connecting computer devices in a series, one-after-another, without each one needing to be directly attached to a motherboard because each device has its own address for receiving data and instructions | **112** |

DDR RAM	Double Data Rate Random Access Memory, a type of RAM that doubles the data transmission speed by making data transfers on both edges of clock cycles (i.e., on their rising and falling edges)	**37**
desktop	a non-portable computer with a separate case, keyboard, mouse, and monitor	**13; 18**
DIMM	Dual In-line Memory Module memory, a chip that is mounted on a small circuit board to form part of a RAM module	**79**
diode	a solid material that allows electrical current to pass in only one direction and emits light when a current passes through it	**125**
DIP switch	dual in-line packaging switch, a type of switch used to make settings on components	**62**
DirectX	a Windows extension that enables fast video animations and other advanced graphical features	**100**
disc/disk	'disc' refers to removable optical media, such as a DVD, whereas 'disk' refers to magnetic media, such as a hard drive	**112**
dongle	a small USB device that enables a peripheral device, such as a keyboard, to send wireless signals to a computer	**188**
DOS	Disk Operating System, the only type of OS before graphical user interface (GUI) OSs	**21**
double pump	the transfer of data on both the rising and falling edges of clock signals, which effectively doubles the data transmission rate	**37**
DRAM	dynamic RAM, a type of memory that stores each bit of data in separate capacitors, which are continually recharged to maintain the data	**35, 36; 80**
driver	a software program that allows an operating system to control a device such as a printer, disk drive, or keyboard	**27**
DSL	Digital Subscriber Line, a high-speed Internet connection	**75**
duplex	the transmission of a signal in both directions, one direction at a time (half-duplex) or both directions simultaneously (full-duplex)	**74**
DVD	Digital Video Disc, a type of removable optical media used for storing large amounts of digital information	**90; 116**
DVI	Digital Visual Interface, an interface used to connect digital monitors to computers	**97; 163**

E

electrostatic	an electrical charge that normally doesn't flow but which can suddenly discharge onto an integrated circuit	**140; 142**
Environmental Audio Extension	EAX, a reverberation engine that can generate immersive 3-D sounds that seem as if they are coming towards listeners from various directions	**95**
ergonomics	the relationship between humans and the tools they use	**131; 134**
Ethernet	a network cabling and protocol system	**16; 75**

F

FireWire	a legacy high-speed peripheral device interface created by Apple	**78; 164**

firmware	instructions and data stored in a read-only memory (ROM) location that cannot be changed without the use of a special flashing program	**67, 175; 180**
FLAC	Free Lossless Audio Codec, a combined hardware and hardware system used to convert analog signals into digital signals and back again	**94**
flashing	up-dating the firmware contained on ROM chips using a special program provided by the chip manufacturers	**180**
form-factor	the specifications of the dimensions, power supply type, mounting hole locations, and other aspects of a component, such as a motherboard	**33, 67, 104; 124**
forum	a public on-line meeting place where anyone may freely and openly report their experiences and share their opinions	**226**
frame buffer	a memory location, usually on a graphic card memory chip used to hold images sent to a monitor	**102**
frame rate	the speed (f/s) at which GPUs can output frames or monitors can display new frames	**98; 126**
FreeSync	an AMD technology that resolves the frame/refresh rate coordination issue — similar to Nvidia's GSync technology	**98**
frequency response	the amplitude (i.e., the volume) of a sound at a particular frequency	**91**
FSB	front-side bus, a data wire on motherboards that connected hardware and the memory controller to CPUs until the 2000s	**59**

G

| Gigabit Ethernet | the most common transmission technology used in local area networks | **74** |
| GPU | graphic processing unit, a type of circuit board that processes video data and controls monitors | **96** |

H

hardware	the physical parts of a computer system including internal and external components and devices	**13; 31**
HDMI	High-Definition Multimedia Interface, a digital audio/video interface for transferring both uncompressed and compressed audio and video data	**18, 97, 99; 103**
header	a group of pins on a motherboard or expansion card to which internal devices can be attached	**17**
heatsink	a block of aluminum or copper attached to a component to passively draw heat from it	**152**
hot-swapping	the installation of components without needing to shut down and reboot systems	**41**
hyperthread	Intel system that allows single CPUs to work like two separate CPUs and to be recognized by OSs and application programs as separate CPUs Intel's, a technology similar to AMD's simultaneous multithreading technology	**48**

I

| I/O faceplate | metal shield that fits around the I/O ports on the backs of the motherboards to prevent dust entering cases and to help control the air flows inside cases | **147** |

microchip	a small flat piece of semiconducting material, such as silicon, containing an integrated circuit, which is used to store computer memory; provide logic circuits, or transmit data signals	**67**
middleware	software that integrates separate programs or hardware devices to enable the exchange of data between them when the system operating system is unable to do so	**100**
Molex connector	a standard pin and electronic socket interconnection produced by the Molex Connector Company, although only the 8981-type with four pins is usually called a Molex connector	**120; 168**
motherboard	the main electronic circuit board in a computer that contains a chipset as well as a CPU socket, RAM slots, ports, and expansion slots	**66**

N

NAND memory	a non-volatile flash storage technology called 'NAND' memory because it uses a 'Not AND' type of digital logic gate	**115**
native support	an ability built into a device or system that enables it to function without the assistance of any additional software or hardware	**100**
Northbridge	a chipset that was used to provide data transfers between CPUs and RAM modules	**59; 61**

O

OEM	original equipment manufacturer, a manufacturer that produces parts that may be used and marketed by another manufacturer	**88; 136**
office suite	a set of office applications that includes a word processor used for producing documents, presentations, spreadsheets, databases, and digital paintings, which is often called 'productivity software' to avoid confusion with MobiSystem's cross-platform OfficeSuite application	**28**
optical disc drive	a disc drive that uses laser light or electromagnetic waves near the visible light spectrum to write or read digital data to or from optical discs	**39**
OS	operating system, the software that controls a CPU and peripheral devices and allows applications to access those devices	**21**
overclock	increasing the clock frequency, and possibly the operating voltage, of a computer component to exceed the clock frequency certified by the manufacturer	**56, 62; 64**
overhead	the extra data carried by signals to provide routing information, error corrections, and directions for carrying out instructions	**75**

P

paging system	a computer memory management system which uses secondary storage for extra main memory	**83**
parallel cable	a ribbon cable with multiple wires arranged side-by-side that transmits signal on all the wires at once	**40; 242**

refresh rate	the number of times per second a monitor can display images on its screen — including the repetition of identical frames	**97; 127**
registered RAM	double in-line memory module technology that uses an error-correcting code (ECC) type of memory which places data in extra registers before CPUs can use it	**80**
registry	an operating system's database that stores application and hardware configuration settings, operating system settings, user passwords, and data that enables applications to exchange information	**206; 249**
resolution	amount of detail (i.e., pixels) displayed on a monitor	**98; 125**
response time	how fast liquid crystal pixels can go from black to white and then return to black again	**128**
Ryzen	a recent revolutionary computer central microprocessors architecture first produced by AMD in February 2017	**26, 48, 55, 63, 67; 115**
	S	
sample rate	the number of sound samples produced by a soundcard per second measured in hertz or kilohertz	**91**
SATA	Serial Advanced Technology Attachment, a computer bus interface for connecting storage devices to motherboards	**41; 71**
SCSI	Small Computer System Interface, a legacy standard for connecting and transferring data between CPUs and peripheral devices	**75; 241**
secondary storage	any removable device such as a hard drive, flash drive, or tape drive that can be used to store large quantities of non-volatile data	**29**
serial transmission	the transmission of bits of data one-after-the-other along a wire or through a port	**40**
server	a computer that delivers data and services to other	**22**
set-off screw	a screw with exterior male threads on one end that screw into a case's chassis, and with interior female threads on the other end that serve as the attachment points for motherboard attachment screws	**148**
SI	*Le Système international d'unités* (International System of Units) the modern form of the metric measurement system	**14**
SNR	Signal-to-Noise Ratio, a measurement describing the level of noise in the sound output by a device in relation to its signal level	**91**
socket	1. a mechanical and electrical connection between a CPU or a RAM module and a motherboard; 2. a female connection for a mains electrical power supply plug	**18**
solder	a metal with a low melting temperature, such as lead or tin, used for joining two pieces of other metals that have higher melting temperatures	**20**
solid-state drive	a secondary storage device that uses integrated circuits, which are actually RAM chips, to store non-volatile data	**113**
source code	the essential parts of a computer program written in a high-level language which can be read and modified by programmers	**22**

volume	a logical drive (which might be different from a physical drive) that is used as a storage area which can be accessed by an operating system	**116; 202**
VRAM	video RAM, originally a term used to refer to a particular type of video RAM, but which is nowadays loosely used to refer to any type of RAM on any graphic card	**97**
W		
warm boot	restarting a computer by using only the operating system — not by turning the power on	**177**
word	a unit of data of a particular bit length that can be moved between RAM and a CPU	**37**
workstation	a powerful desktop computer used by a single person for work	**48; 69**
X		
Y		
Z		
ZIF	zero insertion force socket, a type of socket which allows CPUs to slide into their sockets without any force	**154**

Four signs that Information Technology has taken over your life are:

1. You can no longer sit through an entire movie without having at least one device on your body beep or buzz.

2. When you are in a computer store, you may eavesdrop on salespeople talking with customers, and even butt in to correct them.

3. You sign messages by putting :) next to your signature.

4. You can think of ten keystroke symbols off the top of your head that are far cleverer than :).

Appendix

Notes about things that I want to check some more.

Appendix 1: Software Selection List

Task	Software	Main Use	Some Use	Possible Use
accounting				
audio editing				
computer-aided design				
desktop publishing				
email client service				
game-playing				
Internet browsing				
office suite				
operating system				
photo editing/storage				
programming				
study/research				
video-editing				
virtual reality				
voice dictation/writing				
VoIP calls				
web page design				
other _____				
other _____				
other _____				
other _____				

Appendix 2: Software System Requirements

Task	Software	RAM	Storage	Audio/visual
accounting				
audio editing				
computer-aided design				
desktop publishing				
email client service				
game-playing				
Internet browsing				
office suite				
operating system				
photo editing/storage				
programming				
study/research				
video-editing				
virtual reality				
voice dictation/writing				
VoIP calls				
web page design				
other				
other				

Appendix 3: Selection of Components and Peripheral Devices

Peripherals and Options	Essential	Desirable	Possible
audio card (if not integrated on the motherboard)			
case			
CPU			
Ethernet NIC (if not integrated into motherboard)			
floppy disk drive			
keyboard (wired or wireless)			
memory (RAM)			
microprocessor (CPU)			
modem			
monitor			
motherboard			
mouse(wired or wireless)			
M.2 secondary storage device			
optical drive (CD/DVD or CD/DVD/BD)			
power supply unit			
solid-state drive			
standard spinning hard drive			
surge protector			
Thunderbolt port (mini DisplayPort port)			
USB 2.0 ports			
USB 3.0 ports			
USB 3.1 ports			
graphic card (if not integrated on the motherboard)			
tape drive			
other _____			
other _____			

Appendix 4: Installation of Legacy SCSI System

The SCSI was first developed in 1986. It ran at a speed of 5 MHz and could transmit only 10 MB/s using a 16-bit bus. Since that time, many improved versions have been developed. For example, the SCSI Ultra-640 version, which was released in 2003, supported a transfer speed of 640 MB/s. The latest type of the SCSI is Serial Attached SCSI (SAS). It was first introduced on some motherboard chipsets, and on some SSDs, in 2005. SAS-3 has been available since 2013 and supports a transfer rate of up to 12 Gb/s. The most recent standard specifications for SAS, SAS-4, which supports a transfer rate of 25 Gb/s, was released in 2017.

You can install a SCSI system on an either EIDE or SATA systems, providing the SCSI interface is supported by either the motherboard or by a host controller card. SCSI controller cards, particularly SAS types, are expensive. For example, the LSI's MegaRAID 9361-8i SAS RAID controller card, which supports SAS-3's transmission rate of 12 Gb/s, costs about $ 570. Using a motherboard with a built-in SCSI controller can save some of the cost and complexity of setting up a SCSI system.

If you want to install an older version of SCSI, you will need to know about SCSI ID numbers. That is because the devices in SCSI systems are daisy-chained and SCSI controllers must have some way of identifying which device to send data to. Every SCSI device on a SCSI daisy-chain must have its own SCSI ID number. The SCSI adapter card uses those ID numbers to identify the various SCSI internal devices, such as hard drives, scanners, tape backups, Zip drives, and CD/DVD devices.

Older SCSI-2 cards can only use a range of ID numbers from 0 to 7. However, some later versions of SCSI, such as Ultra 3 SCSI, can use a range of IDs from 0 to15. In either case, the SCSI adapter card or integrated controller uses one of the available ID numbers for itself. A SCSI-2 adapter usually reserves number 7 for itself, and an Ultra 3 SCSI adapter reserves number 15. So, for example, on an Ultra 3 SCSI system, the available addresses for devices would range from 0 to 14. SAS systems can daisy-chain up to 128 devices. Figure A.4.1 shows a typical SCSI system.

SCSI adaptor card on motherboard

daisy-chain cable

daisy chain terminator

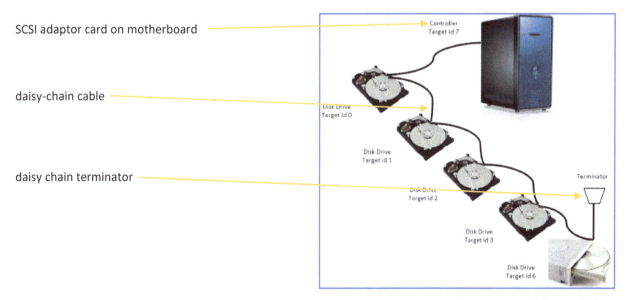

graphic courtesy of Microsoft/Bing

Figure A.4.1: Typical SCSI System

The following instructions are for installing a typical PC SCSI system with a SCSI adapter card.

1. Install the SCSI adapter card into a 32-bit PCI or PCIe card slot on the motherboard just as you would install any other card.

2. Assign each device on the SCSI daisy-chain cable an ID number.

3. Install the SCSI hard drives, or other SCSI devices, into available drive bays in your case's chassis just as you would install a standard type of spinning hard drive. Adapters are available to allow you to connect SCSI drive to IDE cables, if necessary.

4. Connect a cable from the SCSI adapter card to each SCSI hard drive or other device. Use the first open device connector on the cable to connect the first device. You may have to press the connector firmly to fully insert it. This connection can be made upside-down, so take care to align 'Pin 1' on the male connector with 'Pin 1' on the female connector. The odd-colored wire on a SCSI cable indicates 'Wire 1', which corresponds to 'Pin 1'. Different SCSI drives have different pin configurations. However, the most common configuration used in PCs is the 68-pin configuration.

SCSI cables come in a variety of sizes and shapes; so, it is necessary to check that their bus widths and cable types are supported by your system's SCSI devices. Thin serial SAS data cables have less bulky connectors than SATA connectors and can work over much longer distances than parallel cables, such as SATA cables. SATA cables can only be up to 100.6 cm (3.3 feet) long, whereas SAS cables can be up to 10 m (32.8 feet) long.

5. Install a terminator in the last device on the cable. This terminator sends a stop signal to the SCSI adapter card or integrated controller. It informs the adapter card or controller when signals have reached the end of a SCSI daisy-chain. A SCSI device's manual will instruct you how to set its switches to identify it as a terminal device. Some older SCSI devices have removable terminators which are usually located adjacent to their cable connections. Other SCSI devices have DIP switches that are used to make the termination settings. Some SCSI-2 cards have jumpers that are used to set them as terminal devices instead.

6. Connect a power supply cable to each SCSI device.

Appendix 5: Introduction to Case Modeling

Some DIY computer builders enjoy the artistic aspect of building their own computer cases. They have developed that enjoyment into a new art form called 'case modeling'. For them, building a computer is about aesthetics as well as performance. For some of them, the opportunity to create their own cases may even be the main reason they build their computers.

Case modeling usually involves designing the color schemes of cases. Most case modelers use car paints from spray cans because that type of paint doesn't leave brush strokes and stands up well to heat and wear-and-tear. Modelers usually apply clear topcoats over the color coats to provide additional protection for their cases' painted surfaces. Some other case modelers use glow-in-the-dark or ultraviolet-reactive paints on the insides of their cases.

Many case modelers also decorate their cases with decals or airbrush artwork. For instance, samples of modDIY's computer modStickers are shown in Figure A.5.1. The prices of individual stickers typically range from $ 1-2.

Figure A.5.1: modSticker Samples

Most case modelers also attach some sort of LED, plasma or ultraviolet fluorescent lights in their cases. An ordinary 112 cm magnetic strip of LED lights costs about $ 13. However, strips with more features are more expensive. The newest type of RGB LEDs strips, such as BitFenix's Alchemy LED Strips, as shown in Figure A.5.2, provide the ability to program the colors of the lights. LIFX's 1 meter Z LED programmable light straps with eight color zones, which can connect wirelessly to Wi-Fi, cost about $ 30. Other rigid LED strips, such as DarkSide's 5.5" (14 cm) Rigid UV LED Strips are also dimmable. Sophisticated LED light strips usually require expansion kits and controllers, which adds to their costs. A few cases are available with factory-installed programmable LCD lighting. An example is InWin's Infinity HALO case.

Lighting colors should coordinate the exterior and interior colors of cases. Black cases coordinate well with any color of lighting. Some case modelers imagine that white lights would be boring. However, white lights can balance excessive colored lights, which can be overpowering. White cases also reflect internal lights better.

It is best to position lighting sources so that they shine onto components, but not directly at the viewer's eyes. For example, case modelers often insert LED light strips in the spaces created by the set-off screws underneath their motherboards to create a backlighting effect. Others place magnetic LED strips inside the tops of their cases or underneath them. It is usually best to use two lighting strips in different parts of the case so that the light intensity is balanced throughout the case.

Many case modelers install third-party case fans that have integrated LED lights. For example, CoolerMaster's ice-blue SI3 twin 120-mm fan pack, as shown in Figure A.5.2, costs only about $ 15. Alternatively, after-market LED rings that fit around fans are also available.

Figure A.5.2: BitFenix Alchemy Strips and CoolerMaster S13 Fan Pack

People who build computers to use for work, instead of as showpieces, don't mind the traditional dull brown/beige colors of Noctua cooler fans. But, until recently, case modelers usually had to paint their Noctua fans to match the colors of the other components and lights in their systems. That is no longer necessary because Noctua has recently released their Chromax NA-SAVP1 cables, anti-vibration pads, and mounts in black, red, blue, white, green, and yellow, as shown in Figure A.5.3.

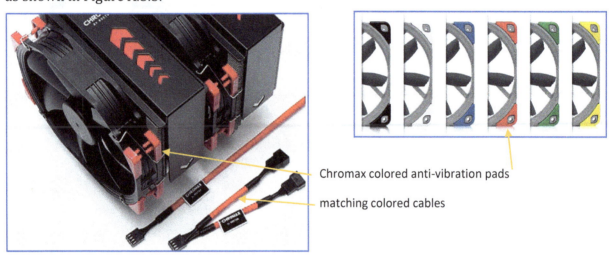

Figure A.5.3: Noctua Chrome Fan Accessories

Most DIY case modelers install custom liquid-cooler systems so that they can use customized colored fittings and colored coolants that show through transparent plastic tubes. These case modelers use liquid-coolers because of their aesthetics, even if their systems don't require the enhanced cooling capacity.

It is best to avoid colored coolants that contain reflective glitter because the glitter will eventually block-up the system pump. Solid color coolants, such as Mayhem's Pastel coolant, last longer. Mayhem coolant also comes in a variety of colors that can be mixed and customized, as shown in Figure A.5.4. Mayhem is even developing a Chameleon color coolant that will change color depending on a cooling system's temperature. Three meters of flexible plastic tubing costs only about $ 7. However, using angled fittings and hard tubing is more secure than using flexible tubing and usually looks better as well. One liter of good-quality coolant, which should last at least three years, costs about $ 20.

The main risk from using custom liquid-coolers is leaking tube joints. To minimize that risk, Thermaltake recently released their C-Pro tube compression fittings in six colors. These fittings have four O-rings, and Thermaltake insists that if their fittings are correctly installed, they will never leak. A diagram of the C-Pro fitting is provided in Figure A.5.5.

Thermaltake also offers complete systems. For example, Thermaltake's Water 3.0 Ring RGB 360 water cooling system with triple 120 mm high-pressure fans, and a smart fan controller costs about $ 175. See Figure A.5.7.

coolant colors

Figure A.5.4: Mayhem Coolant and Tubing   **Figure A.5.5: Thermaltake C-Pro Fitting**

Case modelers typically use other components with integrated lighting as well. For instance, some of the latest graphics cards have LEDs that can be software controlled. An example is MSI's GTX 960 Gaming 2G graphics card. It has a white LED logo on its top edge that fluctuates between bright and dark, as shown in Figure A.5.6. Alternatively, users can select other light-effect modes. Lighted RAM modules, such as AVEXIR's Raiden RAM modules, with plasma lighting, are also available. They are also shown in Figure A.5.6. Two 8 GB DDR 4 Raiden modules cost about $ 140.

Case modelers may now even buy PSUs with pre-installed programmable 256-color RGB fans. The first in the marketplace was Thermaltake's Toughpower DPS G RGB 1250 W Titanium PSU shown in Figure A.5.6. It cost about $ 380.

Case modelers also now have the option of selecting colored braided PSU power cables. For example, CableMod offers its ModMesh C-Series Cable Kit, as shown in Figure A.5.7, for about $ 120. CableMod even offers custom-made designer cables. Another company, Cool Force, offers multi-colored cables as part of its Nanoxia range of cables. Alternatively, case modelers can cover their PSU cables with colored UV-reactive covers such as Darkside's 4 mm (5/32") cable sleeving, as shown in Figure A.5.7. They may also buy ultraviolet light-reactive case cable ties.

MSI GTX 960 GPU   Thermaltake Toughpower Titanium PSU   AVEXIR Raiden RAM

Figure A.5.6: RGB Components

These days, case modelers usually buy motherboards that have some form of integrated RGB lighting. For example, at the time the fourth edition of this book was produced, the ROG Maximus VIII Formula motherboard, with three customizable RGB lighting zones, cost about $ 370. Some modelers also install fan controllers with temperature indicators in their cases' front panels. Two examples of Lamptron fan controllers are shown in Figure A.5.7.

Figure A.5.7: Case Modeling Equipment

Case modelers who go to the trouble and expense of installing lights in factory cases usually select cases with toughened glass side panels so that the lights will be visible. Tinted glass panels reduce the glare from internal lights and provide smoother balances of light around the interiors of cases.

Case modelers often select RGB-equipped peripheral devices that complement the designs of their cases. Even some external speakers are designed with case modeling in mind these days. For one example, the Razer Nommo Chroma speakers shown in Figure A.5.7 have integrated controllable RGB lighting. Another example is the JBL Pulse speaker with LEDs, also shown in Figure A.5.7.

Razer, Logitech, and Corsair have all released other RGB peripheral devices. For example, the Razer Blackwidow Chroma mechanical keyboard with programmable multi-colored RGB lights shown in Figure A.5.7 costs about $ 155. For another example, Kingston Technology Company offers its HyperX Pulsefire Surge RGB mouse, as shown in Figure A.5.7. It is a particularly smooth and accurate mouse — although it is expensive. It costs about $ 140. Razer also offers a Firefly Micro Textured Surface Hard Gaming Mouse Mat, which cost about $ 45, as shown in Figure A.5.7. Phillips has recently produced its Amibglow monitor with changing LED colors around its sides. Case modelers might like this monitor because of its eye-catching lights. However, from a practical point-of-view, those surround-lights could be distracting.

Cooler Master Technology offers online case modeling tutorials and a portal for case modelers. Two examples of modeled cases from the Cooler Master website are shown in Figure A.5.8. The first is VEGA. It was created by S.PiC from Russia and won Cooler Master's 2017 Case Mod World Series. The second is PROJECT ISOLATION. It was built by Australian, Alex Ciobanu, and was awarded 3rd place in the ANZ section of Case Mod's World Series. You will notice that, just like traditional artists, case modelers give their artistic creations titles.

The cases mentioned in the previous paragraph are examples of bespoke DIY-fabricated cases. However, case modeling can also involve using factory-produced cases. For example, the SNOWSTORM case shown in Figure A.5.8. was built by Atheros & Zebralet, also from Russia. It was based on a Fractal Design Define S case, is. The Define S case is one of Fractal Designs' series of cases with transparent side panels, which are built with system designing in mind.

If you are enthusiastic about case modeling, you might like to enter your computer into a case modeling competition. If you do, you will face strong creative competition from high-class competitors around the world. There is no end to the ingenuity of case modelers. At Computex in 2018, a case with fish swimming around a working submerged graphic card was displayed! It is shown in Figure A.5.8. Computex is the main international ICT (Information and Communication Technology) trade exhibition. It is held in Taipei, Taiwan.

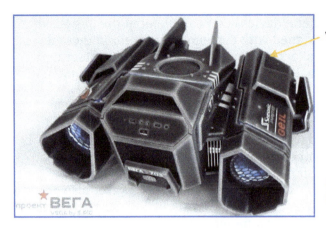

VEGA

PROJECT
ISOLATION

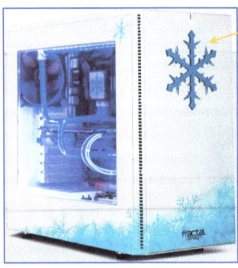

SNOWSTORM

swimming guppies

submerged Aorus
GTX 1080 graphics
card

Figure A.5.8: Case Modeling Examples

Appendix 6: Removing Write-protection with Regedit

To remove write-protection on a USB drive with Windows 10:

1. Plug the flash drive into a USB port.

2. Type 'regedit' into Windows 10's Type here to search dialog box.

3. Click the regedit Run icon command that appears.

4. On the pop-up User Account Control screen, allow Registry Editor to make changes.

5. On the Registry Editor screen, double-click on the Computer folder and then double-click on the HKEY_LOCAL_MACHINE key folder.

6. Continue to navigate to SYSTEM, CurrentControlSet, and Control, as shown in Figure A.6.1.

1. Double-click on 'computer'.

2. Double-click on 'HKEY_LOCAL_MACHINE'.

3. Double-click on 'SYSTEM'.

4. Double-click on 'CurrentControlSet'.

5. Double-click on 'Control'.

Figure A.6.1: Changing Windows' Registry StorageDevice Policies

7. Then, double click on StorageDevicePolicies. That will likely direct you to the WriteProtect tools. There is no 'StorageDevicePolicies' folders in some Windows 10 registries. In that case, you must create one yourself. To do that:
   6.1. Right-click on the Control key folder. Then select 'New' from the pop-up screen and select 'Key' from the next pop-up screen.
   6.2. In the NewKey#1 dialog box that appears, assign the name 'StorageDevicePolicies' to the new folder.
   6.3. Open the newly created StorageDevicePolicies folder.
   6.4. Right-click inside the large white space at the right side of the screen.
   6.5. Click 'New' when it appears. Then select 'DWORD (32-bit) value'.
   6.6. In the NewValue#1 dialog box that appears, name the folder 'WriteProtect'.
   6.7. Double-click on 'DWORD (32-bit) Value'.
   6.8. Set its Value data to '0' if it is not already '0'.

7. Double-click on the WriteProtect value in the right-hand pane of Regedit Editor screen. In the pop-up Edit DWORD (32-bit) value screen, make sure that the Value is '0' and click the OK button to save the change. That should ensure that the write-protection is removed from the USB flash drive. Close Regedit and restart your computer. Connect your USB flash drive again, and you should find that the flash drive is no longer write-protected.

Appendix 7: Installing Windows 10 ISO from USB Device

Setting-up Windows 10 is somewhat different than setting-up previous versions. Systems must also meet Windows 10's new system requirements: a 1 GHz or faster CPU; at least 1 GB of RAM for the 32-bit version, or 2 GB of RAM for the 64-bit version; 16 GB free secondary storage space for the 32-bit version, or 20 GB free secondary storage space for the 64-bit version; a Microsoft DirectX 9 or better graphics device with a Windows Display Driver Model. That driver is Microsoft's Windows graphic card driver architecture, which also supports Internet access.

If you have already installed Windows 10 on a computer, you cannot reinstall it onto the same computer if you change any main components, such as the motherboard or CPU. Windows 10 would see the computer as being a different computer. In that case, you would need to phone Microsoft and request a new activation code.

You can install Windows 10 in two different ways. The first method is to simply use Windows Update if you have Windows 8.1 already installed. The second method is to undertake a clean install of Windows 10 using an ISO image. An ISO image of a file is an exact copy of all its contents, including its file system. The ISO method installs a completely new version, without reusing any old files from a previous version. That is the best method if you are building a new Ryzen-based system because not all previous methods for configuring and optimizing systems still work well with Ryzen-based systems.

You will need access to a computer with an OS already running as well as an Internet connection. You will also need a Windows 10 installed key to activate Windows on a new PC. You wouldn't need an installed key to re-activate Windows 10 on the same computer. The installed key might not be the same as the OEM product key. The installed key (i.e., product activation key) is a unique sequence of twenty-five characters that activates Windows 10. To deter theft, installed keys are no longer printed on product stickers. Instead, these days, installed keys are encrypted and stored on motherboard UEFI firmware chips.

When you install Windows 10, the installed key might be automatically be detected from the UEFI firmware chip. But, if it not detected or you have previously installed Windows 10 but don't remember its installed key, you can download, unzip, extract, and run ShowKeyPlus to discover the key, as shown in Figure A.7.1. The latest version of ShowKeyPlus when this book was produced was 1.0.7060.

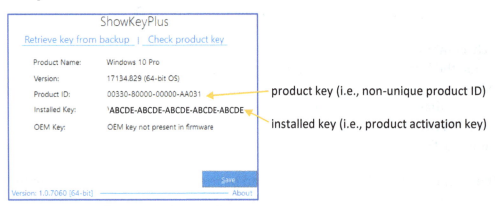

Figure A.7.1: ShowKeyPlus Tool

You can use either a USB device or an optical device as the temporary boot device. Using a USB device is faster than using a CD/DVD; so that method is explained in the following instructions.

1. Plug a USB flash drive (i.e., thumb drive) that has at least 8 GB of storage capacity into a USB port on your computer. It is best to use a USB 3.0 or USB 3.1 port if your computer has one because the process will then be much faster.

2. Check to see if your system's BIOS is a UEFI BIOS, which it most likely is. If it is a UEFI BIOS, it is best to configure the USB drive so that it is a UEFI-bootable Windows 10 drive. Creating a UEFI-bootable USB drive involves formatting it. That means that any data on the USB drive will be lost. So, if you have any files you want to keep on the USB device, make backup copies of them. Most third-party bootable-USB creation software utilities will only create legacy BIOS USB drives. Fortunately, Windows' own USB Tool will automatically create a UEFI-bootable USB drive. Alternatively, you could use a free third-party tool called Rufus to create the UEFI bootable USB drive. Rufus works with both Windows and Linux distributions. To use that Windows tool:

2.1. Download and save the Windows 10 USB download tool from the official Microsoft webpage, http://windowsmicro.com/download-windows-10-media-creation-tool-1809/. Don't download a nonofficial version of Windows from another website because it might carry malware or spyware.

2.2. When the tool has downloaded, click the Run button.

2.3. On the next pop-up User Account Control box, click on the Yes button to allow changes to be made to the computer system.

2.4. In the next pop-up Windows 10 Setup box, select 'Create installation media for another PC', as shown in Figure A.7.2. Then click the Next button. On the next Windows 10 Setup screen, select 'USB flash drive' as shown in Figure A.7.2. Then click the Next button on that screen.

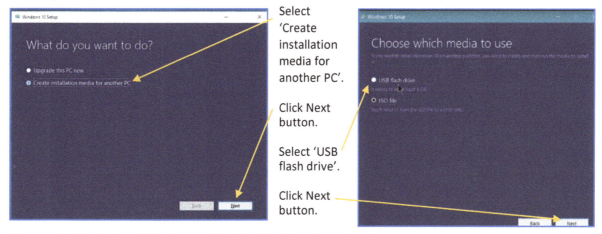

Figure A.7.2: Using Windows 10's Media Creation Option

2.5. On the next pop-up box, select the name of the USB drive from the drop-down menu, and click the Next button, as shown in Figure A.7.3. That will add a file path to the tool. It will take the tool a long time to create the UEFI-bootable Windows 10 USB drive. After the USB drive has been prepared, a 'Your USB flash drive is ready' message will appear on the next pop-up box, as shown in Figure A.7.3. Click the Finish button on the bottom of the screen.

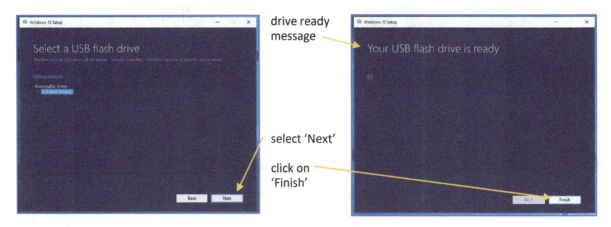

drive ready
message

select 'Next'

click on
'Finish'

Figure A.7.3: Downloading Windows Media Creation Tool to USB Device

Accept 'Use the recommended options for this PC', unless you want to configure your new system differently.

3. Now, cold boot your new PC (i.e., turn the power off and then on again). Then, enter the UEFI-BIOS and configure the USB flash drive as the boot device. Save and apply the new settings.

4. Now cold boot your PC again. It will boot from the Windows 10 ISO image on the USB flash drive. When the files are copied, choose the various setting options you want to use. Then click 'Next' and follow the prompts to sign into your Microsoft account.

5. Click on 'Install'. Enter your Windows 10 product key when prompted, and then click 'Next'. Click on 'I accept the license terms', and then click 'Next'. To make a clean install, click 'Custom: Install Windows only (advanced)'. Select the spinning hard disk partition that you want to save Windows 10 onto, if you want your system to boot from a spinning hard drive and press 'Next'. After installing, the setup routine will reboot your computer at least twice while configuring itself.

6. Log into your account and enter 'Activation' in the Windows Type here to search dialog box. Verify your installation. Then install any available updates. Also, manually install and update any device drivers that are not automatically installed and updated.

Appendix 8: Troubleshooting Checklist

Problem Symptoms	Solutions
power supply unit smoking	1. pull plug from mains and replace PSU.
no motherboard LEDs on; no fans running	1. Check PSU plug is inserted into the unit and the mains power socket. 2. Make sure any power strip switch is turned on. 3. Toggle PSU switch to On. 4. Plug PSU into different mains socket and surge protector. 5. Check that the case's On/Off button is making proper contact with its switch. 6. Replace PSU with known-good unit.
power supply working, but no display on monitor	1. Check that monitor's power cord is securely plugged into the wall socket and into the monitor. Try using a known-good power cable. 2. Turn monitor off, disconnect the data cable, reconnect the cable, and turn the monitor on. Try using a known-good data cable. 3. Check that the monitor's cable is connected to the correct graphic card's or motherboard's port. 4. Remove and then reinstall GPU; then try a known-good GPU. 5. Try using integrated video, if available, instead of GPU. 6. Try using known-good monitor.
RAM not working	1. Remove and fully reinsert modules into their slots. 2. Try using one module at a time.
no sound from system speakers no sound from system	1. Check that all speakers are connected. 2. Check that the correct speaker plugs are inserted into the correct jacks — most likely stereo jacks, not mono jacks. 3. Check that all speaker's switches are turned on. 4. Check that the mute toggle is not turned Off on the sound mixer. 5. Turn sound on using the soundcard's software. 6. Turn computer off and then on again. 7. Check that integrated audio is enabled in the UEFI-BIOS or legacy-BIOS. 8. If using a soundcard, check that it is compatible with the system; then uninstall and then reinstall its driver. 9. Remove and reinstall soundcard if present. 10. Check Windows Control Panel to ensure audio drivers are installed.

wired keyboard not working	1. Check that keyboard is plugged into the correct port. 2. Make sure that 'USB keyboard' is enabled in the BIOS or UEFI. 3. Reboot PC to give it another chance to detect keyboard.
wireless keyboard or mouse not working	1. Make sure devices are turned on. 2. Check for other buttons on the device that need to be pressed. 3. Make sure that battery compartment covers are closed properly. 4. Make sure batteries are good and correctly installed. 5. Remove and reset dongle. 6. Press dongle's reset button if present. 7. Make sure nothing is blocking signal to dongle. 8. Insert dongle into a different USB port. 9. Reinstall good copies of device's driver installed.
motherboard not working	1. Check that 20 or 24-pin power supply is connected correctly and securely. 2. Check that motherboard voltage settings are correct. 3. Check that bus speeds are correct. 4. If the motherboard doesn't pass the POST, it may be because it's BIOS won't recognize the CPU. In that case, return the motherboard to the retailer and ask them to update the BIOS.
secondary storage device not working	1. Check that both the data cable and power cable are connected properly. 2. Try using known-good cables. 3. Try reinstalling the driver, if one has been installed, or try installing a new driver for the device. 4. Uninstall device, disconnect and reconnect cables, and reboot system. 5. Try using known-good device to confirm faulty device.
computer shuts off when a software application runs	1. Uninstall and then reinstall the software.
CPU not working properly, or computer randomly shuts down when you run various software programs	1. Temporarily disconnect UPS if you are using one. 2. Ensure CPU's cooler fan is working correctly. 3. Check that the case fans are installed correctly (i.e., not backwards) and are running correctly. 4. Check CPU temperature in BIOS/UEFI. If cooler fan is working, but CPU is overheating, replace cooler. 5. Try known-good PSU. 6. Reseat CPU correctly in motherboard socket.

If CPU doesn't work at all	1. Make sure CPU's 4 or 8-pin power connection is good and secure.
	2. Try known-good CPU, if all else fails.
no network connection	1. Try installing a known-good Ethernet card — even if the motherboard has an integrated Ethernet NIC.
noisy CPU cooler fan or case fan without sealed bearings	1. Turn the PSU's power switch 'Off'.
	2. Disconnect the power cable to the fan.
	3. Use a Phillips screwdriver to remove the fan's four mounting screws and then detach its power cable.
	4. Lay the fan on a flat surface and peel back the sticker on its back.
	5. Pull out the rubber plug covering the lubrication hole under the sticker.
	6. Squeeze a single drop of sewing machine oil into the hole.
	7. Replace the plug and sticker, and reinstall the fan back onto the heatsink, or the case.
peripheral device possibly preventing system from starting	1. Disconnect all devices expect monitor.
	2. Reattach devices one-at-a-time to identify problem device.

Appendix 9: Audio-Technica Forum Guidelines

Audio-Technica values your questions and answers!
When writing your question or answer, please follow these guidelines:
- *Questions and answers must be written in English*
- *Make sure the question is relevant to the product*
- *Make sure the answer is relevant to the product and relevant to the question being asked*
- *Make sure the answer addresses the question being asked*
- *If applicable, include the model number*
- *All submitted questions and answers are subject to the terms set forth in our Terms of Use. We reserve the right to not post your question or answer if it contains any of the following types of content or violates other internal guidelines:*
- *Full name, email addresses, URLs, phone numbers, physical addresses, or other forms of contact information*
- *Obscenities, discriminatory language, or other language not suitable for a public forum*
- *Advertisements, 'spam' content, or references to other products, offers, or websites*
- *Critical or spiteful comments on other questions or answers posted on the page or their authors*
- *Pricing and promotional details referring to products or services.*

The first computer was built at the time of Adam and Eve.

It was an Apple with limited memory — just 1 byte.

And then everything crashed.

Thanks for using this book.

The goal of a non-fiction writer is to produce a book that people can effortlessly understand and apply. Of course, that goal can never be entirely reached — only strived for. As the famous American football coach, Vince Lombardi, put it:
'Perfection is not attainable, but if we chase perfection, we can catch excellence.'

With that spirit in mind, I thank readers, reviewers, and the editor for their constructive criticisms about previous editions. Any shortcomings in this edition are my own responsibility. I would welcome and answer any constructive criticisms that you might have about this edition at my website, www.Pittman-Progressive-Publishing.com. However, my website is not intended as a computer-building Q&A forum.

If you aren't familiar with the expression 'constructive criticism', I offer the following explanation: A constructive criticism is a thoughtful opinion, civilly expressed, about someone's work. A constructive criticism may include negative comments, as well as positive ones. But all comments should suggest how the work might be improved.

If you purchased the previous edition, I would be happy to mail a free copy of the fourth edition of this book to you. Just send a digital copy of your proof-of-purchase and your postal address to my website. I won't store or pass on your address. You can also find information about the upcoming book, 'Modern International English', at my website.

I support the Book Aid International charity. Perhaps you would like to do likewise?

Hugh Pittman

Books change lives

Email: info@bookaid.org
www.bookaid.org

Book Aid International provides about 1,000,000 new high-quality books to disadvantaged people at libraries, schools, prisons, universities, refugee camps and hospitals each year. These people would not otherwise have access to such books and therefore value them greatly.

As Maha, a West Bank librarian reported, 'Before Book Aid International started supporting our school, getting new books was virtually impossible.' And, as Yvonne, a 23-year-old refugee who was born in a refugee camp said, 'I have read about women who have succeeded. I now believe I can succeed too.'

Harry Boughton, Head of Operations, would be happy to answer your questions about donating books, helping as a warehouse volunteer, or supporting projects such as BAI's community library children's Book Havens program.

BAI is registered charity no. 313868, and a limited company in England and Wales.

Professional Review

This book about building your perfect computer is easy to read and follow. *Build your own Computer*, written by Hugh Pittman, is a book that, unlike many others in the market, goes really deep into the subject matter. The process of personal computer building is explained in detail, showing the author's obvious experience in the field. From the very beginning, the author provides an informative introduction, explaining his reason for writing this book: to provide a practical guide to building a modern personal computer hardware system that runs on a Windows or Linux-based operating system. Pittman makes it clear that his book is intended for people that have limited knowledge of computers. Therefore, he makes sure that complex technical concepts are carefully explained — starting with basic terms such as 'personal computer', 'operating system', 'Hackintosh computers' and the like.

Also, the author chose to make his book more than just a good reference guide by introducing a bit of humor. Therefore, the reader will be able to meet a cartoon character named Ding Duck, who either offers some friendly advice or is annoyed when he points out some common mistakes. The user should listen to advice provided by this charming character, and make sure to avoid mistakes that usually happen when it comes to computer assembly.

Build your own Computer puts a special emphasis on the use of tables full of reference data, in figures that can be found throughout the entire book, and in demonstrating practical examples of the situations in which users can, and most likely will find themselves, following the author's instructions.

Though I'm not part of the audience this book is written for, given my 30+ years of working with computers, I'm pleasantly surprised by the amount and quality of information that can be found within, as well as by the author's knowledge. During careful reading, I could not find a single thing that is incorrect. Though, of course, I have somewhat different opinions about some of the author's views. But, when it comes to software and hardware, that is normal. Therefore, I would say *Build your own Computer* is a book that is intended for, and will be mostly enjoyed by, those readers that know nothing or very little about personal computers. That is because the well-written instructions and good quality pictures make it easy-to-read and easy-to-follow.

On the other hand, even experienced users will find this book interesting because of the exhaustive and comprehensive manner in which the author synthesizes knowledge about the selection of high-quality components to enable users to create the kinds of systems they want to build.

I was given a copy of this book by the author for the purpose of writing an unbiased review, and all the presented information is based on my own.